The First Aid Book

second edition

Alton L. Thygerson

Brigham Young University

Prentice-Hall, Englewood Cliffs, New Jersey 07632

Library of Congress Cataloging-in-Publication Data

Thygerson, Alton L.
   The first aid book.

   Includes index.
   1. First aid in illness and injury. I. Title.
[DNLM: 1. First Aid. WA 292 T549f]
RC86.7.T47 1986   616.02′52   85-16686
ISBN 0-13-318015-8

Dedicated to my family

Editorial/production supervision and
   interior design by *Lisa Halttunen*
Cover design by *20/20 Services, Inc.*
Manufacturing buyer: *Harry P. Baisley*

© **1986, 1982 by Prentice-Hall**
A Division of Simon & Schuster, Inc.
Englewood Cliffs, New Jersey 07632

Printed in the United States of America

10 9 8 7 6 5 4 3 2 1

ISBN 0-13-318015-8   01

PRENTICE-HALL INTERNATIONAL (UK) LIMITED, *London*
PRENTICE-HALL OF AUSTRALIA PTY. LIMITED, *Sydney*
PRENTICE-HALL CANADA INC., *Toronto*
PRENTICE-HALL HISPANOAMERICANA, S.A., *Mexico*
PRENTICE-HALL OF INDIA PRIVATE LIMITED, *New Delhi*
PRENTICE-HALL OF JAPAN, INC., *Tokyo*
PRENTICE-HALL OF SOUTHEAST ASIA PTE. LTD., *Singapore*
EDITORA PRENTICE-HALL DO BRASIL, LTDA., *Rio de Janeiro*
WHITEHALL BOOKS LIMITED, *Wellington, New Zealand*

Contents

Preface

Everyone must expect sooner or later to be on hand when an injury or illness strikes. The outcome of such misfortune frequently depends not only on the severity of the injury or illness but on the first aid rendered. Therefore, first aid knowledge and skills are essential in our society. All people should receive first aid training.

First aid procedures have been tremendously upgraded in recent years. Thanks to advances in medical science, first aid is in a dynamic state of progress. But misinformation still abounds. Numerous techniques are now obsolete, such as applying over-the-counter burn ointments, giving warm salt to induce vomiting in cases of poisoning, and applying cold on a poisonous snakebite. This book contains the most recent, medically accurate first aid information.

The First Aid Book is written for college and university first aid courses, in which it can serve either as the main textbook or as an in-depth companion to the popular American National Red Cross textbook. College and university students need more information than is contained in the ARC textbook. *The First Aid Book* meets or exceeds the American Red Cross standards. Pick a topic (for example, tick removal, ring removal, treatment for nosebleed, or poison ivy itch relief), look it up in this book, and then compare the information with that of other books: Which book would you rather have?

The intent of *The First Aid Book* is to promote confidence by building first aid competence. Both the experienced first aider and those with little first aid training will profit from the material contained herein. Special features include the anecdotal "boxes" providing pertinent world records, historical background, uncommon facts, and other background material.

A book of this kind has to reflect the author's experience. First, like many people, I have been exposed to many first aid situations both as victim and as first aider. I have spent over 20 years teaching first aid at the community, public school, and university level. And I have enjoyed a close association with several professional organizations whose objectives include first aid.

I have also drawn upon long hours of library research. My many years as author of a weekly newspaper column featuring first aid, a monthly feature in *Emergency: The Journal of Emergency Services,* and several books in the safety and health fields have also enhanced this book.

DISCLAIMER STATEMENT

The first aid procedures in this book are based on the most current research and recommendations of responsible medical sources. The author and publisher, however, disclaim any responsibility for any adverse effects or consequences resulting from the misapplication or injudicious use of any of the material contained herein.

Because the circumstances and the victim's physical condition can vary widely from one emergency to another, standards of care will also vary.

Chapter 1

Introduction to First Aid

First aid is the immediate care given to an injured or suddenly ill person. First aid does not take the place of proper medical treatment but consists only of furnishing temporary assistance until competent medical care, if needed, is obtained, or the prognosis for recovery without medical care is assured. Remember, most injuries and illness are corrected with only first aid care. First aid is given to prevent death, counteract shock, prevent further injury, and relieve pain. Certain conditions, such as severe bleeding or asphyxiation, require *immediate* first aid if the victim is to survive. In such cases, seconds might mean the difference between life and death. However, the first aid care of most injuries or other medical emergencies may be postponed safely for the few minutes required to locate a skilled first aider or suitable first aid supplies and equipment.

All people should be prepared to administer first aid. They should have sufficient knowledge of first aid to be able to apply true emergency first aid measures and decide what can be done safely until more skilled assistance arrives. Limitations must be recognized. Procedures and techniques beyond the rescuer's ability should *not* be attempted. More harm than good might result.

A knowledge of first aid and its purposes, when properly applied, may mean the difference between life and death, rapid recovery and long hospitalization, or temporary disability and permanent injury.

1

The person administering first aid should think and act carefully and not become unduly excited or emotionally upset. Unnecessary haste and the appearance of uncertainty or confusion should be avoided.

Haste and hurry are very different things.

Lord Chesterfield (1694–1773)

First aid must be administered *immediately* to:

Restore breathing
Control severe bleeding
Give first aid for poisoning
Prevent further injury to the victim
Treat shock.

A rapid, emergency evaluation of the victim should be made immediately at the scene of the injury to determine the type and extent of the trauma. The rescuer must be prepared to simultaneously observe, speak to the victim, and act.

Always remember that the rescuer will be expected to provide assistance to the victim until the victim is placed in the care of qualified medical personnel or the prognosis is such that the victim will recover without the need of medical assistance.

THE NEED FOR FIRST AID

Despite increased attention and progress in recent years, there are still many people who lack an acceptable level of knowledge and proficiency in first aid. Moreover, these skills are greatly needed. Seventy million people in the United States receive hospital emergency care each year; this number does not include those who receive care for less serious injuries and sickness at home or at a physician's office. The extent of trauma and sudden illness is shown in the following data:

Trauma (accidents) is the fourth largest killer in the United States, claiming over 100,000 lives annually and permanently disabling an additional 400,000 people.

Two million burn accidents occur annually, with 75,000 classified as severe.

About 10,000 to 15,000 spinal cord injuries occur each year, resulting in a lifetime of disability for many victims.

Between one and one and a half million people experience acute myocardial infarction (heart attack) each year. Half of these usually die within two hours of the onset of the symptoms without any prehospital or hospital emergency care.

Five million persons are poisoned annually. Of the victims, 90 percent are children.

Accidental injuries are the most serious public health problem facing the United States and other developed countries.

In the United States, accidental injuries account for the majority of deaths among children and young adults.

Throughout the world, accidental injuries are now the leading cause of death during half of the human life span.

The risk of an accidental injury is such that most people sustain a significant injury sometime during their lives. Few escape the tragedy of fatal or permanently disabling injury to a relative or friend. Accidental injuries are too often taken for granted.

LEADING CAUSES OF DEATH

RANK   CAUSE

1. Heart disease
2. Cancer
3. Stroke
4. Accidents
5. Pneumonia
6. Diabetes mellitus
7. Cirrhosis of liver
8. Arteriosclerosis
9. Suicide
10. Homicide

LEADING ACCIDENTAL CAUSES OF DEATH

RANK   CAUSE

1. Motor vehicle accidents
2. Falls
3. Drowning
4. Fires, burns, and deaths associated with fires
5. Suffocation—ingested object
6. Poisoning by solids and liquids
7. Firearms
8. Poisoning by gases and vapors

National Safety Council, *Accident Facts*

Whatever can go wrong, will.

Murphy's Law

BYSTANDER INTERVENTION

Whatever can happen to one man can happen to every man.

Lucius Annaeus Seneca (4 B.C?–AD. 65)

Virtually everyone will at some time have to make a decision whether or not to help another person. The model presented in Figure 1–1 shows helping behavior as a form of decision making. Also shown in the model are reasons why a bystander may not assist a victim in distress.

Essentially the model involves a sequence of decisions that must be made if an individual is to intervene in another's crisis or emergency. The steps are:

1. Notice something wrong
2. Decide whether the event is an emergency
3. Decide if one should help
4. Decide on the specific mode of intervention.

Notice Something Wrong

The bystander has to notice that something is wrong. The ability to notice something wrong is related to:

1. *Perceived severity of the emergency.* Situations of greater severity (for example, a traffic accident involving several vehicles as opposed to a heart attack) consistently gain attention from a bystander.
2. *Distance between the bystander and the emergency.* There is no published literature relating distance from the victim to willingness to assist. Nevertheless, it does seem that a direct relationship exists between closeness to the event and willingness to help.
3. *The bystander's similarity to and emotional involvement within the victim.* Similarity to and feelings of closeness with the victim increase a bystander's attention to the victim's distress. For example, it is difficult to deny that an emergency involving one's own child would gain more attention than the same emergency involving a total stranger.

Model of Bystander Intervention

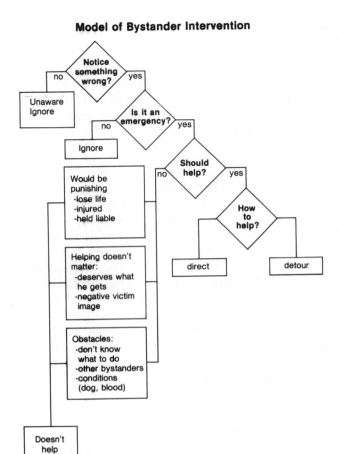

FIGURE 1–1   (Adapted from *Analyzing Performance Problems* by Robert F. Mager and Peter Pipe, © 1984 by David S. Lake Publishers, Belmont, Calif.)

Bystander attention becomes more pronounced when an emergency is witnessed alone. For example, a bystander who witnesses an emergency alone bears 100 percent of the responsibility for intervening; when more than one bystander can help, responsibility may be diffused. Thus, an individual who believes that others can help may be less emotionally involved with the victim.

4. *The length of time of the observer's exposure to the emergency,* if no intervention occurs. Evidence indicates that attention increases as the length of the bystander's exposure to the emergency increases.

Decide Whether the Event Is an Emergency

People influence each other. They depend on the reactions of others around them to tell them what to believe and how to behave.

Decide if One Should Help

Several factors affect this decision: the bystander's assessment of whether or not the victim deserves help, the bystander's competence, the relationship between bystander and victim, and the presence or absence of other bystanders among whom responsibility may be shared. Age, sex, physical condition, and socioeconomic class of the victim can greatly influence the extent of help he or she receives.

Decide on the Mode of Intervention

Once the decision is made, two alternatives are possible: (1) direct intervention (diving into a flood-swollen river or running into a burning house), or (2) detour intervention (calling the fire or police department). Detour intervention consists of reporting emergencies to a relevant authority rather than attempting to cope with the emergency situation directly.

A problem with direct intervention is that it sometimes requires considerable skill (for example, lifesaving, repelling); whereas a problem with detour intervention is that the bystander may not correctly assess the appropriate behavior.

Many well-meaning intentions become aborted at this stage; for example, it is not helpful for a nonswimmer to jump into deep water to save someone from drowning. The alternative to direct action is detour intervention, in which those qualified to help are alerted.

It is chance chiefly that makes heroes.

Carlyle

Deciding Not to Help

There are emergency situations in which a bystander decides not to help. Examples of such inaction are many. For example, the *Titanic* disaster brought out behavior ranging from heroic self-sacrifice to total selfishness. Another example is the famous Kitty Genovese case, in which 38 New Yorkers watched an assailant attack Kitty Genovese several times over a 40-minute period without helping her, until finally a neighbor summoned police.

The following are possible explanations for why people fail to aid others.

1. *It would be punishing.* Bystanders have lost their lives or been severely injured while attempting to rescue others. An example is Oklahoma teacher Ronnie Darden, who lost his left leg and part of his right foot when he tripped over a

power line while attempting to help passengers in a car that had crashed. Another example is Joe Delaney, a star halfback for the Kansas City Chiefs, who died while trying to rescue three drowning boys in Louisiana. The fear of a lawsuit can also act as a deterrent against helping.

2. *Helping doesn't matter.* Some bystanders feel that the victim is getting what he or she deserves. A negative image of the victim (for example, if the victim is poor or drunk) repulses some bystanders.

    Rewards, if any, are not high for rescuers, possibly consisting of a newspaper write-up or a small cash prize. Often the rescuer can expect nothing more than a hurried "Thanks."

3. *Obstacles may prevent helping.* Many bystanders do not know how to help. They can not swim, repel, or perform other necessary rescue skills.

    The more bystanders there are, the less likely it is that one of them will respond. If only one bystander is present, he or she carries all the responsibility, will feel all the guilt for not acting, and will bear all the blame for nonintervention.

    Rescuers have been repulsed by dogs protecting their disabled owners. Some have also been adversely affected by the sight of blood and other appalling conditions normally found at many emergency scenes.

We never know when we may be bystanders or who the victims will be. All adults should prepare themselves for the inevitable emergency situation.

A hero is no braver than an ordinary man, but he is brave five minutes longer.

Emerson

---

911 FOR EMERGENCIES

In communities served by more than one emergency phone number, seldom is more than 10 percent of the population able to recite by heart the phone numbers for police, fire, and ambulance.

The system of a common emergency number was first used in Great Britain in 1937, when "999" was designated the nationwide emergency reporting number. In 1968 the American Telephone and Telegraph Company announced that it would make the digits 9-1-1 available for national implementation.

There are several benefits of 9-1-1:

There is only one number to remember. It is not uncommon for a county to have 40 to 80 emergency numbers listed for various emergency services.

It is true that dialing "operator" only requires dialing one number. However, the operator that a caller gets is generally not in the same town. Because of technological advances, the operator is likely to be in another city or even another state, thus making it difficult to confirm location and determine the correct resources needed for an appropriate response.

Because of the mobility of today's society, it is frequently difficult for emergency providers to determine the correct location of an emergency. In fact, under stress, many longtime residents give incorrect addresses. The mispronunciation of a street can delay help, especially if it is an operator who has been contacted. While telephone operators are minimally trained to respond to emergency calls, the large areas they cover make it difficult to respond effectively. The telephone companies recognize this problem and are among the biggest supporters of 9-1-1 systems.

Calls are received by specially trained persons.   Whether an emergency requires police, fire, and/or emergency medical services (EMS) assistance, a 9-1-1 dispatcher should be capable of determining the location of an incident and coordinating the appropriate response. Many systems require dispatchers to be trained at least to the basic emergency medical technician (EMT-A) level if they handle emergency medical calls.

Response time is potentially reduced.   The fact that the 9-1-1 call immediately goes into a center that has a multitude of emergency resources available can reduce dispatch time. The shorter 9-1-1 number takes less time to dial than seven digits.

Once contact has been made with an emergency center, certain information must be communicated:

1. Exact location. This is probably the single most important piece of information.
2. Circumstances. What has happened—illness, heart attack, drowning, and so on.
3. Number of people involved.
4. Telephone number from which the call was placed. This information is required not only to help prevent false calls but, more important, to allow the center to call back for additional information.

Other tips include:

1. Always be the last to hang up the phone. The police, ambulance, or fire department may need to ask more questions about how to find you. They may also tell you what to do until help arrives.
2. Speak slowly and clearly. Shouting is difficult to understand.
3. If you send someone else to call, have the person report back to you so that you can be sure the call was made.
4. Never call from a dangerous location, such as inside a burning building.

5. Never use an emergency number for nonemergencies.
6. Always carry change in your car, pocket, or purse for phone calls.
7. While traveling, make a mental note of the last telephone or call box location.
8. If you are not in a 911 number system, place the emergency numbers near all the phones in your house. Dialing the operator will get help, too.
9. If possible, have someone waiting in the street to flag down the ambulance and lead the way to the victim.

Pain and suffering can be relieved and lives can be saved through notification of the emergency medical system via the telephone.

LEGAL ASPECTS OF FIRST AID

The possibility of liability affects first aiders who render assistance to the ill or injured. Most people associate the term *liability* or *malpractice* with physicians. It is not, however, a problem of concern only to the medical profession.

This section offers guidelines for the first aider, who should rightfully be concerned about liability and the avoidance of a lawsuit. A person who is faced with a specific legal problem should rely on the advice of his or her own attorney. The attorney can assess all the facts and give the guidance and protection needed.

When You Are Required to Give First Aid

Unless you have a duty to act, you cannot be held responsible because you failed to act. No one is required to render aid when no legal duty exists. As an example, a physician taking a leisurely walk could ignore a stranger suffering a heart attack or bone fracture.

We may all agree that this defies moral obligations. However, morality is not the same as a legally required duty.

Frequently first aiders express concern over the question of when their duty to act does arise. This is an important consideration, for you can be held liable if you have a duty and ignore it. For these reasons you should clearly understand at what point a legal duty does arise. Duty may be imposed under any of the following situations:

1. *When you are under a contractual duty.* If there is a preexisting relationship between parties (such as teacher-student, physician-patient, parent-child, fireman-community, lifeguard-swimmer, driver-passenger), then there is a duty to render aid.
2. *When you begin to act.* Once you start rendering first aid, you cannot stop. This is difficult for most people to understand. The legal reasoning is based on the possibility that the victim has refused aid from others and is relying on your continued assistance.

From a legal viewpoint it is best not to begin caring for a victim unless you plan to render all the aid required of you.

a.   Do not stop or become involved unnecessarily.
b.   Clearly tell a victim that you cannot render aid, so that your position is definite.
c.   If you do start to render assistance, make certain that you stay with the victim and provide all possible aid until the victim is in the hands of other personnel with equal or greater competence.

The only time that duty can be called into question is when you fail to act. However, if a court determines you should have acted but did not, the legal consequences can be severe.

Obtain Consent

Most people think the term *assault and battery* means striking a person or causing the person bodily injury through physical means. This term can also apply to a first aider who provides life-sustaining care to a victim who does not agree to it. It is a well-recognized principle of law that all persons have the right to decide whether to accept or reject treatment.

How granted?   A victim usually indicates consent by voluntarily submitting to treatment. This is referred to as *implied consent*. It is not necessary to ask the victim whether he or she consents, or to obtain written approval.

Informed consent.   For the consent to be valid, victims must have enough information about what they are consenting to.

As a first aider you should tell victims what they should know about the first aid being offered.

What to do when a victim refuses consent.   Though it seldom happens, there are countless reasons for a person to refuse assistance, such as religious grounds, avoidance of possible pain, or the desire to be examined by a physician.

Whatever the reason for refusing medical care, or even if no reason is given, the victim can reject aid or transport provided he or she has the mental capacity to do so.

One exception to this rule is the case in which a victim refuses to be moved, but relocating the victim is necessary to let traffic move or is otherwise necessary for the public good.

In every situation in which a victim refuses assistance or withdraws consent for further assistance, the following procedures should be followed:

1.   Clearly advise the victim of his or her medical condition, what you propose to do, and why the assistance is necessary.
2.   Encourage others at the scene to persuade the victim to seek care.

3. Do not be hasty. A victim may have a change of mind after a short period of time.
4. Make certain you have witnesses. All too often a victim will refuse consent and then deny having done so.
5. Decide whether the victim has the mental capacity to refuse consent.

Mentally incapacitated victim.   Mental incapacity can take many forms, such as unconsciousness or mental distortion through drug or alcohol use. When a victim is not mentally competent to express consent and requires immediate emergency care, you have the implied consent to carry out the assistance. Where immediate emergency care is not required, you must obtain consent from a person authorized to act for the victim before rendering first aid. Consent for an incompetent victim in most states can be obtained from (in order of priority): a spouse, either parent, any adult child, any adult brother or sister, any adult aunt or uncle, any grandparent, or any person who has the obvious responsibility or authority.

Consent problems with minors.   According to the law, minors do not have the ability to consent or refuse consent, no matter how intelligent the minor may be.

The approach to be taken with a minor is the same as with a mentally incapacitated adult. If immediate emergency care is required and prompt consent from a relative cannot be obtained, then you can provide needed first aid. In nonemergency situations, consent will be required from a relative.

Children who are injured while in school or summer camp can pose a problem. Many schools and camps obtain prior permission from parents to care for any injured or suddenly ill child. If such has not been given, effort should be made to obtain consent from a parent at the time it is needed. However, if you cannot reach the parents, it is usually safe to proceed with first aid.

In cases where a parent refuses to give consent, you should advise the parent of the risks and have other bystanders witness the situation. It might be wise to report the incident either to the police or to an appropriate child-welfare agency.

Recognizing what *not* to do is as important as knowing what to do.

Standard of Care

The point at which first aid falls below a required standard is debatable. If a first aider is a defendant, the question may be posed, "Would other first aiders have performed in the same way?" Essentially the court determines the *standard* of behavior by examining the evidence and deciding what others with equal training or certification would have done under the same circumstances. Through this process a *peer standard* is determined, and then the defendant's conduct is evaluated to see whether he or she operated within that standard or below it.

Abandonment

First aiders must remain with the victim until the victim is under the supervision of others of equal or greater competence, or refuses treatment and transport.

Steps which a first aider can take to avoid a negligence suit based on abandonment include:

1. Once you start first aid, remain with the victim until that individual is safely transferred to the care of other providers with equal or greater competence.
2. Do not leave a victim who decides he or she may not require first aid unless you have performed an adequate examination and are convinced that the victim is correct. In most cases a victim is the least qualified person to assess his or her own medical condition.
3. Emergency departments represent a special danger. Never leave a victim in an emergency department (ED) until you have provided the staff with all the required information and are satisfied that the ED staff is attending to the needs of the victim.
4. Always ask yourself this one important question before you leave a victim: Is the victim in capable hands, and did you do everything you could for that person?

GOOD SAMARITAN LAWS

Every state has passed Good Samaritan laws to protect citizens from liability when providing emergency care. The concept is logically based on the premise that a person who voluntarily stops to aid another should not be liable if he or she provides that aid negligently. The best part of the Good Samaritan laws is not only to protect the person providing aid but to encourage people to assist others in distress by granting them immunity. It requires little imagination to predict that few people would risk liability through voluntary involvement without the protection of these laws.

There are notable differences in the range of these laws among different states. First aiders are covered by a Good Samaritan law in some states, but this is not the case in most states. Some state laws cover only physicans and nurses, or only automobile accidents.

The only way to determine whether you are protected and under what circumstances is to look carefully at your state law. Here is an example of a typical Good Samaritan law:

No person who in good faith renders emergency care at the scene of an emergency or who participates in transporting injured persons therefrom for medical treatment, shall be liable for civil damages resulting from any act or omission in the rendering of such emergency care, or in transporting such persons, other than for acts or omissions constituting gross negligence or willful or wanton misconduct.

Volunteer first aid and rescue personnel are usually given protection because there is no profit or expectation of payment involved.

Aside from vagueness, Good Samaritan laws have another weakness. Although they protect covered individuals from negligence, they generally do not protect individuals against the more extreme cases of negligence, which are legally classified as "gross negligence" or "wanton, willful, or reckless conduct."

Even where the Good Samaritan laws clearly apply, a victim has the right to file a lawsuit. Good Samaritan laws do not prevent the start of litigation.

After rendering first aid, record the basic facts pertaining to the emergency for possible future litigation. Information for filing might include:

Victim's name, age, sex, marital status, occupation
Address and telephone number
Time and date of emergency and time when first aid began and ended
When and where the emergency happened
Injuries and/or illnesses observed
First aid rendered
Witnesses to the emergency and to the rendered treatment
Disposition of the victim (released to ambulance, family, friends, physician, others).

I shall pass through this life but once.
Any good, therefore, that I can do
Or any kindness I can show to any fellow
    creature
Let me do it now.
Let me not defer or neglect it,
For I shall not pass this way again.

Etienne de Grellet

Chapter 2

Victim Examination*

A systematic and complete examination of the victim is essential to evaluate the extent of a victim's illness and/or injury in order to provide adequate first aid.

To be effective, an examination should

Quickly discover life-threatening problems
Take only a few minutes to complete
Be appropriate to both illness and injury situations.

You can observe a lot just by watchin'.

Yogi Berra (Former New York Yankee baseball player)

A victim examination described here has two major parts: a primary survey to discover conditions that are immediately life-threatening, and a secondary survey to discover injuries and the complications of illness that

*This chapter is adapted with permission from Grant and Murray, *Emergency Care* (Bowie, Md.: Robert Brady Co, 1978).

do not pose an immediate threat to life but that may eventually become life-threatening if they remain uncorrected.

Accident victims should always be surveyed whether they are conscious or unconscious. Accident victims may have obvious as well as not-so-obvious injuries. Every unconscious person should also be examined regardless of whether coma has been produced by trauma or illness.

We don't see things as they are, but as we are.

THE PRIMARY SURVEY

Many conditions can become life-threatening if they remain uncorrected. However, two of them require immediate attention if a person is to survive—airway obstruction and severe bleeding. An obstructed airway quickly leads to respiratory arrest, which could lead shortly to cardiac arrest and death. Profuse bleeding causes a condition of severe shock. In either case, death will occur in a very few minutes if no attempt is made to correct the problem. Thus, it is imperative that a survey for conditions that pose an immediate threat to life be carried out as soon as a sick or injured person is reached.

As you start a primary survey, bring to mind any significant observations made as you approach the victim. If (1) statements from bystanders, relatives or witnesses; (2) your observation of the mechanism of injury; (3) deformity; or (4) characteristic signs such as upraised arms cause you to suspect a spinal injury, treat the person with extreme care as you carry out the steps of the survey. If an object is impaled in the person, take care not to disturb it during the examination procedure. Be careful not to move deformed or dislocated limbs. In short, do nothing that may aggravate existing injuries or introduce new ones unless movement is necessary for a life-saving effort.

First, assure an open airway.   A person who stops breathing has only a few minutes to live. Thus it is imperative that you check the victim for an open airway before doing anything else.

Take a position at the person's side. Place one hand on the individual's forehead and your other hand under the neck. With hands so positioned, push down on the forehead and lift up the neck (Figure 2–1). This hyperextends the neck and places the airway in the most favorable position. If a spinal injury is suspected, use an alternative method for establishing an airway, one that does not involve hyperextension of the neck. An alternative technique will be discussed in a later chapter (see page 50 and Figure 3–2).

Next, check for adequate breathing.   Knowing that the victim's airway is open is not enough. Check to assure that there is a sufficient air exchange.

Look for the chest movements that are associated with breathing and listen and feel for air movement at the victim's mouth and nose (Figure 2–2).

If the victim is breathing, go on with the survey. If the victim is not, however, quickly begin artificial respiration with four quick breaths by either the mouth-to-mouth or mouth-to-nose technique (Figure 2–3) and clear away any airway obstruction. If the person does not start to breathe after four quick breaths given without pause through an unobstructed airway, then very quickly check for circulation.

Check for circulation.   If the person has been in respiratory arrest for a few minutes, he or she may have developed cardiac arrest as well.

Determine if there is heart action and blood circulation by palpating a carotid pulse point in the neck (Figure 2–4). Remember that the carotid arteries are large vessels that lie close to the surface on both sides of the neck, just away from the midline. If a carotid pulse can be felt, continue to give mouth-to-mouth resuscitation to the victim until respiration begins again or until the victim is transported to a medical facility.

If there is no carotid pulse, however, start cardiopulmonary resuscitation (CPR) without delay. With every second that the brain goes without an adequately oxygenated blood supply, the chance for the person's recovery decreases sharply. The technique of CPR is more fully explained in Chapter 3.

If the victim's airway is open and if he or she is breathing and has a carotid pulse, then look for bleeding.

FIGURE 2–1

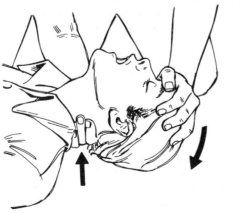

FIGURE 2–2 Recognition of airway obstruction. Look, listen, and feel for air exchange.

The carotid arteries along the neck convey the blood to the head, and if pressure is applied to them, the individual drops off into a stupor or slumbers. Hence, the Greeks, who knew of this, called these arteries the "karotides" from the Greek work *karoun*, meaning to stupefy.

Look for profuse bleeding.   Bleeding wounds are not always as severe as they first appear. Many grotesque wounds involve extensive damage to soft

FIGURE 2–3

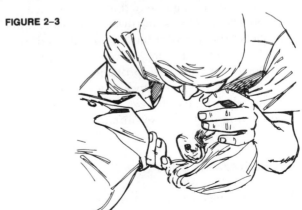

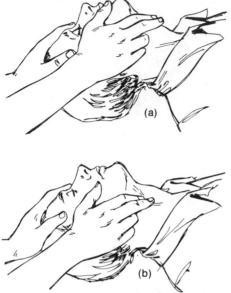

FIGURE 2–4

tissues but do not present an immediate threat to life unless bleeding is profuse. Prompt direct-pressure control of external bleeding is essential in any injury situation, but if bleeding is not life-threatening, the haste that often leads to the aggravation of other injuries can be avoided.

Severe or profuse bleeding means that blood must be spurting or flowing rapidly from a wound. Such bleeding indicates that heart action is still present. Apply direct pressure while looking for signs of breathing—the emphasis is on an open airway and adequate breathing.

Control serious bleeding by direct pressure on the wound and elevation of the injured part. Use a tourniquet only as a last resort when all other attempts at controlling the bleeding have failed.

It is often suggested that the absence of a distal pulse indicates a severed artery. This is not always the case. A pinched—not severed—artery may cause the loss of a pulse in an injured extremity.

When the primary survey for life-threatening problems has been completed (and any such problems have been attended to), proceed to the next phase of the victim evaluation. Where there is more than one victim, conduct all primary surveys and control all life-threatening problems before moving on to any secondary survey.

THE SECONDARY SURVEY

Recall the objective of a secondary survey—to discover problems that do not pose an immediate threat to survival but may do so if they remain uncorrected. The secondary survey has two parts: a subjective interview and an objective examination. The *subjective interview* is not unlike that conducted by a physician prior to a complete physical examination. During the interview you use the victim as a source of information. You ask the person who he or she is, what happened, and what current medical problems may complicate either emergency care or later medical care measures. The *objective examination*, on the other hand, is a comprehensive hands-on survey during which you check virtually every part of the victim's body for less-than-obvious injuries or the effects of an illness. From the findings of the interview and examination you can make an assessment of the victim's condition and form a plan of emergency care.

TABLE 2–1   Victim Evaluation

PRIMARY SURVEY

   Airway?
   Breathing?
   Circulation: Pulse? Bleeding?

SECONDARY SURVEY

Subjective
1. Introduce self and reassure
2. Main complaint?
3. Victim's name?
4. Past health?
5. Current medications?
6. Allergies?

Objective
1. **Vital signs:**
   Pulse: rate
   Respiration: rate
   Temperature
   Skin color

2. **Head-to-toe:**
   Head and scalp: Bleeding? Deformity?
   Pupils: Equal? Reactive?
   Eyelid color: Pink or pale?
   Ears and nose: Fluid or blood?
   Mouth: Clear?
   Neck: Spine tenderness?
   Chest: Pain? Penetration?
   Abdomen: Penetration? Tenderness?
   Lumbar spine: Tenderness?
   Pelvis: Compression pain?
   Legs: Injury? Deformity or tenderness? Pedal pulse?
          Foot wave? Toe touch sensation?
   Arms: Injury? Deformity or tenderness? Radial pulse?
          Hand wave/grasp? Finger touch sensation?
   Back: Wound?

Source: Adapted from Phillips, *Basic Life Support Skills* (Bowie, Md.: Robert J. Brady Co., 1977).

To do a victim examination, a few tools are useful though not essential:

A flashlight or *pen light* is useful when a survey must be conducted under poor light conditions, when it is necessary to look into a person's mouth, and when you are checking for pupillary response.

Heavy-duty scissors can be used to cut away clothing that may obscure an injury site; they are also required when boots or high top shoes must be removed to expose an injury site.

A *piece of paper* can be used to record the results of a survey; thus, accurate information can be passed on to medical personnel.

A *pen* or *pencil* is necessary.

A *watch with a second hand* is required for accurate measurement of pulse and respiration rates.

Signs That Are Significant to the Examination

A number of examination signs are noticeable during the secondary survey. For practical purposes these signs are divided into vital signs and other examination signs. Vital signs are especially important because they indicate the status of basic life processes. The vital signs that first aiders should know are respiration, pulse, skin color, and temperature.

Throughout the discussion of the secondary survey, the term *normal* appears many times. Reference will be made to normal respiratory rate and to normal pulse rate. It is important to know what the normal vital signs are in a healthy and uninjured person. Then, when examining a sick or injured person, you will have a basis for comparison. Keep in mind that it is the abnormalities in examination signs that provide clues about a person's condition.

A *sign* is something the rescuer sees, hears, or feels—for example, a pale face, no respiration, cold skin.

A *symptom* is something the victim tells the rescuer about—the person feels nauseated, has back pain, or has no sensation in the extremities.

The Subjective Interview

Recall that a subjective interview is actually a conversational information-gathering effort. When a person is unconscious, there is neither need nor time for conversation or for the usual introductory amenities characteristic of an effective first aider. The survey for life-threatening problems and subsequent first aid must start without delay. However, when a sick or injured person is conscious and coherent, being close to the person and speaking a few kind and reassuring words can do much to reduce apprehension and promote cooperation.

First, position yourself close to the victim. The person should be able to see you. You should not be just a voice without a face.

Depending on the victim's situation, kneel or stand close by. If at all possible, position yourself so that the sun or other bright light is not behind your back.

Introduce yourself and reassure the victim. It is important for sick or injured people to know right from the start that they are in competent hands. Tell the victim your name. Maintain eye contact as you speak. If another person is recording information, rest your hand gently on the victim's shoulder or arm, or place your hand over the victim's hand as you ask questions during the subjective interview. The simple act of touching is comforting to most people, but especially to children or the elderly.

Eliminate trite phrases from your conversation. Comments like "Everything is all right," "You're fine," and "Don't worry" are meaningless to a sick or injured person. Obviously everything is not all right; the person is not fine or else he or she would not be lying there suffering pain. Explain what you are going to do.

Learn the victim's name. Knowing who the victim is also allows you to address him or her by name—a personal touch that is often reassuring in itself. Once you have learned the person's name, repeat it to yourself a few times and then use it in conversation.

Seek out the main complaint. Unless the pain of one injury masks that of another, or unless a spinal injury has interrupted nerve pathways, an injured person will be able to tell of painful areas. A sick person, of course, will be able to tell of pain or discomfort.

If the victim has been injured in an accident, ask whether there is numbness, tingling, burning, or any other unusual sensation in the arms or legs. Such sensations in extremities suggest damage to the spinal cord and warn against moving the victim any more than necessary during the remainder of the survey procedure.

Learn of any previous relevant experience. Accidents and illness alike can sometimes be attributed to a past medical condition. Ask the victim if a similar experience was ever encountered.

Determine the current medical status. Ask injured victims if they are presently under a doctor's care. If yes, ask for the doctor's name and for what condition the victim is being treated. The information is usually important to the staff of the emergency department to which the person will be delivered.

Find out what medications the victim is taking.   Although this information will have little or no bearing on your first aid measures, it may be extremely important to the emergency department staff as they formulate definitive care procedures.

Finally, determine any known allergies.   This may be important to the emergency department staff or in the emergency handling of anaphylactic shock.

Some may question the need for a subjective interview and even argue the merit of asking questions that have no direct bearing on the first aid measures. It takes only a minute to conduct the interview, however, and the brief history that is obtained may be extremely valuable to the emergency department physician, especially if the victim loses consciousness during the trip to the hospital.

The Objective Examination

Like a subjective interview, an objective examination is conducted to discover injuries or the effects of illness. However, during the objective examination you learn about the victim from personal observation rather than from the responses to your questions—responses that may be vague, incomplete, or even misleading. This portion of a secondary survey begins with a determination of vital signs and continues with a head-to-toe examination during which you systematically employ your physical senses.

Determine vital signs.   Remember that the vital signs are pulse, respiration, temperature, and skin color. By following a simple procedure, you can quickly check both the victim's pulse rate and rate of respirations.

In 1707, Sir John Floyer, an English physician, invented the second hand on watches. He called his watch the "physician's pulse watch." Until Floyer's invention, watches were capable of recording only the hours.

A number of attempts to estimate the pulse rate were made by early observers before the second hand on watches was invented.

Determine the pulse rate.   Each time an electrical impulse causes a person's heart to contract or beat, blood is forced from the organ into a network of vessels that leads to all parts of the body. Because the pumping action is rhythmic, blood moves through the arteries in pressure waves, not smoothly and continuously like water flowing through a pipe. A fingertip held over an artery where it either crosses a bone or lies close to the skin surface can easily feel characteristic pulsations as the pressure wave causes the vessel wall to expand; hence the term *pulse*.

Rate varies among individuals (see Table 2-2). The normal pulse rate in an adult at rest is usually between 60 and 80 beats per minute.

Normal pulse rates in children are faster than in adults, between 80 and 100 beats per minute. Along with age (mild increases in old age), several other factors influence a person's pulse rate, including the individual's sex (women's are faster), physical condition, degree of exercise just completed, body size, and emotional stress at the time of measurement.

Pulse rate can be determined at a number of points throughout the body, but the usual method is to palpate a radial pulse point.

Find the radial pulse point by placing the tips of your index and long fingers on the middle of the victim's wrist (Figure 2-5). Move your fingertips slightly off center (toward the victim's thumb) until pulsations of the underlying artery can be felt. It may be necessary to press rather firmly, especially if the pulse is weak. Be careful not to press too firmly, however, because interference with blood flow could occur. Count the pulse rate for 30 seconds and multiply the count by 2, or count for 15 seconds and multiply by 4 to determine the number of beats per minute.

If you have difficulty in finding a radial pulse point, you can determine pulse rate by feeling a carotid artery in the neck.

CRITICAL PULSE RATES (AT REST):

< 50 beats per minute
> 120 beats per minute

TABLE 2-2   Normal Pulse Rate

60–70	Men
70–80	Women
80-90	Children over seven years
80–120	Children from one to seven years
110–130	Infants

Pulse Classified in Adults

60 and below	Slow or subnormal
60–80	Normal (men, women)
80–100	Moderate increase
100–120	Quick
120–140	Rapid
140 and above	Running (hard to count)

Source: U.S. Public Health Service, *The Ship's Medicine Chest and Medical Aid at Sea*.

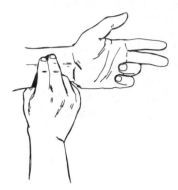

FIGURE 2-5

Locate a carotid pulse point by placing the tips of the index and middle fingers on the victim's Adam's apple. It may be prominent in some people, not so prominent in others. Slide your fingertips off the midline to the side of the neck nearest you and you will feel pulsations in the carotid artery. Learn to locate carotid pulse points quickly. Remember that quick identification of the carotid pulse is essential in CPR efforts. Don't press both carotid arteries at the same time. Do not use your thumb to feel the pulse—it has its own pulse (see Figure 2-4).

Visible pulsations can normally be seen at the carotid artery in a victim lying down; pulsations disappear as the victim is elevated to a sitting position (usually 45°).

Never put too much pressure on the carotid, especially in victims who have had a heart attack—the heart's electrical conduction system may be disturbed.

Variations in pulse are significant of a number of disorders, as shown in Table 2-3.

Determine the rate of respiration.   As with the pulse, the only concern for respiration during a primary survey is that the victim is breathing through an unobstructed airway. In the secondary survey, however, you should be concerned with the rate of respiration. Stated simply, respiration is the process of breathing.

Rate refers to the number of breaths that a person takes each minute, a breath being the complete inhalation and exhalation cycle. Normal breathing rates for adults at rest vary from 12 to 18 breaths per minute. Children breathe faster (20 times or more per minute)—the rate in infants varies from 35 to 50 breaths per minute. Older persons breathe more slowly. Aside from age, a number of factors influence a person's respiratory rate, including body size, sex, the degree of exercise just completed, and emotional state. Pulse rate and internal temperature also influence the rate of respirations.

TABLE 2–3   Pulse Variations and Medical Conditions

OBSERVATION	POSSIBLE CAUSE OF ABNORMALITY
Rapid, regular, and full pulse	May be caused by nothing more than exertion, may also be caused by fright, hypertension (high blood pressure) or first stage of blood loss
Rapid, regular, and thready pulse	Reliable sign of shock; often evident in later stage of blood loss
No pulse	Cardiac arrest leading to death

Source: Grant and Murray, *Emergency Care* (Bowie, Md.: Robert J. Brady Co., 1978).

CRITICAL RESPIRATION RATES (AT REST):

Adults > 28 breaths per minute
Child (5–12 years), > 36 breaths per minute
Child (1– 5 years), > 44 breaths per minute
Under 8 breaths per minute in any victim.

Start counting respirations as soon as you have determined the pulse rate. In most cases you need not move your hand from the victim's wrist. Continue to grasp the wrist as if you were still measuring pulse rate. Count for 30 seconds and double the number as you watch the victim's chest movements and listen to his or her respirations.

If the person is supine and there is a problem in seeing chest movements or hearing respirations, fold the victim's arms over the chest as you continue to grasp the wrist. Count respirations as chest movements cause the victim's arms to move up and down.

Subtlety in checking respirations while appearing to be measuring pulse rate may be advantageous in some situations. Respiratory rate in an apprehensive victim can change simply because the person knows that you are watching him or her breathe. As you determine the rate and condition of respirations, also listen for distinctive sounds that are characteristic of airway obstructions, such as snoring, crowing, or gurgling. Any noisy breathing is obstructed breathing.

Several observations of respiration that may be indicative of possible abnormalities are listed in Table 2-4.

Determine body or skin temperature.   The third vital sign is temperature—the balance between heat produced in the body and heat lost. There are times when the measurement and recording of internal temperature is

TABLE 2-4   Variations in Respiration and Medical Conditions

OBSERVATION	POSSIBLE CAUSE OF ABNORMALITY
Deep, gasping, labored respiration	Airway obstruction; heart failure; asthma
Rapid, shallow respirations	Shock; cardiac problems; hyperventilation
Painful, difficult, labored respirations	Dyspnea (labored or difficult breathing)
Difficulty in breathing while lying down	Heart failure
Snoring	Stroke, fractured skull, drug influence and alcohol intoxication, soft tissue obstruction
Gurgling respirations (as though the breaths are passing through water)	Foreign matter in throat; pulmonary edema (accumulation of fluid in lungs)
Crowing (birdlike sounds)	Spasms of the larynx; foreign body
Temporary cessation of respirations	Anoxia (lack of oxygen)
No respirations	Respiratory arrest
Wheeze	Spasm or partial obstruction in bronchi (asthma, emphysema)

Source: Grant and Murray, *Emergency Care* (Bowie, Md.: Robert J. Brady Co., 1978).

important, as in cases of heat stroke or when a child has a high fever. Body temperature is often recorded when a person will not be receiving medical care for some time, as in a rural situation when snow or high water prevents the immediate transfer of a sick or injured person to a medical facility.

Body temperature is measured with a *thermometer* that is held for a short time under the tongue, within the rectum, or in the armpit. The techniques are referred to as oral, rectal, and axillary, respectively. A standard glass thermometer should not be used when there is any chance that the victim will bite through it.

Although 98.6°F is considered to be normal (see Table 2-5), the body temperature of healthy individuals may vary from 97°F to 99°F. Temperature at the axilla is usually a degree lower than that measured under the tongue, and rectal temperature is generally a degree higher.

If you include measurement of body temperature in your victim evaluation procedure, record the determination as, for example, "Body temperature is 98.6°F orally."

Skin temperature is not actually a vital sign, but it may be an indicator of abnormally high or low internal temperature. A quick determination can be made during the measurement of vital signs or at any time during the remainder of the victim evaluation procedure.

Determine skin temperature with the back of your hand; your fingertips may be somewhat insensitive because of calluses. If your victim's skin temperature is near normal, you will note no significant difference between the person's own skin surface and the back of your hand. However, if the person's skin is hot or cool, the difference between your skin temperature and that of the victim will usually be quite noticable.

TABLE 2–5 Comparable Readings—Fahrenheit and Centigrade Scales

FAHRENHEIT (F)		CENTIGRADE (C)
108°	Usually Fatal	42.2°
107		41.7
106	Critical Condition	41.1
105		40.6
104		40.0
102	High Fever	39.4
103		38.9
101		38.3
100	Moderate Fever	37.8
99		37.2
98.6	Healthy (Normal) Temperature in Mouth	37.0
98		36.7
97	Subnormal Temperature	36.1
96		35.6
95		35.0

Source: U.S. Public Health Service, *The Ship's Medicine Chest and Medical Aid at Sea.*

CRITICAL BODY TEMPERATURE CONDITION:

Over 104°F in an adult
Over 105°F in a child
Under 95°F in any victim

Observations of a person's skin temperature and the meaning of those observations are summarized in Table 2–6.

Observe the victim's skin color.   A great deal of emphasis is often placed on the significance of a sick or injured person's skin color. Skin color does suggest a variety of medical problems, as shown in Table 2–7. However, changes in coloration are difficult to notice in a person whom you do not know, because you have no basis for comparision. When a person has deeply pigmented skin, it may be necessary to look for color changes in the tongue, nailbeds, or mucous membranes. Note any variations in skin color but do not draw a conclusion as to the nature or extent of a person's illness or injury solely on the basis of this observation. Cyanosis is the bluish color coming from a reduced amount of oxygen in the blood vessels. The best

TABLE 2–6 Temperature Variations and Relevant Medical Conditions

OBSERVATION	POSSIBLE CAUSE OF ABNORMALITY
Cool, clammy skin	Usual sign of shock, heat exhaustion
Cold, moist skin	Body is losing heat
Cold, dry skin	Body has been exposed to cold and has lost considerable heat
Hot, dry skin	Excessive body heat (as in heat stroke and high fever)
"Goose pimples" accompanied by shivering, chattering teeth, blue lips and pale skin	Chills caused (among other things) by malaria, communicable disease, pneumonia, pain or even fear, hypothermia

Source: Grant and Murray, *Emergency Care* (Bowie, Md.: Robert J. Brady Co., 1978).

place to look for cyanosis is under the tongue or on the inside cheek membranes. Lips and nailbeds vary too much to be useful, and besides, peripheral blood flow can be unrelated to the adequacy of respiration.

The Head-to-Toe Survey

During this final portion of the secondary survey, you systematically use your physical senses in a number of ways as you make an all-inclusive body survey. Not all first aid situations may require such a complete survey.

Inspection is the visual examination of a body part. During the examination you look for deformities, wounds, an opening in the neck, chest movement, and so on.

Palpation is examination with the fingers or hands. Through your fingers you can learn of tenderness, pulsations of blood vessels, and grating bone ends.

Check the scalp for wounds.   Extreme care must be exercised during this step to avoid moving the person's head any more than is absolutely necessary; movement may aggravate a spinal injury. In addition, be careful

TABLE 2–7 Medical Significance of Changes in Skin Color

OBSERVATION	POSSIBLE CAUSE OF ABNORMALITY
Red skin	High blood pressure, stroke, heart attack, alcohol intoxication, sunburn, infectious disease, simple blushing, fever, allergic reactions
White skin	Shock, heart attack, fright, anemia, simple fainting, emotional distress, blood loss
Blue skin	Asphyxia (suffocation), anoxia (lack of oxygen), heart attack, poisoning, cold exposure
Black and blue skin	Seepage of blood under skin surface

Source: Grant and Murray, *Emergency Care* (Bowie, Md.: Robert J. Brady Co., 1978).

not to drive in any bone fragments or force dirt into a wound that may be associated with a skull fracture. Always keep in mind that the brain is easily contaminated by foreign matter. Resultant infection may be fatal.

If blood is seen or felt, separate strands of hair so that you can determine the location and extent of bleeding. When the victim is lying face up, check the part of the scalp that is hidden by placing your fingers behind the neck and sliding them upward toward the top of the head. Note any "goose egg" that may be the sign of bleeding under the scalp (Figure 2–6).

Examine the pupils for equality and reactivity.   The pupils of a healthy person's eyes are regular in outline and of the same size. They are also reactive to light; that is to say, they *constrict* (become small) in response to a bright light and they *dilate* (become large) when the light source is removed. There are also conditions that cause the pupils to constrict and remain constricted, or to become unequal in size (Figure 2–7). Some observations of pupil abnormalities and their possible causes are summarized in Table 2–8. A small percentage of people normally have unequal pupil size (anisoria).

Examine both of the victim's pupils. If the victim is unconscious, it will be necessary to slide the upper eyelids back. First determine if the pupils are constricted or dilated and if they are equal in size. Then use a small bright light source (such as the beam from a pen light) to determine if the pupils are reactive (Figure 2–8).

If there is no flashlight, cover the eye with your hand and notice the pupil reaction when the eye is uncovered.

As you check for pupil equality and reactivity, look for contact lenses. Prompt removal of contact lenses from the eyes of an unconscious patient may be important to the preservation of the patient's eyesight. See page 124 for contact lens information.

Look at the inner surfaces of the eyelids.   The moist inner surfaces of the eyelids are pink in a normal healthy person. When the hemoglobin content

FIGURE 2–6

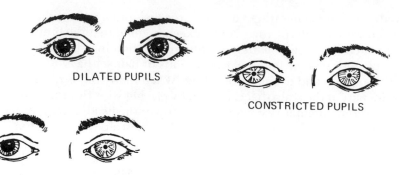

DILATED PUPILS

CONSTRICTED PUPILS

UNEQUAL PUPILS

FIGURE 2–7   Dilated/constricted pupils.

of a person's blood is low, however, the inner eyelids become pale. This is a significant sign. Hemoglobin is an important substance within the red blood cells. It combines with oxygen and enables the blood to carry the life-sustaining fuel to all parts of the body. A reduction in hemoglobin may be the result of anemia or blood loss.

Gently pull down either eyelid and check the color of the inner surface. Remember that it will be either pink or pale (Figure 2–9).

Inspect the ears and nose for blood or clear fluid.   The brain and spinal cord are somewhat cushioned and nourished by a clear, waterlike fluid called *cerebrospinal fluid.* A break in the skull can result in the loss of this fluid into nearby cavities and finally out through the ears or nose or both. Loss of fluid is an important sign both of skull fracture and of underlying brain damage. Blood mixed with this fluid is an indication of skull fracture.

TABLE 2–8   Medical Significance of Changes in Pupil Size

OBSERVATION	POSSIBLE CAUSE OF ABNORMALITY
Dilated pupils that are not responsive to light	Cardiac arrest, influence of drugs such as LSD and amphetamines, unconsciousness from numerous causes
Constricted pupils	Central nervous system disease or disorder; influence of narcotic such as heroin, morphine, or codeine; bright light
Unequal pupils	Stroke; head injury; normal (2–4 percent of the population)
Lackluster pupils that do not appear to focus; dilated	Shock
No pupil response to light; eyes rolled back in head	Death; coma; cataracts in older person; artificial eye

Source: Grant and Murray, *Emergency Care* (Bowie, Md.: Robert J. Brady Co., 1978).

FIGURE 2–8

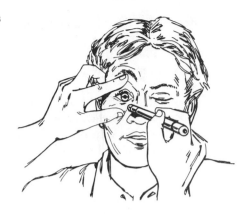

Simply observe the ears and nose for blood and/or clear fluid. Be aware, however, that blood alone coming from the nose often results from nothing more than damage to nasal tissues.

Inspect the mouth for possible causes of airway obstruction and for blood.   The tongue can serve as an anatomical obstruction to one's airway. A variety of foreign objects can obstruct the airway as well, including broken natural teeth, broken dentures, a wad of chewing gum, a bolus of food, vomitus, a ball or other toy, and so on.

Carefully open the victim's mouth and look inside for any possible cause of airway obstruction other than the tongue. If you can reach the object with your fingers, remove it. Take care not to move the person's head in the process. Remember, there still is no indication whether or not the victim has sustained a spinal injury.

If blood is observed during the check for a foreign object, carefully look into the person's mouth for the source of bleeding. If you can find no such source, assume that the blood is coming from the back of the nose or from the lungs or digestive tract. Frothy red blood is an indication of bleeding within the lungs or airways.

FIGURE 2–9

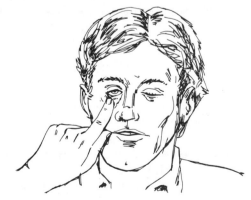

Begin the examination of the victim's neck, body, and extremities. During the remainder of the survey, however, clothing may obscure examination areas and injury sites. As you make your way from head to foot, expose examination areas and injury sites, if necessary, when you come to them.

Exposing examination areas.   There are parts of the body that should be exposed so they can be examined properly.

The neck should be exposed so that you can check for a stoma or a tracheostomy incision. Both are openings in the neck through which a person may breathe. A stoma is a permanent opening, while a tracheostomy incision is a temporary incision that is held open with a tube.

The abdomen can be exposed to: (1) check the abdomen for penetration; and (2) palpate the abdomen for tenderness. In male victims there is usually no problem. A shirt can be unbuttoned or pushed up at the waist. When the victim is female, however, exposing the examination area can be complicated by the type of clothing being worn. Remove whatever clothing may be obscuring the examination area, but do so in such a way that the victim will be neither offended nor embarrassed by the stares of onlookers. First aiders usually have little need to remove the victim's clothing during the head-to-toe examination. Always explain to a female victim what you are doing to her clothing and why. Some male first aiders prefer to have a female do the actual contacting and examining of a female victim. However, do not delay if such assistance is not available.

Be very discreet while examining the victim for injuries. Exposing or touching sexual parts may be offensive to the victim, family, and/or bystanders. It is suggested that the first aider inform the victim and any overly concerned bystander (spouse, child, others) regarding the first aid procedure about to be performed and the reasons it is needed.

Check the corresponding parts of the victim's body as a comparison. For example, compare the right eye with the left eye, right arm with the left arm, and the right side of the chest with the left side.

Where there is a lower extremity injury, it will be necessary to feel the pedal pulse in the foot of the injured side to determine if circulation is impaired. This will present no problem when your victim is wearing dress shoes or low-cut sport shoes. If the victim is wearing high top gym shoes, high top work shoes, or boots, however, it will be necessary to cut the footwear away if manipulation of the foot during unlacing and removal efforts will aggravate an injury. Refer to page 269 for procedures for removing a boot. An exception to the rule of removing high top footwear is when a person is wearing ski boots. These should not be removed unless you are completely familiar with the procedure.

Exposing injury sites.   Clothing covering an injury site must be removed except in the case of severe burns. Extreme care will be necessary, otherwise the removal will be painful and injuries can be aggravated. Clothing should not be forcibly ripped nor should extremities be manipulated in an effort to remove clothing. Instead, material should be cut with scissors.

Feel the cervical spine for point tenderness and deformity.   Point tenderness is a painful response to gentle finger pressure.

Prepare the victim for a possible increase in pain by explaining beforehand what you intend to do. Steady the person's chin with one hand and check the cervical spine for midline point tenderness with your other hand. As you check for point tenderness, be alert for deformity as well.

If point tenderness or deformity is noted in the cervical spine, a sound practice is to stop the survey and temporarily immobilize the victim's head with sandbags or a rolled blanket. The tenderness or deformity indicates the possibility of spinal column damage, and the temporary immobilization reduces the likelihood of dangerous head movement until the survey is completed.

Examine the chest for penetration.   Look for an impaled object or a wound that suggests penetration of the chest wall.

Feel the chest for pain.   Continue examining the victim's chest by gently compressing the sides of the rib cage (Figure 2–10). Tell the person beforehand what you are going to do and explain that it may cause momentary pain. Compression pain is an indication of fractured ribs.

FIGURE 2–10

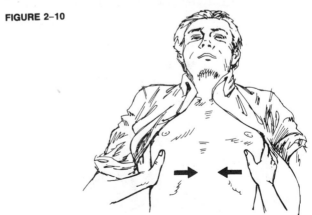

Inspect the abdomen for penetration.   If something is protruding from the abdomen, it will be obvious. Less obvious and perhaps even difficult to see will be a wound produced by a small-caliber bullet or a long, thin weapon such as an ice pick. In either case, external bleeding may not be present because of the self-sealing nature of the abdominal muscles and surrounding fatty tissues.

Feel the abdomen for tenderness.   Once again, preparation of the victim is important. If there is an abdominal injury or illness, the procedure may be painful. Avoid sudden pokes and cold hands.

Lightly feel the victim's abdomen (Figure 2–11). If there is an injury or illness, tenderness may be *local* (confined to one spot) or *diffuse* (spread over a wide area). The victim who has tenderness may guard the painful area by tightening abdominal muscles. A truly rigid abdomen feels boardlike. Feel the four abdominal quadrants. Always examine the abdomen with the victim supine—if the victim is not supine and spinal cord injury is suspect, do not move him or her.

Feel the lower back for point tenderness and deformity.   Preparing the victim for a possible increase in pain is important once again.

Gently slide your hand under the void created by the curve of the spine. As you check for point tenderness, feel for deformity as well.

Feel the pelvis for fractures.   This is another potentially painful procedure, so warning the victim beforehand is in order.

Gently compress the pelvis (Figure 2–12). Painful compression suggests a fracture in the bony structure.

Check each leg for injury and paralysis.   Inspect the leg from thigh to foot. Look for deformity, bleeding, bone protrusion, swelling, and discol-

FIGURE 2–11

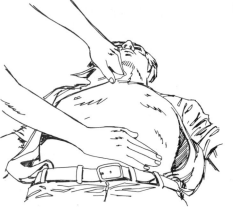

FIGURE 2–12

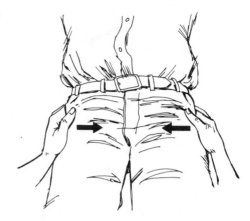

oration. Gently palpate any suspected fracture site for point tenderness.

Knowing that a fracture has been sustained is important, to be sure, but knowing whether circulation has been impaired or nerve pathways have been interrupted is equally important. Feel the pedal pulse either behind the inside ankle bone or at the junction of the great and second toes (Figure 2–13). Presence of a pulse indicates that circulation is intact, while absence of a pulse suggests that the major artery supplying the limb has been pinched or severed by a broken or displaced bone end.

When you have established the presence (or absence) of the pedal pulse, ask the victim to alternately extend and flex the foot (Figure 2–14). Foot wave—the ability to move the foot in this manner—is an indicator that nerve pathways are intact, and inability to move the foot suggests that nerve pathways have been interrupted by injury.

Confirm the continuity (or interruption) of nerve pathways by touching a toe and asking the victim to identify the toe that you touch. Sensation in the toes indicates that nerve pathways are intact.

Finally, check for paralysis in the leg by having the victim press the sole of the foot against the palm of your hand. Inability to do this suggests that motor functions have been impaired by a spinal cord injury.

FIGURE 2–13

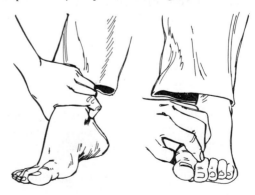

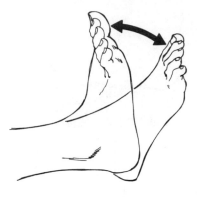

FIGURE 2-14

Reposition an uninjured leg so the other leg can be examined. Examine the leg in the position in which it was found. Once a fractured leg is moved, manual traction will have to be maintained until it can be properly immobilized. Often when first aid efforts are initiated before a secondary survey is complete, the remaining steps of the survey are disregarded; hence, hidden injuries remain undetected.

The previous procedure is repeated for the other leg after the leg is straightened, with the pant leg cut if needed.

The previous tests serve to discover closed fractures; they also serve to discover damage to the spinal cord. Loss of sensation and paralysis in one leg can usually be attributed to a pinching or severing of a major nerve pathway by a broken or displaced bone end. But when both legs are paralyzed, it is likely that the spinal cord has been damaged. The approximate location of such an injury can be determined by a series of similar tests performed on the upper extremities as well.

Check each arm for injury and paralysis.   Inspect the arm from clavicle to fingertips. Look for deformity, bleeding, bone protrusion, swelling, and discoloration. Gently feel any suspected fracture site for point tenderness. Feel the radial pulse point. As in the legs, circulation is intact when the distal pulse is present.

Ask the victim to flex and extend the hand. Hand wave is a sign that nerve pathways are intact (Figure 2-15). Confirm the continuity of nerve pathways by asking the victim to identify fingers as they are touched. Finally, ask the victim to grip your hand. Note the force of the grip. A strong grip indicates that motor functions have not been impaired by a spinal cord injury. The procedure should be repeated for the other arm.

If both upper and lower extremities are paralyzed, damage to the spinal cord has most likely occurred in the neck. If movement and sensations are noted in the arms, however, cord damage has been sustained below the neck.

Needless to say, an unconscious person cannot be tested for a possible

FIGURE 2–15

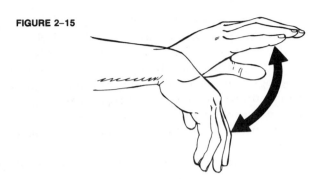

spinal cord injury in the manner just described. However, you may determine whether cord damage has been sustained by watching the person's response to a stimulus. A sharp-pointed object such as a pin should not be used.

Scratch the soles of an unconscious person's feet (Figure 2–16) with a disengaged ball point pen or similar object that is not sharp. If the muscles are not paralyzed, the leg will quickly be pulled away in response. If the muscles are paralyzed, there will be no such reflex action.

Determine the approximate location of cord damage by repeating the prodecure on the person's hands. If the hands jump in response to the stimulus, the injury is below the neck. On the other hand, if there is no reflex action noted in the hands either, it is likely that the person has sustained injury to the cord in the neck.

Another stimulus for testing for nerve damage is pressing your fingernail into the victim's nailbed. Nailbeds are extremely sensitive. This causes no injury, and it eliminates multiple bruising from pinching the skin.

FIGURE 2–16   Surveying the unconscious victim.

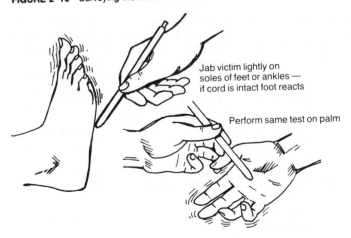

Jab victim lightly on
soles of feet or ankles —
if cord is intact foot reacts

Perform same test on palm

Finally, inspect the back surfaces. Provided there are no injuries to either the spine or the extremities, logroll the victim onto one side so that you can check the back surfaces for wounds.

The victim evaluation procedure is now complete. On the basis of the findings, conclusions as to the nature and extent of the injuries or illness can be drawn and complete first aid can be provided. Table 2–1 (page 19) presents a systematic outline for a complete victim examination. Obviously, for many first aid situations such a complete victim evaluation is not needed.

The victim is entitled to a certain degree of privacy during and after first aid. Confidentiality can be maintained by being discreet in conversations about the victim, especially to bystanders, during first aid care.

Be quick to act in emergencies, but slow to discuss them afterwards.

Evaluating the Unconscious Victim. Although the specific cause of the unconsciousness may not be known at once, an orderly routine is urgent. Immediate findings may call for first aid measures. Some general rules follow:

1. Breathing and bleeding are top priorities. First, make sure that the airway is open; if there is no breathing, begin artificial respiration at once. Make a quick overall check for serious bleeding; if found, bleeding must be stopped.
2. Unless the victim is lying in a dangerous spot, do not move him or her until first aid is completed.
3. Remove spectacles or dentures, and loosen tight clothing around neck, chest, and abdomen.
4. Look into the victim's wallet for a *card*, or elsewhere on the body for a *metal tag* or *bracelet* that shows the *Emergency Medical Identification Symbol* (see Figure 2–18). The symbol identifies people with special medical problems that might be neglected in an emergency or aggravated by usual emergency treatment. (See page 40 for additional information.) If looking in a purse or wallet, have a reliable witness whom you have informed about the reason for looking through the victim's purse or wallet. This will help protect against later theft accusations. Some states have laws against such searches.
5. If the victim is breathing, lay him or her on one side so that vomitus will run out of the mouth and the tongue will be kept from falling back into the throat, which could cause choking (Figure 2–17).
6. If breathing seems difficult, extend the head by pushing the jaw forward with fingers pressing behind the angle of the jaw. This will keep the tongue from falling back into the throat.
7. Put blankets or coats over and under the victim for warmth. Use special care if spinal cord injury is suspected.

FIGURE 2-17

8. Give nothing by mouth until the victim regains consciousness.

9. Keep the victim under continuous observation, noting color of face and rates of pulse and respiration. If the face is pale, the head should be lowered. If the face is flushed, use a pillow, rolled clothing, or towels underneath the head and shoulder to raise these a few inches.

10. If the victim is restless, restrain gently any movements that might be injurious—but do not use force.

11. As conscousness returns, treat for shock (see page 110).

12. Question observers of the incident as to what caused the unconsciousness before taking a history or making a more detailed examination.

13. Get medical advice.

The Unconscious Victim

Even though no emergency care measures are indicated, care for an unconscious person involves more than transportation to a medical facility. If you do nothing more, you should care for the eyes, properly position the injured for drainage of fluids, and prevent accidental ingestion of any liquids or solids. Because of the danger associated with aspiration of fluid into the lungs, an unconscious person should never be given liquids or solids by mouth.

Care for an unconscious victim's eyes. The eyes of an unconscious person are especially vulnerable to injury. If your victim evaluation procedure indicates that the person is not wearing contact lenses, you need only keep the person's eyes closed until you can deliver him or her to a medical facility. This requires a little effort but is vitally important to the preservation of an unconscious person's eyesight. Eye surfaces are kept moist by normal tear production and are continually swept clean of any airborne debris by the blinking action of the eyelias. Neither tearing nor blinking occurs when a person is unconscious, and if the eyes remain open, the surfaces dry quickly and ulcerate. Injury is permanent, and the result is blindness.

When caring for an unconscious person whose eyes are open, gently close the lids and either hold them closed with strips of clear tape or secure water-moistened dressings over the closed lids with a bandage.

See p. 124 for contact lens information.

Positioning an unconscious victim.   If you have established by a complete victim evaluation procedure that there are no injuries to be cared for, you can prepare your unconscious victim for transportation to a medical facility. Proper positioning is important.

When an unconscious person is placed in the usual supine position (on the back), the tongue may drop back into the throat and block the airway. Placing a pillow under the victim's head only increases the probability of an obstructed airway. However, obstruction of the airway by the tongue is not the only danger when an unconscious person is transported on the back. If the person vomits, it is likely that the contents will be aspirated into the lungs. Fluid in the lungs can cause lethal complications and, of course, the vomitus itself can cause airway obstruction.

The coma position—uninjured victim.   To prevent the possibility of airway obstruction by the tongue and aspiration of vomitus, prepare an unconscious and uninjured victim as shown in Figure 2–17 (page 39).

Assure that the airway is open by feeling for air exchange with your cupped hand. Carefully monitor respirations.

The traumatic coma position.   Traumatic coma is the state of profound unconsciousness that may be noted in severely injured persons. Initial care for a comatose accident victim is slightly more complex because the possibility of a spinal fracture must be assumed.

Emergency care textbooks have traditionally recommended immobilizing and transporting unconscious accident victims supine on a spine board because of the possibility of a cervical fracture. In his book *Basic Life Support Skills Manual,* Dr. Charles Phillips argues that an unconscious accident victim should be transported on the side rather than on the back. He states: "Since the chance for a cervical fracture is about 1 percent and the possibility of immediate death from asphyxiation and delayed death due to aspiration pneumonia is greater than 1 percent, airway consideration dictates the side position."

Because of the danger associated with aspiration of fluid into the lungs, an unconscious person should never be given any liquid or solid by mouth.

EMERGENCY MEDICAL IDENTIFICATION SYMBOL

The *Emergency Medical Identification Symbol* (Figure 2–18) is worn or carried by many people. The American Medical Association designed the symbol to identify people who have medical problems that might be neglected in an emergency or aggravated by usual emergency treatment.

It may save a life or lessen disability. Worn as a bracelet, necklace, or

TABLE 2-9 Causes of Unconsciousness and Emergency Medical Management

CATEGORY	PROBLEM	CAUSE	PATHOPHYSIOLOGY	MANAGEMENT	CHAPTER REFERENCE
General	Loss of consciousness	Injury or disease	Shock, head injury, other injuries/diabetes, arteriosclerosis	Need for CPR; triage, priority one	2
Diseases	Diabetic coma	Hyperglycemia and acidosis	Inadequate use of sugar, acidosis	Complex treatment for acidosis	12
	Insulin shock	Hypoglycemia	Excess insulin	Sugar	12
	Myocardial infarct	Damaged myocardium	Insufficient cardiac output	Oxygen, CPR, transport	12
	Stroke	Damaged brain	Loss of arterial supply to brain or hemorrhage within brain	Support, *gentle* transport	12
Injury	Hemorrhagic shock	Bleeding	Hypovolemia	Control external bleeding, recognize internal bleeding, CPR, transport	4, 5
	Respiratory shock	Insufficient O_2	Paralysis, chest damage, airway obstruction	Clear airway, supplemental O_2, CPR, transport	5
	Anaphylactic shock	Acute contact with agent to which patient is sensitive	Allergic reaction	Intramuscular epinephrine, support, CPR, transport	5, 8, 12

41

TABLE 2-9 Causes of Unconsciousness and Emergency Medical Management (continued)

CATEGORY	PROBLEM	CAUSE	PATHOPHYSIOLOGY	MANAGEMENT	CHAPTER REFERENCE
	Cerebral contusion, concussion, or hematoma	Blunt head injury	Bleeding into or around brain, concussive effect of blow	Clear airway, supplemental O$_2$, CPR, careful monitoring, transport	6
Emotions	Psychogenic shock	Emotional reaction	Sudden drop in cerebral blood flow	Place supine, make comfortable, observe for injuries	5
Environment	Heatstroke	Excessive heat, inability to sweat	Brain damage from heat	Immediate cooling, support, CPR, transport	10
	Electric Shock	Contact with electric current	Cardiac abnormalities, fibrillation, standstill	CPR, transport; *do not treat until current controlled*	3
	Systemic hypothermia	Prolonged exposure to cold	Diminished cerebral function, cardiac arrhythmias	CPR, rapid transport, warming at hospital	10
	Drowning	O$_2$; CO$_2$; breath holding, H$_2$O inhalation	Cerebral damage (O$_2$)	CPR, transport	3

Category	Condition	Mechanism/Cause	Pathophysiology	Treatment	
	Air embolism	Intravascular air	Obstruction to arterial blood flow by air bubbles	CPR, recompression	—
	Decompression sickness ("bends")	Intravascular nitrogen	Obstruction to arterial blood flow by nitrogen bubbles	CPR, recompression	—
Injected or ingested agents	Alcohol	Excess intake	Cerebral depression	Support, CPR, transport	14
	Drugs	Excess intake	Cerebral depression	Support, CPR, transport (bring drug)	14
	Plant poisons	Contact, ingestion	Direct cerebral or other toxic effect	Support, recognition, CPR, identify plant, local wound care, transport	8
	Animal poisons	Contact, ingestion, injection	Direct cerebral or other toxic effect	Recognition, support, CPR, identify agent, local wound care, transport	8
Neurological disease	Epilepsy	Brain injury, scar, genetic predisposition, disease	Excitable focus of motor activity in brain	Support, protect patient, transport in status epilepticus	12

Source: American Academy of Orthopaedic Surgeons, *Emergency Care and Transportation.*

FIGURE 2-18   Emergency Medical Identification Symbol.

anklet, the symbol means that the person has special health needs that must not be ignored if the person is injured or suddenly taken ill. A card in a pocket, wallet, or purse will explain the victim's special needs. Everyone with special medical problems, or who takes medicines regularly, or has dangerous allergies, or who requires special medical attention of any kind—such as the hard-of-hearing, heart patients, contact lens wearers, epileptics, diabetics, or non-English speakers—should wear the *Emergency Medical Identification Symbol* and carry an *Emergency Medical Identification* card.

   EMI cards and emblems.   Pocket or wallet cards are available from the American Medical Association or some voluntary health agencies that deal with special health problems. Bracelets and necklaces may be obtained from several sources.

SIGNS OF DEATH

To everything there is a season . . . a time to be born, and a time to die . . .

Ecclesiastes 3:1-2

   Modern methods of resuscitation have been spectacularly successful—so much so that the point at which death occurs is difficult to determine. First aiders should be equipped with a knowledge of how to recognize death. The signs of death may be divided into two classes, depending upon whether they arise *shortly after death* (presumptive signs) or *sometime later* (positive signs).

   Early signs (presumptive) of death are absence of heartbeat and breathing for at least 20 minutes. It is difficult for a first aider to determine with certainty when the heart stops beating. Besides feeling for the pulse, the first aider should search for the heart sounds by listening with an ear applied directly to the chest, just to the left of the breastbone.

The following is considered a time-honored test if breathing is not superficially apparent: Obtain a clean mirror, make sure it is cooler than body temperature, and hold it before the victim's mouth and nostrils. If the victim is breathing, even shallowly, the mirror will fog; that is, moisture from the breath will condense on its cool surface. If a polished mirror is not available, a wisp of cotton placed on the slightly opened lips of the person or before a nostril opening should indicate air current if there is life and breathing.

It never should be forgotten that a person may appear to be dead when he or she is still alive. *Death* is the cessation of life beyond the possibility of resuscitation. *Suspended animation (or death trance)*, which imitates death, is total unconsciousness with scarcely any respiration, heartbeat, or other obvious signs of life. Suspended animation may occur as a part of such things as neuropsychiatric disorders (hysteria, for instance), debilitating disease, submersion, gas poisoning, electric shock, or any major injury followed by shock, whether or not there are large wounds, massive hemorrhage, or extensive tissue damage. Breathing may be so shallow that it cannot be distinguished by ordinary methods, or breathing may stop before the heart stops beating. Heart sounds may be so faint that they cannot be heard by ordinary means. The pulse may be so feeble that it cannot be detected by touch. The pupils of the eyes may be dilated and fail to react to light. The eyelids may be half-closed and the cornea (the transparent covering of the front of the eyeball) insensitive to touch.

Therefore, if the circumstances suggest suspended animation, resuscitation efforts should not be stopped until the fact of death is definitely established—even if one or more of the early signs of apparent death are present. Unless the person is unquestionably dead, time should not be wasted in looking for the early, minute signs of death. Instead, every effort should be centered on resuscitation.

In most cases, death is unmistakable when it occurs. It will not be necessary to wait for the later signs to confirm death. From legal and other points of view, the record of the case should include a description of those later signs of death that were observed. The later conclusive signs (positive) of death include:

Drop in body temperature. In doubtful cases, a clinical thermometer (usually not readily available) should be placed in the rectum. Occasionally the temperature remains stationary or rises for a short time after death. However, cooling soon occurs and usually the body temperature drops several degrees Fahrenheit each hour after death, except in the tropics or under circumstances where the room temperature approaches body temperature ($98.6°F$

or 37°C). The rate of fall depends upon the temperature at the time of death, the amount of fatty tissue under the skin, the amount of clothing worn, and weather conditions.

Rigor mortis. A stiffening of the muscles and rigidity of the body usually appears within two to eight hours after death and lasts 16 to 24 hours. However, the onset of rigor mortis and its duration are subject to wide variation. Rigor mortis usually begins in the facial muscles, extends gradually to the legs, and disappears in the same order.

Care must be taken not to confuse rigor mortis with the muscular spasm and rigidity that sometimes occur almost immediately after an electric shock or in some cases of poisoning. Early rigidity is not a reason for discontinuing artificial respiration or other attempts at resuscitation.

Postmortem lividity. The skin upon which the body rests—usually at the buttocks, back, and shoulders—gradually becomes discolored several hours after death. This discoloration is due to the settling of blood into the lowest parts of the body as it lies in one position. These purplish or reddish-violet spots are known as "death spots," corpse lividity, postmortem lividity, or cadaveric lividity.

These spots, sometimes mistaken for bruises, usually can be distinguished from bruises in two ways: (1) *lividity spots* would not have been present before death; and (2) *bruises* will show considerable blood or perhaps a clot, while the lividity spots will not. Lividity spots provide a sure sign of death.

Putrefaction (rotting, decomposition). This is absolute proof of death. Putrefaction occurs after rigor mortis has disappeared. Ordinarily its onset is not apparent for at least one day after death; and it may be delayed for several days, depending upon such circumstances as the cause of death and whether the body is in a cold or hot and moist climate.

Any man's death diminishes me, because I am involved in mankind; And therefore never send to know for whom the bell tolls; It tolls for thee.

John Donne (1572–1631)

Chapter 3

Artificial Respiration and Cardiopulmonary Resuscitation (CPR)*

Resuscitation is the term that covers measures taken to reverse the dying process in acute, life-threatening conditions. These measures include artificial respiration, which is performed to restore breathing, and external cardiac compression, performed to restore circulation.

CAUSES OF RESPIRATORY FAILURE

Anatomical obstruction can cause respiratory failure or inadequacy.

> *Obstruction by the tongue* is the most common cause of a respiratory emergency. Ironically, it is probably the most easily solved problem.
>
> *Medical problems* that can cause respiratory failure or inadequacy include laryngospasms (spasms of the larynx) and acute asthma, among others.
>
> *Accident-related problems* can cause respiratory failure. A severe blow to the throat can collapse the rigid tracheal tube. Swelling that results from burns of the face and the inhalation of heated air can effectively block air exchange. Corrosive poisons can cause the airways to close.

*This chapter is based on "Standards and Guidelines for Cardiopulmonary Resuscitation (CPR), *The Supplement to the Journal of the American Medical Association*, August 1, 1980. Copyright 1980, the American Medical Association. Reprinted with permission of the American Heart Association.

Mechanical Obstructions result from the introduction of a foreign object into the airway.

A solid foreign body, such as a toy or a piece of meat, can partially or completely block any part of the airway.

Liquids that accumulate in the back of the throat of an unconscious, supine person can block the air passages.

Vomitus that is not quickly removed can also block the airway.

An *insufficient oxygen supply* causes respiratory arrest.

Asphyxiation occurs when a person is forced to breathe in an air mixture that lacks oxygen.

Toxic fumes cause respiratory arrest either by a poisoning effect or because the fumes have displaced the normal air.

Other causes of respiratory failure include:

Drowning
Hanging
Shock (inadequate circulation)
Electrocution
Chest compression (as in a cave-in situation)
Disease that affects respiration, such as pneumonia or emphysema
Injury to the chest, such as a penetrating chest wound
Poisoning by respiration-depressing drugs, such as codeine, morphine, barbiturates, and alcohol.

The world record for voluntarily staying underwater is 13 minutes 42.5 seconds by Robert Foster of Richmond, California, who stayed under 10 feet of water in San Rafael, California, in 1959. He hyperventilated with oxygen for 30 minutes before his descent. The longest breath-hold without oxygen was 6 minutes 29.8 seconds by Georges Pouliquin in Paris in 1912. It must be stressed that record-breaking of this kind is extremely dangerous.

Guinness Book of World Records

BEGINNING RESUSCITATION

Speed is essential once the need for resuscitation has been recognized (see Figure 3-1). After four to six minutes without respiration or circulation, irreversible brain damage will probably have occurred. Because the duration of absence of heartbeat and breathing is usually not known by the

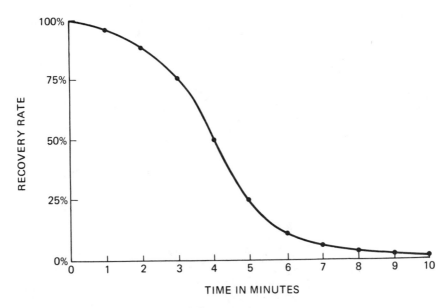

FIGURE 3–1   Recovery rates for resuscitation.

rescuer, resuscitation efforts should be started at once. Three exceptions are the victim with a terminal illness (as determined by a doctor), the victim known to have been in cardiac arrest for ten minutes (except the rapid-onset hypothermic victim, see page 227), and a victim in whom definite signs of death (for example, rigor mortis; see page 46) are obvious.

Examination of the Victim

A collapsed or unconscious victim must be examined immediately to determine the adequacy or absence of breathing and circulation. Follow the ABC's—airway, breathing, and circulation—in examination and setting the priorities for action.

Airway

Establishing an open airway is the most important step in resuscitation. Spontaneous breathing may occur as a result of this simple measure. Place the victim in a face-up position on a hard surface. Put one hand beneath the victim's neck and the other hand on the forehead (head-tilt-neck-lift method). Lift the neck with the one hand, and apply pressure to the forehead with the other to tilt the head backward (see Figure 3–2, Method 1). This extends the neck and moves the base of the tongue away from the back of the throat. The tongue is the most common cause of airway obstruction in the unconscious victim. *The head should be maintained in this position during the entire resuscitation procedure.* If the airway still is

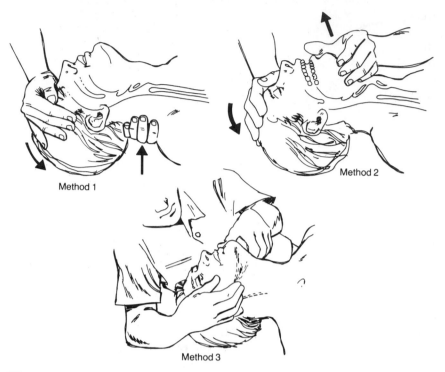

Method 1

Method 2

Method 3

FIGURE 3–2 Three ways to open an airway.

obstructed, any foreign material in the mouth or throat should be removed immediately.

Occasionally, there may be an incomplete opening of the air passages even with a properly performed head-tilt. In such cases, further opening of the air passages can be achieved by lifting the chin (Figure 3–2, Method 2). The tips of the fingers of one hand are placed under the lower jaw on the bony part near the chin, bringing the chin forward and helping to tilt the head back. The chin should be lifted so the teeth are nearly brought together, but avoid closing the mouth completely. Rarely should the thumb be used when lifting the chin. The chin lift is superior in some ways and may eventually replace the more popular head-tilt–neck-lift method. First aiders should learn one method well, yet both should probably be learned.

For a victim with a suspected neck injury, the jaw thrust without tilting the head should be attempted (Figure 3–2, Method 3).

Look, listen, and *feel* for any movement of air, because the chest and abdomen may move, in the condition of an *obstructed airway*, without moving air. The rescuer's face should be placed close to the victim's nose and mouth so that any exhaled air can be felt against his cheek. Also, the rise and fall of the chest can be observed and the exhaled breath heard.

A partially obstructed airway is characterized by noisy breathing.

There is usually a snoring sound when the airway is obstructed by the tongue and a crowing sound when it is obstructed by foreign matter, such as phlegm, blood, or vomit (see Table 2–4). *Respiratory failure* is characterized by the absence of respiratory effort and movement and the absence of air movement through the mouth or nose.

Breathing

If the victim does not resume adequate spontaneous breathing promptly after the head has been tilted backward, artificial respiration should be given by mouth-to-mouth or mouth-to-nose techniques. Regardless of the method used, an open airway is essential. Give four quick, full breaths. Keep the head tipped.

The four quick, full breaths should be given as fast as you can without allowing the lungs to deflate fully (this prevents collapse of the small air sacs of the lung). The space between the four quick breaths should allow the rescuer to get a fast breath of air for the next exhalation.

Circulation

After the four quick, full breaths, the pulse of the carotid (neck artery) and breathing should be checked. A head tilt should be maintained with one hand. With the index and middle fingers of the other hand, gently locate the voice box (Adam's apple) and slide the fingers flat into the groove at the side of the neck nearest you where the carotid pulse can be felt. The carotid pulse area should be felt, not squeezed (see Figure 3–3). Check the pulse for at least five seconds.

FIGURE 3–3 Checking the carotid pulse.

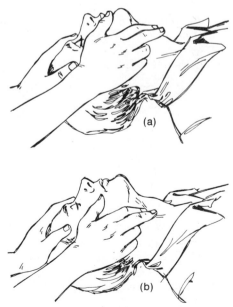

(a)

(b)

The pulse in a child can be felt over the carotid artery in a manner similar to that described for the adult. In infants, their very short and at times fat neck makes the carotid pulse difficult to feel. Therefore, in infants the brachial pulse should be used.

The infant's brachial pulse is located on the inside of the upper arm, midway between the elbow and shoulder (Figure 3–4). The rescuer's thumb is placed on the outside of the arm, between the shoulder and the elbow. The tips of the index and middle fingers are placed on the opposite side of the arm. These fingers are pressed lightly toward the bone.

If the victim is not breathing but has a pulse, give mouth-to-mouth breathing. Cardiopulmonary resuscitation (CPR) is given if the victim is neither breathing nor has a pulse. When properly performed, both techniques can support life.

MOUTH-TO-MOUTH RESPIRATION

Advantages of mouth-to-mouth resuscitation:

> Quickly applied
> Can be given in most situations and in unusual positions
> Moves the most air to lungs
> Easy to detect airway obstruction
> Easy to gauge effectiveness.

Techniques for mouth-to-mouth resuscitation:

> Keep the victim's head at a maximum backward tilt with *one hand* under the neck. (See Figure 3–2, Method 1.)

FIGURE 3–4 Brachial pulse, infant.

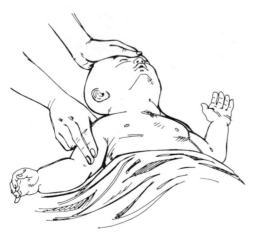

Place the heel of *the other hand* on the forehead, with the thumb and index finger toward the nose. Pinch together the victim's nostrils with the thumb and index finger to prevent air from escaping. Continue to exert pressure on the forehead with the palm of the hand to maintain the backward tilt of the head.

Take a deep breath, then form a tight seal with your mouth over and around the victim's mouth. (See Figure 3–5a.)

Blow four quick, full breaths in first without allowing the lungs to deflate fully. Then continue the procedure. The reason for beginning artificial respiration by delivering four quick, full exhalations is to fill the lungs with oxygenated air and at the same time increase the air pressure, which will help to open the smaller airways in the lung that have collapsed.

Blow forcefully and smoothly into the victim's mouth. Do not use sudden, excessive force. Too much sudden pressure might damage the person's lungs.

Watch the victim's chest while inflating the lungs. If adequate ventilation is taking place, the chest should rise and fall.

Remove your mouth and allow the victim to exhale passively. If in the right position, the victim's exhalation will be felt on your cheek. (See Figure 3–5b.)

Take another deep breath, reform a tight seal around the victim's mouth and blow into the mouth again. Repeat this procedure 10 to 12 times a minute, once every five seconds, for adults and children over four years.

Air that the first aider inhales contains 21 percent oxygen, and air that is exhaled contains about 16 percent oxygen. In air that is forced into the victim from the rescuer, enough oxygen remains to support life. As long as other life-supporting body functions are working, mouth-to-mouth resuscitation will keep a victim alive.

If there is no air exchange and an airway obstruction exists, make sure the head is tilted well back and the jaw is jutting up and out. If there is still no exchange of air, attempt the Heimlich maneuver (see page 70).

FIGURE 3–5a
Rescuer blows forcefully into victim's mouth, after his mouth forms a tight seal around the victim's mouth.

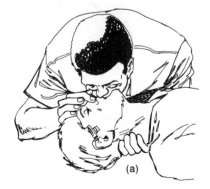

(a)

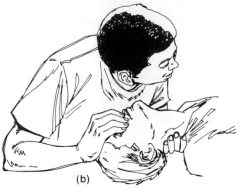

FIGURE 3–5b
Rescuer removes his mouth and allows the victim to exhale.

(b)

It may be necessary to reach into the victim's throat to remove foreign matter; be careful not to force it deeper. Clean any vomit from the victim's mouth and resume artificial respiration.

Mouth-to-Nose Respiration

The mouth-to-nose technique should be used when it is impossible to open the victim's mouth, when it is impossible to ventilate through the victim's mouth, when the mouth is severely injured, or a tight seal around the lips cannot be obtained. (See Figure 3–6.)

Keep the victim's head tilted back with one hand. Use the other hand to lift up the victim's lower jaw to seal the lips.

Take a deep breath, seal your lips around the victim's nose, and blow in forcefully and smoothly until the victim's chest rises. Repeat quickly four times.

Remove your mouth and allow the victim to exhale passively (it may be neces-

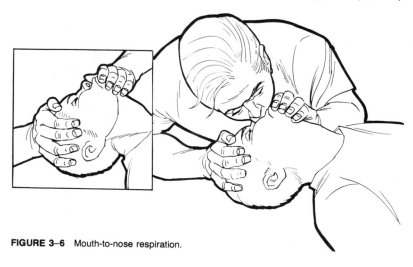

FIGURE 3–6   Mouth-to-nose respiration.

sary to open the victim's mouth during exhalation to allow exhaled air to escape).

Repeat the cycle 10 to 12 times per minute, or approximately every five seconds.

Special Situations

Children.   Resuscitation is performed in essentially the same way for children. Open the airway by the head-tilt–neck-lift method, which can be augmented by the chin-lift method. For infants and small children, the child's nose and mouth should be covered with the rescuer's mouth. (See Figure 3–7.) The rescuer should blow gently, using less volume to inflate the lungs. Babies require only small puffs of air from the rescuer's cheeks. The rate of inflation should be 20 to 30 times per minute, or once every three seconds. The neck of an infant is so pliable that forceful backward

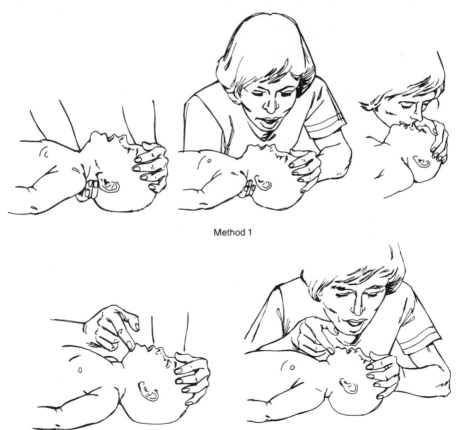

Method 1

Method 2

FIGURE 3–7

tilting of the head may obstruct breathing passages ("kinking" effect). Therefore the tilted position should not be exaggerated.

Foreign bodies.   A foreign body should be suspected if you are unable to inflate the lungs, despite proper positioning and a tight air seal around the mouth or nose. The first blowing effort should tell whether or not any obstruction exists. For removal of foreign objects, see Choking, page 68.

Stomach distention.   Artificial respiration (exhaled air) frequently causes distention of the stomach, especially in children. It is most likely to occur when excessive pressures are used for inflation or if the airway is not clear. Stomach distention may be harmful because it promotes vomiting (material can be aspirated into lungs) and reduces lung volume by elevating the diaphragm.

If the stomach becomes distended during rescue breathing, recheck and reposition the airway, observe the rise and fall of the chest, and avoid excessive airway pressure. Continue rescue breathing without attempting to expel the stomach contents. Attempting to relieve stomach distention by manual pressure over the upper abdomen may cause vomiting, and when suctioning equipment is not available, aspiration of stomach contents into the lungs may occur. Therefore, stomach distention relief by first aiders should not usually be attempted.

TYPES OF ASPIRATION (NOT ALWAYS A CATASTROPHIC EVENT):
1.   particulate matter (small, solid material which can obstruct airway)
2.   nongastric liquid (mainly in fresh and salt water drownings)
3.   gastric acid (can be similar to a chemical burn)

Vomiting.   Vomiting presents two critical problems: mechanical obstruction of the larynx or bronchial tree, and aspiration of acidic gastric juices into the small airways, which can cause severe and widespread pneumonitis.

If the victim aspirates, continue applying resuscitation efforts as vigorously as if the victim had not. If vomitus obstructs the airway, rapidly turn the entire body on its side for drainage and clear the throat and mouth with your fingers. Then resume resuscitating.

Suspected neck injuries.   In accident cases it is imperative to use caution to avoid extending the victim's neck when there is a possibility of a neck fracture. A fractured neck should be suspected in diving or automobile accidents when the victim has lacerations of the face and forehead. If a fracture is suspected, all forward, backward, lateral, or turning movements should be avoided. *To open the airway in cases of suspected neck injury, the routine head-tilt and neck-lift technique should not be used. Instead, the following modified jaw-thrust technique should be employed* (Figure 3-2):

> Place a hand on either side of the victim's head to maintain it in a fixed neutral position without the head extended.
>
> Use the index fingers to displace the jaw forward. Do not tilt the head in any direction.
>
> Artificial ventilation usually can be successful in this position. If not successful, tilt the head very slightly and make another attempt to ventilate, using the modified jaw-thrust.

Laryngectomees (mouth-to-stoma method used).   In the United States, several thousand individuals have had the larynx completely or partially removed by surgery. The surgical operation is called a *laryngectomy*. Persons who have had the operation are called *laryngectomees*. Laryngectomees breathe through an opening (stoma) that is made into the front of the neck to connect with the windpipe (trachea). They do not use the nose or mouth for breathing.

Direct mouth-to-stoma artificial ventilation should be used to resuscitate people who have had a laryngectomy. Neither head-tilt nor jaw-thrust maneuvers are required. The same general procedure for mouth-to-mouth resuscitation is used except that the rescuer's mouth is placed firmly over the victim's stoma. Then the rescuer blows into the stoma at the same rate as a person who breathes normally while watching the victim's chest for the inflow of air. It is not necessary to close off the victim's mouth or nose or to be concerned with the victim's tongue or dentures. Keep the victim's head straight and avoid twisting it. Twisting the head might change the shape of the stoma or close it.

CARDIOPULMONARY RESUSCITATION (CPR)

Some experts believe between 100,000 and 200,000 lives could be saved in the United States each year if enough people could apply cardiopulmonary resuscitation (CPR). Therefore, every adult who is physically capable should know how to give CPR to a cardiac arrest victim.

The American Heart Association says that more than 40 percent of victims with ventricular fibrillation out-of-hospital can be successfully resuscitated if CPR is provided promptly. In certain situations, successful resuscitation has been accomplished in 60 percent to 80 percent of cases.

Cardiopulmonary resuscitation (CPR) is a life-saving procedure that requires exactness and good physical coordination. Book knowledge only on how to administer CPR is not enough. Correct practice at frequent intervals is required. A manikin should be used during practice sessions on CPR. A formal course of instruction, certified by either the American Heart Association or the American National Red Cross, is strongly suggested.

All material on CPR in this chapter should be used primarily to refresh those first aiders who are certified to apply CPR or as a supplement to CPR instruction.

Sudden death from myocardial infarction (heart attack) is the most important medical emergency today.

American Heart Association

Technique for External Cardiac Compression

Compression of the sternum produces some artificial ventilation, but not enough for adequate oxygenation of the blood. For this reason artificial respiration is always required whenever external cardiac compression is used. Nevertheless, CPR is only 25 percent to 33 percent as effective as the action of a normal heart.

The victim should be in a horizontal position (elevating the legs while keeping the rest of the body horizontal may help circulation).

Effective external cardiac compression requires sufficient pressure to depress the victim's lower sternum 1½ to 2 inches in an adult. *For chest compression to be effective, the victim must be on a firm surface. If the victim is in bed, a board or improvised support should be placed under the back. However, chest compression must not be delayed to look for a firmer support.*

Kneel close to the side of the victim. With the middle and index fingers of the hand closest to the feet, the rescuer locates the lower margin of the victim's rib cage on the side next to the rescuer. The fingers are then run up along the rib cage to the notch where the ribs meet the sternum in the center of the lower part of the chest (see Figure 3–8). With one finger on the notch, the other finger is placed next to the first finger on the lower end of the sternum. The heel of the hand closest to the head is placed on the lower half of the sternum just next to the index finger of the first hand that located the notch. The heel of the rescuer's hand should be placed on the long axis of the breastbone. This will decrease the chance of rib fracture.

PRESSURE
POINT

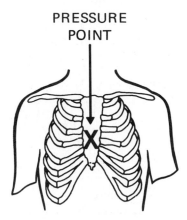

FIGURE 3–8
The rescuer hand position for closed chest heart massage is located above the xiphoid process on the sternum.

The first hand is then removed from the notch and placed on the top of the hand on the sternum so that the heels of both hands are parallel and the fingers are directed straight away from the rescuer. The fingers may be either extended or interlaced but must be kept off the chest.

> Lean forward so that your shoulders are almost directly above the victim's chest.
>
> Keep your arms straight (lock the elbows), and exert adequate pressure almost directly downward to depress an adult's lower sterum 1½ to 2 inches.
>
> Depress the sterum 60 times per minute for an adult (when two rescuers are used). This is usually rapid enough to maintain blood flow and slow enough to allow the heart to fill with blood. Also, it avoids fatigue and aids timing at the rate of one compression per second. The compression should be regular, smooth, and uninterrupted, with compression and relaxation being of equal duration. Avoid bouncing compressions because they are less effective and are more likely to cause injury.

Two rescuers preferred. It is preferable to have *two qualified rescuers*, because artificial circulation must be combined with artificial ventilation (see Figure 3–9). When possible, the rescuers should not be on the same side of the victim. The most effective ventilation and circulation are achieved by quickly giving one lung inflation after each five chest compressions (5:1 ratio). *The compression rate should be 60 per minute for two rescuers.* One rescuer should perform external cardiac compression while the other remains at the victim's head, keeps it tilted back, and continues rescue breathing (exhaled air ventilation). *Supplying the breaths without any pauses in heart compression is important, because every interruption in cardiac compression results in a drop of blood flow and blood pressure to zero.*

Switch positions when necessary without serious interruption in the 5:1 sequence.

Single rescuer. A *single rescuer* must perform both artificial ventilation

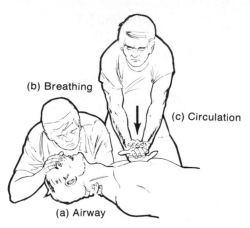

(b) Breathing

(c) Circulation

(a) Airway

FIGURE 3–9
Two-Rescuer Cardiopulmonary Resuscitation
(CPR). 5 chest compressions at a rate of 60
per minute, with no pause for ventilation; 1 lung
inflation after each 5 compressions, interposed
between compressions.

and artificial circulation using a 15:2 ratio. (See Figure 3–10.) *Two very quick lung inflations should be delivered after each 15 chest compressions, without waiting for full exhalation of the victim's breath. A rate equivalent to 80 chest compressions per minute must be maintained by a single rescuer* in order to achieve 50 to 60 actual compressions per minute because of the interruptions for the lung inflations. Most CPR is rendered by a single rescuer rather than two rescuers.

Children and infants.   *The technique is similar for children* (one to eight years of age), except that the heel of only one hand is used for children, and only the tips of the fingers for infants (under one year of age). The heart of infants and small children lies higher in the chest, so external pressure should be applied over the midsternum. The danger of injuring the liver is greater in children because of the smallness and pliability of the chest and the high position of the liver under the lower sternum. In infants the brachial pulse should be used.

FIGURE 3–10a
One-Rescuer Cardiopulmonary Resuscitation (CPR). 15 chest
compressions at a rate of 80 per minute, then 2 quick lung inflations.

FIGURE 3–10b
Proper positioning for performing cardiac compression on an adult.

In an *infant* the midsternum should be compressed one half to three fourths of an inch at 100 compressions per minute, and in a *child*, three fourths to one and one half inches at 80 compressions per minute. Breaths are placed between each five compressions. A backward tilt of the head arches (lifts) the back in infants and small children. A firm support for external cardiac compression can be provided if the rescuer slips one hand beneath the child's back while using the other hand to compress the chest.

Checking Effectiveness of CPR

The carotid (neck) pulse should be felt after the first minute of cardiopulmonary resuscitation and every few minutes thereafter. The pulse will indicate the effectiveness of the external cardiac compression or the return of a spontaneous effective heartbeat. Checking the pulse should take no longer than five seconds.

Other indicators that show CPR effectiveness are the following:

Expansion of the chest each time the operator blows air into the lungs
A pulse that can be felt each time the sternum is compressed
Return of color to the skin
A spontaneous gasp for breath
A return of a spontaneous heartbeat
A pupil that constricts when exposed to light indicates that the brain is receiving adequate oxygen and blood. When the heart stops beating, the pupils will begin to dilate within 45 to 60 seconds. They will stay dilated and will not react to light.

Terminating CPR

The decision to stop cardiopulmonary resuscitation is a medical one that depends upon an assessment of the cerebral (brain) circulation. Deep unconsciousness, the absence of spontaneous respiration, and fixed, dilated pupils for 15 to 30 minutes indicate cerebral death, and further resuscitative efforts are usually futile.

In the absence of a physician, CPR should be continued until

The victim's heart resumes normal beating

Resuscitation has been transferred to another responsible person who is trained in CPR to continue basic life support

A physician or other properly trained person responsible for emergency medical services assumes responsibility for the victim.

The rescuer is exhausted and unable to continue

The victim is dead beyond any doubt (see page 44) for signs of death).

Mistakes in CPR Performance

CPR may be ineffective in providing basic life support when performed improperly. The following points should be remembered when performing cardiopulmonary resuscitation:

Never interrupt cardiopulmonary resuscitation (CPR) for more than five seconds for any reason except when moving a victim up or down a stairway. In this situation effective CPR can be performed best at the head or foot of the stairs. On a given signal, interrupt CPR and move quickly to the next landing, where it can be resumed. Such interruptions should only occur under emergency conditions when the victim must be relocated and then should never exceed 30 seconds.

Never move a victim for convenience until the victim has been stabilized or until arrangements have been made for uninterrupted CPR during movement.

Never compress the xiphoid process at the tip of the sternum (Figure 3–8). Pressure on it may tear the liver and lead to severe internal bleeding.

Although pressure *must* be completely released between compressions, the heel of the hand should remain in constant contact with the chest wall over the lower half of the sternum.

The rescuer's fingers must *never* rest on the victim's ribs during compression. This increases the possibility of rib fractures. Interlocking the fingers of the two hands may help avoid this.

Never use sudden or jerking movements to compress the chest. The action should be smooth, regular, and uninterrupted, with 50 percent of the cycle compression and 50 percent relaxation.

Never maintain continuous pressure on the abdomen to decompress the stomach. This traps the liver and may cause it to rupture. Also, such pressure may lead to regurgitation and aspiration of stomach contents.

The rescuer's shoulders should be directly over the victim's sternum, elbows straight, and pressure applied vertically downward on the lower sternum. This provides maximum thrust, minimal fatigue for the first aider, and reduces the chance of complications to the victim.

The lower sternum of an adult *must* be depressed 1½ to 2 inches for CPR to be effective.

Improperly applied CPR may cause trauma, such as rib fractures. Careful adherence to details of performance will minimize complications. It must be remembered that effective CPR is required during cardiac arrest even if traumatic conditions do result, because the alternative is death.

Because even with the best currently accepted technique, cardiac output with external compression is only about a third of the normal output, improper application of techniques can put the cardiac arrest victim in greater jeopardy during CPR.

Skills that are not used regularly can be easily lost. Nevertheless, do *not* withhold CPR in an emergency situation even if you have not practiced recently. Some assistance is better than none at all, and even the rescuer with rusty skills has been known to save lives.

There is no known case in which a layperson who has performed CPR reasonably has been sued successfully.

American Heart Association

The best way to learn CPR is to focus not only on *what* the rescuer is doing but *why*. An approved CPR course that meets either the American Heart Association or the American National Red Cross standards is highly recommended.

Many victims who die as a result of heart attack and accidental causes such as drowning, electrocution, suffocation, or automobile accidents could be saved by the prompt and proper application of CPR. Failure to resuscitate a victim may be due to one of several reasons:

A delay in starting CPR
Using improper techniques
The advanced stage of an underlying disease.

CPR MISCONCEPTIONS:

Misconception 1—The purpose of CPR is to get the heart started.
Fact: In the vast majority of the cases of cardiac arrest, CPR alone will not bring about return of cardiac function.

Misconception 2—Prolonged CPR is impractical.
Fact: It is now well established that good CPR technique can maintain good victim viability for long periods of time.

RESUSCITATION IN ELECTRIC SHOCK

The type and the extent of an injury from electric shock will depend upon the amount and frequency of the current, the duration of contact with the current, and the pathway through the tissue. The resistance of the body primarily is centered on the skin. A dry, well-keratinized, intact skin provides a higher resistance to electricity than moist thin skin, and electrical contact is more easily established.

The resulting injuries from electric shock may range from benign to fatal ones. Burns, injuries from falls, paralysis of respiration, and ventricular fibrillation are all possible emergency conditions.

The *cardiopulmonary status* of the victim should be determined as soon as the electrical object has been cleared. Cardiopulmonary resuscitation should be started immediately if spontaneous respirations or circulation are absent. The procedure for CPR starts on page 57.

Effective CPR can only be performed with the victim in a horizontal position on a hard surface.

Some 200 people are killed annually (some believe the actual number may be double this amount) by lightning in the United States, and some 300 are injured. Death is usually due to heart failure or inability to breathe. The lightning bolt may kill, but it seldom does serious damage to the heart of the survivor. Cardiopulmonary resuscitation is important in saving the lives of those struck by lightning.

The only living man in the world to be struck by lightning 7 times is former Shenandoah Park Ranger Roy C. Sullivan (US), the human lightning-conductor of Virginia. His attraction for lightning began in 1942 (lost big toenail) and was resumed in July 1969 (lost eyebrows), in July 1970 (left shoulder seared), on April 16, 1972 (hair set on fire) and, *finally*, he hoped, on August 7, 1973: as he was driving along a bolt came out of a small, low-lying cloud, hit him on the head through his hat, set his hair on fire again, knocked him 10 feet out of his car, went through both legs, and knocked his left shoe off. He had to pour a pail of water over his head to cool off. Then, on June 5, 1976, he was struck again for the sixth time, his ankle injured. When he was struck for the *seventh* time on June 15, 1977, while fishing, he was sent to Waynesboro Hospital with chest and stomach burns.

Guinness Book of World Records

Excluding lightning bolts, the highest reported voltage electric shock survived was one of 230,000 volts by Brian Latasa, 17, on the tower of an ultra-high voltage power line in Griffith Park, Los Angeles, November 9, 1967.

Guinness Book of World Records

DROWNING

Types of Drowning

Four types of drowning are now recognized: dry, wet, secondary, and immersion syndrome.

Dry drowning.   An estimated 10 percent of all victims drown without aspiration of water because of a prolonged laryngospasm. Because no water enters the tracheal airway, dry drowning responds readily to mouth-to-mouth resuscitation, and victims of this type of drowning account for 90 percent of those successfully resuscitated.

Wet drowning.   About 80 percent of drownings are of this type. After the larynx relaxes, the lungs become partially flooded with water. Fresh and salt water diminishes the oxygen-absorbing areas of the lungs.

Fresh water in the lungs can chemically alter the capillary membrane and alter the normal pulmonary surfactant. Surfactant is a chemical in the alveoli of the lung that is responsible for the stability of the alveoli. The fresh water also passes through the lungs to the bloodstream and may cause hemodilution. Authorities disagree as to what proportion of victims die in ventricular fibrillation because of hemodilution, because it has been difficult to document.

Salt water draws water from the bloodstream into the lungs. Salt-water aspiration has been shown to be twice as lethal as fresh-water aspiration. Victims drown in their own fluids as much as in the salt water itself.

Emergency care for fresh and salt water drowning are the same.

Secondary drowning.   This drowning type describes the case where a person has been resuscitated yet dies hours or days later of secondary complications. Some authorities prefer to call it pulmonary edema. One study reported death in 25 percent of the victims of near-drownings. Pulmonary edema is seen more often following salt-water near-drownings, but can also follow fresh-water near-drownings. Aspiration pneumonia is a late complication of near-drowning episodes, occurring after 48 to 72 hours have elapsed.

Immersion syndrome.   This refers to sudden death from cardiac arrest as a result of contact with very cold water.

Resuscitation in Drowning.

Basic life support resuscitation principles, which were presented previously, should be performed immediately.

A drowning victim must be rescued as quickly as possible. Most incidents occur within reach of a rescuer; thus, even a nonswimmer can be of assistance.

Artificial respiration should be started *immediately*. Although mouth-to-mouth respiration may be performed while in the water, it may be difficult or impossible because of the depth of the water and the lack of good swimming skills by the rescuer. In such situations, a flotation device may be used to support the head of the victim, while performing mouth-to-mouth respiration. Rescuers may have to postpone artificial respiration until they can stand in shallow water. *Effective cardiac compression cannot be performed in the water unless one has had special training.*

Vomiting is common in drowning victims and poses a significant problem for the rescuer.

At the drowning scene, no revival efforts are made in seven out of ten drownings. This may be because there was no one skilled in administering artificial respiration when the victim was first pulled out of the water. When resuscitation is attempted, it is usually by police officers or firefighters.

Water in the Lungs

Water remaining in the lungs makes mouth-to mouth respiration ineffective for treating most drowning cases. You cannot get air into the lungs until you get the water out.

Several successful cases have been reported that used the Heimlich maneuver for removing water from the lungs of a drowning person before mouth-to-mouth respiration was attempted.

Over the centuries various methods have used the principle of compressing the lungs, which then elevate the diaphragm. Rolling a drowning person over a barrel dates back to the sixteenth century. In Europe, drowning victims were draped face down in a jackknife position over the back of a trotting horse. In parts of the United States, lifeguards were once taught to jackknife the victim face down over the shoulder and then jog before performing mouth-to-mouth respiration. All of these methods resulted in forcing water from the victim's lungs.

The Schafer (back pressure) method of artificial respiration received wide acceptance from 1928 to 1959. This method is not even found in present-day first aid textbooks. Yet like the other methods (trotting horse and barrel roll) it forced water from the lungs by "performing" the Heimlich maneuver.

From 1961 to the present, first aid textbooks and the medical literature on drowning have stressed that rescuers should waste no time attempting to remove water from the lungs but should proceed immediately with mouth-to-mouth respiration. According to the research and recommendation of Dr. Henry J. Heimlich, the drowning person should have the Heimlich maneuver administered first.

How to perform the Heimlich maneuver.   Place the victim on his or her back in the lying-down position of the Heimlich maneuver (see Figure 3–13), with the victim's head in a sideways position to prevent aspiration of the stomach contents. Remember that for choking cases, the victim's head should remain upward rather than toward the side. This position helps prevent rib fractures and places the victim in the best position for mouth-to-mouth resuscitation after the water has been expelled from the lungs. The Heimlich maneuver should be repeated until no water flows from the mouth.

It is conceivable that many of the thousands of drowning fatalities who received resuscitation might have been saved if a technique to remove water from their lungs had first been applied.

Therefore, evacuation of water from the lungs by the Heimlich maneuver should be the first step in resuscitating a drowning person.

Cold-Water Drownings

Immersion in cold water (defined as below 70°F) presents a special problem. In recent years much has been written about the seemingly miraculous survival times of some victims of cold-water drowning. The rule that says four to six minutes without oxygen results in irreversible brain damage does not usually apply if the drowning occurs in cold water.

It is believed that there are two major factors accounting for these extended survival times. The first is *hypothermia* (lowering of the body temperature below 95°F). The second factor is a body reaction known as the *diving reflex*.

The diving reflex is the body's reaction to immersion of the facial area in cold water, which results in an oxygen-conserving action. The body reacts by shunting blood from the extremities to its core. However, many experts have discounted this theory.

The longest submersion time on record for a human being who was without oxygen and survived with no neurological damage is 40 minutes. One study found a dozen well-documented cases of persons submerged between 15 and 40 minutes who were revived and recovered fully. Many other cases appear in medical literature, and no doubt there are many unrecorded cases. Perhaps there are many other drowning fatalities who might have been saved if their rescuers had known what to do.

A controversy exists over using cardiopulmonary resuscitation (CPR) when the heart is very cold and appears to have ceased beating. Some experts believe that under such circumstances pressure on the heart may cause the heart to fibrillate; others argue that CPR should be attempted anyway. If CPR is started, continue it until the victim arrives at the hospital and starts receiving appropriate treatment.

Nevertheless, in the case of cold-water drownings in which the victim's heart has stopped beating, CPR should be applied immediately, but only if the victim has been submerged for less than one hour.

Recovery has occurred even after two hours of intensive continuous resuscitation because of trained, capable rescuers. All victims saved from drowning should be transported to a medical facility for hospitalization and close observation.

Do not fail to look for other possible problems such as a suspected spinal cord injury, head injury, allergic reactions to stings, and cardiac arrest.

Whenever a neck or back injury is suspected, the victim must be removed from the water on a back support. If available, a backboard should be slipped underwater and allowed to float up under the victim. If a backboard is not available, such items as a wide board or door may be used. The victim should be secured to the support with any available material to prevent sliding or rolling. The victim should be kept as level as possible while being removed from the water. When materials or assistance are not available, the victim should remain in the water until they do arrive. If removal is urgent because of excessive bleeding, cardiac arrest, or very cold water, the victim's back should be kept as level as possible.

Do not forget the victim's family. They will naturally be upset or hysterical. Provide comfort and information whenever possible, but your first responsibility is to the victim.

CHOKING EMERGENCIES

First aid for a choking victim has received considerable attention of late, and intense discussion and debates have been frequent. The subject is a controversial one.

Foreign-body airway obstruction leading to death is fairly uncommon. In recent years, the National Safety Council has reported about 3,000 deaths annually. During the same period more than 550,000 deaths annually have been attributable to cardiac arrest resulting from heart disease. Hence the relative risk of death from airway obstructions as compared to cardiac arrest is about one in 180.

In 1963 the term *cafe coronary* was coined in response to nine sudden deaths in restaurants. At first these deaths were listed as heart attacks; however, later autopsies showed that the actual cause of death was choking caused by food obstruction. A relationship between choking and excessive alcohol intake, poorly chewed food, or loose-fitting dentures was also noted.

Dr. Henry J. Heimlich became interested in the problem and first published his technique (the Heimlich maneuver) in 1974. In 1976 Dr. A.S. Gordon concluded from his own studies that back blows would be helpful in dislodging a foreign body. Thus arose the controversy as to which is the best method to aid choking victims—back blows or abdominal thrusts.

Because of these conflicting opinions a conference was held in 1976, and out of this came the recommendation that a sequence of back blows as well as manual thrusts to the abdomen or chest should be used as the emergency treatment for the obstructed airway.

The reason behind this recommendation was evidence that indicated that back blows might be helpful in certain circumstances in relieving airway obstruction. In addition, because back blows require only a few seconds to apply, there is no serious delay in treating the victim. Moreover, it was further recommended that, following the back blows, abdominal or chest thrusts be utilized and the sequence repeated until airway obstruction is relieved. Because no data existed to say how many back blows or thrusts should be performed, conference members suggested that four back blows, then four thrusts, be administered, because that would be easier to remember.

These recommendations were incorporated into the teaching programs of both the American Heart Association and the American Red Cross.

At another national conference, in 1979, the controversy was again debated. From this meeting the standards of the 1976 conference were upheld, except that either back blows or abdominal thrusts could be used first in the sequence.

Following other studies on first aid for choking that appeared in 1982 medical journals, the American Medical Association Council on Scientific Affairs concluded that it "agrees with most authors on the subject that there is no evidence based on experimental or upon case reports that is adequate to settle the controversy that has arisen. The ultimate support or abandonment of back blows must await development of more persuasive scientific data than has yet been published."[1]

The Council on Scientific Affairs recommended that the American Medical Association adopt the following position with regard to care of the choking victim: "In first aid management of the obstructed airway, it ap-

[1]William H. Montgomery, "Airway Controversies," *JEMS: Journal of Emergency Medical Services*, 9, no. 7 (July 1984), 35.

pears that a combination of back blows and abdominal thrusts is more effective than either one alone. The abdominal thrusts may precede the back blows and, if both of these fail, there should be a finger sweep of the mouth, and then a repetition of the maneuvers."[2]

Kinds of Choking

Dr. Edward A. Patrick has identified four kinds of choking:

Type 0: Choking that all of us have experienced—the sensation of something in the airway relieved by coughing; it is not life-threatening.

Type 1: Obstruction on the mouth side of the epiglottis (also known as the "lid" type because it may hold the epiglottis down over the larynx like a lid). There are two subtypes: non-life-threatening and life-threatening.

Type 2: Life-threatening choking with airway obstruction on the lung side of the epiglottis (also known as the "plug" type because the obstruction closes up the trachea like a plug; a reflex laryngospasm may complicate the situation).

Type 3: Subacute choking—a foreign body resides in the bronchi, but is not acutely life-threatening. For many cases the foreign body must be removed surgically.

The epiglottis is a thin, leaflike valve guarding the opening of the trachea. It closes when food or liquids are present in the pharynx, except in an unconscious person when it may fail to work.

A physician at the scene of a choking incident could cut an opening into the throat (tracheotomy or tracheostomy) to reach the trachea, or insert a large-caliber hypodermic needle (cricothyroidotomy) to provide a temporary airway. Such expertise is seldom available to provide the immediate action required. First aiders should not attempt such procedures. If you find yourself with a choking victim, the following techniques are suggested. Moreover, physicians will try the procedures that follow before attempting more elaborate medical techniques.

Heimlich Maneuver (Abdominal Thrust)[3]

The abdominal thrust procedure is performed as follows, according to Dr. Henry J. Heimlich, inventor of the procedure:

1. Rescuer standing—victim standing or sitting (Figure 3–11):
   Stand behind the victim and wrap your arms around the victim's waist
   Place your fist, thumb side, against the victim's abdomen slightly above the navel and below the rib cage
   Grasp your fist with your other hand and press into the victim's abdomen and with a quick upward thrust
   Repeat several times if necessary.

[2] *Ibid.*

[3]The content of this section is based upon the research findings of Dr. Henry J. Heimlich and others.

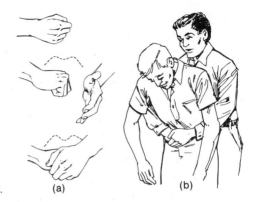

FIGURE 3–11 Heimlich maneuver.   (a)   (b)

2. When the victim is sitting, the rescuer stands behind the victim's chair and performs the maneuver in the same manner (Figure 3–12).
3. Rescuer kneeling—victim lying face up (Figure 3–13):
   Victim is lying face up
   Facing victim, kneel astride the victim's hips
   With one of your hands on top of the other, place on the abdomen slightly above the navel and below the rib cage
   Press into the victim's abdomen with a quick upward thrust
   Repeat several times if necessary.

The choking victim has four minutes to live from the onset of choking; however, a victim who is on the floor unconscious has not the full four minutes but rather a matter of seconds. It is necessary to straddle the thighs immediately and apply the Heimlich maneuver without delay. The rescuer should be prepared to retrieve the foreign object from the victim's mouth with the fingers—especially if the victim is lying face up.

There have been reported incidents when it was necessary to perform the procedure eight or nine times to dislodge the foreign object. In a few instances a poorly informed rescuer did not succeed, only to be followed by a second rescuer whose efforts expelled the obstruction. Also, there have

FIGURE 3–12

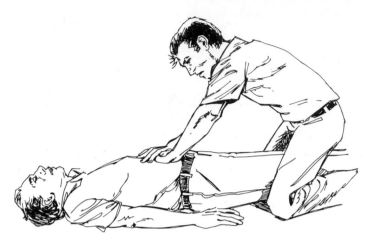

FIGURE 3–13

been many occasions when choking victims have self-administered the Heimlich maneuver—punching the upper abdomen with the fists or pressing the abdomen against the edge of a table or the back of a chair.

Rescuers should remember to press inward and upward with the hands—they should not squeeze with the arms—and properly locate the hands just above the victim's naval. The abdominal thrusts are applied with increasing force until the object is dislodged from the victim's throat. Often the first thrust is a tentative one whereby the rescuer gauges the force that is necessary.

Infants and children. The rescuer should not interfere with a victim's coughing attempts to expel a foreign object. Infants and children have been saved from choking to death by the abdominal Heimlich maneuver. Some experts recommend chest thrusts instead of abdominal thrusts— there are no known scientific reports of a child's being saved from choking by a chest thrust. Besides, injuries and deaths are more likely to result from chest thrusts than from abdominal thrusts. A modified abdominal thrust technique is required for infants and children. For example, two fingers from each of the rescuer's hands may be used (see Figure 3–14). Remember, the initial thrust is slight, with succeeding thrusts gaining more force.

Pregnant women, obese victims, and small or weak rescuers. In cases of advanced pregnancy or obesity, when the rescuer's arms cannot circle the victim's abdomen, the abdominal thrust technique may be used with the victim on the floor flat on the back, face up, and the rescuer kneeling astride the victim's hips. A pregnant woman should not practice the maneuver, but it should be used to save her life. Should the uterus extend to

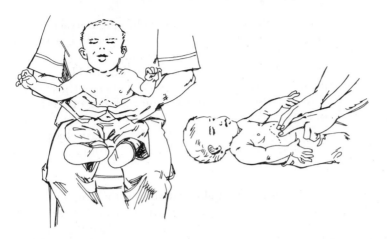

FIGURE 3–14

the margin of the rib cage, it may be necessary to compress the chest at the midsternum (breastbone) level. The same technique should be considered for the obese victim when the rescuer's arms cannot encircle the abdomen. Small or weak rescuers can apply more force with their body weight than circling their arms around the victim.

Other Techniques for Choking

Back blows.   The principle behind the use of back blows is that they may help to dislodge a foreign object. Back blows are rapid, hard hand blows over the spine and between the shoulder blades. Back blows may be given with the victim sitting, standing, or lying. The American Heart Association and the American Red Cross advocate giving abdominal thrusts before back blows. It is recommended that abdominal thrusts be given first, then if unsuccessful, try back blows.

> Abdominal thrust (Heimlich maneuver) given before back blows is recognized as an acceptable first aid procedure for choking victims.
>
> *American Heart Association*

Finger sweep (only for unconscious victims).   Finger sweeps have been discouraged. Critics claim that the foreign object may not be visible, and even it it were, it is likely to be pushed down and cause a partial obstruction to become complete. Another criticism is that the technique detracts from more effective methods. Therefore a rescuer should use the finger sweep as a last desperate effort to save an unconscious choking victim.

The finger sweep technique requires that the head be up. The victim's mouth is opened by grasping the tongue and lower jaw between the thumb and fingers and then lifting. Insert the index finger of the other hand down along the inside of the cheek and deeply into the throat to the base of the tongue. Then use a hooking action to dislodge the foreign object and maneuver it into the mouth so it can be removed. Be careful not to force the object deeper into the airway.

Tongue technique.   As another final alternative in removing a foreign object, tell the conscious victim to sit up straight with the head forward and to stick out the tongue. Grasp the tongue with a napkin or handkerchief to get a firm grip; pull it forward as far as possible. If the object has popped out at this point, maintain your grip on the tongue, then use the index and middle fingers like tweezers to grasp the obstruction and pull it out.

Suction (reverse mouth-to-mouth resuscitation).   There is no scientific substantiation available for the sanctioning of this technique. The first aider attempts to suck out a foreign object, placing a napkin or handkerchief over the victim's mouth, then placing his mouth over the victim's in a manner similar to mouth-to-mouth resuscitation. While pinching the nose, the rescuer sucks rather than blows.

It is probably more important for the first aider to know what *not* to do than what to do in assisting the victim. A simple maneuver may move a foreign object from a dangerous position out into the mouth. On the other hand, a simple maneuver may endanger the victim's life.

The simplicity of the Heimlich maneuver has made it possible for people who have only heard of it to apply it to save a life.

Hanging an infant by its feet in an effort to dislodge a foreign object is a dangerous maneuver and should not be attempted. If the foreign object has passed through the vocal cords into the trachea, it may not produce complete obstruction, but hanging the infant by its feet may move the foreign body back into the vocal cords, creating complete obstruction and possible death.

Most foreign objects are normally removed by the body's own protective mechanisms, such as coughing or sneezing. However, foreign objects that are not removed usually result in two major complications—infection and obstruction. Obstruction is a dangerous situation if it is located in the respiratory tree and impairs the normal oxygen flow essential to life.

A wide variety of foreign objects have been found and removed from the respiratory system, including ammunition, bones, buttons, pins, coins, dental objects, foods, hardware, jewelry, rocks, nuts, seeds, shells, and toys.

The longer the foreign object is left in place, the more chance for edema, swelling, and inflammation to develop in the tissues and the less chance for removal of the foreign object by the first aider.

HYPERVENTILATION

Fear or stress can set off an attack of *hyperventilation*. Hyperventilation is extremely rapid or deep breathing that overoxygenates the blood.

Examples of situations that can induce hyperventilation include the death of a loved one, a broken romance, or anticipated stress, such as having to give a speech or appear at a job interview. Often at rock concerts teenage girls have hyperventilated during the excitement of seeing and hearing their favorite singers. The person experiencing hyperventilation does not do it on purpose.

Another situation that can be dangerous is purposeful hyperventilation. A swimmer planning to swim underwater, for example, may take deep breaths to "store up oxygen." This removes the carbon dioxide from the lungs (carbon dioxide is the substance that triggers our breathing mechanism). Then the swimmer dives underwater and uses up the oxygen in the blood. Unfortunately there is not enough carbon dioxide left to trigger breathing, and this causes the swimmer to black out and possibly drown.

Young, anxious persons are the main victims of hyperventilation. Besides too rapid and too deep breathing, victims usually experience numbness or tingling around the mouth and the hands and feet. They often complain of dizziness and may also report stabbing chest pains.

Unless the person says that hyperventilation problems have happened before, the rescuer may be fooled into believing that the victim is having a heart attack. Some hyperventilating victims will have not only sharp chest pains but many of the other signs of a heart attack. Not every victim who is breathing deeply or rapidly is actually hyperventilating.

Hyperventilating victims do not show a blue coloration to the skin, lips, or nailbeds. This clue can be used to separate hyperventilation from the latter stages of most other severe respiratory distresses.

One in ten people will experience at least one episode of hyperventilation during a lifetime. Most cases are temporary, and by breathing carbon dioxide (easily obtained by breathing into a paper bag—*never* a plastic bag), the victim will return to normal.

If the victim's hyperventilation is uncontrollable, a more serious physical condition may exist that requires immediate medical attention.

Chapter 4

Wounds
and Bleeding

A wound is an injury caused by external physical forces. Considerable force is needed to penetrate the human skin. An *open wound* is one where the skin or mucous membranes have been broken. A *closed wound* occurs when underlying tissues are involved and the skin and mucous membranes are intact. In open wounds there is an immediate risk of hemorrhage, after which the greatest danger is infection. Thus, disinfection of the wound should follow first aid procedures. Other concerns will be shock, nerve injury and the extent of tissue destruction.

TYPES OF WOUNDS

Abrasions

An abrasion is an open wound that is caused by rubbing or scraping the skin. (See Figure 4–1.) The wound may be quite painful when large areas of skin are scraped off. An abrasion usually is not very deep and bleeding is limited to an oozing from damaged capillaries and small veins. There is a danger of infection from bacteria, usually ground into the wound with dirt, grease, and other foreign matter.

If foreign matter is left in any wound, especially in an abrasion, it will

FIGURE 4–1 Abrasion.

remain as a permanent, blue-black "traumatic tattoo." Superficial abrasions can be carefully cleaned by the first aider with soap and water, but deep abrasions should be cared for by a physician.

Avulsions

An avulsion is an open wound that may be caused by explosions, accidents from vehicles, heavy machinery, and animal bites. (See Figure 4–2.) Tissue is separated forcibly or torn with loss of skin and soft tissue. Heavy bleeding usually follows immediately.

If an amputated part can be recovered, it should be saved for possible reimplantation. It should be wrapped in a wet dressing or towel, then placed in a plastic bag, which is then placed on ice to be carried with the victim to the hospital (see Figure 4–14). Fingers, toes, feet, hands and scalp have all been saved by microvascular surgery.

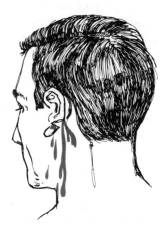

FIGURE 4–2 Avulsion.

Contusions (Bruises, Blood Blisters)

A contusion is a closed, superficial wound usually caused by a blow from a blunt object, a bump against a stationary object, or a crush. Blood seeping into soft tissue from injured vessels and capillaries causes swelling and pain that may be severe at the site of the injury. If the injury is over a bone, there is the possibility of a fracture.

Incisions

An incision is an open wound caused by sharp objects such as knives, broken glass, and sharp metal edges. (See Figure 4–3.) The wound is smooth-edged and bleeds freely. The amount of bleeding depends upon the depth, location, and size of the wound. There may be severe damage to muscles, nerves, and tendons if the wound is deep.

Lacerations

A laceration is an open wound caused by objects such as dull knives, broken glass, stones, moving parts of machinery, and direct blows. (See Figure 4–4.) The edges of the wound are usually jagged and irregular, and pieces of tissue may be partly or entirely pulled away. Bleeding may be scant or rapid and extensive. Contamination of the wound with dirt, grease, or other material increases the chance of infection.

Punctures

A puncture is an open wound caused by such objects as wooden or metal splinters, knives, nails, fishhooks, ice picks, and bullets. (See Figure 4–5.) Although the opening of a puncture wound may be small with minor external bleeding, the object may penetrate far into the body to cause

FIGURE 4–3 Incision.

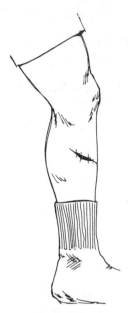

FIGURE 4-4   Laceration.

internal hemorrhage and injure organs. Because the wound is not cleansed by external bleeding, the chance of infection is increased, including possible tetanus (lockjaw). (For a summary of the types of wounds, see Table 4–1.)

BLEEDING

Hemorrhage from major blood vessels of the arms, neck, and thighs may occur so rapidly and extensively that death occurs in a few minutes. Bleeding must be controlled immediately to prevent excessive loss of blood. In most medical emergencies, only the restoration of breathing takes priority over the control of bleeding.

FIGURE 4-5   Puncture.

TABLE 4–1   Types of Wounds

TYPE	POSSIBLE CAUSES	SIGNS AND SYMPTOMS	SPECIAL EMERGENCY CARE
Abrasion (scrape)	Rubbing or scraping from falls, floor burns, rope burns, etc.	Only the surface of skin affected Little bleeding Danger of infection	Remove all debris Wash away from wound with soap and water
Contusion (bruise)	Major force applied to area from heavy objects, falls	Discoloration of skin Swelling Internal bleeding Skin not punctured Pain	Do not puncture skin Support, compress, apply ice Massage and heat after 48 hours
Incision (cut)	Sharp objects that slice the skin such as knives, broken glass, paper edges, etc.	Area of skin surface and arteries or veins Smooth edges Severe bleeding	Control bleeding Wash wound Do not attempt to wash deep parts
Laceration (tearing)	Heavy blunt object tearing skin from dull knives, metal bars, wooden poles, etc.	Area of skin surface and arteries or veins Torn, bruised tissue Severe bleeding Danger of infection Foreign materials in wound	Wash wound Use "butterflies" to pull edges together
Puncture (piercing)	Sharp pointed object driven into skin from nails, arrows, etc.	Narrow, deep into veins and arteries Embedded objects Danger of infection	Do not remove but immobilize impaled objects
Avulsion (torn off)	Guns, explosives, machinery accidents, animal bites that tear skin	Whole piece of tissue torn off or left hanging Severe bleeding	Control bleeding Take avulsed part to hospital Do not replace protruding organs

Source: Alan N. Rabe. Reprinted with permission.

Arteries received their name (literally, "windpipe") because the Greek physician Praxagoras thought they carried air. (In corpses they are usually empty and that was probably where his observations were made.)

Blood is a very special juice.

Goethe (1749–1832)

The total blood volume in an average-sized individual is between 5 and 6 quarts (4500 to 5500 cc), or about 5 to 8 percent of body weight. Although the average healthy adult can easily tolerate a loss of one pint, the amount usually taken from blood donors, rapid loss of one-third or more of the total blood volume often leads to irreversible shock and death.

The blood is the life.

Deuteronomy 12:23

Structure of Blood

Blood is a red, sticky fluid that normally has a capability of clotting in 6 to 7 minutes. The sticky portion is called *plasma*. Blood also contains a particulate portion, the *blood cells*. The latter, suspended in the plasma, include the red blood cells, the white blood cells, and the platelets.

Blood plasma.   Blood plasma is mainly a water solution containing a vast number of proteins, inorganic salts, blood-clotting factors, vitamins, and many other organic molecules. Plasma delivers oxygen and nutrients to the body cells and at the same time carries away carbon dioxide, urea, and waste products.

The red blood cell.   The red blood cell, or *erythrocyte*, has an average life span of 115 to 120 days; thereafter it is destroyed in the spleen or liver and replaced by newly constructed red cells from the bone marrow. The red blood cell functions primarily as a transport vehicle, delivering oxygen from the lungs to individual tissue cells. Red cells give color to the blood.

Human blood is all one color.

Old proverb

The white blood cells.   The white blood cells are also formed in the bone marrow and are not truly white but colorless. The majority of white blood cells function principally to ingest, digest, destroy, and thus over-whelm invading bacteria and even nonbacterial foreign particles, such as an imbedded thorn.

Blood platelets.   Blood platelets are formed within the bone marrow. They accumulate at any site of blood vessel injury, and by virtue of their adhesive surface properties they adhere to the damaged area. The platelets then disintegrate and release chemical agents that cause the blood vessel to constrict and also promote rapid clot formation in order to prevent blood loss. Clotting normally takes 6 to 7 minutes.

Judging Blood Loss

The amount of blood loss is often underestimated in the clinical situation (by the physician, nurse, and other medical personnel) and overestimated in the field (by the first aider, emergency medical technician, and others). Studies have indicated that the majority of medical personnel have difficulty in accurately estimating the amount of observed blood loss. Perhaps the explanation is that many medical personnel receive little or no feedback on how accurate their estimates are, regardless of how much experience they have. For practice in estimating blood loss, pour a pint of water on clothing or a towel and compare it to the dry articles.

The Committee on Trauma of the American College of Surgeons has classified the signs and symptoms involved in bleeding into four classes:

Class I: This class includes blood loss up to 15 percent of the victim's predicted blood volume, or about 750 ml (milliliter) loss in volume. The victim is dizzy upon sitting up, the pulse rate ranges between 72 to 84 beats per minute, and the skin is slightly cool. This amount of blood loss is slightly more than a single unit blood bank donation. People who have donated blood may feel dizzy and experience an increased heart rate when they suddenly sit up after giving blood. The capillary blanch test shows that the nailbed refills within the normal two seconds.

Class II: This is a loss of 20 to 25 percent of the blood volume, or about 1000 to 1250 ml. The pulse rate is greater than 100 beats per minute. The victim is cool, sweating, and thirsty. The capillary blanch test exceeds the normal two seconds.

Class III: The victim has lost 30 to 35 percent of total blood volume (1500 to 1800 ml). The pulse rate exceeds 120 beats per minute. The victim's skin is cold and clammy, and skin coloration is pale to white.

Class IV: This is massive blood loss of over 40 to 50 percent of the blood volume (2000 to 2500 ml). Nailbeds remain blanched when pressed. Pulse rate is over 140 beats per minute. The victim is either semiconscious or unconscious.

Types of External Bleeding

External bleeding is classified as:

Arterial.   Blood from an artery spurts and is bright red in color because it is rich in oxygen. Arterial bleeding is less likely to clot than other types of bleeding. When completely severed, arteries often constrict and seal themselves off. However, if an artery is not completely severed but is torn or has a hole in its wall, it will probably continue to bleed. Blood loss is often rapid and profuse, as blood spurts from the wound. Unless a very large artery has been severed, it is unlikely that a person will bleed to death before control measures can be taken.

Unlike bleeding from other vessels, arterial bleeding, unless it is from only a small artery, will not clot, for a blood clot can form only when there is a slow flow or no flow at all. It is for this reason that arterial bleeding is dangerous; hence, some external means of control must be used to bring about the cessation of the blood flow.

Some vessels are so large and carry such pressure that even if a clot did form, it would be forced out. This can happen if inept handling of a wound disturbs a clot or if pressure is released too soon. Therefore, once arterial bleeding is stopped, control must be maintained long enough for the injured person to be safely transported to an adequate medical facility.

Venous.   Bleeding from a vein is steady and the blood is dark bluish-red in color. This type of bleeding may be profuse, but it is easier to control than arterial bleeding.

One danger associated with venous bleeding, particularly from a large vein, is that of an air bubble or air embolism. This can happen because the blood in the larger veins is being sucked back toward the heart; hence, when a large vein is cut, air may actually be sucked into the opening in the vein. If the air bubble is large enough, the heart cannot pump the blood freely because of the air block that is formed. This is one reason for controlling venous bleeding quickly.

Veins are usually located closer to the body surface than are arteries. Most veins will collapse when they are cut; however, bleeding from deep veins can be as profuse and as hard to control as arterial bleeding.

Capillary.   Blood oozes from a capillary; it is similar in color to venous blood. Capillary bleeding is usually not serious and is easily controlled. It is characterized by a general ooze from the tissues, the blood dripping steadily from the wound or gradually forming a puddle in it. This type of bleeding is not immediately dangerous. Often this type of bleeding will control itself by clotting spontaneously.

Blood Clotting

Very simply, the changes leading to clot formation are brought about by the release of *thromboplastin* from the injured tissues and the blood platelets. This acts upon a substance present in the blood, known as *pro-thrombin*, in such a way as to convert it, with the help of calcium, to *thrombin*. Another substance in the blood, known as *fibrinogen*, is converted by the thrombin into a sticky network of *fibrin*, which forms the basic network of a blood clot.

What wound did ever heal but by degrees?

William Shakespeare (1564–1616)

In *hemophilia*, the tendency to bleed, as well as the inability of the blood to clot, may be so great as to be a hazard to life. Bleeding in a person with this condition is especially difficult to control because the problem is in the failure of the blood-clotting mechanism itself, and there is as yet no known specific curative measure. Hospitalization will be required. As an emergency care measure, the first aider should put firm compression on the bleeding site.

Internal Bleeding

Internal bleeding may occur as a result of a direct blow to the body, fractures, strains, sprains, and from diseases such as bleeding ulcers. When vessels are ruptured, blood leaks into tissue spaces and body cavities. Internal bleeding should be suspected in all cases that involve penetrating or crushing injuries of the chest and abdomen.

The signs and symptoms of excessive loss of blood are weakness or actual fainting; dizziness; pale, moist, and clammy skin; nausea; thirst; fast, weak and irregular pulse; shortness of breath; dilated pupils; ringing in the ears; restlessness; and apprehension. The victim may lose consciousness and stop breathing. The number of symptoms and their severity is generally proportionate to how fast the blood is lost and the amount.

Once the bleeding has been controlled, the victim should be placed in a reclining position, encouraged to lie quietly, and treated for shock (see page 110). *Fluids should not be given by mouth when internal injury is suspected.*

CONTROL OF BLEEDING

Bleeding may be controlled by direct pressure, elevation, and pressure at pressure points. A tourniquet should be applied *only* when every other method fails to control the excessive bleeding.

Direct Pressure

The simplest and preferred method to control severe bleeding is to place a dressing over the wound and apply pressure directly to the bleeding site with the palm of the hand. (See Figure 4-6.) Although a sterile dressing

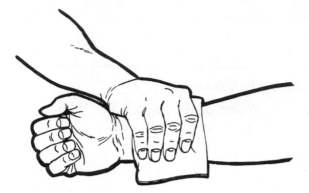

FIGURE 4–6   Applying direct pressure to a wound.

should be applied, none may be available at the time of the emergency, so the cleanest cloth available may have to be used. In the absence of a dressing or cloth, the bare hand may be used until a dressing is available. If the dressing becomes soaked with blood, another dressing should be applied over the first one with firmer hand pressure. The initial dressing should *never* be removed because this will disturb the clotting process, which usually takes about six minutes.

A pressure bandage can be applied over the dressing to hold it in place while additional emergency care is given to the victim. The center of the bandage should be placed directly over the dressing on the wound. A steady pull should be maintained as the ends of the bandage are wrapped around the injured part of the body. (See Figure 4–7.) As in the normal bandaging of wounds or the splinting of fractures, the bandage should be

FIGURE 4–7   Applying a pressure bandage.

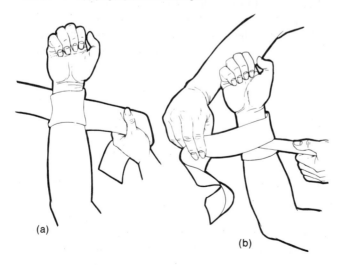

(a)

(b)

tied over the dressing to provide additional pressure to the bleeding area. Do *not* cut off the circulation. A pulse should be felt on the side of the injured part away from the heart. If the bandage has been applied properly, it could be allowed to remain in place undisturbed at least 24 hours. If the dressings are not soaked with blood and the circulation beyond the pressure dressing is adequate, they need not be changed for several days.

Elevation

When there is a severely bleeding wound of an extremity or the head, direct pressure should be applied on a dressing over the wound with the part elevated. The force of gravity then lowers the blood pressure in the affected part and the flow of blood is lessened (Figure 4-8).

Pressure Points

When direct pressure and elevation cannot control severe bleeding, pressure should be applied to the artery that supplies the area. Because this technique reduces the circulation to the wounded part below the pressure point site, it should be applied only when absolutely necessary and only until the severe bleeding has lessened. A pressure point site is where a main artery lies near the skin surface and directly over a bone. There are a large number of pressure point sites where pressure may be applied to help control bleeding. However, the brachial artery in the upper arm and the femoral artery in the groin are the most effective pressure points.

The pressure point for the brachial artery is located midway between the elbow and the armpit on the inner arm between the large muscles (Figure 4-9). To apply pressure, one hand should be around the victim's arm with the thumb on the outside of the arm and the fingers on the inside. Pressure is applied by moving the flattened fingers and the thumb toward one another. The pressure point for the femoral artery is located on the front of the upper leg on the crease between the body and the leg itself (Figure 4-9). Before pressure is applied, the victim should be placed face

FIGURE 4-8

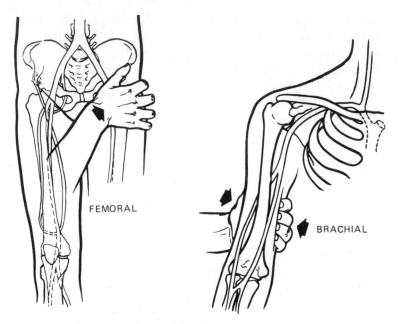

FEMORAL

BRACHIAL

FIGURE 4-9 Proper hand position for applying femoral and brachial pressure.

up. Pressure should be applied with the heel of the hand while keeping a straightened arm.

Pressure point control of bleeding is *not* as satisfactory as direct pressure exerted on a wound because bleeding rarely comes from a single major artery. Therefore, always continue to use direct pressure and elevation if you use a pressure point. When bleeding stops, keep using direct pressure and elevation, but slowly release the pressure point.

Tourniquet

In 1674 during the siege of Besancon, the French military surgeon Morel devised an arrangement for applying pressure over a large artery to stop the flow of blood. The word *tourniquet* was originally applied to the stick or handle that was turned in order to tighten the bandage, and later the term was extended to include the entire device. The term was adopted into English in 1695 from the French and literally means "an instrument for turning."

When to use?   The use of a tourniquet is rarely necessary to control bleeding. If direct pressure, elevation of a limb, pressure points, and pressure dressings are not effective in controlling life-threatening bleeding, a tourniquet may be used as a *last resort*. An amputation of an arm or leg may leave no other choice.

What to use?   Use strong, wide (3 to 4 inches), flat materials only, such as a cravat or folded towel. Never use rope, wire, or other narrow materials that might cut into the skin and damage the underlying tissues.

How to apply?

Place the wide, flat, strong band in the proper location and around the limb twice. Tie a simple overhand knot. The proper location is discussed later in this section.

Place a strong, unbreakable stick of wood or similar material about 6 inches long over the knot and secure it in place with a square knot.

Twist the stick of wood several times to exert enough pressure to stop the bleeding.

Loop or tie a strip of cloth around the end of the stick and tie it to the arm or leg so that the tourniquet will not unwind. Use the ends of the tourniquet, another strip of cloth, or tape.

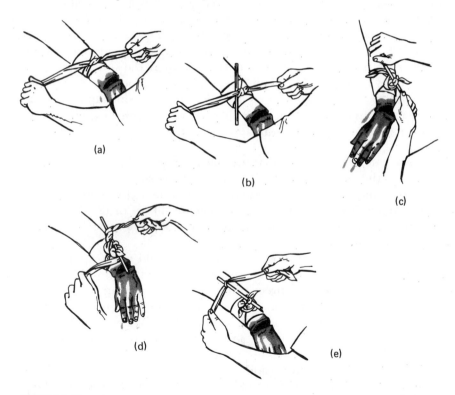

(a)

(b)

(c)

(d)

(e)

FIGURE 4–10

How tight should a tourniquet be?   Obviously the tourniquet should be tight enough to stop the bleeding. A loose tourniquet will restrict the flow of blood in the veins without stopping the flow of blood in the arteries. This will cause *more* blood loss, because the blood will pass from the heart and through the arteries into the wounded area but will not return to the heart through the veins.

If a tourniquet is applied too tightly, injury to underlying nerves and blood vessels may result. It is now known that most of the resultant injuries to nerves are due to compression (too great of a force) rather than from a lack of blood supply.

Should a tourniquet be loosened?   It was formerly believed that a tourniquet should never be left on for more than 20 minutes without loosening it. It is now known that a tourniquet, once applied, should be left in place until it can be loosened under conditions where immediate surgical and supportive care can be carried out, as in a hospital.

Two reasons for this are: (1) Frequent loosening of a tourniquet may dislodge clots and result in sufficient bleeding to produce shock resulting in death; (2) so-called tourniquet shock is recognized as a very real cause of shock to people to whom tourniquets have been applied. This type of shock is thought to be caused by harmful substances released by the injured tissue, which are held back by a tourniquet, and then are allowed to enter the body's circulation in large concentration when the tourniquet is released. Unless measures are taken to control shock, loosening of a tourniquet may be fatal. Studies show that leaving the tourniquet in place causes more limbs to be lost but more lives saved. Therefore, do not loosen the tourniquet until a doctor evaluates the victim.

Where to apply?   Tourniquets are always applied between the bleeding site and the heart, since their purpose is to stop arterial bleeding. Disagreement on the proper location of a tourniquet exists. Two questions arise: (1) Should it be placed above the knee or elbow? or (2) should it be placed as close as possible to the edge of the wound regardless of the wound's location on the limb?

On one side there are those who say one should never apply a tourniquet below the elbow or knee. These sources claim that most bleeding in these areas is controlled by direct pressure and/or pressure points, thus never necessitating a tourniquet. Another argument favoring this point of view is that bones of the lower arm and lower leg disallow complete stoppage of severe bleeding. Moreover, the forearm and foreleg are more likely to have nerve injury because nerves are located superficially in these areas and may be injured by compression.

On the other hand, other sources believe a tourniquet should be as close as possible to, but not flush to, the proximal edge of the wound. The logic behind this view takes into account the possibility that the limb may need to be sacrificed and, thus, if the tourniquet is as far down on the limb as possible, more of the limb will be salvageable for fitting an artificial limb. This method is the one recommended.

Are there other precautions?

Write "TK" on the victim's forehead in ink and attach a note to the victim's clothing or extremity, giving the location of the tourniquet and the time it was applied.

Never cover the tourniquet with clothing or bandages, or hide it in any way.

If tourniquets are left on for too long, gangrene can occur. Thus, whenever possible, evacuation of the injured victim should not be delayed.

If the wound is in a joint area or just below it, place the tourniquet immediately above the joint.

Once a tourniquet is applied, treatment by a physician is imperative.

Remember: A tourniquet can save a life, but the victim may lose a limb.

FIRST AID FOR WOUNDS

Removal of Foreign Matter

Wood splinters, glass, wood and metal fragments, clothing threads, dirt, and other foreign matter that remain in a wound should be removed if they are near the surface and visible. Such materials in a wound may not cause discomfort to the victim but may result in bacterial infection if allowed to remain. However, deeply embedded material should *not* be removed for fear of causing additional damage.

Sterile tweezers may be used to remove foreign matter; also, irrigation of the wound with clean water is helpful. The tip of a sterile needle can be used to remove small particles of matter.

Large objects. Large penetrating objects should *never* be removed from the body. Also, the body should not be removed from a fixed object, such as a fence post. Medical advice and assistance needed to remove the object should be obtained immediately. Any movement of an impaled object should be prevented. If it cannot be broken off close to the body, dressings should be placed around the object to immobilize it. Doughnut-shaped dressings are most effective because they fit securely around the object and are less likely to come undone. The dressing should not be added until the object's position is stabilized. Then, a dressing should be placed over the area and a bandage applied to hold the object securely in place. Plans should be made to evacuate the victim to the nearest medical facility as soon as possible.

Fishhooks.   A fishhook can be removed easily by backing the hook out when only the point and not the barb penetrates the skin. If the barb of the hook enters the skin, there are several techniques suggested:

1. If medical care is near, transport the victim and have a physician remove the hook.
2. If medical care is distant, remove the hook by one of two methods.

Method A

Use cold or hard pressure to provide temporary anesthesia.

Loop a piece of fishline (about 18 inches long) around the hook near the skin surface (see Figure 4–11a). Wrap the other ends of the line around your forefinger.

Grasp the eye of the hook with one hand and press down about one-eighth of an inch to disengage the barb (see Figure 4–11b).

While still pressing the hook down (barb disengaged), jerk the line parallel to the skin surface with the other hand so that the hook shaft leads the barb out of the skin (see Figure 4–11c).

Wash the wound thoroughly with soap and water, and cover with a dressing.

Method B

Use cold or hard pressure to provide temporary anesthesia.

Push the barb until it penetrates the skin on the opposite side (Figure 4–12b).

Cut the barb wire off with a wire cutting instrument (Figure 4–12c) and remove the rest of the hook through the original hole (Figure 4–12d).

Wash the wound thoroughly with soap and water, and cover with a dressing.

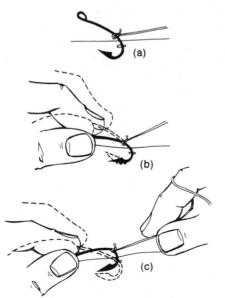

FIGURE 4–11   Removing a fishhook—Method A.

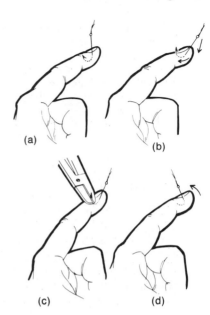

(a)　(b)

(c)　(d)

FIGURE 4–12 Removing a fishhook—Method B.

Cleaning a Wound

Most wounds can be handled safely without professional medical care. The following steps can be taken to prevent or reduce the chance of infection when caring for wounds:

1. When possible, wash hands with soap and water.
2. Allow the wound to bleed slightly. Apply direct pressure to the wound with a clean cloth. Continue pressure for 3 minutes (clotting may take 6 to 7 minutes).
3. Using a sterile gauze pad or a clean cloth saturated with soap and water, gently wash dirt away from the wound edges. Hydrogen peroxide (3 percent solution) helps to bubble away old blood and clots—not to disinfect the wound or destroy anaerobic bacteria as is often thought. Foreign bodies, such as dirt or gravel, must be removed to avoid infection and tatooing after the skin has healed.
4. Flush the wound liberally with large quantities of water.
5. Those who feel they must use an antiseptic should avoid name-brand products, choosing instead isopropyl (rubbing) alcohol. It should be applied, if at all, on the intact skin around the wound, *not in the wound*. First aid antiseptic salves, sprays, and solutions do little good and may even retard healing by burning the tissue.
6. Cover the wound with a sterile gauze dressing and bandage. A band-aid is commonly used on small cuts. The dressing should not be airtight because it might trap moisture given off by the skin and encourage the growth of bacteria. If the wound is more a scrape than a cut, a plastic "nonstickable" covering may be helpful because it does not adhere to the wound.
7. Small (less than 1 inch) lacerations heal faster and with less scarring if the

wound edges are brought together by one or more pieces of tape. Commonly known as "butterfly" bandages, these can be made or purchased.

8. If the wound bleeds after a bandage is applied and the bandage becomes stuck, it is best to leave it on as long as the wound is healing normally. Pulling the scab loose to change the dressing can only retard healing and increase the chances of infection. If a bandage must be removed, soaking it in warm water or hydrogen peroxide can help soften the scab and make removal easier. If a dressing is changed too often, it can prolong the healing process.

Dressings for a wound are usually most needed in the first 24 hours after an injury. During this time the fibrin seal has not yet formed, and the wound is especially susceptible to infection.

Dressings serve a number of functions, including

1. Protecting the wound from outside contamination
2. Shielding the wound from further injury
3. Preventing the spread of germs, blood, and other wound materials to surrounding areas
4. Preventing the wound from getting either too wet or too dry
5. Increasing the comfort of the victim and at the same time covering the wound site so the victim and others are not disturbed by the wound's appearance.

Gauze is still widely preferred as a dressing. Utilize elastic bandages with caution. Most experts say dressings should be impervious to water but allow in air; others feel this is not necessary.

A dressing must be changed if it becomes wet. A wet dressing is an excellent site for bacteria. Dressings that are dry on the surface may be wet at the point of contact with the wound. Dirty dressings should be changed for the sake of appearance.

In recent years several types of dressing materials designed to minimize sticking to wound surfaces have been developed. One of the first was Telfa, which consists of a thin sheet of perforated plastic attached to a backing of absorbent material.

Various antibiotic creams were once shown to be of some value in the mid-1950s, but their use has decreased as bacteria became more resistant. Elastic bandages, when applied improperly or left on for extended periods, can complicate healing because they impair circulation.

None can speak of a wound with skill, if he hath not a wound felt.

Sir Philip Sidney (1554–1586)

Hematoma Under Fingernail

Blood trapped under a fingernail as a result of a blow is very painful. If a hole is made in the nail to allow the blood to escape, the victim will obtain some relief.

As soon as possible after the injury, apply cold to minimize swelling. One of two methods might be tried for a blood blister (hematoma) after the victim's hand is cleansed with soap and water.

Method A (Figure 4–13)

Straighten a paper clip and heat the tip until it glows—then carefully place the tip of the paper clip on the center of the discolored area of the nail and let it burn through the nail into the center of the blood blister. The nail has no nerves, thus there will be no pain. If this is done carefully, a tiny opening will be made in the nail and the hot paper clip will not penetrate into underlying tissues because the hematoma offers protection. The hole releases pressure, drains the blood blister, and gives the victim prompt relief from pain. A sterile dressing should be placed over the area.

Method B

Use a small pocketknife blade as a drill. The tip should be sharp and the blade sterilized. This method is slow and may be painful. Place the knife tip at the center of the discolored area of the nail and gently turn the blade in a back and forth drilling motion. When a hole is made through the nail, a small drop of blood will appear. Apply a sterile dressing over the area.

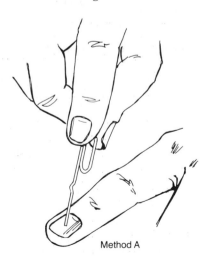

Method A

FIGURE 4–13 Hematoma under fingernail—Method A.

Human Bites

A severe infection may develop in a wound caused by human teeth because the mouth abounds with potentially harmful bacteria. In most cases, human bites involve the nose, ears, and fingers. Self-inflicted bites of the tongue and lip are tolerated well.

The bite treatment consists of washing with running water. Cover the wound with a sterile dressing and observe carefully for any infection. Treatment for tetanus is not needed because the tetanus germ is not found in the human mouth.

Animal Bites

Over one million people are bitten by dogs each year. Such bites are responsible for 1 percent of all emergency room visits. The most likely victims are males under age 20. Victims over 50 are at greatest risk for infections. So are those who delay medical care for more than 24 hours. About one bite in ten will require stitches, but all bites need complete cleaning, which may not be possible by a first aider.

From a first aid standpoint, the main concerns in animal bites are bleeding and infection. Considerable bleeding may occur, for the jaws of many dogs are powerful enough to puncture sheet metal. The crushing nature of a bite often deposits bacteria deep beneath the surface of the skin, where it is hard to clean.

A dog's mouth may carry more than 60 different species of bacteria, some of which are very dangerous to humans. Cat bites are equally contaminated and dangerous. Only human mouths contain more bacteria.

The location of a bite is a critical factor both in producing infection and in determining whether the bite requires medical treatment. Often, the better the blood supply to the bitten area, the safer the bite, because it is less likely to become infected (only 4 percent of facial bites studied became infected, while 33 percent of the hand bites did). Puncture-type wounds have the greatest chance of developing infection, as compared to lacerations. All bites to the face, neck, and head should receive medical treatment for two reasons: the close proximity of these wounds to the brain, and the fact that bites to these regions often must be irrigated and stitched to prevent scarring. However, some wounds from bites, especially on the hand, are left open because of their high infection potential. Once the wound closes, harmful germs can grow where they can't be reached by cleaning.

First Aid

Proper first aid for an animal bite begins by controlling bleeding. Use direct pressure and elevation. Next, the wound must be vigorously washed with lots of soap and water for at least 10 minutes. Puncture wounds can be encouraged to bleed. This helps remove bacteria deposited deep in the tissues. Most bites should be treated in an emergency room or physician's office because of the danger of infection and the need for a tetanus shot.

Signs of infection may include redness, swelling, and sensations of heat around the wound. If the infection spreads, lymph nodes in the armpit, neck, or groin may become swollen and painful.

Rabies

Only three people have been known to survive rabies after its onset. Fortunately, over the past 50 years in the United States, the incidence of rabies in humans has continued to decrease.

Though rabies is a consideration in all animal bites, rabies is most commonly found in wild animals: skunks, bats, raccoons, and foxes. Since nine out of ten bites are caused by domestic animals, the chances of contracting rabies are low.

Rabies is caused by a virus that passes from saliva through an opening in the skin of a human or animal. The virus can be found in the brain of the animal. That is why it is important to prevent damage to the animal's head.

If a wild animal bites a human, the only certain way to rule out rabies is to examine the animal's brain. If the animal can't be found or the brain can't be examined, the human who was bitten will have to undergo rabies shots.

Bites from domestic animals that are not warm-blooded, such as birds, snakes, and other reptiles, do not carry the danger of rabies. But these, too, may become infected. Such bites should be thoroughly washed and cleaned and watched for signs of infection.

It is interesting to note the prevalence of rabies in cats. The reason for this may be that stray cats are frequently adopted into a household without much consideration for their immunization status. Cats are not as subject to prelicense vaccination laws as dogs and are not actively restricted by leash laws or other control measures.

Dogs are the other common source of rabies that humans can contract from domestic animals. Even though the incidence of the disease appears to be decreasing in this group, dog bites still constitute an estimated 1 percent of all hospital emergency department visits.

Wild animals remain the primary source of rabies, and raccoons represent a particular danger because significant numbers of them carry rabies. All wild animals should be left alone. They should not be fed, played with, or picked up, especially the young.

If bitten.　If an animal does bite, efforts should be made to capture the animal for observation without further endangering the captors. Every attempt should be made to avoid destroying the animal. If it is killed, the animal's head and brain should be protected from damage. It is best to transport the animal intact to prevent exposure to potentially infected secretions or tissues. If necessary, the animal's remains can be refrigerated (avoid freezing).

Bites that break the skin should be vigorously cleansed and washed with large amounts of soap and water. Medical care is of utmost importance, not only for repair of the wound but for consultation regarding further treatment.

Many people still believe that treatment for rabies involves a long and painful series of injections. Until 1980, rabies treatment required a series of 23 injections, sometimes in the abdomen. However, a new vaccine has been found to be safer, less painful, and more effective than the old type. It requires only five injections in the arm within a 30-day period.

Each year at least one million Americans are bitten by dogs. This means that, annually, one out of every 200 Americans can expect to be the victim of a dog bite.

Rabies in humans has been regarded as uniformly fatal when associated with the hydrophobia symptom. A 25-year-old woman of Brazil was believed to be the first ever to survive the disease in 1968. Some sources give priority to Matthew Winkler, age 6, who on October 10, 1970 was bitten by a rabid bat. Once common, rabies is now rare.

Guinness Book of World Records

Severed Body Part

As microsurgical procedures and instrumentation have improved, successful reimplantation of amputated body parts, especially of the extremities, has become common.

Blood loss in cases of complete amputations is often surprisingly quite minimal. Blood vessels at the injured ends tend to retract into the traumatized body parts and to contract in diameter. This is nature's mechanism of preventing life-threatening bleeding. Bleeding-control efforts should start with direct pressure along with elevation. Tissue, vessel, and nerve damage that could result from the application of a tourniquet will be avoided if these techniques are used.

The amputated part should be transported with great care. In most cases the severed part is recovered at the accident scene by emergency medical technicians or paramedics, but in multicasualty cases or in reduced lighting conditions, or when untrained people transport the injured, someone may be requested to locate and transport the missing body part to the hospital emergency ward after the victim's departure.

Studies indicate that severed parts that have been without oxygen as a result of the loss of blood supply for more than six hours, and have not been cooled, have little chance for survival; 24 hours is probably the maximum time allowable for an adequately cooled part (32° to 39°F). The severed part should not be packed in ice, however, as reimplantation of frozen parts is usually unsuccessful.

The following procedures should be followed in caring for severed body parts:

1. Soak a clean gauze with clean water. If gauze is unavailable, use a clean towel, washcloth, or similar material. Do not wash, rinse, scrub, or apply antiseptic solution to the wound or severed part.
2. Wrap the amputated part with the wet gauze or towel. Do not immerse the body part in water.
3. If a plastic bag is available, put the wrapped severed part in it.
4. Place the wrapped, amputated part on a bed of ice, but do not submerge.
5. Transport immediately to the emergency department.

If the injured part is still partially attached to the stump by a tendon

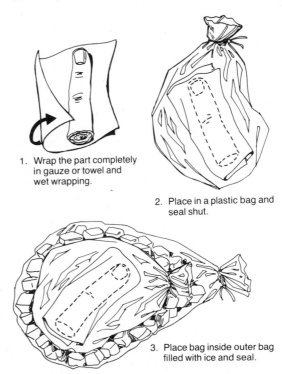

1. Wrap the part completely in gauze or towel and wet wrapping.

2. Place in a plastic bag and seal shut.

3. Place bag inside outer bag filled with ice and seal.

FIGURE 4–14　Care of severed part.

or a small skin "bridge," the treatment is essentially the same. The part can still be wet-wrapped and placed on ice.

A well-preserved part without a large amount of muscle tissue (which necroses quickly) can be replanted up to 24 hours after the amputation. However, a nonpreserved part can remain viable for six hours at the most.

Avulsed Scalp

The amputated scalp should be loosely wrapped in a manner similar to that described for a severed part. The denuded skull should be kept moist and covered with a dressing.

Gunshot Wounds

Guns are abundant in the United States. It is estimated that about one-half of all American homes have a firearm. It has also been established that the ratio of serious, nonfatal gunshot wounds to accidental gunshot deaths is 13:1.

In a typical recent year, guns were involved in nearly 2,000 fatal accidents, about 16,000 suicides, and over 13,000 homicides in the United States. Each year about 100,000 people are injured in firearm accidents.

A bullet causes injury in the following ways depending on its velocity:

1. *Laceration and crushing.* When the bullet penetrates, the tissue is crushed and forced apart. This is the main effect of low-velocity bullets. The crushing and laceration caused by the passage of the bullet is not usually serious unless vital organs or major blood vessels are directly injured. The bullet only damages tissues with which it comes into direct contact, and the wound is comparable to those caused by weapons such as knives.

2. *Shock waves and temporary cavitation.* When a bullet penetrates, a shock wave exerts outward pressure from the bullet's path. This pushes tissues away. This has been described as a "blowing out" and results in bursting of tissue. A temporary cavity is created, which can be as much as 30 times the diameter of the bullet. As the cavity is formed, a negative pressure develops inside, creating a vacuum. This vacuum draws debris in with it.

    This temporary cavitation occurs only with high-velocity bullets, and it is the main reason for their immensely destructive effect. The cavitation lasts only one millisecond but can damage muscles, nerves, blood vessels, and bone.

In a *penetrating* wound, there is an entry of the bullet but no exit. In a *perforating* wound, there is both an entry and exit point. The exit wound of a high-velocity bullet is larger than the entrance wound; the exit wound from a low-velocity bullet is about the same size of the entry wound. In a bullet wound at very close range, the entrance wound may be larger than the exit wound because the gases in the blast contribute to the surface tissue damage.

Bullets sometimes hit hard tissue (for example, bone) and may bounce around in the body cavities and cause a great deal of damage to tissue and organs. Moreover, bone chips can be forced to other body areas and cause damage. A split or misshapen bullet does greater damage because it tumbles, exerting its force over a greater diameter than a smooth bullet going in a straight line.

First Aid

The victim of a gunshot wound often gets initial care from a first aider. What is done in giving immediate treatment and in anticipating and preventing complications may very well determine whether the victim has prolonged hospitalization or rehabilitation difficulty, or even survives at all.

Regardless of the type of wound, initial care follows roughly the same pattern. Wound treatment is limited to inspection and covering the wound to control and monitor the amount of bleeding. In addition to the point of entry, try to find the point of exit, if any. Generally, efforts are concentrated on attempting to stabilize the victim's condition.

Begin the assessment with the primary examination (best known as the ABCs). First, an open airway should be established. If the airway is uninjured but there is breathing difficulty, efforts are limited to maintaining an extension of the neck.

The second priority provides for proper respiration assistance, if needed.

Another area of concern is circulation. If the heart has stopped, start regular cardiac resuscitation (CPR). Bleeding should be covered with a sterile dressing and direct pressure applied. (Do not apply direct pressure on head wounds, where pressure may drive debris and bone into the brain. This may prevent blood from escaping, thus causing pressure against the brain.) Be sure to prevent shock and care for existing shock. Elevate the legs (8 to 12 inches) if there are no head or chest wounds, no vomiting, and the victim is conscious; give no fluids; maintain body warmth.

While taking care of these priorities, monitor bleeding and vital signs. Measure the amount of bleeding. Make an estimate by how quickly a dressing becomes saturated. The amount of blood loss is often underestimated.

Legal aspects. Gunshot wounds will involve contact with the law-enforcement agencies and possibly testifying in court. Therefore, keep a careful record of what you did and when you did it. Preserve possible evidence, such as bullets. Always check for powder burns around the wound, both on the skin and on the clothing. The distance between the victim and the firearm may be important in determining if the shooting was a suicide or a homicide. In most states, gunshot wounds *must* be reported to the police.

The rich and famous as well as the poor and obscure can be gunshot victims. Gunshot wounds are all too common, as viewing the evening television news shows us. How well the first aider handles this emergency will have a direct bearing on what happens to a gunshot victim.

Wounds Requiring Medical Care

Arterial bleeding.

Bleeding that cannot be controlled.

Any deep incision, laceration, or avulsion that:
(1) goes into the muscle or bone
(2) is located on a body part that bends and puts stress on the cut (elbows, knees)
(3) tends to gape widely
(4) is on the thumb or palm of hand (because nerves may be cut, later affecting the sense of touch). Wounds requiring sutures should be seen by a physician within the first eight hours.

Any puncture that: is large or deep; is made by a dirty object; or does not bleed freely.

Large embedded objects.

Deeply embedded objects of any size.

Foreign matter left in a wound.

Human and animal bite wounds.

Wounds where a scar would be noticeable. Sutured cuts usually heal with less scarring than unsutured ones.

Cuts to eyelids need sutures to prevent later drooping.

A slit lip needs suturing because it scars easily.

Any closed wound worse than a bruise.

Any wound that the first aider is not certain how to care for.

Wounds Not Requiring Sutures

Cut edges of the skin that tend to fall together.

Cuts less than one inch long that are not deep.

Gaping Wounds

Gaping wounds may be closed by using the *butterfly* bandage method (Figure 4–15). Close a gaping wound only if all of the following are found:

The wound is less than 8 to 12 hours old;

The wound is very clean; and

It is impossible to get to a physician to suture it the same day the wound occurred.

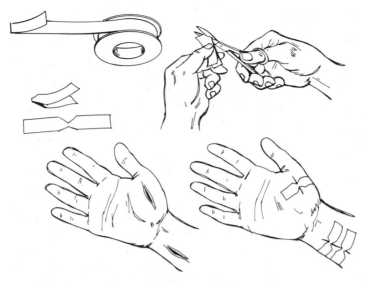

FIGURE 4–15

Internal Bleeding (Closed Injuries)

Closed injuries may range from damaged tissue beneath the skin to severe internal injuries.

Signs of internal bleeding include the following:

1. The pulse becomes weak or rapid.
2. The skin becomes cold and clammy.
3. The eyes are dull; the pupils may be dilated.
4. The victim is usually thirsty.
5. The victim may be nauseated and may vomit.
6. A bruise may be external evidence of a more serious internal injury.
7. Bleeding from the respiratory or digestive tracts (see pages 285–288).

First Aid

The principles for first aid care of suspected internal bleeding at any body site are:

1. Treat the victim for shock.
2. Anticipate vomiting; therefore, give nothing by mouth. Keep the victim lying down, preferably on the side.
3. Blood may collect in damaged tissue and from a lump, if an extremity is injured; a pressure bandage should be applied in such cases.
4. Transport to a medical facility as quickly, gently, and efficiently as possible.

For contusions (bruises) elevate the injured leg or arm. Apply cold, wet compresses or ice to the bruise. Try to avoid causing cold injuries with improper use of ice. If there is increasing pain and tenderness or the bruise has increased in size four or more hours after the injury, seek medical care. Warm compresses may be applied after 12 to 18 hours. The bluish discoloration characteristic of a bruise will turn greenish or yellow after a few days.

INFECTION

All open wounds contain bacteria. The potential for an infection to develop is dependent upon the type and quality of bacteria present, the adequacy of the blood supply to the area, and the amount of damaged tissue within the wound. Normal body tissues are capable of destroying large numbers of some bacteria. However, other bacteria resist destruction by the body's defense mechanisms. Careful cleansing of a wound and removal of foreign matter will help to prevent an infection.

Wound infections usually do not become evident until some time after the injury. During the first two or three days there may be throbbing pain, swelling, redness, and excessive warmth in the area of the wound. These are symptoms of infection; they also occur following most extensive injuries. The symptoms tend to diminish toward the end of the first 48 hours if the wound is healing satisfactorily. However, if the symptoms increase, infection may have set in. As an infection progresses, the victim will develop a rising temperature and pulse rate. Pus may develop beneath the skin or drain from an open wound. The size of the inflamed area will increase as surrounding tissues become involved. Red streaks that radiate upward from the infected area indicate the spread of infection through the lymphatic circulation taking away debris and germs from the wound site. Swollen lymph glands may appear as tender nodes in the groin, armpit, or neck; this indicates that the infection has spread beyond the immediate site of the injury. An infection of this type is very serious and medical advice from a physician should be obtained.

First Aid

Medical attention should be sought. When medical advice is delayed, the following may be done. The victim should be kept lying down with the infected body part elevated, if possible. This will reduce swelling and pain. To improve the circulation, warm, moist packs should be applied to the wound four times daily for periods of 30 minutes. Do not squeeze the infected wound. Daily redressing of the wound is necessary to remove the infected discharge from the surface of the wound.

TETANUS

Although the incidence of tetanus has declined in the last 20 years, thanks largely to the use of tetanus toxoid, no really effective treatment exists. Once the disease has occurred, the mortality rate runs between 50 percent to 60 percent. Most fatalities occur among infants, very young children, and the elderly, usually within the first ten days after the development of symptoms.

Tetanus occurs worldwide and causes more than one million deaths each year. It is more prevalent in agricultural regions and developing countries that lack mass immunization programs. In the United States, about 100 cases occur annually, with about 75 percent of all cases occurring between April and September.

Tetanus is an acute infectious disease caused by toxin produced by the bacillus *Clostridium tetani*, a bacterium that grows in the absence of air at the site of an injury. The spores of *Clostridium tetani* are found almost everywhere. They can exist—harmlessly—in the intestinal tracts of humans and animals and are found in soil where animals have pastured. The spores are readily blown about and settle in dust everywhere—city and country. These spores are tough and can survive for many years as long as they are not exposed to direct sunlight. Given the proper anaerobic conditions to stimulate growth, the bacillus produces the deadly toxin that affects the central nervous system.

Tetanus bacteria almost always enter the body through wounds. They are likely to thrive in deep puncture wounds, from a nail, splinter, or pitchfork; wounds in which the flesh is bruised, crushed, or torn; wounds into which dirt or soil is forced; or wounds from foreign objects driven deeply into the flesh, such as gunpowder, bullets, or pieces of clothing. Other types of injuries that are tetanus-prone include burns, insect bites, neonatal infections from the umbilical site, contaminated heroin, animal bites, and frostbite.

The tetanus bacillus is dangerous because it produces one of the most powerful toxins known, far more toxic than the most deadly snake venom. The toxin gradually passes along the nerves from the wound to the spinal cord. There it becomes anchored to the motor nerve cells, which it stimulates so that muscles become rigid and the victim is thrown into terrible convulsions. The jaw muscles are involved early. Stiffness occurs and the mouth cannot be opened; hence, the common name of the disease is lockjaw.

Prevention

All wounds are possible breeding beds for tetanus. Even the smallest injury, such as a puncture or scratch from a rose thorn, is suspect. For this reason, the old-fashioned but extremely effective precaution of thoroughly washing even minor cuts with plenty of soap and water is recommended. The tetanus spore may be present, but it can be washed away before the bacteria begin to grow.

A person can be protected (immunized) against tetanus by injections of tetanus toxoid. All individuals should obtain their primary immunizations and updated booster shots.

First aiders are rarely involved with a tetanus victim. Their primary role is in prevention of the disease. Therefore, all first aiders should understand the importance of strongly encouraging any wounded victim to obtain protection against tetanus by seeking medical assistance if the victim has not been receiving booster shots.

Tetanus immunization is virtually 100 percent effective. Most persons who have tetanus nowadays have been either incompletely immunized or not immunized at all.

According to the American Medical Association, only one of every four Americans has been properly immunized against tetanus.

Protective antibodies persist for five to ten years following complete immunization. Thus more frequent booster doses are not necessary, and in fact, people who receive repeated immunizations may develop serum sickness.

Tetanus remains an important health problem because the tetanus organism is found throughout the world. Tetanus is rare today in the United States (but common throughout the rest of the world). However, the causative bacterium—*Clostridium tetani*—is not extinct, thus necessitating the need for immunizations.

Tetanus would never occur if all people were immunized with tetanus toxoid and received a booster as recommended. Remember—no one should have tetanus. It results in a painful and horrible death.

Chapter 5

Shock

When people are injured, the blood flow in their entire body is disturbed. To overcome this difficulty, the heart beats faster and the blood vessels near the skin and in the arms and legs constrict, thus sending most of the available blood supply to the vital organs of the body and to the nerve centers in the brain that control all vital functions.

While this is going on, the other body cells do not receive enough blood and therefore do not get enough oxygen or food. The blood vessels suffer from this lack, and eventually they lose their ability to constrict. When this happens, the vital organs and the brain do not receive enough blood because it rushes back to fill dilated vessels away from the vital organs. If this situation continues, the damage becomes so extensive that recovery is impossible. In less severe cases, prompt first aid treatment for shock may mean the difference between life and death. In mild cases of shock, recovery usually occurs naturally and rather quickly.

Basically, then, shock is a failure of the circulatory system to provide sufficient circulation of blood to every body part. The measures used to combat shock are aimed at helping the body to recover from this disturbance of the blood flow.

CAUSES OF SHOCK

Serious shock occurs as a result of serious injury to any part of the body. Crush injuries, fractures, burns, poisoning, and prolonged bleeding are very likely to cause serious shock. An interruption of breathing, from whatever cause, is almost always followed by severe shock. In short, any damage to the body is accompanied by or followed by some degree of shock.

A number of factors affect the seriousness of shock. Age, for example, is often a determining factor. Very young children and very old people do not usually have as much resistance to shock as young or middle-aged adults. Pain can produce shock or increase its severity. People who have been starved, deprived of water, or exposed to extremes of cold or heat go into shock very easily. Excessive fatigue can increase the severity of shock. As a general rule, people who have any kind of chronic sickness are likely to go into shock more easily than healthy people. In addition to these factors, there are some unexplained differences between individuals in regard to their resistance to shock; an injury that might cause mild shock in one person could cause serious, perhaps fatal, shock in another. Remember that shock is sure to accompany or follow any serious injury, and that it is often the most serious consequence of the injury.

HOW TO RECOGNIZE SHOCK

A person who is going into shock may show quite a few signs or symptoms. Some of these are indicated in Figure 5-1 and are discussed below. Remember, however, that signs of shock do not always appear at the time of the injury; indeed, in many very serious cases they may not appear until hours later.

The symptoms shown by a person suffering from shock are, directly or indirectly, due to the fact that the circulation of the blood is disturbed. The pulse is weak and rapid. Breathing is likely to be shallow, rapid, and irregular, because the poor circulation of the blood affects the breathing center in the brain. The temperature near the surface of the body is lowered because of the poor blood flow; so the face, arms, and legs feel cold to the touch. Sweating is likely to be quite noticeable. A person in shock is usually very pale, but in some cases there may be a bluish or reddish color to the skin. The pupils of the eyes are usually dilated (enlarged).

The conscious victim may complain of thirst, have a feeling of weakness, faintness, or dizziness, or feel nauseated. Also, shock victims may be very restless and feel frightened and anxious. As shock deepens, these signs gradually disappear and victims become less and less responsive to what is going on around them. Finally, they may become unconscious.

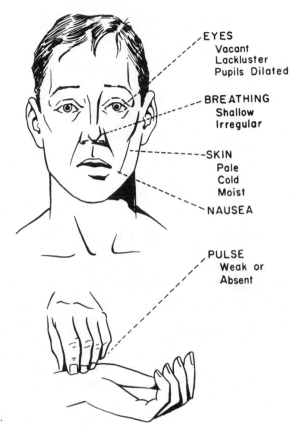

EYES
Vacant
Lackluster
Pupils Dilated

BREATHING
Shallow
Irregular

SKIN
Pale
Cold
Moist

NAUSEA

PULSE
Weak or
Absent

FIGURE 5–1 Symptoms of shock.

It is not likely that you will see all these symptoms of shock in any one case. Some of them appear only in late stages of shock, when the disturbance of the blood flow has become so great that the victim's life is in serious danger. Sometimes the signs of shock may be disguised by other signs of injury. It is important to know what symptoms indicate the presence of shock, but don't ever wait for symptoms to develop before beginning the treatment for shock. Remember, every seriously injured person is likely to develop serious shock.

TYPES OF SHOCK

1. Hemorrhagic (hypovolemic) shock (blood loss). There is insufficient blood in the system to provide adequate circulation to all body organs.
2. Respiratory shock (inadequate breathing). There is an insufficient amount of oxygen in the blood.
3. Neurogenic shock (loss of vascular control by the nervous system). Damage to the spine and brain, which control heart and blood vessels, result in decreased blood supply to the brain.

4. Psychogenic shock (fainting). Temporary dilation of the blood vessels results in decreased blood supply to the brain.
5. Cardiogenic shock (inadequate functioning of the heart). The heart muscle no longer imparts sufficient pressure to the blood to drive it through the system.
6. Septic shock (severe infection). This form of shock is caused by toxins released during infection, which may cause blood vessels to dilate.
7. Anaphylactic shock (allergic reaction). This is a severe allergic reaction caused by foods, drugs, insect stings, or inhaled substances. It can occur in minutes or even seconds following contact with the substance to which the victim is allergic.
8. Metabolic shock (bodily loss of fluid). A severe fluid loss occurs from a severe untreated illness (diarrhea, vomiting, or urination).

PREVENTION AND FIRST AID FOR SHOCK

In many emergency situations, the most helpful thing you can do for an injured person is to begin treatment for shock. If shock has not yet developed, the treatment may actually prevent its occurrence; if it has developed, you may be able to keep it from reaching a critical point. Shock creates a vicious circle—the worse it is, the worse it gets. It is extremely important that you begin the treatment at the earliest possible moment. Although shock is often not as obvious as other emergencies, it should be treated before all other emergency problems except absence of breathing, cardiac arrest, and profuse bleeding.

In order to give first aid treatment to those in shock, you will need to know how warm they should be kept, what position is best for them, and what you may do to relieve pain.

Fluids

A person in shock is often thirsty. No particular harm will be done if you allow the victim to moisten the mouth and lips with cool water, if it will make the victim more comfortable; but, in general, there is no need to give anything to drink unless you are in a position in which medical personnel will not be available for an excessively long period of time.

If medical care will not be available (over one to two hours), you should give small amounts of warm water, preferably mixed with 1 level teaspoon of salt and ½ level teaspoon of baking soda per quart or liter if the victim is conscious, able to swallow, has not suffered internal injuries, and is not nauseated. Adults may be given ½ (4 oz.) glass over a 15-minute period; children (ages 1 to 12) ¼ (2 oz.) glass; infants ⅛ (1 oz.) glass.

Do not give fluids if the victim is unconscious, having convulsions, likely to need surgery, has a brain injury, has a stomach wound, or is vomiting. Stop fluids if vomiting does occur.

In the case of burns, an exception must be made to the rule of not giving liquids. A seriously burned person has an overwhelming need for fluids. It is therefore a desirable part of first aid treatment for burns to give water or other liquids. Fruit juices or sugar water may be given if the victim is conscious and able to swallow, has no internal injuries, and is not vomiting.

One final precaution must be given concerning the use of liquids: Never give alcohol to a person in shock or one who may go into shock. Alcohol increases the blood supply to surface vessels and so diminishes the blood supply to the brain and other vital organs.

Heat

Heat is important in the treatment of shock to the extent that the injured person's normal body temperature must be conserved. Exposure to cold, with resulting loss of body heat, can cause shock to develop or to become worse. You will have to judge the amount of covering to use by considering the weather and the general circumstances of the accident. Often a light covering will be enough to keep the victim comfortable. Wet clothing should be removed and dry covering provided, even on a hot day. Use blankets or any dry material to conserve body heat. Artificial means of warming (hot water bottles, heated bricks, heated sand) should not ordinarily be used. Artificial heat may cause loss of body fluids (by sweating), which brings the blood closer to the surface, thus defeating the body's own efforts to supply blood to the vital organs and to the brain. Also, the warming agent may burn the victim.

Keep injured victims warm enough for comfort, but do not overheat them. Whenever possible, have a layer of covering underneath the victim as well as on top to preserve body heat.

Position

The best position to use for the prevention or treatment of shock is one that encourages the flow of blood to the heart. If it is possible to place the injured person face up, you can raise the legs and feet 8 to 12 inches so that the feet are higher than the heart (Figure 5-2). If the circumstances of the accident make it impossible to do this, it might still be possible for you to raise the feet and legs enough to help the blood flow to the heart. Sometimes it is possible to take advantage of a natural slope of ground and place the casualty so that the heart is lower than the feet. Do not lift a stretcher or bed at the feet since this makes breathing more difficult, and increases the heart's work. Some experts suggest elevating the head 15 to 30 degrees with elevating the legs 30 degrees. Excessive (over 12 inches) elevation of the legs may cause the bowels and other viscera to fall against the underside of the diaphragm and adversely affect the victim's breathing.

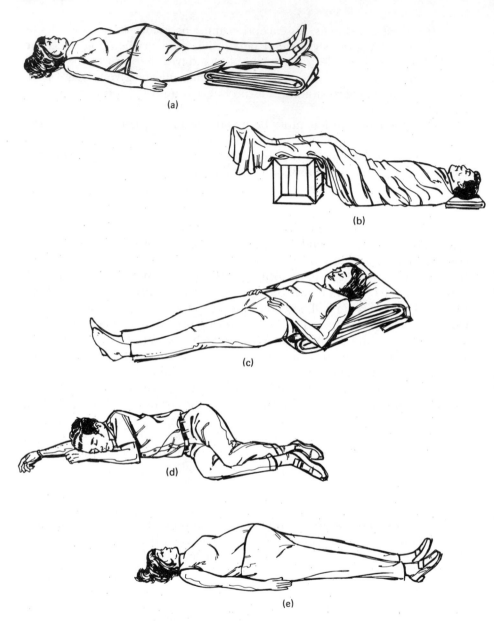

FIGURE 5–2 Positions for traumatic shock. To improve circulation, individuals suspected of being in shock are usually positioned with feet elevated, as in (a) and (b). If the individual is having respiratory difficulty, the head and shoulders should be elevated (c). If the individual is unconscious, place the person on the side (d). And if circumstances dictate, the individual should be left in the position found (e).

In every case, of course, you will have to consider what type of injury is present before you can decide on the best position. For example, a person with a chest wound may have so much trouble breathing that you will have to raise the victim's head slightly. If the face is flushed rather than pale, or if you have any reason to suspect a head injury, do not raise the feet; instead, you should keep the head level with, or slightly higher than, the feet. If the victim is unconscious, place the person on the side with the head extended to keep the airway open. If there is a chance the victim may vomit, place the victim on the side. If the person has broken bones, you will have to judge what position would be best both for the fractures and for shock. A fractured spine must be immobilized before the victim is moved at all if further injuries are to be avoided. If you have any doubts about the correct position to use, have the victim lie face up. The basic position for treating shock is one in which the heart is lower than the feet. Do the best you can, under the particular circumstances, to get the injured person into this position. In any case, never let a seriously injured person sit, stand, or walk around.

If the face is red,
Raise the head.
If the face is pale,
Raise the tail.

Old first aid axiom

Relief of Pain

A long-accepted but false generalization is that all extensive injuries are associated with severe pain and that the more extensive the injury, the worse the pain. In reality, severe and even fatal injuries may be considerably less painful than a mashed fingertip, which can cause agony.

Another generalization is that, with similar injuries, everyone experiences the same amount of pain. This, too, is incorrect. Some feel pain far more severely than others. Also, those who would not be in much pain from a wound when rested, relaxed, and confident might experience severe pain from the same wound if exhausted, tense, and fearful. Persons in shock tend to feel less pain. However, pain, unless relieved, may cause or increase shock.

Injured victims should be reassured and made to realize that their injuries are understood and that they will get the best possible care. They should also be told of plans to get medical help or plans to move them to a place where medical assistance is available.

Support for an Injury

Pain can often be relieved by furnishing adequate support for an injury. Fractures of bones in which the surrounding tissue swells rapidly are extremely painful when left unsupported. Adequate immobilization of fractures not only relieves pain but prevents further tissue damage and shock. Needless suffering can often be eliminated by unlacing or slitting a shoe or loosening tight clothing in the region of the injury. Often a simple adjustment of a bandage or splint will be of much benefit, especially when accompanied by a few encouraging words.

Once shock occurs, there is no way for the rescuer to *reverse* a shock state with current first aid methods; rescuers can only keep the state from worsening—the victim needs medical care.

It is especially important that severe shock be *prevented* in all emergency cases; preventing shock means caring for the whole victim.

Chapter 6

Specific Body Area Injuries

ABDOMINAL INJURIES

Open Wounds

A wound that penetrates the abdominal cavity is extremely dangerous because of possible damage to internal organs. Rupture of hollow organs (for example, digestive system organs) spills contents into the abdominal cavity, resulting in infection. Bacteria may be introduced into the abdominal cavity from the outside or from a perforated intestine. Rupture of a solid organ (for example, the liver) may result in severe bleeding. Usually there is intense pain, severe shock, nausea, and vomiting; a spasm of the abdominal muscles may occur. The victim prefers to lie still with legs drawn up.

First Aid

As soon as possible, plans should be made to evacuate the victim to the nearest medical facility, because immediate surgical treatment generally is required.

Victims should be placed on the back. If the intestine is exposed or protruding, a pillow or bulky material should be put under the victim's knees to relax the abdominal muscles. *Because of the danger of infection, no attempt should ever be made to push the protruding intestine back into the abdominal cavity.*

The intestine should be covered with a sterile dressing that is dampened with sterile cool water. The dressing should be large enough to cover the wound and surrounding skin and should be held in place with a bandage. Care should be taken *not* to fasten the bandage so tight that it interferes with circulation. When the intestines are not protruding, a dry, sterile dressing may be applied to the wound. Some experts feel that covering the wound with a sterile dressing and then wetting the dressing with water will wash contaminants deeply into the abdominal cavity, thus increasing the danger of severe infection. Therefore, they suggest that the wound and the protruding organ be covered with a piece of nonadhering material, such as plastic wrap or aluminum foil because both will retain moisture.

The victim should be treated for shock (see page 110). *No fluids should be given by mouth* because surgery will be necessary as soon as the victim reaches a medical facility.

When there is an impaled object, do not remove the object, because serious bleeding and further damage may occur. Stabilize the impaling object with bulky dressings in the manner suggested for chest injuries (see page 118).

Closed Wounds

Closed wounds from severe blows or crushing injuries may be extremely dangerous. Serious injury to internal organs, internal hemorrhage, and shock may occur. Complications might develop within the first 48 hours that will be as serious as the immediate effects of the injury.

Soon after an injury, a victim may have no signs of abdominal injury, so it is important to come back to check for injury later.

Often victims with closed abdominal injuries have other injuries that can distract the first aider from the abdominal injury and that can also distract the victim from complaining about abdominal pain. Therefore, especially with blunt trauma to the abdomen, the first aider should carefully check the abdomen by gently pressing the four quadrants of the abdomen (see page 294).

The signs of abdominal injury are often not very dramatic—sometimes a slight increase in size or tenderness. Guarding of the abdomen by the victim is a good sign of a closed injury.

First Aid

Treatment for a closed wound is the same as for an open wound, except for the application of a dressing.

BACK INJURIES

First Aid

Closed injuries to the spine are covered on page 257. These injuries are usually the result of falls, crushing accidents, and sharp blows across the back. Severe pain in the side, blood in the urine, muscle spasm, and shock may indicate an injury to a kidney.

Open injuries to the back usually are the result of stabbings, bullets, and flying debris from explosions. The treatment for an open wound should be followed for this type of injury. (See page 85.)

Plans should be made as soon as possible to evacuate the victim to a medical facility. Injury to the spinal cord should be suspected and handled accordingly.

CHEST INJURIES

Sucking Wounds

Because of the lower internal pressure, an open wound into the chest cavity permits air to flow in and out as the victim breathes (see Figure 6-1). This may cause the lung to collapse and fail to function (pneumothorax). Also, there is a danger of internal hemorrhaging if the lung, heart, or large blood vessels have been punctured. A sucking chest wound *always* should be suspected when there is an open chest wound.

The victim may have increasing difficulty in breathing, blueness of the skin (cyanosis), faintness, dizziness, thirst, and a rapid pulse. If the lung, heart, or large blood vessels have been punctured, the victim may

FIGURE 6-1 Treatment of a sucking chest wound.

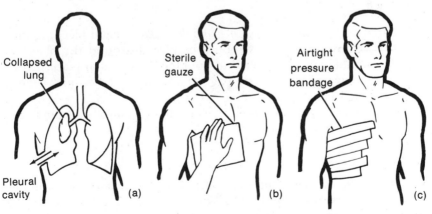

Collapsed lung

Sterile gauze

Airtight pressure bandage

Pleural cavity

(a)   (b)   (c)

cough up frothy, bright-red blood, have a weak pulse, faint heart sounds, and distention of the neck and arm veins. There may be a "sucking" or "hissing" sound as the air flows in and out of the chest cavity.

First Aid

The wound opening must be sealed off immediately. An effective dressing can be made from a piece of plastic wrap or aluminum foil, which will serve to seal off the opening. As the victim forcibly exhales, secure the material in place with overlapping strips of wide adhesive tape. Be sure that all edges of the seal are held down by the tape. A large dressing of sterile gauze can also be applied and the area sealed off with overlapping strips of adhesive tape. (See Figure 6–1.) If sterile gauze dressings are not available immediately, the palm of the hand could be used temporarily. The victim should be placed on the injured side so the uninjured lung can expand more freely and keep the airway free of blood and vomitus. The victim can be treated for shock, if it occurs. (See page 110.) An airway should be maintained and artificial respiration administered, as necessary. (See page 48.) If the lung on the injured side has been damaged, then covering the wound will force the air from the lung to collect in the chest cavity (tension pneumothorax) and put pressure on the heart. In this event, the first aider should remove the dressing applied earlier to allow the air that was built up in the chest cavity to escape. Reseal the wound after the air has escaped.

Plans should be made to evacuate the victim to the nearest medical facility as soon as possible. This injury should not be fatal. Many people have undergone removal of one lung and are still capable of life-sustaining respiration.

Protruding Objects

First Aid

Never remove the impaled object if it is still in place. Fatal bleeding may occur if it is removed. Dressings should be placed around the object to immobilize it and a bandage applied to hold the dressings in place. Artificial respiration may be required (see page 48). Treatment for shock should be given (see page 110).

Plans should be made as soon as possible to evacuate the victim to the nearest medical facility.

Rib Fractures

Rib fractures usually result from blunt trauma or compression. The upper four ribs are rarely fractured because they are protected by the shoulder. The fifth to tenth ribs are the ones most commonly fractured. Fracture of the eleventh and twelfth ribs, because they are the "floating" ribs attached only to the vertebrae, is not likely because of their freedom of movement.

The victim can usually point out the exact injury site with tenderness if you palpate the area. The victim may also guard the injured side by leaning toward the injured side and holding a hand over the fracture site in an effort to immobilize the ribs and ease the pain.

First Aid

Place the arm of the injured side across the chest as shown in Figure 11–17, page 263. This will help prevent bone ends from overriding each other. Tighten the cravats as the victim forcefully exhales.

Flail Chest

When a blunt or crushing injury fractures several adjacent ribs in two or more places, the victim has a flail chest.

The flail segment is detached from the strut of the ribs, which rise and fall with breathing. The result is "paradoxical breathing" where the loose chest wall segment does not move in and out with the rest of the wall. Instead, it moves in the opposite to the normal direction as the victim breathes.

First Aid

Flail chest is treated with external stabilization of the chest. In an emergency, a hand can be applied to the flail segment to prevent the paradoxical movement. Also, the victim can lie on the side of the flail segment. The segment can be supported with sandbags. A more effective method is to place a small pillow or bulky pad over the flail segment. Tape the pillow or pad in place with large strips of tape as arranged in Figure 6–2.

Transport the victim on the affected side.

FIGURE 6–2   Flail chest.

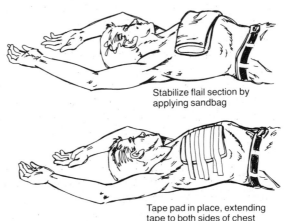

Stabilize flail section by applying sandbag

Tape pad in place, extending tape to both sides of chest

Compression of the Lung

Because of sudden compression of the chest, blood, air, and other fluids may enter the chest cavity and compress the lung. *Immediate medical attention is necessary*, and plans should be made as soon as possible to evacuate the victim to the nearest medical facility.

First Aid

The victim may have difficulty breathing. An airway should be established and artificial respiration applied, if necessary.

Crushing Injuries

These injuries usually result from vehicle accidents and falls. The severe pain from the injuries, often intensified by broken ribs, tends to cause the victim to restrict breathing. Also, the chest wall may collapse between the multiple fractures on each side of the chest (flail chest), which prevents an adequate amount of air from being exchanged.

First Aid

To make breathing easier, the victim should be placed in a comfortable position with the head and shoulders elevated. If the victim has a flail chest, the rib cage should be splinted (see page 119). Plans should be made to evacuate the victim to the nearest medical facility.

EAR INJURIES

Cuts and Lacerations

Cuts and lacerations of the ear occur frequently, and occasionally a section of the ear may be severed.

First Aid

The treatment of these cuts and lacerations is the same as for regular wounds (see page 77). If there is excessive bleeding, direct pressure should be applied (see page 85), and the bleeding controlled before the area is bandaged. Refer to page 98 for care of severed or avulsed body parts.

Perforation (Rupture) of the Eardrum

An injury to the eardrum generally occurs as a result of a blow to the ear, explosion or blast, or a sudden change in the pressure on the ear, as from a dive into deep water. Also, an infection in the middle ear may cause the eardrum to rupture.

First Aid

The ear should not be tampered with, and no instrument should be inserted into it. A small piece of cotton should be placed loosely into the ear canal to protect the injured area until medical assistance can be obtained.

When the eardrum has been perforated as a result of a skull fracture, the flow of the cerebrospinal fluid should not be stopped. Also, nothing should be inserted into the ear canal because of the danger of causing a brain tissue infection. The victim should be placed on the injured side, with the shoulders and head propped up. This will allow the fluid to drain freely until medical assistance can be obtained.

Foreign Bodies in the Ear

Various foreign bodies, such as insects, seeds, matchsticks, and cotton, can become lodged in the ear canal.

First Aid

Don't try to kill a lodged insect by poking something in the ear. Insects are attracted to light, so it may be coaxed out with light. If outdoors, pull the ear lobe gently to straighten the canal and turn the ear toward the sun. If indoors, turn off all lights, then shine a flashlight into the ear while pulling gently on the ear lobe. This will induce the insect to crawl out toward the light.

If the light method fails, a little oil (mineral, baby, or olive oil) may cause the insect to float out. Do not use this method if you are not absolutely sure that the foreign body in the ear is an insect, because if it is a bean, popcorn, etc., the object may swell and be difficult to remove. Do not use if there are signs of eardrum rupture.

Do not go into the ear canal to remove foreign bodies.

Foreign bodies can occasionally be jarred loose from an ear by gently pounding with the hand on the opposite side of the head with the affected ear held down.

If the foreign object cannot be seen, or if any of the above techniques do not work, consult a physician.

EYE INJURIES

The goals of the first aider who cares for a victim of an eye emergency are to identify the problem, provide appropriate initial care, and decide whether medical attention is required. One eye emergency that requires immediate care is a chemical burn; the rest may be successfully treated by an opthalmologist hours or even days later. No eye emergency requires immediate surgery; for example, even repair of eyelid lacerations or removal of most foreign bodies may be postponed for hours.

Initial examination

The initial examination of the victim should include:

Step 1: A history.   This is essential for accurate diagnosis by a physician and for legal purposes.

Step 2: Examination.   If a perforation of the eye is suspected, it is best not to examine the eye. Have the victim voluntarily open the eyes. If the victim cannot, elevate the upper lid by either sliding the lid upward with care to avoid pressure on the globe, or grasping the upper eyelashes between thumb and forefinger. Cotton-tipped applicators may also be used to expose the eye. A flashlight with the beam directed at the eye from the outside toward the nose can be of great assistance. Do not shine the beam directly at the injured eye from the front since the light can cause discomfort.

Step 3: Measure visual acuity.   Determine the approximate visual acuity of each eye separately (with glasses if the victim wears them), using some standard printed material such as a book or newspaper. This information can be helpful to the physician. Some injuries will be too severe to allow for this evaluation.

Step 4: Eye patching.   Do not patch chemical burns. There are two methods of eye patching: loose patch or shield. Small gauze pads or slightly moist cotton may be used in place of the eye pad.
For an unconscious victim, keep the eyes closed because drying of the tissues can cause permanent injury and blindness. Cover the lids with a moist bandage or tape them closed; normal tears will then keep the tissues moist.

Taking the History

Date, time, and place?
What did the victim first notice?
Are both eyes affected? In what way?
Did a foreign body or object strike the eye?
If a chemical is involved, how long was the exposure?
Note: The victim should be briefly but thoroughly questioned.

Eye Patching

Do not patch chemical burns or eye infections.
Moist 2″ by 2″ gauze pads may be substituted for eye pads.
A loose patch reduces light sensitivity.

An eye shield:

> Prevents accidental injury after trauma.
>
> May consist of the cutoff bottom of a paper drinking cup. (See Figure 6–3.)

Cover both eyes to minimize their movement (sympathetic eye movement).

Eyelid Laceration

In all cases:

> Search for laceration of globe and foreign body.
>
> Search for penetration of globe.
>
> Save avulsed portion of eyelid in moist gauze.

Apply gentle direct pressure (if the globe is not cut) to stop bleeding. Apply a patch over eyes.

Transport victim to medical facility. Sutures will prevent later drooping of eyelid.

Foreign Bodies (Superficial)

"Foreign body" sensation, blurred vision, red conjunctiva, and excessive watering.

Evert lid if necessary. A wet, sterile cotton-tipped applicator may be used to remove the foreign object.

If foreign body does not come off easily, patch both eyes and transport victim to medical facility.

FIGURE 6–3

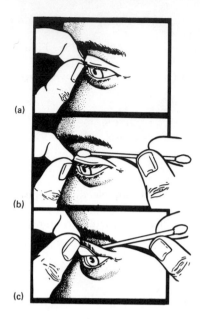

(a)

(b)

(c)

FIGURE 6–4

Foreign Bodies (Penetrating)

Don't attempt to remove a penetrating foreign body.

Cover the injured eye with a paper cup, cover the other eye, and gently transport victim supine to medical facility. (See Figure 6-3.)

Contact Lens Emergencies

Determine if victim is wearing contact lenses:
>Ask the victim.
>Check for medic-alert information or driver's license.
>Look for contact lenses by gently separating the victim's eyelids. (Shining a small flashlight on the eye from the side will help.)

If lenses are suspected to be still on the eye:
>Apply adhesive tape strip to victim's forehead and label "contact lenses."
>Alert other emergency personnel to the need for lens removal.

Remove the victim's contact lenses (or at least slide them off the cornea and off to the side of the eye) if victim cannot do it and if professional help is delayed.

Chemical Burns

The first few minutes after injury are crucial, and prompt action may prevent blindness—alkali penetrates the globe in seconds and produces corneal scars, while acid produces more superficial injury.

Instruct the victim to hold eyelids open, and copiously irrigate the eyeball directly with any water available for 20 minutes—no neutralizing solutions are necessary. It may be necessary to force the eyes open.

Do not patch, because there may be residual chemical in the eye.

Obtain exact identification of chemicals from the package label.

Reassure the victim and explain the importance of the continuous irrigation.

Transportation to a medical facility is essential.

Ultraviolet Burns

Common causes:
> Welder's flash
> Sunlamp
> Snow "blindness"

History: four to six hours after exposure, severe eye pain begins.

Refer to a physician who may prescribe eyedrops. Analgesic may be prescribed.

Rest in a darkened room with cold compresses on the eyes and forehead.

Eye patches may be necessary for comfort during the first 24 hours.

Blunt Eye Injuries

Common causes:
> Automobile accidents
> Athletic injuries
> Fistfights

Every "black eye" should have a complete eye examination.

Eyelid contusion:
> Apply cold compresses
> Clearing will take place during two to three weeks.

Orbital Fractures

Definition: fracture of one or several of the bones of the skull that form the orbits (eye sockets).

Victim may complain of double vision and may lose sensation above the eyebrow or over the cheek from associate nerve damage.

Transport victim in a sitting position.

Cold packs may be used to diminish swelling if there is no globe injury suspected.

Ophthalmologic consultation is required.

Eyeball Lacerations

"Cut" appearance of cornea or sclera (white part of eye).

Such a laceration is severe injury. Inner portions (vitreous humor) of the eye may come out through the wound, possibly resulting in the loss of sight.

Do not exert pressure on the eyeball. Vitreous fluid can be lost. This can result in the loss of sight.

A loose dressing may be placed over the uninjured eye in order to prevent sympathetic eye motion. A shield may be used.

Transport to an ophthalmologist.

Extruded Eyeball

Never apply pressure on the eye.
Cover with a paper cup for protection. (See Figure 6–3.)
Bandage both eyes.
Transport the victim to medical facility.

The first aider may encounter eye emergencies which are usually not life-threatening. Prompt and appropriate care, however, can relieve the victim's pain and reduce the possibility of permanent damage to the vital sense of vision.

Any victim with an injury or medical problem involving the eye will be anxious and upset. It is important for the first aider to maintain a calm, reassuring attitude when dealing with victims who fear the loss of one of their most important senses.

To avoid making a mistake in treatment, remember the following guidelines:

1. Do not wash the injured eye—except in the case of chemicals. There is nothing to be gained by washing, regardless of how dirty the object might be.
2. Do not put salves or other medication in an injured eye. The reason for this is the same as for not washing an injured eye. Such solutions are no more effective than plain water.
3. Do not remove any blood or blood clots from the eye. There is not enough blood loss to concern the first aider.
4. Do not try to force the eyelids open. Let victims open their own eyelids; however, in the case of chemical burns, victims may need assistance in order to obtain proper irrigation of the eyeball.
5. Do not feed the victim before transporting to the hospital. If surgery has to be performed under general anesthesia, food in the stomach can make anesthesia hazardous. Food that is regurgitated by the semiconscious victim can be aspirated into the lungs.
6. Do not panic. Remember that other than chemical burns of the eye, most types of eye injures can usually be treated hours after the injury has occurred.
7. Do not allow the victim to use the injured eye. Movement by the uninjured eye allows movement of the injured eye; therefore, cover the uninjured eye whenever the injured eye is shielded or covered.
8. Do not attempt to remove a penetrating foreign object.
9. Do not exert pressure on a lacerated eyeball.
10. Do not try to remove a foreign object with a match, toothpick, or other object.

HEAD INJURIES

Almost one out of every 25 people in the United States suffers head trauma annually. Considering the incidence of head trauma, every first aider should be prepared to handle it.

Types of Head Injuries

Skull fracture. A blow to the head can result in a variety of skull fractures, ranging from a simple skull fracture to a severely depressed fracture in which bone fragments that are driven into the brain cause a cerebral laceration.

A skull fracture does not necessarily mean there is brain damage, and it is immaterial in judging whether or not actual brain damage has occurred. However, the absence of a fracture does not mean that brain damage can be ruled out. In fact, the absence of a fracture usually results in more severe brainstem contusions because fractures absorb some of the energy of the blow.

The types of skull fractures are:

Linear fracture. This type of fracture does not involve any pieces of bone driven into the brain. Rather, it is a line fracture in the skull. Most skull fractures are of this type.

Comminuted fracture. This consists of multiple cracks radiating from the center of impact. They look like a cracked eggshell.

Depressed fracture. Pieces of bone are pressed in toward the brain and sometimes cause tearing of brain tissue.

Basal fracture. The base of the skull is fractured.

A fractured skull indicates that a sizable force was delivered to the head; however, nothing can be said about the condition of the brain merely by the presence or absence of a skull fracture. As many as 30 percent of fatal head injuries are associated with an intact skull.

Of interest is the fact that it requires about twice as much accelerative force to fracture the skull as it does to produce a concussion. Another complication with a fractured skull is that bacteria can enter the central nervous system.

Impalement injury. Objects such as knives, sticks, and pencils may penetrate the skull and lodge in the brain. Any foreign body protruding from the skull should be left in place until a neurosurgeon can remove it.

Scalp wounds. Though the scalp has three distinct layers (skin, superficial fascia, and galea), it can be considered as one layer because these layers adhere tightly to one another. Scalp wounds will not gape open unless all three layers have been cut.

Because most of the blood vessels are in the outer scalp layer, bleeding can be controlled by direct pressure. If the underlying skull is unstable, pressure should be applied to the periphery of the wound over intact bone.

Dress and bandage open wounds with minimum pressure.

Do not attempt to stop the flow of blood or cerebrospinal fluid from the ears or the nose.

Scalp avulsion.   The amputated scalp should be loosely wrapped in a manner similar to that for any other severed part. Wrap the scalp completely in gauze or towel and wet the wrapping. Then place the wet wrapping containing the scalp in a plastic bag and seal shut. Next, place the bag inside another bag that is filled with ice, if available, or cold water. Do not immerse the part directly in the water or ice. The denuded skull should be kept moist and covered with a dressing. For a partial avulsion, place the severed part in a normal position, then apply dry, sterile dressings and elevate the head. Cold packs can be applied to the outside of the dressing.

Gunshot wound.   High-velocity weapons, such as military and hunting rifles, are especially destructive. Most handguns and .22-caliber rifles are low-velocity weapons and produce somewhat less damage.

The caliber of the bullet is of little consequence in low-velocity injuries. In fact, a .22-caliber handgun can create just as devastating a wound as a .45-caliber pistol.

Brain damage results from shock waves and from the temporary cavity that is formed by tissue displacement from the shock waves surrounding the bullet as it passes through the brain. The path of a bullet is impossible to predict, although bullets almost always completely perforate brain substance and become lodged in the skull or soft tissues of the scalp.

Although some victims may live for a short time following severe gunshot injuries to the head, only about 10 percent will live longer than one day.

For more information on gunshot wounds, refer to pages 100–102.

Concussion of the brain.   The symptoms associated with this type of injury are directly related to the severity of the blow. In moderate injuries, the brainstem twist is not too severe. It recovers rapidly; unconsciousness lasts only seconds or minutes to at most, an hour, and rapid recovery follows. This injury is known as a *concussion* and is the least serious form of brain trauma.

Concussion is a jostling of the brain's soft substance without contusion. Concussion can leave the victim dazed or unconscious.

Repeated concussions are cumulative and can lead to the blunted behavior of the "punch-drunk" boxer. However, for most concussive victims, symptoms disappear altogether, even within a couple of hours. Headache or dizziness may persist for several weeks.

Recognizing concussion.   It is not necessary to be hit on the head to receive a concussion, which is what most first aiders look for in a victim with head injury. Concussion can occur simply from sudden deceleration of the head (for example, in an automobile crash).

In the absence of unconsciousness (one of the best signs), a glassy-eyed look, lack of coordination, the inability to walk correctly, or obvious disorientation provide clues to the victim's condition. The victim may complain of dizziness, light-headedness, blurred vision, and disorientation.

Headache may or may not follow head injury. Headache immediately after a head injury is a significant symptom. On the other hand, it is common for people suffering a concussion to develop headache a day or two and sometimes even as long as a week after the injury.

The severity of a brain injury can be judged by the duration of unconsciousness and loss of memory (amnesia). Remember, however, that unconsciousness is not a prerequisite for concussion and that some concussions are manifested only by memory loss.

Seizures that follow a head injury are serious and may complicate the injury.

Contusion of the brain.   Direct brain injury occurs instantly. A sudden force to the head starts the brain in motion. There is a swirling as well as a back-and-forth motion. It is helpful to imagine the brain as jello wrapped in plastic wrap (called the *dura*) sitting in a bowl (the skull). When the bowl is pushed across the floor and hits the wall, the jello hits the side of the bowl that hit the wall (coup reaction) and pulls away from the opposite side (contracoup reaction). This results in a contusion on both sides of the impact.

As the brain moves back and forth, it is also swirling because it floats in the cerebrospinal fluid. This swirling causes twisting (like a wet washcloth) of the brainstem.

If the head blow is powerful enough, severe brainstem twisting with hemorrhage and tissue disruption can occur. Loss of consciousness is prolonged, lasting many hours, even days, weeks, months, or for as long as the victim lives. Multiple bruising of the brain occurs, and this is considered even more serious than a concussion.

The brain is surrounded by bony irregularities. Hence, sudden jar-

TABLE 6–1 Guidelines for Returning to Activity After a Concussion

TYPE	DESCRIPTION	GUIDELINES
Mild	Momentary or no loss of consciousness	Delay return until medical evaluation has been made.
Moderate	Unconscious for less than 5 minutes	Avoid vigorous activity for a few days or longer. Resume activity only when associated symptoms of headache, visual disturbances, etc., have been resolved.
Severe	Unconscious for more than 5 minutes	Avoid rigorous activity for 1 month or longer. Clearance from a neurosurgeon is advised.

ring against these rough bone projections results in injury. Extensive swelling of the brain after a contusion can damage brain tissue.

The victim may be paralyzed on one side of the body or in all four limbs. One pupil may dilate.

Initial Physical Evaluation

A cardinal rule for head trauma is that all victims with head injuries must be considered to have neck or spinal injuries until it has been proven otherwise. Therefore, before assessing any victim with a head injury, immobilize the head and neck to prevent further damage to a possibly injured neck. The use of a cervical collar and backboards is crucial.

Other essential evaluation points to be considered include:

Check for a clear airway and victim breathing
Check for bleeding
Note location of abrasions, lacerations, contusions on the head
Check for deformity of the skull (depression or swelling)
Check pupils for equality and reaction
Check for blood or cerebrospinal fluid in ears and nose
Check for Battle's sign (look behind the victim's ears (mastoid area) for a bruise)
Look for raccoon eyes (bruising of the eyelids without any direct eye injury)
Check vital signs initially and every five minutes thereafter.

Pupil response.   In a brightly lit room or in the bright sunlight, pupils may show minimal or no response to light because they are already constricted. Dim the room lights or cover the eyes to evaluate victim's reaction to light.

Pupil dilation occurs on the same side as the brain injury. It is important to remember that a common cause of pupil dilation is direct eye injury.

Mental status tests.   It is important to ask the victim simple questions, for example, the sum of two numbers or what he or she had for breakfast, as a short-term memory test. Studies show that short-term memory is the first to show deficits after concussion. Also ask the victim what day it is, where he or she is, and personal questions such as birthday and home address. If the victim cannot answer these questions, a significant problem may be present.

Another useful test is to give a list of five or six numbers and ask the victim to repeat the numbers back in that order. Lists of objects can also be used as short-term memory tests. If a victim fails on these tests, you can be sure the person has a concussion.

A victim who loses consciousness should not participate again that day in any sport or activity. Anyone who remains unconscious for more than several minutes should be transported to the hospital immediately.

Leakage of cerebrospinal fluid and blood.   Blood or fluid coming from the ear or nose should alert the first aider to a probable skull fracture. Most cerebrospinal fluid leaks close spontaneously within two weeks. Surgery is rarely required. However, such information should not minimize the seriousness of blood or fluid leakage.

Because of associated bleeding it is sometimes difficult to detect cerebrospinal fluid. The "halo sign" is a test for cerebrospinal fluid. On linen or a pillowcase, the fluid will often look like a slightly blood-tinged center spot surrounded by a ring of a lighter color. Save all stains on pillowcases and linen for the physician to see. You could save a victim's life simply by observing one spot on a pillowcase.

If the victim's nose is running, instruct the person to wipe it, *not* blow it. If the ear is draining, cover it lightly with a sterile 4″ by 4″ gauze pad, changing it periodically to examine for drainage.

When there is a leak, keep the victim prone with the head elevated 30 degrees. This puts the brain at atmospheric pressure and promotes healing of the leak. If the victim's head is higher than 30 degrees, there will be negative pressure within the cranial cavity; lower than 30 degrees, there will be increased intracranial pressure; both are dangerous.

Do not attempt to stop bleeding and cerebrospinal fluid from the nose or ears when a skull fracture is suspected. Doing so may cause increased pressure on the brain or an infection around the brain.

Airway and breathing.   Correct life-threatening problems by maintaining respiration. Adequate ventilation is essential for the preservation of cerebral function in the severely injured victim. The nose and mouth should be cleared of blood and mucus either by bulb syringe or by the most common first-aider method—sweeping the fingers through the mouth. Do not leave the unconscious victim alone.

The airway of a victim with a suspected cervical spine injury must be maintained by the modified jaw thrust technique. Maintaining an open airway is essential since any oxygen deprivation contributes to brain swelling (edema). The brain stores only a ten-second oxygen supply.

The traditional head-tilt method of opening an airway could render those with cervical fractures immediately and permanently quadriplegic. Immobilization through the use of a cervical or hard plastic collar or sandbags should be done at once to prevent this possibility.

Victims with head injuries frequently vomit, and if the victim is unconscious, vomitus may be aspirated and cause a chemical pneumonitis.

Position.   An unconscious victim who is lying on the back should initially be considered to have an obstructed airway, not only from the tongue but also from secretions, blood, and vomitus. The proper position is to place the victim face down or on the side. Assume that the victim has a cervical spine injury until it has been proven otherwise. Therefore, the head and neck should be immobilized before moving the victim. All moving should consist of log-rolling the victim with the head stabilized.

For a conscious victim, the head and upper body should be elevated at an angle if possible (no pillows), and the first aider should be prepared for victim vomiting.

Convulsions. If convulsions occur, remove harmful objects from around the victim. Do not place anything between the victim's teeth. Usually the first aider is too late to place a bite-stick between the teeth, and there is no point in forcing the mouth open. Attempts to do so often cause damage to the teeth and/or gums. Broken teeth from such attempts could even be aspirated into the lungs during a deep breath before the victim becomes conscious.

Head injury follow-up. Within 48 hours after a head injury, signs may appear that indicate a need for medical attention. These are:

1. *Headache.* A headache is to be expected. If it lasts more than one or two days or increases in severity, medical advice should be sought.
2. *Nausea, vomiting.* This is frequent after head trauma, especially in children. If nausea lasts more than two hours, medical advice must be sought. Vomiting once or twice after a severe head injury, especially if the victim is a child, may be expected. Vomiting does not tell anything about the severity of the injury. However, if vomiting begins again hours after one or two episodes have ceased, consult a physician.
3. *Drowsiness.* If the victim wants to sleep, allow him or her to do so, but awaken the person periodically to assess state of consciousness and sense of orientation by asking name, address, telephone number; the day, date, and year. If the victim can't answer correctly or appears confused or disoriented, call the doctor. For a small child the questions will have to be modified.

   Experts disagree on the time intervals for waking a sleeping victim to check the person's state of consciousness. Some say to do so every 30 minutes to an hour, and others say every two to three hours. On the night following the head injury, or during any nap, the victim should be awakened at least every two hours for assessment of consciousness and other signs listed below.
4. The victim "sees double" or the eyes fail to move together.
5. One pupil appears to be larger than the other.
6. The victim cannot use arms or legs as well as before or is unsteady in walking.
7. The victim's speech is slurred or the victim is unable to talk.
8. Convulsions occur.

Head injuries are common, but the vast majority of children and adults who injure their heads fully recover. The head-injured victim needs to be monitored carefully at home for the first 24 to 48 hours. Remember—never hesitate to seek medical advice.

FACE AND JAW INJURIES

Injuries to the face and jaw are generally a result of fights, falls, vehicle accidents, and other violent accidents. Obstruction of the air passage with blood and other secretions is common and requires immediate treatment. Teeth may be loose, deformed, or missing. This type of victim may have difficulty opening and closing the mouth, speaking, and swallowing.

First Aid

An open airway should be established immediately (see page 49). Open wounds should be treated like regular wounds (see page 85). *Unless a neck injury is suspected, a conscious victim without a neck injury* should be positioned to lean forward, so secretions can drain out. Sterile dressings should be applied. *An unconscious victim without a neck injury* should be turned toward the side with the head and shoulders elevated to let secretions drain out. Treatment for shock should be given (see page 110). Artificial respiration (page 52) should be administered as required.

CHEEK INJURIES

An impaled object in the cheek should be removed. As long as the object remains impaled in the cheek, it will be impossible to control blood flowing into the mouth and throat, and if it is dislodged it may pose a threat as an airway obstruction.

The cheek is the only location from which a first aider should remove an impaled object. If the cheek is perforated, carefully remove the impaled object by pulling it out in the direction it entered. If this cannot be easily done, leave the object in place. Once the object is removed, pack the space between the cheek and gums with gauze pads and apply pressure against the backing with a dressing held against the outside of the cheek.

NOSEBLEED

Severe nosebleed (epistaxis) is frightening to the victim, occurs at inopportune times, and often challenges the skill of the first aider.

Minor nosebleeds are usually self-limiting (about 90 percent of them) and seldom require medical attention unless they become recurrent.

Causes of Nosebleed

Most people, regardless of age or gender, develop a nosebleed at some time in their lives. Especially prone, however, are these individuals:

Children who habitually pick or rub their noses.

Persons with upper respiratory infections. Nasal secretions result in forceful nose-blowing, with bleeding from the delicate nasal vessels.

People in their fifties or older who have cardiovascular disease, including hypertension. They tend to have a posterior nosebleed that appears in the middle of the night; the victim wakes up gagging on a mouthful of blood.

People taking an anticoagulant or aspirin.

People with blood dyscrasias (disorders such as leukemia and aplastic anemia).

People living in low relative humidity. Dry household air during the winter months may dry the nasal membrane lining and precipitate bleeding in an otherwise healthy person.

People with allergies. Dilated vessels and congestion make the victim more vulnerable to nosebleeds.

Persons receiving trauma to the nose and sinuses. In cases of head trauma, be alert for bleeding from the nose (or ear). This may indicate an underlying skull fracture with leakage of cerebrospinal fluid. The presence of cerebrospinal fluid can be verified by allowing the blood to drop on a paper towel. The drainage will separate into two zones—an outer zone of cerebrospinal fluid and an inner zone of blood. If cerebrospinal fluid is present, do not try to stop the bleeding because pressure on the brain may be increased.

If you've ever wondered why people who break their noses always end up with black eyes as well, consider that not all bleeding is external and that some of it settles into the soft tissues. The loosest tissue is under the lids, so blood tends to settle there.

Assessment

The history of a nosebleed is important and should include:

Time of onset
Duration of the bleeding
Severity
Answers to these questions:
    Does the blood appear to be coming from one or both sides?
    Have nosebleeds occurred before? If so, how frequently? When was the last one?
    Has there been any trauma?
    Were there symptoms of nasal congestion or sinusitis?
    Is there a history of allergy?
    Is the victim being treated for hypertension, heart disease, a blood disorder, or other major ailment? Has the victim undergone recent oral or nasal surgery?
    Is the victim currently taking medication for any of the above conditions? If "yes," what is it?

Types of Nosebleeds

Nosebleeds can be divided into anterior and posterior types: those that bleed through the nose and those that bleed backward into the mouth or down the back of the throat into the nasopharynx. Anterior bleeding is by far the most common, found in nine cases out of ten.

You are most likely to see nosebleeds among children, and the great majority of these cases—about 90 percent—originate from Kiesselbach's plexus (also called Little's area), the vascular junction of three blood vessels located in the anterior septum of the nose. Nosebleeds that originate in Kiesselbach's plexus generally resolve spontaneously and are easy to control.

The information contained in Table 6–2 may help the first aider differentiate between anterior and posterior nasal bleeding.

In older persons, bleeding most commonly occurs in the posterior part of the nose. Nearly all nosebleeds in children are in the anterior part of the septum.

Stopping a Nosebleed

Most nosebleeds from the anterior nasal septum can be stopped by simple procedures:

1. Reassure the victim. Explain that most nosebleeds are not serious. Keep the victim quiet. Though a large amount of blood may appear to have been lost, most nosebleeds are not likely to be serious.
2. The victim should be in a sitting position. To reduce blood pressure, keep the head in an upright position or tilted slightly forward, so that the blood can run out the front of the nose instead of down the back of the throat, where it can cause either choking or nausea, with vomiting of dark clots. These could be aspirated into the lungs.
3. Check for a foreign object in the nose by looking into the nose, but do not probe with finger or swab.
4. With thumb and forefinger, apply steady pressure to both nostrils for five

TABLE 6–2   How to Differentiate Between Anterior and Posterior Nosebleeds

	ANTERIOR	POSTERIOR
History:	Frequent brief bouts of nosebleeds controlled by pressing the nose nares.	Massive uncontrollable bleeding. Never had it before.
Location:	Usually one side.	Starts on one side, then comes out both sides and down throat.
Quantity:	Continuous significant blood loss, 1 to 2 handkerchiefs.	Towel or basin full of blood.

minutes before releasing. Ideally, place a 4" by 4" gauze to serve as a cushion against the nose. Remind the victim to breathe through the mouth and to spit out any accumulated blood.

5. If bleeding persists, have the victim gently blow the nose to remove any clots or excess blood, and to minimize sneezing. This is a new concept for most first aiders. Then press the nostrils again for five minutes.

6. Some experts recommend soaking a cotton ball in hydrogen peroxide, a nasal decongestant (nose drops or spray), or plain water; wring out the excess fluid, and gently insert the cotton ball inside the bleeding nostril. A potential problem with this step is the lack of time and/or materials. When the five minutes are up, slowly and gently remove the cotton.

7. Place a roll of gauze between the victim's upper lip and gum and press against it with the fingers.

8. Some experts recommend applying a cold compress over the nose.

9. If the victim is unconscious, place the victim on the side to prevent aspiration of blood; begin the procedures listed above.

Seek medical care if:

1. The procedures do not stop the bleeding after a second attempt.
2. The signs and symptoms indicate a posterior source of bleeding.
3. The victim has hypertension (high blood pressure).
4. The victim is taking anticoagulants (blood thinners) or large doses of aspirin.
5. The bleeding occurred after an injury to the nose.

Nose Care After a Nosebleed

After a nosebleed has stopped, suggest that the victim

1. Sneeze through an open mouth, if there is a need to sneeze.
2. Avoid stooping or physical exertion.
3. Elevate the head with two pillows when lying down.
4. Keep the nostrils moist by applying a little petroleum jelly just inside the nostril for a week, and increase the humidity in the bedroom during the winter months with a cold-mist humidifier.
5. Avoid picking or rubbing the nose. If a child has an uncontrollable habit, trim the youngster's nails frequently.
6. Avoid hot drinks and alcohol beverages for a week.
7. Stop smoking and taking aspirin for a week.

Most victims with nosebleeds never need medical care. Most nosebleeds are self-limiting, and victims can control the bleeding themselves. However, such episodes should not be minimized, and the first aider should be prepared to handle nosebleed cases properly by making correct decisions in judging the severity of the bleeding and applying appropriate emergency care procedures.

Foreign Object in Nose

A foreign object in the nose can usually be removed by one of several methods:

1. Blowing it out as the opposite nostril is compressed.
2. If it is easily visible, tweezers may be used to pull the object out. Be careful not to push on it and lodge it further in the nostril.
3. Sometimes it can be sneezed out. Induce sneezing by sniffing pepper or tickling the opposite nostril.
4. If the object cannot be expelled, consult a physician.

MOUTH INJURIES

Small wounds of the lips, tongue, and cheeks usually heal quickly without serious infection. Large lacerations and gaping wounds require suturing. Plans should be made to transport the victim to the nearest medical facility.

Bleeding can be controlled by direct pressure (see page 85) with a sterile gauze dressing. When there is a small wound, the mouth should be rinsed well with sodium bicarbonate mouthwashes several times a day. Good oral hygiene must be maintained.

Dental Emergencies

A neglected area in first aid training is the care of certain dental and dental-related injuries. Many teeth that could have been saved have been lost unnecessarily because appropriate care was not initiated at the scene of the injury.

In order to provide appropriate care for dental emergencies, the American Dental Association has developed an easily understood chart of appropriate first aid procedures (see Figure 6–5).

Knocked-out tooth. In remote areas with no dentist nearby, reinsert a knocked-out tooth by gently rinsing the tooth to remove any dirt (avoid scrubbing the tooth) and gently repositioning it into the socket, using adjacent teeth as a guide. If you are unable to reinsert the tooth, it should be kept in a moist environment—water, milk, or a clean wet cloth—and sent with the victim to a medical facility. The victim may hold the tooth in the mouth under the tongue or against the cheek so that the saliva keeps it moist. Be sure it is not swallowed. A dentist should always be consulted as soon as possible for all cases of knocked-out teeth.

Successful replanting occurs best within 30 minutes of the accident, but replants have worked even after 24 hours. Reimplanted teeth rarely survive as long as undisturbed teeth.

Dental Emergency Procedures

Type of Injury	First Aid
Toothache 	Rinse the mouth vigorously with warm water to clean out debris. Use dental floss to remove any food that might be trapped within the cavity (especially between teeth). If swelling is present, place cold compresses to the outside of the cheek **(Do Not Use Heat)**. **Do Not** place aspirin on gum tissue or aching tooth. Take the individual to the dentist.
Orthodontic Problems (Braces & Retainers) 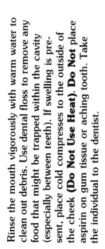	A. If a wire is causing irritation, cover the end of the wire with a small cotton ball or a piece of gauze and take the individual to the orthodontist. B. If a wire is imbedded in the cheek, tongue or gum tissue, **Do Not** attempt to remove it. Take the individual to the orthodontist immediately. C. If there is a loose or broken appliance, take the individual and the piece to the orthodontist.
Knocked Out Tooth 	Place tooth only in water or wrap in clean wet cloth. **Do Not Clean Tooth**. Take the individual **and tooth** to the dentist immediately.

Type of Injury	First Aid
Broken Tooth 	Try to clean dirt or debris from injured area with warm water. Place cold compresses on face next to injured tooth to minimize swelling. Take individual to the dentist immediately.
Bitten Tongue or Lip	Apply direct pressure to bleeding area with a sterile or clean cloth. If swelling is present, apply cold compresses. If bleeding doesn't stop readily or the bite is severe, take the individual to the hospital emergency room.
Objects Wedged Between Teeth 	Try to remove the object with dental floss. Guide the floss in carefully so as not to cut the gums. If unsuccessful, take the individual to a dentist. **Do Not** try to remove with sharp or pointed objects.
Possible Fractured Jaw ☆	If suspected, immobilize jaw by any means (handkerchief, cravat, towel) and take the individual to the hospital emergency room.

P43 © 1979 American Dental Association

FIGURE 6-5 Dental emergency procedures chart (Copyright by the American Dental Association. Reprinted by permission.)

Toothache.   Probably the most common dental emergency is a toothache. Have the victim rinse the mouth vigorously with warm water. Next, gently remove any debris lodged between the teeth in the painful area with dental floss. You can also place a pellet of cotton dipped in oil of cloves in the area where there is pain. This will provide temporary relief until a dentist can be seen.

If swelling is present, apply a cold compress to the area on the outside of the cheek. Do *not* use heat! Do *not* place an aspirin or aspirin substitute on the gum tissue or aching tooth, as this can cause a serious chemical burn. See a dentist as soon as possible.

NECK INJURIES

First Aid

Because the jugular veins, in addition to deeper major arteries and veins, are on each side of the neck, lacerations and puncture wounds can be extremely serious. If one of these blood vessels is damaged, direct pressure must be applied immediately, and maintained until the victim is seen by a physician. *Victims must be evacuated immediately to save their lives.* A small wound is treated as a regular wound (see page 85).

If pressure is applied forcibly to the throat or if the throat is struck by a blunt force, collapse, swelling, or a serious spasm of the larynx may occur. Artificial respiration should be administered immediately (see page 48). The victim's head and shoulders should be elevated if there are no suspected fractures of the back or neck. If the condition appears serious, plans should be made as soon as possible to evacuate the victim to the nearest medical facility for treatment of a possible fractured neck.

If a large vein is injured, air embolism (air entering the circulatory system) becomes a distinct possibility. These victims should be transported in a supine position. Placing the victim upright may decrease venous bleeding, but it also increases the risk of air embolism.

HAND INJURIES

Many injuries occur to the hands owing to the variety of uses to which the human hand is put. In fact, the hand may be the most frequently injured part of the body. The psychological reaction to hand injuries may be much greater than that for injury to any other body part, with the possible exceptions of the eyes and the genitalia.

First Aid

Minor wounds to the hands are common and should be treated like regular wounds (see page 85). If there has been a crushing type of injury and a fracture is suspected, the hand should be treated for a fracture (see page 253).

Extensive wounds should not be cleansed. A roll of gauze or fluffed-up gauze dressings should be applied over the injured area, and a pressure bandage applied (see page 86) to control the bleeding. Then the arm should be placed in a sling and elevated above the level of the heart to reduce the swelling. If the victim is face up, pillows should be placed under the hand to elevate it.

For additional treatment, medical advice should be obtained. Plans should be made as soon as possible to evacuate any victim with an extensive wound or fracture of the hand to the nearest medical facility. Amputations of fingers or hands should be handled in the following manner (see Figure 4–14, page 99):

1. Do not attempt to wash, rinse, scrub, or apply antiseptic solutions to the wound.
2. Apply dry sterile dressing. Apply pressure and elevate.
3. Do not wash, rinse, scrub, or apply antiseptic solution to the severed part. Wrap it in a wet, sterile gauze or towel, depending upon size, place it in a container, and place the container in a separate plastic bag that contains cold water or ice. Don't make the decision as to the viability of the severed part; this is a physician's decision.
4. For a partial amputation, place severed part(s) in a functional position. Apply dry sterile dressing, splint, and elevate. Apply coolant bags to the outside of the dressing.
5. If possible, control bleeding with pressure. If a tourniquet is necessary, place it close to the amputation site.
6. The amputated part must not be submerged directly in ice or cold water. Do not allow the ice to melt; replace with another bag of ice.

GENITAL INJURIES

Injuries to the genitalia usually are the result of kicks, blows, falling astride rails or similar objects, machinery accidents, and being struck by flying missiles. Severe pain, faintness or fainting, considerable swelling, and bleeding usually occur. If the urethra or bladder is damaged, urine and blood will leak into the injured area. Severed tissues should be saved by preserving the avulsed part (see page 98), and it should be sent with the victim to a medical facility.

In general, these injuries are extremely painful but usually are not life-threatening. Control bleeding by direct pressure; do not remove impaled objects.

First Aid

Bleeding should be controlled by direct pressure (see page 85). To ease the pain and reduce the swelling, the victim should lie quietly with cold compresses applied to the injured area. The victim should be treated for shock as necessary. If there is an open wound, a dressing should be applied (see page 142). Medical advice should be obtained if the injury appears serious.

Testicular Trauma

First Aid

A blow to the testicles is acutely painful. Have the victim sit up on the ground or floor. Lift him about four inches and allow him to drop. This sudden drop will usually eliminate the spasm and provide instant relief from pain and discomfort.

Next, if necessary, have the victim lie on his back. Push his thighs up to his chest, keeping his knees about 15 inches apart. Applying cold packs to help prevent swelling and reduce pain is also suggested.

Chapter 7

Bandaging

Dressings and bandages are two different first aid supply items. Dressings are applied directly over the wound to control bleeding and prevent contamination. Bandages hold the dressings in place. A dressing should be sterile or as clean as possible; bandages need not be.

BUTTERFLY BANDAGE

A butterfly strip may be applied to hold together the gaping edges of a small wound (see Figure 7-1). When commercially produced butterfly strips are not available, they can be improvised from adhesive tape (see Figure 4-15). If a dressing is needed, it may be applied directly over the strips. A splint or sling may be applied to prevent reopening a wound when it is near a joint or an area where movement might separate the edges.

ROLLER BANDAGE

A roller bandage is applied to hold a dressing securely in place over a wound. For this reason it should be applied snugly, but not tightly enough to interfere with the circulation. Fingers and toes should be checked

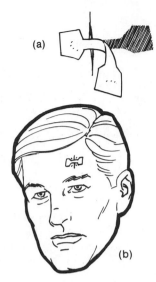

FIGURE 7–1 Applying a butterfly strip.

periodically for coldness, swelling, blueness, and numbness. If any of these symptoms occur, the bandage should be loosened immediately.

Anchoring a Roller Bandage

Hold the roll of bandage in the right hand with the loose end in the other hand (Figure 7–2). The left hand may be used if you are left-handed.

Place the outside surface of the loose end at any angle on the body part. (See Figure 7–3a.)

Roll the bandage around in a direction away from the body part.

Bring the bandage from under to over the body part, and turn down the uncovered triangle on the end. (See Figure 7–3b.)

Roll the bandage over the end two more times to anchor it and begin circling the body part. (See Figure 7–3c.)

Applying a Roller Bandage

Continue to circle the body part with the bandage, using spiral turns. On tapered body parts (for example, forearms and legs), it is best to use a spiral reverse turn (see Figure 7–25).

FIGURE 7–2 How to hold a roller bandage.

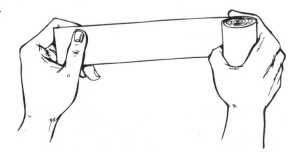

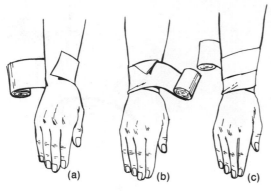

FIGURE 7–3 Anchoring a roller bandage.

Space the turns so that they overlap and completely cover the skin.

Always anchor the roller bandage at the lower portion of the arm or leg to be covered and proceed upward to prevent slippage.

Fastening a Roller Bandage

Roller bandages may be fastened with such items as clips, safety pins, or tape. Two methods of fastening them by tying follow.

Method 1

Reverse the direction of the bandage by looping it around a thumb or finger and continue back to the opposite side of the body part. Encircle the part with the looped end and the free end; tie them together (see Figure 7–4).

Method 2

Split the end of the bandage lengthwise for approximately 12 inches, and tie a knot to prevent further splitting (see Figure 7–5). Pass the ends in opposite directions around the body part, and tie.

FIGURE 7–4 Fastening a roller bandage, Method 1.

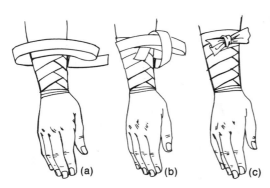

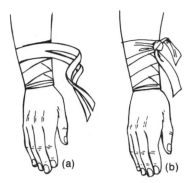

FIGURE 7–5 Fastening a roller bandage, Method 2.

TRIANGULAR AND CRAVAT BANDAGES

Triangular and cravat bandages (Figure 7–6) are made from the triangular piece of preshrunk muslin (about 55 inches across at the base and from 36 to 40 inches along the sides). If this bandage is applied without folding it, it is called a triangular bandage. If it is folded into a strip, it is called a cravat bandage.

FIGURE 7–6 Triangular and cravat bandages.

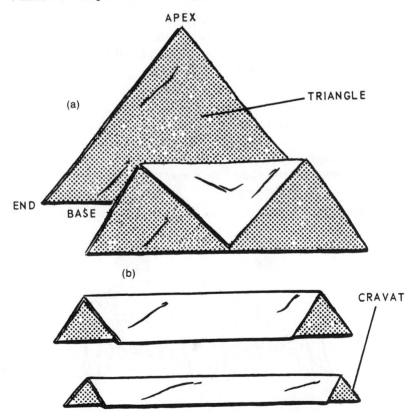

These bandages are valuable in an emergency because they are easily applied. They can also be improvised from a piece of shirt, sheet, or any other pliable material of a suitable size. To improvise a triangle, cut a square of material somewhat larger than three by three feet and fold it diagonally. If two bandages are needed, cut the material along the fold.

Chest or Back Bandage

A triangular bandage may be used to secure large dressings on wounds and burns.

> Place the point (apex) of the bandage over the shoulder. Let the rest of the bandage drop down over the chest or back with the middle of the base under the point. (See Figure 7–7a.)
>
> Fold the base of the bandage up far enough to secure the dressing and tie the ends in the back below the shoulder blade. One long and one short end will be left. (See Figure 7–7b.)
>
> Bring the long end up to the shoulder and tie it to the point of the triangle. (See Figure 7–7c.)

Chest or Abdomen Bandage

This bandage may be used to secure large, bulky dressings in place on the abdomen or chest. It may be improvised from a piece of cloth, a bedsheet, or large bath towel. The bandage should be placed under the victim and pinned securely in the front. (See Figure 7–8.)

Shoulder or Hip Bandage

This bandage is used to secure a dressing in place over a wound or burn on the shoulder or hip. A triangular bandage and a cravat bandage together should be used. The cravat bandage may be made by folding a triangular bandage into a narrow band, or it may be improvised from such items as a roller bandage, tie, or belt.

FIGURE 7–7　Triangular bandage for the torso.

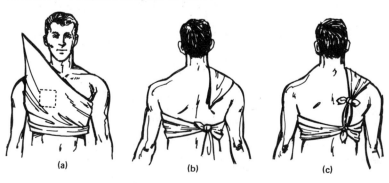

(a)　　　(b)　　　(c)

FIGURE 7–8 Bandage for chest or abdomen.

Place the cravat bandage on the point of the triangular bandage and roll them together several times. Fold the remainder of the triangular bandage and place it on top of the cravat. (See Figure 7–9.)

Place the center of the cravat over the injured shoulder. Bring the back end of the cravat under the opposite armpit and tie slightly in front of it.

Bring the base of the folded triangular bandage down and over the dressing on the shoulder.

Fold up the base of the triangular bandage. Wrap the ends around the arm and tie in front.

A view of the bandage applied to the hip is shown in Figure 7–10.

Triangular Bandage Applied to Head

Note: Some experts feel that this bandage does not apply enough pressure.

Turn base of bandage up and place center of base on center of forehead, letting apex fall on back of neck; then take ends backward (Figure 7–11a).

FIGURE 7–9 Bandage for shoulder.

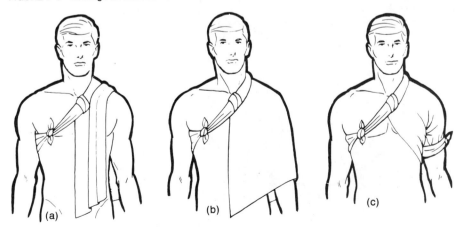

(a)   (b)   (c)

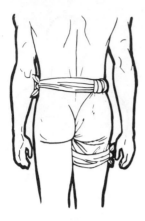

FIGURE 7–10   Bandage for hip.

Cross ends over apex, then take them over forehead and tie with square knot (Figure 7–11b and c).

Tuck apex behind crossed part of bandage and further secure it with safety pin, if available (Figure 7–11d).

Cravat Bandage Applied to Head

Place middle of bandage over dressing (Figure 7–12a).

Pass the two ends of the bandage in opposite directions completely around the head, and tie them with a square knot over the dressing (Figure 7–12b and c).

FIGURE 7–11   Triangular bandage for the head.

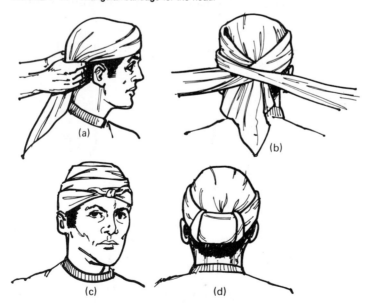

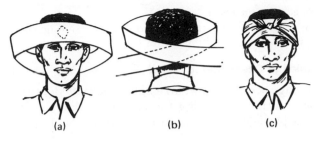

FIGURE 7-12 Cravat bandage for the head.

Cravat Bandage Applied to the Ear or Forehead

The cravat bandage (Figure 7–13) is applied to the ear or forehead as follows:

Place middle of bandage over the dressing (Figure 7–13a).

Cross ends, take them in opposite directions around head, and tie them with square knot (Figure 7–13b and c) over the dressing.

If possible, place some dressings between the ear and the side of the head to avoid crushing the ear against the head when the bandage is applied.

Cravat Bandage Applied to the Eyes

Even if only one eye is injured, both eyes must be bandaged. Because both eyes move together, any movement of the uninjured eye would cause the same movement and further damage to the injured eye.

Bandages are applied to the eyes as follows:

FIGURE 7-13 Applying cravat bandage to ear area.

Place middle of bandage over the eyes.

Cross ends, take them in opposite directions around the head, and tie them with a square knot over the bridge of the nose.

Cravat Bandage Applied to Cheek, Ear, or Head

Before applying bandage around a jaw, take any removable dentures (full or partial) from the mouth. In applying the bandage, allow the jaw enough freedom to permit passage of air and drainage from the mouth.

Place bandage under chin and carry ends upward. Adjust bandage to make one end longer than the other (Figure 7–14a).

Take longer end over top of head to meet short end at temple. Cross ends (Figure 7–14b).

Take ends in opposite directions to other side of head and tie them with square knot over part of bandage applied first (Figure 7–14c).

Cravat Bandage Applied to Shoulder or Armpit

Be aware that most cravat bandages will be too short for this bandaging technique.

Place middle of cravat bandage under armpit so that front end is longer than back end (Figure 7–15a).

Cross ends on top of shoulder (Figure 7–15b).

Take one end across back and under arm on opposite side and other end across chest. Tie ends with square knot (Figure 7–15c).

Cravat Bandage Applied to the Elbow

The cravat should be wide (six to eight inches) in order to avoid gaps. The cravat bandage (Figure 7–16) is applied to the elbow as follows:

FIGURE 7–14   Cravat bandage for the jaw.

(a)   (b)   (c)

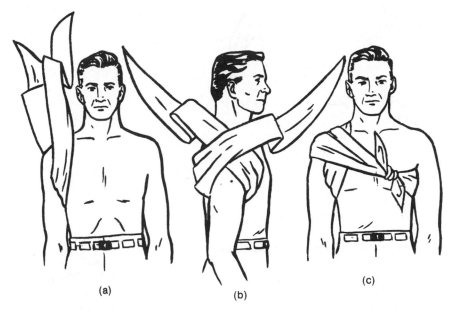

(a)

(b)

(c)

FIGURE 7–15   Applying cravat bandage to shoulder or armpit. (This bandage usually takes an unusually long cravat.)

Bend arm at elbow and place middle of cravat at point of elbow (Figure 7–16a).

Bring ends up and across, extending one downward and one upward (Figure 7–16b).

Take each end around arm and tie with square knot at front of elbow (Figure 7–16c).

FIGURE 7–16   Applying cravat bandage to elbow.

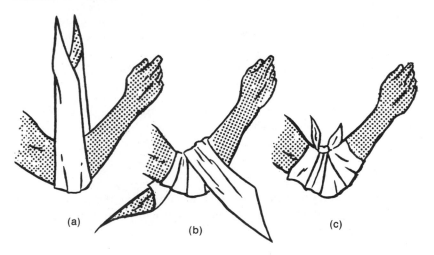

(a)

(b)

(c)

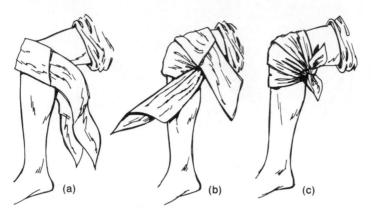

(a)   (b)   (c)

FIGURE 7–17   Applying cravat bandage to knee.

Cravat Bandage Applied to the Knee

Apply cravat bandage to knee as illustrated in Figure 7–17, using the same technique described for the elbow. A key to successful bandaging of the knee or the elbow is the utilizing of a wide cravat (six to eight inches) bandage so that gaps will be covered.

Cravat Bandage Applied to the Leg or Arm

The cravat bandage is applied to the leg or arm by one of three methods.

Method 1

Place center of cravat over dressing (Figure 7–18a). Take one end around and up the leg in a spiral motion and the other end around and down the leg in a spiral motion, overlapping part of each preceding turn (Figure 7–18b). Bring both ends together and tie with square knot (Figure 7–18c).

Method 2

For a small area, place the cravat bandage over the center of the dressing. Bring the ends around the back, cross them, bring back around to the dressing, and tie over it.

Method 3

For a large area, hold one end of the bandage above the dressing and lay the other downward across the dressing, then wind it spirally upward. Tie a knot where both ends meet (Figure 7–19).

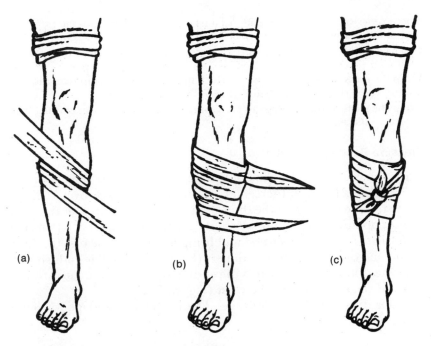

FIGURE 7–18   Applying cravat bandage—Method 1.

Triangular Bandage Applied to Hand or Foot

One triangular bandage may be used to secure large dressings in place on the hand or foot. Criticism against this bandage is the lack of pressure against a wound; however, it meets the need for covering a burn.

FIGURE 7–19   Applying cravat bandage—Method 3.

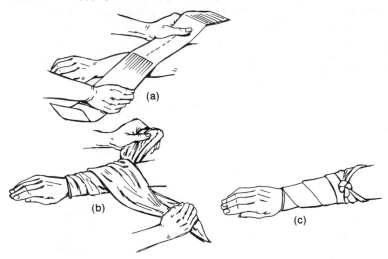

Place the wrist or heel in the center of a triangular bandage with the finger or toes pointing toward the point. (See Figure 7–20a.)

Fold the point of the bandage up and over the fingers or toes. (See Figure 7–20b.)

Wrap the ends of the bandage across the hand or foot to the opposite side and around the wrist or ankle. (See Figure 7–20c.)

Bring the ends of the bandage to the front of the wrist or ankle, and tie. (See Figure 7–20d and e.)

Pressure Bandage for Palm

Place a sterile pad in the palm of the hand and close the fingers over it firmly (Figure 7–21a). Lay the center of a cravat bandage over the up-turned wrist. Take the end on the thumb side and bring it up over the back of the hand, opposite the thumb side, and over the two fingers on that side (Figure 7–21b). Take the other end and bring it diagonally across the back of the hand and over the other two fingers (Figure 7–21c). The ends should cross over the upturned wrist. Cross the ends in opposite directions around the wrist and tie at the side of the wrist (Figure 7–21d).

Use this dressing for a short time. The preferred bandage for hand wounds exposes all fingertips.

ROLLER BANDAGE USES

Roller Bandage for Elbow or Knee

Make several anchoring turns above the joint, overlapping the top edge of the dressing. Proceed diagonally across the dressing (Figure 7–22a). Circle below the joint and diagonally back across the dressing (Figure 7–22b) to complete the figure-of-eight. Repeat the figure-of-eight process until the area is sufficiently covered. Complete by tying off. This may be used on the knee or the elbow.

FIGURE 7–20   Triangular bandage for hand or foot.

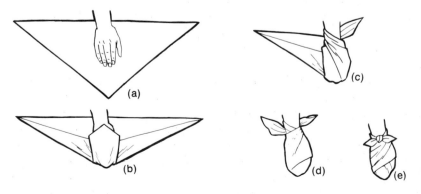

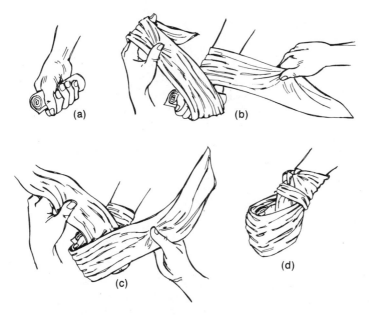

FIGURE 7–21   Pressure bandage for palm of hand.

Roller Bandage for Ankle

Anchor the bandage on the instep and take two or three additional turns around the instep. Carry the bandage diagonally upward across the front of the foot, then around the ankle (Figure 7–23) and diagonally downward across the foot and under the arch. Make several of these figure-of-eight turns, each turn overlapping the previous one by about two-thirds the width of the bandage (Figure 7–23b, c, and d).

It should be remembered that this is a bandage used to hold a dressing and is not for supporting the ankle or foot.

Roller Bandage for Hand

Method 1

Anchor the bandage with one or more turns around the palm of the hand. Carry it diagonally across the back of the hand and then around the wrist (Figure 7–24). Again carry it diagonally across the back of the hand and back to the palm. This figure-of-eight maneuver is repeated as many times as is necessary to fix the dressing properly.

Method 2

Make several anchoring turns around the wrist. Proceed diagonally across the dressing. Circle around the lower ends of the fingers and diag-

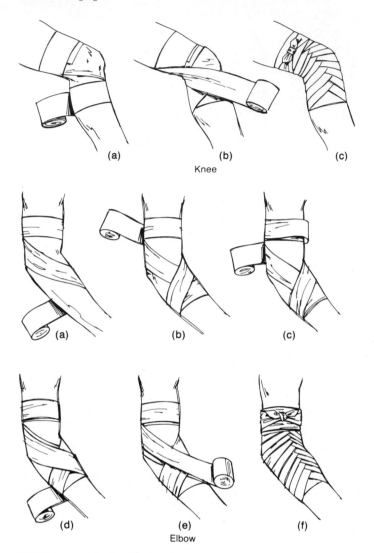

FIGURE 7–22   Roller bandage for elbow and knee.

onally back across the dressing to complete the figure-of-eight. Repeat the figure-of-eight process until the area is sufficiently covered. Complete by tying off. This bandaging technique will look similar to the figure illustrating the roller bandage for elbow or knee (Figure 7–22).

Roller Bandage for Forearm or Leg (Spiral Reverse)

The forearm and leg are tapered; thus a spiral reverse bandage technique is needed to keep the bandage flat and even.

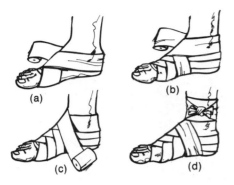

(a) (b) (c) (d) **FIGURE 7–23** Figure-of-eight bandages.

Anchor the bandage and make two or three circular turns around the lower part of the limb. Then start upward by bringing the bandage diagonally around the limb, overlapping about one-third to one-half of the width of the bandage. Use the spiral reverse technique by holding the lower edge of the last turn, then loosely make a neat half-turn. Continue the spiral reverse technique up the limb (see Figure 7–25).

Two useful maneuvers will aid in bettering the spiral reverse technique: (1) on the front side of the limb (facing you), bring the bandage up diagonally; and (2) remember that the half-turn is not a twist and that the bandage should be turned (folded) down.

Recurrent Bandage

Usually used on fingers, this technique may be adapted on toes, scalp, or stumps of limbs. This technique consists of a series of back-and-forth turns (recurrent turns), then circular turns hold the bandage in place (Figure 7–26). For fingers, a narrow (one-inch) roller bandage should be used.

FIGURE 7–24 Figure-of-eight bandage for the hand and wrist.

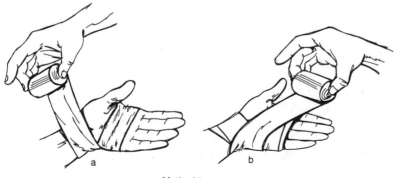

a b

Method 1

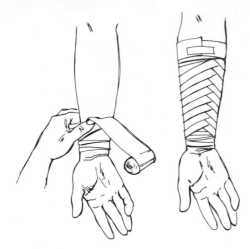

FIGURE 7-25 Spiral reverse bandage for legs and forearms.

BANDAGING PRINCIPLES

If the bandage does what it is supposed to do and does it well (controls bleeding and prevents contamination), the materials used and the knots tied are of little consequence. Regardless of what bandaging techniques are used, certain rules should be followed:

FIGURE 7-26 Recurrent finger bandage.

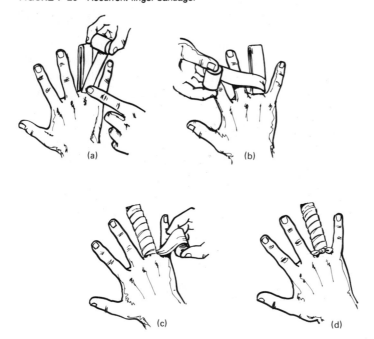

Do not bandage so tightly as to restrict blood supply.

Do not bandage loosely enough to allow dressing to slip. This is the most common bandaging error. Bandages tend to stretch after a short time.

Leave fingers and toes exposed to allow observation of color change. Pain, pale skin, numbness, and tingling are all signs of a bandage that is too tight.

Elastic bandages should not be used for applying pressure because of possible complications from unevenly distributed pressure and a tendency for first aiders to apply them too tightly.

Never apply a circular bandage around a victim's neck because strangulation may occur.

Tie the knot over the wound for compression.

Sterile dressings are preferred over the wound: However, it may become necessary to use the cleanest dressings available. To sterilize a dressing, iron a clean cloth with a hot iron. Placing a dressing in aluminum foil for three hours in an oven (350°F) or boiling for 15 minutes then drying are other techniques.

After a dressing is applied to a bleeding wound, do not remove it, even if it is saturated with blood.

ADHESIVE TAPE*

Being unable to tear adhesive tape quickly can be a frustrating experience for a first aider. Moreover, removing adhesive tape can be painful to a victim. Below are suggestions for alleviating the frustrating inability to tear a piece of tape and alleviating some of the pain from hair being ripped off the skin.

TEARING ADHESIVE TAPE

1. Back (nonsticky side) of the tape should face the first aider.
2. Place thumbs close together on back of the tape, index fingers directly under the thumbs (on sticky side).
3. Quickly snap by one of the following methods:
    Snap right hand away and snap left hand toward the body, or vice versa.
    Hold firm with the left hand and snap with the right hand, or vice versa.
4. The secret is to break the first thread. If unable to break the thread, move to another spot on the tape and try again.

REMOVING ADHESIVE TAPE

1. Gently but firmly, peel the tape from the skin in a direct line with the body (tape back to back). Don't jerk at right angles to the skin.
2. The pull should be in the same direction as the hair growth.

For extremely tender areas, follow the previous points plus:

*Adapted from *The First Aider* (Gardner, Kansas: Cramer Products, Inc.)

1. Firmly hold the skin from which the tape is pulled away.
2. Slap the skin with your hand prior to the removal of the tape.

FIRST AID SUPPLIES

First aiders rarely have all the necessary materials needed for treating injuries and illness in an emergency. Table 7–1 presents a list of suggested first aid items available from most pharmacies. These items should be kept in a convenient container (for instance, fishing tackle box) for accessibility, yet not within the reach of children. Check supplies regularly and replace them as they are used up or become outdated.

TABLE 7–1   Suggested First-Aid Kit Contents

FIRST-AID ITEM	USE
Activated charcoal	To bind and/or absorb poison
Adhesive bandages (Band-Aids)—different sizes; plastic-coated to avoid sticking	Open wounds
Adhesive tape—1- and 2-inch rolls—1 roll of each size	To hold dressings and bandages in place
Alcohol (70%)—1 pint bottle	For poison ivy; to sterilize; to cool body (except infants)
Alcohol wipes—towelettes—12	To clean hands
Aspirin—5 gr.—and Tylenol	Depress pain
Baking soda—small container	In case of delayed medical attention for third-degree burns and/or shock
Bandage—3 1-inch rollers	Finger bandages
Bandage—3 2-inch rollers	To hold dressings in place
Bulb aspirator	Suck blood and other secretions from back of throat
Calamine lotion—bottle, 4 to 6 ounces	Poison ivy, poison sumac, poison oak, and soothe minor bites and stings
Constriction band made of rubber tubing	Bites and stings
Cotton applicators—1 package	To make swabs
Cotton (sterile) half-ounce package	Swabs
Dimes and quarters	For pay-telephone calls
Elastic wraps (Ace bandages) 2- and 3-inch width, 1 can	To hold dressings
Emergency telephone numbers: doctor, fire and police departments, hospital, poison control center	To reach those who can assist
Epsom salts	For a laxative in case of poisoning
First-aid book	As a guide on what and what not to do
Flashlight and extra batteries	To examine throat; for vision in darkness, signaling
Hot-water bottle	Relief of pain
Ice bag (plastic)	To reduce swelling; for burns; for relief of pain; the bag itself without ice can cover third-degree burns or sucking chest wounds

TABLE 7–1   (Continued)

FIRST-AID ITEM	USE
Kerlix gauze rolls—two	To cover wounds
Kwik Kold, 5″ by 10″—two	For instant cold pack
Matches	To sterilize needles, scissors, dressings
Measuring cup and spoons	For measuring
Medicine dropper	To rinse eyes
Needles	To remove splinters
Oil of cloves	To place on cotton for toothache
Paper and pencil	To record information and send messages
Paper drinking cups	To give drinks; to cover eye injuries
Penlight	For contraction of eyes; to examine nose and throat
Plastic bag—(Ziploc)—1 gal. size	Carry water, waterproofing, airtight dressing
Rescue ("space") blanket	Body temperature control, signaling, water repellent protection
Safety pins—12, various sizes	To tie bandages
Salt (table)—dilute with water before administering	For delayed treatment of shock and burns; for treatment for heat cramps
Scissors—1 pair	Cutting
Sharp knife or razor blade	Cutting
Snakebite kit	Treatment of snakebite
Soap (mild)	Cleaning wounds
Splints—2 or 3, different lengths	Splinting broken arms and legs
Sterile dressings (gauze)—2 by 2, 4 by 4, 6 by 6 inches	To cover wounds
Sterile eye pads—3 or 4	To cover injured eyes
Sterile gauze (also called roller gauze)— rolls in widths up to 3 inches, 1 each	To cover wounds
Sterile soap—liquid, 4 to 6 ounces	Cleaning
Sugar cubes—small container	Insulin shock
Syrup of ipecac—one ounce	To induce vomiting in poison cases
Tackle box	To store and transport supplies listed
Thermometer—1 oral, 1 rectal	To determine body temperature
Tongue blades	To splint broken fingers
Towel	Drying
Triangular bandages—at least 4, with material for making more	Bandages, tourniquet, sling, splint stabilization
Tweezers—1 pair	To remove small splinters
Wire ladder splints—1	For splinting fractures

Not Recommended

(See Consumers Union, *The Medicine Show*, New York: Pantheon Books.)
   Mercurochrome, Merthiolate, iodine
   Ammonia—aromatic spirit, inhalant ampules
   Boric acid
   Over-the-counter burn ointments

Source: Alton L. Thygerson, *Study Guide for First-Aid Practices*, Englewood Cliffs, New Jersey: Prentice-Hall, Inc., 1978. Reprinted by permission.

Chapter 8

Poisoning

Poisoning is defined as a reaction to any chemical substance that may result in impaired health, permanent injury, or death. Poisonings occur by ingestion (for example, aspirin), contact (poison ivy), inhalation (carbon monoxide), or injection (snakebite).

INGESTED POISONING

Poisoning may be confused with other medical emergencies. The diagnosis of poisoning is made from

1. A history of witnessed ingestion or the finding of the victim with an emptied container. The use of a toxicity-rate scale (Table 8–1) to classify the degree of toxicity of a substance is common. The amount ingested has to be known; unfortunately, in the majority of cases the amount is not known.
2. The label on the poison container.
3. Characteristic, suspicious, or suggestive signs and symptoms in the victim.

Identifying the Poison

Usually the agent that poisoned the victim is known. By calling a poison control center, you can obtain an estimate of toxicity and the suggested treatment.

There are over 600 poison control centers. The American Association of Poison Control Centers has designated the centers appearing on pages 164–166 as Regional Centers.

TABLE 8–1   Toxicity Ratings for Common Household Products

CLASS 1 (PRACTICALLY NONTOXIC)	CLASS 2 (SLIGHTLY TOXIC)	CLASS 3 (MODERATELY TOXIC)	
Foods	Cosmetics (most)	Polishes (metal wood, shoe, stove)	Motor fuels
Candles	Adhesives (most)		Lighter fluids
Mucilages and pastes	Lubricating oils	Cosmetics (hair dyes, tonics, permanent	Repellents (insect, cat, dog)
	Lubricants (most)	waves; liquid lipstick;	Antifreeze
Cosmetics (especially baby products)	Soap products and detergents	nail polish, enamel, remover; perfumes)	Brake fluids
	Waxes (general, wood, window)	Cleaners (window, stain removers)	Mothballs (most)
Abrasives	Polishes (porcelain, some furniture)	Adhesives (rubber, linoleum, roofing,	Preservatives (brush, canvas, roof)
Pure soaps	Inks (some)	plastic cement)	Matches
Lead pencils	Incense	Bleaches	Inks
Modeling clays			Agricultural chemicals (many)

CLASS 4 (VERY TOXIC)	CLASS 5 (EXTREMELY TOXIC)	CLASS 6 (SUPERTOXIC)
Disinfectants (most, such as those for garbage cans)	Drain and sewer cleaners (caustics)	Insecticides
Dry cleaner solvents (some)	Fireplace flame colors (blues and greens)	Fungicides (a few)
Degreasers (metal, etc.)	Insecticides and fungicides (some)	Rodenticides
Depilatories (some)	Rodenticides (some)	Herbicides
Drain cleaners (some)	Herbicides (some)	
Naphthalene moth repellents		
Rust removers		
Radiator cleaners		
Leather dyes		
Indelible inks		
Fire extinguisher liquid		
Agricultural chemicals (many)		

RATING		PROBABLE LETHAL DOSE (150 LB HUMAN)
Class 1	Practically nontoxic	More than 1 quart
Class 2	Slightly toxic	Between 1 pint and 1 quart
Class 3	Moderately toxic	Between 1 ounce and 1 pint
Class 4	Very toxic	Between 1 teaspoon and 1 ounce
Class 5	Extremely toxic	Between 7 drops and 1 teaspoon
Class 6	Supertoxic	A taste (less than 7 drops)

Source: Robert E. Gosselin, "How Toxic Is It?," *Journal of the American Medical Association,* vol. 163, April 13, 1957, p. 1334. Copyright 1957, American Medical Association.

Regional Poison Control Centers

ALABAMA

Alabama Poison Center
809 University Blvd., East
Tuscaloosa, AL 35401
(800) 462-0800

ARIZONA

Arizona Poison Control System
University of Arizona Health
  Science Center
Tucson, AZ 85724
(602) 626-6016

CALIFORNIA

Regional Poison Center
University of California Medical
  Center
225 Dickinson St.
San Diego, CA 92103
(619) 294-6000

Regional Poison Center
University of California Davis/
  Sacramento Medical Center
2315 Stockton Blvd.
Sacramento, CA 95817
(916) 453-3414

San Francisco Bay Area
  Regional Poison Control
  Center
San Francisco General Hospital
1001 Potrero Ave.
San Francisco, CA 94110
(415) 666-2845

COLORADO

Rocky Mountain Poison Center
645 Bannock St.
Denver, CO 80204
(303) 893-7774

FLORIDA

Tampa Bay Poison Control Center
P.O. Box 18582
Tampa, FL 33679
(813) 251-6995

GEORGIA

Georgia Poison Control Center
Grady Memorial Hospital
Box 26066, 80 Butler St. SE
Atlanta, GA 30335
(404) 589-4400

ILLINOIS

Central and Southern Illinois
  Poison Center
St. John's Hospital
800 East Carpenter St.
Springfield, IL 62769
(217) 753-3330

INDIANA

Indiana Poison Center
1001 W. Tenth St.
Indianapolis, IN 46202
(317) 630-7351

IOWA

University of Iowa Poison
  Center
University of Iowa Hospital
Iowa City, IA 52242
(319) 356-2922

LOUISIANA

Louisiana Regional Poison
  Control Center
1501 Kings Highway
P.O. Box 33932
Shreveport, LA 71130
(318) 425-1524

KENTUCKY

Kentucky Regional Poison Center
of Kosair Children's Hospital
P.O. Box 35070
Louisville, KY 40232
(502) 562-7270

MARYLAND

Maryland Poison Information
Center
20 Pine St.
Baltimore, MD 21201
(301) 528-7701

MICHIGAN

Western Michigan Poison Center
1840 Wealthy SE
Grand Rapids, MI 49506
(800) 442-4571

Poison Control Center
Children's Hospital of Michigan
3901 Beaubien Blvd.
Detroit, MI 48201
(313) 494-5711

MINNESOTA

Minnesota Poison Control Center
640 Jackson St.
St. Paul, MN 55101
(612) 221-2113

MISSOURI

St. Louis Poison Center
Cardinal Glennon Memorial
Hospital for Children
1465 S. Grand Blvd.
St. Louis, MO 63104
(314) 772-5200

NEBRASKA

Omaha Regional Poison
Control Center
Children's Memorial Hospital
8301 Dodge St.
Omaha, NE 68114
(402) 390-5434

NEW JERSEY

New Jersey Poison Information
and Education System
201 Lyons Ave.
Newark, NJ 07112
(201) 926-8005

NEW MEXICO

New Mexico Poison, Drug
Information and Medical
Crisis Center
University of New Mexico
Albuquerque, NM 87131
(505) 843-2551

NEW YORK

Poison Control Center
Nassau County Medical Center
2201 Hempstead Turnpike
East Meadow, NY 11554
(516) 542-2323

New York Poison Control
Center
Department of Health
455 First Ave. Room 123
New York, NY 10016
(212) 340-4494

NORTH CAROLINA

Duke University Medical Center
Durham, NC 27710
(919) 684-8111

OHIO

Central Ohio Poison Control Center
700 Children's Drive
Columbus, OH 43205
(614) 461-2012

Southwest Ohio Poison Control
Center
University of Cincinnati
231 Bethesda Ave.
Cincinnati, OH 45267
(513) 872-5111

PENNSYLVANIA

Pittsburgh Poison Center
125 DeSoto St.
Pittsburgh, PA 15213
(412) 647-5600

UTAH

Intermountain Regional Poison
   Control Center
University of Utah
50 N. Medical Dr.
Salt Lake City, UT 84132
(801) 581-2151

WASHINGTON

Poison Control Center
Children's Orthopedic Hospital
   and Medical Center
4800 Sand Point Way, NE
Seattle, WA 98105
(206) 526-2121

WASHINGTON, D.C.

National Capital Poison Center
Georgetown University Hospital
3800 Reservoir Rd., NW
Washington, DC 20007
(202) 625-3333

Busiest Poison Control Centers

Children's Hospital of Los Angeles, Los Angeles, CA
Georgia Poison Control Center (Grady Memorial Hospital), Atlanta, GA
Nassau County Medical Center, East Meadow, NY
Children's Memorial Hospital, Omaha, NE
Finger Lakes Poison Control Center (LIFE LINE, University of Rochester Medical Center), Rochester, NY
Children's Mercy Hospital, Kansas City, MO
University of California, Irvine Medical Center, Orange, CA
Santa Clara Valley Medical Center, San Jose, CA
University of Connecticut Health Center, Farmington, CT
Children's Hospital National Medical Center, Washington, DC
Maine Medical Center, Portland, ME
Oklahoma Poison Control Center (Children's Memorial Hospital), Oklahoma City, OK
Duke University Medical Center, Durham, NC
Children's Hospital, Columbus, OH
Charity Hospital of New Orleans, New Orleans, LA
Division of Emergency Medical Services, Springfield, IL

Source: National Clearinghouse for Poison Control Centers.

There are a number of steps one can take to confirm a poisoning. Probably the most important of these is a search of the place where the victim was found or any place recently visited by the victim. In the accidental poisoning of a child, evidence will usually be found in a partially emptied, spilled container. When an adult attempts suicide, there may or may not be a note, but somewhere there will always be a container from which the poison was taken.

When it is found, the container and all of the remaining contents should be brought to the emergency department with the victim. It may even be necessary to send someone back after them. The importance of this step cannot be overemphasized: Accurate identification may hinge upon the precise spelling of a brand name; the label frequently will identify the contents; treatment information may even be provided (although this is sometimes wrong or may be of limited usefulness); and the label will almost certainly provide at least the name of the manufacturer, who may need to be contacted.

In addition, the container and its contents provide perhaps the best clue to an estimate of the dose that was taken. Children under four years old usually take only one swallow or a small bite. Poisoning in a person aged six or over is rarely accidental, so suspect larger doses.

TABLE 8–2   Substances Most Frequently Ingested by Children Under Five Years of Age—Reported by Poison Control Centers

RANK	SUBSTANCE	RANK	SUBSTANCE
1.	Plants	8.	Insecticides
2.	Soaps, detergents, cleaners	9.	Miscellaneous analgesics
3.	Perfume, cologne, toilet water	10.	Miscellaneous internal medicines
4.	Antihistamines, cold medications	11.	Fingernail preparations
5.	Vitamins, minerals	12.	Liniments
6.	Aspirin	13.	Household bleach
7.	Household disinfectants, deodorizers	14.	Miscellaneous external medicines
		15.	Cosmetic lotions, creams

Source: National Clearinghouse for Poison Control Centers.

When dealing with unidentified poisons,

Ensure the ABCs of life support (airway, breathing, circulation) before instituting any treatment for poisoning
Do not spend valuable time attempting to identify a specific poison or its antidote
Do not induce vomiting in victims with a deteriorating level of consciousness
Save all vomitus for analysis.

FIRST AID FOR POISONING

Perhaps the most important thing to remember about treating a poisoned victim is not to make the victim any worse. Minutes can spell the difference between life and death; thus, first aid should be started immediately. First aid will be most effective when you

Identify the drug or chemical that caused the poisoning
Contact a poison control center for medical advice

Evacuate the poison from the victim's stomach upon poison control center's or physician's advice

Give activated charcoal if available and indicated by the poison control center or physician.

Unfortunately, much of the first aid advice available is misleading or simply wrong. Be wary of labeling advice unless it is confirmed by a poison control center.

Inducing Vomiting

Medical advice should be obtained, preferably from a poison control center. For a poison that has been taken by mouth, empty the stomach as quickly as possible. This is the most important treatment that can possibly be used. Most poisons will produce vomiting themselves, but if vomiting does not occur spontaneously, it should be induced if possible (exceptions to this rule are listed later in this section).

There is now evidence that forceful vomiting is actually more effective than lavage done by a physician, probably because portions of the small intestine as well as the stomach are emptied. The forcefulness of induced vomiting is also more efficient than spontaneous vomiting, so an emetic may be worthwhile even in the victim who has already vomited. Ipecac can evacuate 30 to 50 percent of stomach contents within 15 to 30 minutes.

Syrup of ipecac can be given in doses of one tablespoonful for children under five years and two tablespoonfuls for older children and adults. Infants under one year old receive two teaspoonfuls; however, most toxicologists prefer to make a young infant vomit in a medical facility rather than at home. Repeat once in 30 minutes if vomiting has not occurred. The victim should also be given warm water (one to two glasses) immediately after the syrup of ipecac is swallowed because vomiting may not occur if the stomach is empty. (Never substitute carbonated drinks for water or use milk, because it will delay vomiting.) Larger amounts of water should be avoided because it may defeat the ipecac's purpose. Agitation of the ipecac and water in the stomach by gently bouncing an infant up and down may produce vomiting earlier. Have a large receptacle at hand when ipecac has been given. A small basin is usually inadequate to contain the volume expelled when vomiting occurs.

The word *ipecac* is a shortening of the word *ipecacuanha*, which is the Portuguese version of a native Brazilian term. The name refers to the emetic properties of this South American perennial shrub and is said to mean literally "the roadside sick-making plant." Syrup of ipecac is derived from this shrub.

Syrup of ipecac is very effective (97 percent of victims will vomit). It is safe to use, may be obtained without prescription, is inexpensive, and unlikely to aggravate the poisoning. Bear in mind, though, that syrup of ipecac should never be given without medical advice; thus, a poison control center or physician should be contacted before inducing vomiting.

Syrup of ipecac can induce vomiting by acting in two different ways. First, it produces gentle irritation of the lining of the stomach, leading to vomiting. This is how most victims vomit. If this fails, the active ingredients are absorbed by the stomach and stimulate the vomiting center in the brain.

Rarely will victims fail to vomit following a second dose. The major cause of failure is the giving of insufficient amounts of water. Another cause is inaccurate measuring of the dosage of ipecac. When using household tablespoons as the measuring tool, large errors can occur. A medical tablespoon contains 15 ml. Household tablespoons, in general, hold 10 ml or less. Therefore, whenever liquid medications are being measured, use measuring tablespoons such as the type used for cooking.

Never induce vomiting in the following types of victims:

Those who are unconscious or semiconscious. There is a risk of aspiration into the lungs; also, syrup of ipecac only works when the vomit-control center of the brain is functioning.

Those who have taken sedative drugs and who give indication that they might go into coma before the vomiting occurs.

Those who have swallowed caustics (strong acids and alkalis), which would expose the gastrointestinal tract to further chemical damage.

Those who have swallowed petroleum products or hydrocarbons (for example, gasoline, lighter fluid, furniture polish, and so on), which poses the threat of lipoid pneumonia if aspirated into respiratory passages.

Those who have ingested iodides, silver nitrate (styptic pencil), or strychnine. Accompanying seizures would increase in frequency and severity.

Those who have ingested poison four or more hours before the availability of syrup of ipecac. For them, vomiting will have little positive effect. However, medications such as aspirin remain in a lump or in the stomach for 8 to 36 hours (or sometimes several days) and thus may still be susceptible to removal by vomiting.

Those with advanced heart disease or those likely to have a heart attack.

Those who have convulsed or have had a seizure.

Women in late pregnancy.

When syrup of ipecac is not available, alternative methods of inducing vomiting are not very reliable and may be dangerous. Gagging the victim by sticking a finger down the victim's throat is usually ineffective in causing vomiting, and it wastes time. One study found gagging to be successful in less than 15 percent of cases. If syrup of ipecac is unavailable and vomiting should be induced, transport the victim to a medical facility. If the distance is great, stop for ipecac on the way but be prepared with a large container to receive the vomitus. Gagging is a last resort. If fingers are used, be extremely careful, for severe bites may occur. To avoid bites, push the victim's cheeks in between his or her teeth as you are inserting your fingers in the mouth.

Using warm salt water or mustard water to induce vomiting is impractical and can be dangerous in children. Besides, most children will refuse to drink such a concoction. Salt water can produce a rapid increase in the sodium concentration of the blood, leading to brain cell damage, intracranial bleeding, and cardiac arrhythmias. Numerous deaths have been reported in the medical literature as a result of using salt water to induce vomiting. Most children, fortunately, refuse to drink the concoction, and valuable time is lost trying to coax them to do so.

Lay the victim on the side when transporting to prevent aspiration of any vomitus. This is especially important with unconscious victims.

Activated Charcoal

Ingested poisons usually require the removal of as much of the poison as possible from the stomach by inducing vomiting with syrup of ipecac. However, ipecac is only partially effective. Syrup of ipecac removes only 30 to 50 percent of the ingested poison and leaves the remaining 50 to 70 percent to be absorbed, to produce possible toxic effects.

Therefore, a first aid procedure to counteract the remaining amount of poison should be followed. The most effective substance found to retard absorption of drugs and chemicals from the gastrointestinal tract is activated charcoal.

Activated charcoal is a fine, black, odorless, tasteless powder produced primarily from wood pulp and specially treated so that it has a huge capability to bind chemical substances. Charcoal must be "activated" to bind drugs and chemicals; therefore, substances such as burnt toast, fireplace ashes, and charcoal briquetts are all ineffective in the treatment of poisoning.

Ordinary charcoal is "activated" by heating it in carbon dioxide. Each grain of charcoal powder expands like a sponge, enormously increasing its surface area. In the stomach and intestine, poisons diffuse through the pores and bind to the absorbent (activated charcoal) so that they can't enter body tissue. The poison is then eliminated through the bowels together with the charcoal.

Activated charcoal should be administered as soon as vomiting has been induced. It must not be given before syrup of ipecac because it will absorb the ipecac and vomiting will not occur. The dose of charcoal should be eight to ten times the amount of the poison ingested. When the exact quantity of the poison ingested is unknown, a general guideline is to administer 50 grams to children and 100 grams to adults. Fifty grams is roughly about one-half a lightly packed 8-ounce cup. The charcoal should be mixed in 400 ml of water (about the same as 1⅔ cups; consistency of a thin milkshake) so that the victim can drink it. Put the charcoal and water together in a jar and shake it until the two are well mixed. For best results, the mixture must be given within 30 minutes of the poisoning episode but after vomiting has occurred.

The unpleasant taste of the black, gritty charcoal is the major drawback to its use. Attempts to improve the taste or consistency of the charcoal with additives, such as ice cream, sherbet, mineral oil, or milk, all result in decreased absorptive capacity of the charcoal.

Crushed charcoal tablets are less effective than the powered form. Another substance that should never be used in place of activated charcoal powder is the so-called universal antidote, a combination of activated charcoal, tannic acid, and magnesium oxide. This has been proven to be less effective than activated charcoal alone.

Activated charcoal is highly effective in decreasing the absorption of ingested drugs and/or chemicals into the body. It should be used in all cases of oral poisonings where a potentially life-threatening amount of poison has been ingested. For first aid use, it can be used following the induction of vomiting and when the time needed to transport the victim to the hospital is unduly long.

Despite the fact that activated charcoal is effective against ingested poisons and should be used more frequently, most pharmacies do not stock it because of lack of demand. The reasons for this neglect stem partially from a lack of knowledge.

The trouble with first aid for poisoning is the emphasis on antidotes and the failure to recognize that there is not an antidote for every poison. In addition, many of the antidotes printed on labels are in error and should not be followed.

Epsom salts, used as a laxative, is advocated by some poison authorities. There is disagreement about its effectiveness in ridding the body of poisons—and concern about its safety. If not handled correctly, its critics contend, epsom salts can cause massive diarrhea and fluid problems, especially in small children. Consult a physician before giving epsom salts to a poisoned victim.

POISONING DON'TS

Don't induce vomiting without medical advice, preferably from a poison control center.

Don't administer a salt and water solution, especially to a small child. Salt water is relatively ineffective as an emetic and potentially dangerous. If given repeatedly—as some label directions suggest—it can cause salt intoxication, seizures, and even death.

Don't attempt to "neutralize" the ingested substance by, for example, giving fruit juice or vinegar after an alkali has been swallowed, or sodium bicarbonate, chalk, or soap after an acid ingestion. In the first case (an acid to neutralize an alkali), studies have shown that heat is produced, compounding the possibility of burn injury. In the second case (giving an alkali to neutralize an acid), carbon dioxide gas is released and may stretch the stomach and even cause it to rupture.

Don't give the victim milk to coat the digestive tract. Milk may bind syrup of ipecac and delay vomiting. If a petroleum product has been ingested, milk may promote vomiting, undesirable because there is danger of aspirating the substance into the lungs. Some poison experts believe that milk, with its fat content, may actually increase the body's absorption of petroleum products, and that water is a safer choice. Giving milk to coat the digestive tract is not desirable unless a corrosive or highly irritating substance has been swallowed.

One of the first treatments that is often suggested for poisoning is to dilute the poison with water or milk. For corrosives, the administering of water or milk is appropriate. Milk or water will dilute the corrosive agent and decrease its potential to damage tissues. However, for other types of poisons, the administering of water or milk may actually increase the rate of absorption of the poison by causing the tablets or capsules to dissolve more rapidly. A distended stomach (one filled with water or milk) will force contents through the sphincter between the stomach and the small intestines, where absorption is faster. Dilution, therefore, should *not* be a standard first aid treatment unless a corrosive is ingested. However, it is necessary for syrup of ipecac to work, and therefore water should be given when ipecac is administered.

Unfortunately, over the past several decades many of the recommendations for the first aid of poisoned victims have now been shown to be either outdated, easily subject to misinterpretation, blatantly wrong, or, in some cases, dangerous.

In treating any poisoning, don't place too much reliance on first aid instructions on package labels. They are often out-of-date and inaccurate and may increase the likelihood of serious or fatal injury. Only on the advice of the poison control center or a physician should such instructions be followed.

Poisonous Plants

Surprisingly few plant species account for the majority of plant poisonings. Furthermore, plants are the leading household poisoners, overtaking aspirin, which once was the leading child poisoner. Children who balk at spinach apparently have no hesitancy in sampling leaves from the family's potted plants. Small children do not have a highly developed sense of taste, so they are not able to recognize a bad-tasting plant and spit it out.

Many plants can cause illness when consumed in sufficient amounts, but not all are poisonous. Poisonous plants are those that contain specific substances that produce symptoms when small amounts are ingested. While most plants are not deadly, many can cause discomfort.

It would be convenient to be able to label a plant as "poisonous" or "not poisonous," but this is not always possible. The toxins in many species known to cause significant illness have not been isolated. Also, plants that cause poisoning in animals may or may not be harmful to humans.

The toxicity of some plants is conditional. Only certain parts of some plants, often the berries or bulbs, concentrate the toxin in dangerous amounts, and then perhaps only during certain times of the year.

Individuals react as differently to plants as to drugs, with underlying disease, age, and weight among the factors influencing reaction to a plant's toxin.

First Aid

Find out when the plant was eaten and what symptoms, if any, have appeared (see Table 8–3). If the plant was ingested more than 12 hours before and no symptoms have appeared, there is no problem. Symptoms usually appear within four hours. Only with mushrooms do you sometimes find symptoms delayed for more than 12 hours.

TABLE 8–3 Common Poisonous Plants

PLANT	TOXIC PART	SYMPTOMS AND COMMENT
House Plants		
Castor bean	Seeds	Burning sensation in mouth and throat. Two to four beans may cause death. Eight usually lethal. Death has occurred in U.S.
Dieffenbachia (dumbcane), caladium, elephant's ear, some philo-dendrons	All parts	Intense burning and irritation of mouth, tongue, lips. Death from dieffenbachia has occurred when tissues at back of tongue swelled and blocked air passage to throat. Other plants have similar but less toxic characteristics.
Mistletoe	Berries	Can cause acute stomach and intestinal irritation. Cattle have been killed by eating wild mistletoe. People have died from "tea" of berries.
Poinsettia	Leaves, flowers	Can be irritating to mouth and stomach, sometimes causing vomiting and nausea, but usually produces no ill effects.
Vegetable Garden Plants		
Potato	Vines, sprouts (green parts), spoiled tubers	Death has occurred from eating large amounts of green parts. To prevent poisoning from sun-burned tubers, green spots should be removed before cooking. Discard spoiled potatoes.
Rhubarb	Leaf blade	Several deaths from eating raw or cooked leaves. Abdominal pains, vomiting and convulsions a few hours after ingestion. Without treatment, death or permanent kidney damage may occur.
Ornamental Plants		
Atropa belladonna	All parts, especially black berries	Fever, rapid heartbeat, dilation of pupils, skin flushed, hot and dry. Three berries were fatal to one child.
Carolina jessamine, yellow jessamine	Flowers, leaves	Poisoned children who sucked nectar from flowers. May cause depression followed by death through respiratory failure. Honey from nectar also thought to have caused three deaths.

TABLE 8–3   (Continued)

PLANT	TOXIC PART	SYMPTOMS AND COMMENT
Ornamental Plants (continued)		
Daphne	Berries (commonly red, but other colors in various species), bark	A few berries can cause burning or ulceration in digestive tract causing vomiting and diarrhea. Death can result. This plant considered "really dangerous," particularly for children.
English ivy	Berries, leaves	Excitement, difficult breathing and eventually coma. Although no cases reported in United States, European children have been poisoned.
Golden chain (laburnum)	Seeds, pods, flowers	Excitement, intestinal irritation, severe nausea with convulsions and coma if large quantities are eaten. One or two pods have caused illness in children in Europe.
Heath family (some laurels, rhododendron, azaleas)	All parts	Causes salivation, nausea, vomiting and depression. "Tea" made from two ounces of leaves produced human poisoning. More than a small amount can cause death. Delaware Indians used wild laurel for suicide.
Holly	Berries	No cases reported in North America, but thought that large quantities may cause digestive upset.
Jerusalem cherry	Unripe fruit, leaves, flowers	No cases reported, but thought to cause vomiting and diarrhea. However, when cooked, some species used for jellies and preserves.
Lantana	Unripe greenish-blue or black berries	Can be lethal to children through muscular weakness and circulatory collapse. Less severe cases experience gastrointestinal irritation.
Oleander	Leaves, branches, nectar of flowers	Extremely poisonous. Affects heart and digestive system. Has caused death even from meat roasted on its branches. A few leaves can kill a human being.
Wisteria	Seeds, pods	Pods look like pea pods. One or two seeds may cause mild to severe gastrointestinal disturbances requiring hospitalization. No fatalities recorded. Flowers may be dipped in batter and fried.
Yew	Needles, bark, seeds	Ingestion of English or Japanese yew foliage may cause sudden death as alkaloid weakens and eventually stops heart. If less is eaten, may be trembling and difficulty in breathing. Red pulpy berry is little toxic, if at all, but same may not be true of small black seeds in it.
Trees and Shrubs		
Black locust	Bark, foliage, young twigs, seeds	Digestive upset has occurred from ingestion of the soft bark. Seeds may also be toxic to children. Flowers may be fried as fritters.

TABLE 8–3 (Continued)

PLANT	TOXIC PART	SYMPTOMS AND COMMENT
Trees and Shrubs (continued)		
Buckeye, horsechestnut	Sprouts, nuts	Digestive upset and nervous symptoms (confusion, etc.). Have killed children but because of unpleasant taste are not usually consumed in quantity necessary to produce symptoms.
Chinaberry tree	Berries	Nausea, vomiting, excitement or depression, symptoms of suffocation if eaten in quantity. Loss of life to children has been reported.
Elderberry	Roots, stems	Children have been poisoned by eating roots or using pithy stems as blowguns. Berries are least toxic part but may cause nausea if too many are eaten raw. Proper cooking destroys toxic principle.
Jatropha (purge nut, curcas bean, peregrina, psychic nut)	Seeds, oil	Nausea, violent vomiting, abdominal pain. Three seeds caused severe symptoms in one person. However, in others as many as 50 have resulted in relatively mild symptoms.
Oaks	All parts	Eating large quantities of any raw part, including acorns, may cause slow damage to kidneys. However, a few acorns probably have little effect. Tannin may be removed by boiling or roasting, making edible.
Wild black cherry, chokecherries	Leaves, pits	Poisoning and death have occurred in children who ate large amounts of berries without removing stones. Pits or seeds, foliage and bark contain HCN (prussic acid or cyanide). Others to beware of: several wild and cultivated cherries, peach, apricot and some almonds. But pits and leaves usually not eaten in enough quantity to do serious harm.
Yellow oleander (be-still tree)	All parts especially kernels of the fruit	In Oahu, Hawaii, still rated as most frequent source of serious or lethal poisoning in man. One or two fruits may be fatal. Symptoms similar to fatal digitalis poisoning.
Flower Garden Plants		
Aconite, monkshood	Roots, flowers, leaves	Restlessness, salivation, nausea, vomiting, vertigo. Although people have died after eating small amounts of garden aconite, poisoning from it is not common.
Autumn crocus	All parts, especially bulbs	Burning pain in mouth, gastrointestinal irritation. Children have been poisoned by eating flowers.
Dutchman's breeches (bleeding heart)	Foliage, roots	No human poisonings or deaths, but a record of toxicity for livestock is warning that garden species may be dangerous.

TABLE 8–3   (Continued)

PLANT	TOXIC PART	SYMPTOMS AND COMMENT
Flower Garden Plants (continued)		
Foxglove	All parts, especially leaves flowers, seeds	One of the sources of the drug digitalis. May cause dangerously irregular heartbeat, digestive upset and mental confusion. Convulsions and death are possible.
Larkspur, delphinium	Seeds, young plant	Livestock losses are second only to locoweed in western United States. Therefore, garden larkspur should at least be held suspect.
Lily-of-the-valley	Leaves, flowers, fruit (red berries)	Produces glycoside like digitalis, used in medicine to strengthen the beat of a weakened heart. In moderate amounts, can cause irregular heartbeat, digestive upset and mental confusion.
Nicotiana, wild and cultivated	Leaves	Nervous and gastric symptoms. Poisonous or lethal amounts can be obtained from ingestion of cured smoking or chewing tobacco, from foliage of field-grown tobacco or from foliage of garden variety (flowering tobacco or nicotiana).
Wild Plants		
Baneberry (doll's-eyes)	Red or white berries, roots, foliage	Acute stomach cramps, headache, vomiting, dizziness, delirium. Although no loss of life in United States, European children have died after ingesting berries.
Death camas	Bulbs	Depression, digestive upset, abdominal pain, vomiting, diarrhea. American Indians and early settlers were killed when they mistook it for edible bulbs. Occasional cases still occur. One case of poisoning from flower reported.
Jack-in-the-pulpit, skunk cabbage	All parts, especially roots	Contains small needle-like crystals of calcium oxalate and causes burning and severe irritation of mouth and tongue.
Jimsonweed (thornapple)	All parts, especially seeds and leaves	Thirst, hyper-irritability of nervous system, disturbed vision, delirium. Four to five grams of crude leaf or seed approximates fatal dose for a child. Poisonings have occurred from sucking nectar from tube of flower or eating fruits containing poisonous seeds.
Mayapple (mandrake)	Roots, foliage, unripe fruit	Large doses may cause gastroenteritis and vomiting. Ripe fruit is least toxic part and has been eaten by children—occasionally catharsis results. Cooked mayapples can be made into marmalade.
Nightshades, European bittersweet, horse nettle (solanum)	All parts, especially unripe berry	Children have been poisoned by ingesting a moderate amount of unripe berries. Digestive upset, stupefication and loss of sensation. Death due to paralysis can occur. Ripe berries, however, are much less toxic.

TABLE 8-3   (Continued)

PLANT	TOXIC PART	SYMPTOMS AND COMMENT
Wild Plants (continued)		
Poison hemlock	Root, foliage, seeds	Root resembles wild carrot. Seeds have been mistaken for anise. Causes gradual weakening of muscular power and death from paralysis of lungs. Caused Socrates' death.
Pokeweed (pigeonberry)	Roots, berries, foliage	Burning sensation in mouth and throat, digestive upset and cramps. Produces abnormalities in the blood when eaten raw.
Water hemlock (cowbane, snakeroot)	Roots, young foliage	Salivation, tremors, delirium, violent convulsions. One mouthful of root may kill a man. Many persons, especially children, have died in United States after eating this plant. Roots are mistaken for wild parsnip or artichoke.

Source: National Safety Council, *Family Safety*, Spring 1979, pp. 18–19.

Find out what the victim ate—try to identify the plant and determine how much was ingested. Difficulty in identifying the plant eaten is the rule, not the exception. The only safe thing to do in plant swallowing cases is to obtain positive identification and check the plant's toxicity.

Most people need help in plant identification. Some helpful sources might include: (1) a college or university botanist; (2) a local florist; (3) an older person who gardens and grows various types of plants; and/or (4) plant identification books. Remember that popular plant names can be misleading.

If the victim has no symptoms but did eat part of a plant less than four hours earlier and you know it is poisonous or it is not known if the plant is poisonous, give the victim syrup of ipecac to induce vomiting. Follow the proper procedure on administering syrup of ipecac as discussed earlier in this chapter.

Ipecac evacuates only 30 to 50 percent of stomach contents; therefore, afterward, give activated charcoal, which absorbs most plant toxins except cyanide (for example, apricot seeds) quite efficiently.

When only mild to moderate gastrointestinal upset is expected, the use of ipecac is not necessary. There are few specific antidotes for plant poisons.

CONTACT POISONING

Poison Plant Dermatitis

Two million Americans suffer allergic contact dermatitis from poison ivy, poison oak, or poison sumac annually. All three are members of the *Rhus* genus, and their allergen is urushiol oleoresin.

Individuals often know when they have been exposed to an offending plant, but this is not always the case. Many people cannot identify poison ivy, oak, or sumac (Figure 8–1). The characteristic burning, itching, rash, and edema resulting from poison ivy, oak, or sumac contact may not follow for as many as ten days after exposure. A day or two is the usual interval between exposure and onset of signs and symptoms.

Leaflets three—let it be.
Berries white—poisonous sight!

Old first aid axiom

Poison ivy has three light green, shiny leaflets. In the fall, poison ivy has clusters of white berries and its leaves take on bright colors. Poison oak looks like poison ivy, but its leaflets resemble oak leaves.

Clothing may become contaminated and is often a source of prolonged infection. Dogs and cats can carry the oleoresin on their fur. Smoke can transport enough to cause contact dermatitis.

Allergic plant dermatitis may be limited to a small spot or it may involve the entire body. Consider any reaction involving the face or genitals severe. Edema (swelling) in these areas can be disabling.

First Aid

Many potions and treatments have been proposed to prevent and cure the allergic reaction to poison ivy. Among the many agents at one time thought to be beneficial in relieving poison ivy eruption were bromine, kerosene, gun powder, iodine, buttermilk, cream, and marshmallows, as well as a large number of botanical preparations.

It has been demonstrated that washing thoroughly with soap and water within minutes after exposure can help. If delayed, washing may be useless. Moreover, little benefit is obtained from the use of tincture of green soap or other soaps derived from alcohol or similar solvents.

Generally, the local treatment should be adapted to the stage or severity of the lesions. During the acute weeping and oozing stage, sodium bicarbonate solution should be used as an astringent soak, bath, or wet dressing for 30 minutes, three or four times a day. "Shake" lotions (calamine, zinc oxide) are used at night or when wet dressings are not desirable. Greasy ointments should not be used during active oozing. During the healing phase, application of a neutral soothing cream (such as cold cream) helps prevent crusting and scaling.

Recognize common poison plants:

Poison Ivy
Small plant, vine, or shrub common throughout U.S. except California. Shiny leaves grow in clusters of three, turning red and yellow toward Fall.

Poison Oak
Western variety grows in California and portions of adjacent states as shrub or vine closely resembling poison ivy.
More common variety grows in other areas, usually as a shrub with clusters of hairy, yellowish berries and undersides of leaves covered with hair.

Poison Sumac
Woody shrub or small tree (5-25 feet) grows in eastern U.S., especially in moist climates.
Each leaf stalk has 7-13 leaflets with smooth edges, which turn red in Fall, and cream-colored berries which hang from branches in loose clusters.

FIGURE 8–1 Poisonous contact plants in the United States. (From *Emergency Medical Procedures for the Backpacker.* Copyright © 1979, Patient Care Publications, Inc., P.O. Box 1245, Darien, Conn. All rights reserved.)

Studies indicate that not one over-the-counter medication tested was more effective than tap water compresses and "shake" lotions containing a soothing ingredient, such as zinc oxide or calamine. Antihistamines appeared to have no value when taken either orally or in ointments and lotions. In fact, ointments and lotions can cause their own allergic reactions.

When the dermatitis eruption affects a large part of the body, severely affected victims may benefit from corticosteroids taken under the care of a physician. Another useful method of obtaining relief is a hot bath or hot shower. Heat releases histamine, the substance in the cells of the skin that causes the intense itching. Therefore, a hot shower or bath will cause intense itching as the histamine is released. Continue the heat until the itching has subsided. This process will deplete the histamine cells and the victim can obtain up to eight hours of relief from itching. An advantage of this method is that it does not require the frequent applications of ointment.

Reassure the victim that the dermatitis is not contagious and that it won't spread to other parts of the body if the person touches the affected areas. Any apparent spread is a new outbreak caused by a fresh contact with the oleoresin. However, because some oleoresin may remain on the skin after contact with the plant, tell the victim to wash the affected areas and launder clothing. Such a precaution may help prevent the residual oleoresin from coming in contact with unaffected skin areas.

Cases of contact with poison ivy, oak, or sumac generally do not require medical attention unless the lesions become infected. Instruct the victim not to scratch the rash—scratching opens the skin and introduces bacteria into the sores, resulting in infection.

INHALED POISONING

The mortality rate from poisoning by gases and vapors is increasing. These fatalities are due chiefly to poisoning by carbon monoxide produced by the incomplete combustion of fuels used by standing motor vehicles, cooking stoves, and heating equipment.

Carbon monoxide is an odorless, tasteless, nonirritating gas. It is produced during the incomplete burning of any carbon-containing (organic) material. Thus, it can be produced by fuels such as wood, gasoline, oil, natural gas, or coal whenever they are burned in an atmosphere that provides insufficient oxygen to allow for complete combustion.

Carbon monoxide has a peculiar effect on the body that makes it especially dangerous. Carbon monoxide and red blood cells (hemoglobin) have an affinity for each other. The red blood cell will pick up carbon monoxide, when it is present, in preference to oxygen; the affinity for carbon monoxide is about 250 times greater than for oxygen. As the blood's ability to pick up oxygen from the lungs and to carry it to the tissues of the body declines, health quickly becomes impaired and death may occur rapidly.

Carbon monoxide (CO) produces its toxicity by depriving the cells of the body of necessary oxygen. It combines with hemoglobin, the oxygen-carrying pigment in red blood cells, to form carboxyhemoglobin, which is unable to carry as much oxygen as normal hemoglobin. In addition, the CO alters the hemoglobin so that any oxygen that is carried is more firmly bound to the hemoglobin and is not released in the tissues.

Signs and Symptoms

Effects of various concentrations of carbon monoxide range from mild headache to death, and are described briefly in Table 8–4.

Carboxyhemoglobin has a bright red color; this has led people to say that you can diagnose CO poisoning by noting "cherry-red" coloration of the victim's lips, nailbeds, and skin. It has been shown, however, that the cherry-red color occurs only with carboxyhemoglobin levels that are not compatible with life. It is essentially observed only at autopsies.

It is important that the first aider *not* depend upon the oft-cited (and actually rare, if not nonexistent, in living victims) sign of carbon monoxide —the cherry-red cyanosis.

First Aid

The most important step in first aid is to remove the victim from exposure to carbon monoxide and to provide access to fresh air immediately.

TABLE 8–4   Symptoms of Carbon Monoxide Poisoning

PERCENT CARBOXY-HEMOGLOBIN	SYMPTOMS
10%	Shortness of breath on mild exertion, headache with throbbing temples
20%	Shortness of breath on mild exertion, headache with throbbing temples, nausea, vomiting
30%	Severe headache, irritability, impaired judgment, dizziness, nausea, vomiting
40–50%	Severe headache, confusion, collapse, nausea, vomiting
60–70%	Loss of consciousness, convulsions, respiratory failure. Death if exposure continued.
80% or greater	Rapid death

Source: Anthony S. Manoguerra, "Carbon Monoxide Poisoning," *Emergency: The Journal of Emergency Services,* January, 1980. Reprinted with permission.

If the victim is conscious, transport to a medical facility where a blood test will determine the level of carbon monoxide.

If the victim is unconscious yet breathing, place on the side. Loosen tight clothing. Transport to a medical facility.

If the victim is unconscious and has stopped breathing, administer mouth-to-mouth respiration and/or cardiopulmonary resuscitation (CPR) if necessary. Transport to a medical facility.

The victim needs pure oxygen as quickly as possible. This will improve oxygenation and will also disassociate the carboxyhemoglobin (the linkage between the carbon monoxide and the red blood cell). Either transport the victim to a medical facility for the pure oxygen or call for an ambulance that carries oxygen.

Even when there are only mild symptoms such as headache or nausea, it may be a good idea to check with a physician if you suspect carbon monoxide poisoning.

Be careful not to become a victim yourself by exposure to carbon monoxide.

INJECTED POISONING

Snakebite

About 8,000 people a year are poisoned by snakes in the United States. It is estimated that 45,000 snakebites occur annually in the United States. Ten to 15 deaths occur each year (a death rate of less than 1%), but the large number of permanent deformities and amputations are also of major concern.

The only poisonous snakes indigenous to the United States are the rattlesnake, cottonmouth, copperhead, and coral snake (see Figure 8-2). No other native snake can cause anything worse than a small infected laceration.

The first three of the above are pit vipers, and each has three common characteristics:

1. A vertically slit pupil like the eye of a cat
2. A triangular, flat head wider than its neck
3. An infrared heat-sensitive "pit" between each eye and nostril.

FIGURE 8-2 Poisonous snakes found in the United States. (From *Emergency Medical Procedures for the Backpacker.* Copyright © 1979, Patient Care Publications, Inc., P.O. Box 1245, Darien, Conn. All rights reserved.)

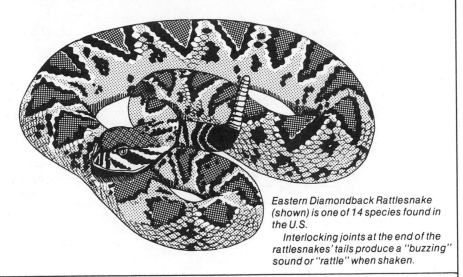

Eastern Diamondback Rattlesnake (shown) is one of 14 species found in the U.S.

Interlocking joints at the end of the rattlesnakes' tails produce a "buzzing" sound or "rattle" when shaken.

Eastern Diamondback Rattlesnake

Description Dark diamonds with light borders along a tan or light brown background. Diamonds gradually changing to bands in tail. Diagonal brown lines on the sides of face, vertical on snout.
Habitat Lowland thickets, palmettos, flatwoods.

Canebrake and Timber Rattlesnake

Description South: Dark streak from canebrake snake's eye to mouth; dark chevrons and rusty stripe along midline. Pink to tan ground color darker toward tail, which is black in adults. North: timber rattlesnake has yellowish ground color and a dark phase in part of its range
Habitat Canebrake: lowland brush, and stream borders. Timber rattlesnake: rocky wooded hills.

Western Diamondback Rattlesnake

Description Light brown to black diamond-shaped blotches along light grey, tan, and, in some localities, pink background. Black and white bands of about equal width around tail and black basal rattle.
Habitat Diverse terrain: dry, sparsely wooded, rocky hills, flat desert and coastal sand dunes. Often found in agricultural land and near towns.

Copperhead

Northern Copperhead (shown here) and other Copperheads in the U.S. vibrate their tails rapidly when alarmed.

Description Large chestnut brown cross bands on a pale pinkish or reddish-brown surface; and coppery tinge of head.
Habitat North: wooded mountains; hills; wild, damp meadows; along stone walls; in slab or sawdust piles. South: Lowland swamps and uplands; sometimes found in wooded suburbs.

Coral Snakes

Eastern Coral (below) and Texas Coral are dangerously poisonous although their small mouths and short fangs make it difficult to bite most parts of the body.

Description Red and black rings, wider than the interspaced yellow rings. Black snout, round pupils; no facial pits.
Habitat East: grassland; dry, open woods; and frequently suburban areas. West: (much less dangerous), desert and semidesert where there is loose soil and rocks.

Cottonmouth (water moccasin)

Eastern Cottonmouth (below), Florida and Western Cottonmouths, are frequently confused with several non-poisonous water snakes.

Description Dark blotches on brown or olive body. Heavy body and broad flat head.
Habitat Semiaquatic.

FIGURE 8–2 Poisonous snakes found in the United States. (*cont.*)

The most venomous snake is the sea snake *(Hydrophis belcheri)*, which has a venom 100 times as toxic as that of the Australian taipan *(Oxyuranus scutellatus)*. The snake abounds around Ashmore Reef in the Timor Sea, off the coast of northwestern Australia.

The most venomous land snake is the small-scaled or fierce snake *(Parademansia microlepidotus)* of southwestern Queensland and northeastern South Australia and Tasmania. One specimen yielded 0.00385 oz of venom after milking, a quantity sufficient to kill at least 125,000 mice. Until 1976, this 6 ft. 6 in. long snake was regarded as a western form of the taipan, but its venom differs significantly from the latter.

It is estimated that between 30,000 and 40,000 people (excluding Chinese and Russians) die from snakebite each year, 75% of them in densely populated India. Burma has the highest mortality rate with 15.4 deaths per 100,000 population per annum.

Guinness Book of World Records

The coral snake has a black snout and yellow rings that always separate the black and red rings.

The two most dangerous pit vipers are the western diamondback and the eastern diamondback rattlesnakes. The eastern diamondback is the most dangerous snake in the country, but of the two, snakebites from the western diamondback occur most often.

Signs and symptoms.   The severity of local and generalized reactions to a snakebite will vary in relation to the kind and size of the snake, the amount of venom it injects, the location, depth, and number of bites, the age and size of the victim, and the kind of first aid and medical care given. Venom from some snakes is more toxic than from others, and some inject more venom. If some venom was discharged in a recent strike, the remaining amount will produce a milder reaction.

The location of the bite will influence the reaction. Venom injected into a muscle is absorbed faster than venom injected into subcutaneous (beneath the skin) tissue. A healthy adult will have a milder reaction than a child. The amount of time it takes before antivenin therapy can be started influences the severity of the reaction. Clothing such as gloves and shoes may have provided some protection.

Venom from *pit vipers* such as rattlesnakes and water moccasins affects the victim's circulatory system (chemotoxin). Pit vipers eject venom with fangs that are used to stab the victim. The skin becomes discolored because of destruction of red blood cells and interference with clotting. There is pain at the site, swelling, usually two fang marks, a rapid pulse, and general weakness. The swelling tends to progress and the entire extremity may be

SNAKES: WHICH ARE MOST DANGEROUS?

Any effort to judge the venomous native snakes according to lethality is unrealistic, because of many factors. Some snakes have highly toxic venom but inefficient "delivery systems." The coral snake is an example. Coral snake venom is among the most toxic of the native venoms, but the small size of the reptile, its blunt head and jaw, and small fangs usually limit venom delivery to a small quantity.

As a rule, only the Eastern and Western diamondback, canebrake, timber, and Mojave rattlesnakes—and some other subspecies—can be considered life-threatening. They account for about 95 percent of the national death toll from snakebite. Diamondbacks inject the largest quantity of venom.

Less dangerous are the cottonmouth (water moccasin) and rattlesnakes not already mentioned; even less dangerous are the pigmy rattler and copperhead. The copperhead delivers more bites than any other native venomous snake, despite its unaggressiveness, because its habitat often overlaps that of humans—dwellings, farmlands, barns, etc.—increasing the likelihood of provocation.

Patient Care, Patient Care Publications, Inc.

swollen if the victim does not receive treatment for a period of time after the bite. Nausea, vomiting, breathing difficulty, and shock may occur gradually over one to two hours. The cause of death is associated with the destruction of the lining of blood vessels and red blood cells, especially in the pulmonary system. Hypovolemic shock and pulmonary edema appear to cause most fatalities. Death usually happens two days after the bite.

The heaviest venomous snake is the Eastern diamondback rattlesnake, found in the southeastern United States. A specimen 7 feet 9 inches in length weighed 34 lbs. Less reliable weights up to 40 lbs. and lengths up to 8 feet 9 inches have been reported.

Guinness Book of World Records

First Aid

The victim will almost certainly have been bitten on the arm or leg (95 percent of the time). The first aider's course of action will be based upon:

1. The signs and symptoms
2. The distance from a medical facility with antivenin
3. The first aider's treatment capability.

Despite the well-documented history of bites, the problem of how to treat them is clouded with disagreement and confusion.

Contradictions such as use ice, do not use ice; use a tourniquet, use a constriction band; cut and suck, do not cut and suck, abound and must be confusing to both first aiders and medical professionals. Over 200 first aid procedures for snakebite have been recommended. Consensus even among the experts is lacking.

All these are offered in first aid and medical literature as proper first aid procedures for snakebite. With the maze of confusion about what to do in the event of a poisonous snakebite, it is amazing that only about a dozen people die yearly from snakebite out of the 8,000 annually poisoned.

The emphasis in treating snakebite poisoning should be placed upon early and adequate medical care. First aid, as practiced by some, should not be overemphasized, for it can be dangerous. First aid should never be considered a substitute for antivenin treatment.

Dr. Charles Watt (upon whom the American National Red Cross bases its protocol) recommends:

1. Get away from the snake—back off 2 to 3 feet. Snakes can strike about half their body length, and most snakes are less than 5 feet in length. Some victims have been bitten more than once by the same snake. Quickly and carefully bring the victim and the dead snake to the physician. Identification of the snake species is important because of the variations in venom toxicity among the species, which in turn determines the amount of antivenin required for treating the victim. If killing the snake will be risky or the snake is elusive, don't delay treatment and/or transportation by pursuing the snake. If a positive snake identification is needed, rescuers can usually find the snake within a 20-foot radius of the bite site even after several hours. Be careful around a decapitated snake head since head reactions persist for at least 20 minutes and sometimes up to 60 minutes.

2. Apply a constriction band above the bite area and be sure that a finger can pass under the constriction band, ensuring that it is not too tight. Don't apply a band around a bitten finger. The band should be ¾ to 1½ inches wide. The band's purpose is to retard the spread of toxins through the lymph system. Do not periodically release it before seeing the physician if you are 1½ hours' travel time or less from a physician. However, as swelling appears, the band can be loosened but not released, because the band can usually stay on safely for about one hour. Periodically check the pulse in the extremity beyond the bite (Figure 8-3). The constriction band is effective only if applied within 30 minutes of the bite.

3. Apply an improvised splint if it can be done within one or two minutes, and keep the limb in a horizontal position. If feasible, do not allow the victim to do any walking; this will lessen the spread of the venom.

4. If the victim is more than four hours from a medical facility with antivenin (most snakebites occur within a short distance from medical care) or if a large snake is the offender, immediately use incision and suction, because 20 to 50 percent of the venom can be removed with this method, if done within three

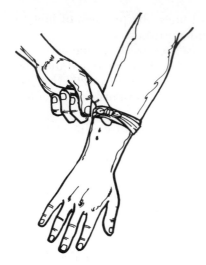

FIGURE 8–3 Constriction band for snakebite.

minutes. Don't attempt this procedure 30 minutes after the bite because little venom will be extracted. The incision need not be more than ¼ inch long and need only be carried through the skin. Cuts should not be deeper (⅛ inch) than the skin because of the closeness of nerves and muscles. Cross-cuts are not recommended. Cuts should be made along the long axis of the limb. Do not make cuts on the head, neck, or trunk. Apply suction with a suction cup for 30 minutes. Incision over the fang marks without suction is of no value. Do not cut over an area of advancing swelling because little or no venom will be recovered (Figure 8–4).

Use mouth suction only if no suction cups are available. There is little risk to the rescuer who uses the mouth, but it is recommended that the venom not be swallowed. The mouth should be rinsed out between suctions. Sucking the venom out with your mouth is questioned by some experts. Critics of mouth suction cite these reasons: (1) likelihood of wound infection from germs in the rescuer's mouth; (2) venom may be introduced to the rescuer through tooth

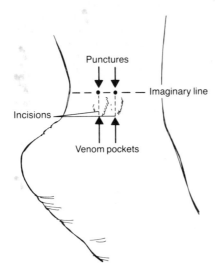

FIGURE 8–4

Incising the snakebite wound. New incision technique calls for two parallel slits starting at the punctures and extending downward (along the presumed path of the fangs) at right angles to an imaginery line connecting the punctures. Because of the shallow implantation of venom, the incisions need be only about ⅛ inch deep and about ⅛ to ¼ inch long. These incisions should reach the main concentration of venom, thought to lie in two parallel oblong pockets. (Some authorities, however, believe the venom spreads rapidly and uniformly in the subcutaneous tissue, so the pockets don't exist for long; they thus include the puncture in the *middle* of the incision.)

cavities or mouth sores; and (3) mouth suction is not as effective as commercial suction cups.

5. Transport the victim as quickly as possible to a physician. It has been said that a set of car keys with a car is the best first aid item. If the victim is alone, he or she should walk slowly, resting periodically.

6. If the victim stops breathing or has no pulse, perform cardiopulmonary resuscitation (CPR).

7. Use absolutely no form of cooling. Some medical experts believe that cooling the bite with ice packs will slow the spread of the venom. The cold treatment of snakebite has fallen into disrepute. When it was thought that the only harmful substance in venom were enzymes, use of cold seemed reasonable. However, the more toxic effects of peptides in venom were overlooked and it was found that they are not affected by cold temperature. A second problem with using ice is that tissue may freeze; thus the snakebite victim may receive frostbite as well. A third reason for not using cold is that the enzymes produced in any animal body generally are active at that animal's average body temperature. Snakes are cold-blooded animals. Thus, enzymes produced by cold-blooded animals are active at low temperatures. Lastly, valuable time could be wasted seeking a form of cooling.

Coral snakebite.   Venom from a *coral snake* affects the nervous system (neurotoxin) of the victim. The coral snake has short fangs and "chews" its venom into the wound. Because of its small mouth and teeth and limited jaw expansion, the coral snake usually bites its victim on a small part of the body—a hand, a foot, and especially fingers. Usually only a slight burning pain and slight swelling may be present at the bite. However, slurred speech, blurred vision, drowsiness, drooping eyelids, sweating, and increased salivation occur. Additional symptoms might include breathing difficulty, nausea, vomiting, convulsions, paralysis, and coma.

Red and yellow
Kill a fellow
Red and black,
Venom lack. (*or* Friend of Jack)

This is a description of the coral snake, the most toxic of any poisonous snake in the United States, which accounts for 1 to 2 percent of snakebites in the United States. Red and yellow bands touching each other identify the coral snake.

First Aid

When possible, it is important that the coral snake be brought to the physician for positive identification. Frequently, there is no sign of an envenomation at first. The following is recommended:

1. Wash the bitten area promptly and gently.
2. Transport the victim to the emergency medical facility as soon as possible.
3. Do not apply a constriction band or perform an incision or suction since neither is effective.
4. Do not give the victim solid foods en route to the medical facility.

Antivenin. Intravenous antivenin is the preferred snakebite treatment. Only qualified medical personnel should administer antivenin because many people are allergic to it. Antivenin can be helpful if given within four hours but is of doubtful value if delayed beyond that.

Remember, a snakebite is a relatively unusual medical emergency, and the medical expert treating it is frequently emotionally and intellectually unprepared. Unfortunately, most readily available information concerning the treatment of this problem is conflicting and arbitrary.

Fortunately, the chance of living if bitten by a poisonous snake in the United States is over 99 percent.

Spider Bites

Just about all spiders are venomous—that is how they paralyze and kill their prey. Very few spiders, however, have fangs long enough or venom toxic enough to endanger the lives of human beings.

In the United States, the black widow, brown recluse, and tarantula spiders attract the most attention.

Black widows (Figure 8-5) are easily recognized—they have coal black bodies with a distinct red hour-glass-shaped spot on their abdomens. They range in size from ¾ to 1½ inches. They are found throughout the continental United States. By volume, their venom is more deadly than the rattlesnake's, but fortunately is injected in much smaller amounts. The venom is neurotoxic, which means the toxin attacks the junctions between the nerves, and the muscles they control. The black widow is a shy spider and one almost has to roll on it to be bitten.

About 5 percent of those bitten by the black widow die; its bite can present an emergency situation. Several factors determine the outcome of a black widow spider bite: the amount of venom injected, the size of the spider itself, the size and health of the victim, where the bite occurs, and even the season of the year.

Initially, the bite produces little pain, not much more than a pinprick. However, it is soon followed by a dull ache. Redness and swelling along with two tiny fang marks may be observed at the bite site. Occasionally the area around the fang marks may blanch.

Within 15 to 30 minutes, symptoms develop, beginning usually with severe abdominal pain and rigidity of the abdomen; this is especially true if the bite is on a lower extremity. If the bite is on an upper extremity, the pain is often in the back, chest, and/or the shoulders, and is felt strongly

Black Widow Spider

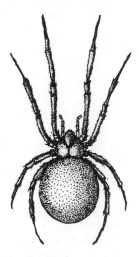

Coal-black, bulbous spider ³/₄ to 1¹/₂ in. long. Bright red hourglass on abdomen. (Be especially cautious in latrines, where these spiders inhabit underside of seats.)

Possible Signs & Symptoms
- sensation of pinprick or minor burning at time of bite
- appearance of small punctures (but sometimes none)
- within 15 to 60 minutes, intense pain at site spreading quickly
- profuse sweating
- rigid abdominal muscles without abdominal tenderness
- other muscle spasms
- breathing difficulty
- slurred speech, poor coordination
- dilated pupils
- generalized swelling of face and extremities

FIGURE 8–5 (From *Emergency Medical Procedures for the Backpacker.* Copyright © 1979, Patient Care Publications, Inc., P.O. Box 1245, Darien, Conn. All rights reserved.)

while exhaling. Cold sweats, tremor, weakness, nausea and vomiting, respiratory difficulties, discoloration of the skin, and convulsions all may follow. The victim may groan a great deal and may become delirious and slip into shock.

In general, the rigidity and extreme restlessness of the victim are signs of black widow bites. However, if possible, the spider should be caught to confirm its identity.

Antivenin is available. Therefore, the victim should be taken to a physician or hospital as quickly as possible.

The black widow spider is credited as being the most venomous spider in the world. Females—male spiders cannot inject a lethal dose of venom into the human body—have a bite capable of killing a human, but fatalities are rare. This is because it is timid by nature and bites only when frightened.

The fang marks should be disinfected (rubbing alcohol will do), but because the black widow venom's action is swift, there is little to be gained by trying to slow absorption with ice packs or even a constriction band. Warm baths may bring some relief for the victim.

The antivenin brings relief of symptoms within one to three hours, especially if given as soon as possible after the victim was bitten.

The brown recluse spider is now believed to be more numerous than was originally thought, but fortunately it is shy and tries to avoid contact with humans, preferring dark, quiet places under debris or in closets. Having a light brown body about ¼ inch long (Figure 8–6), it is more difficult to recognize than the black widow. It has a dark-brown, possibly purplish, violin-shaped figure on its back. Ordinary house spiders may have dark areas on their backs, but they will not have the violin configuration.

Frequently, a victim will not feel the bite (venom is necrotoxic) of the brown recluse spider, or if there is severe pain, the origin of the injury may be overlooked because the spider looks so harmless. It was not until the late 1950s that the spider was found to have a poisonous bite.

The brown recluse's bite is recognized by a small blister, and the surrounding tissue becomes reddened and warm to the touch. Its venom is a powerful necrotoxin causing a blister that develops into an indented ulcer, followed by necrosis and tissue sloughing. The wound can be gangrenous, and infections are common. The ulcer takes about six weeks to heal and will leave a depressed scar, sometimes so extensive that skin grafting is necessary. Anxiety, fever, and a generalized rash may develop.

Ice packs should be applied to slow absorption of the toxin and lessen pain, but early medical treatment should be sought to prevent scarring and possible death.

The tarantula (Figure 8–7) is far more ominous-looking than the other two poisonous spiders discussed, but its bite rarely produces symptoms other than mild to moderate pain. Secondary infections may develop, so this bite should be cleansed thoroughly.

Scorpion Stings

The scorpion of the Southwest inflicts severe pain with a stinger at the tip of its tail, and it is especially dangerous to young children. Its venom is neurotoxic. The deadly scorpion is smaller than the nondeadly variety (all

Brown Recluse Spider

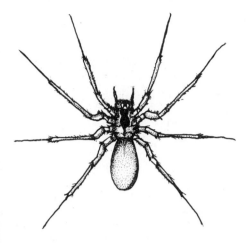

Brownish, rather flat, 1/2-5/8 in. long. Dark brown "violin" on underside. Unlikely in the wilderness; usually found in clothes closets and dark locations in buildings.

Possible Signs & Symptoms
- blister at site
- generalized rash
- joint pain
- chills
- fever
- nausea & vomiting
- pain may become severe after 8 hours

FIGURE 8–6
(From *Emergency Medical Procedures for the Backpacker.* Copyright © 1979, Patient Care Publications, Inc., P.O. Box 1245, Conn. All rights reserved.)

are poisonous to a degree), with a straw-colored, slender body of about two inches (Figure 8–8). It causes severe localized pain, but very little redness or inflammation will occur. Restlessness, drooling of saliva, muscular spasms, and rapid pulse can develop within 30 minutes to an hour. Fever may register as high as 104°F. Labored breathing or shortness of breath with accompanying cyanosis develops and grows more severe with the passage of time, and death can occur within 12 hours. A constricting band should be applied for five minutes, then released about three inches from the bite. Pack the wound with ice and take the victim to a medical facility for antivenin.

The nondeadly scorpion has a stubbier and darker body. Its sting is painful and will cause swelling and discoloration.

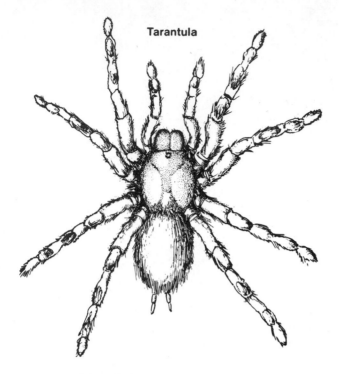

Tarantula

Large, hairy spiders . . . dark brown
to black. Up to 7 in. long.

Possible Signs & Symptoms
● may be similar to Black Widow
  Spider; however, tarantula bites
  are generally no worse than a bee
  sting.

FIGURE 8–7   (From *Emergency Medical Procedures for the Backpacker.* Copyright © 1979, Patient Care
Publications, Inc., P.O. Box 1245, Darien, Conn. All rights reserved.)

Tick Bites

Ticks are small, flat, and oval-shaped and about ⅛ to ¼ inch long (see
Figure 8–9). They are gray or brown in color. Once attached and left to
feed undisturbed, a tick will suck many times its body weight of blood or
body fluids, swelling up like a miniature balloon before dropping off after
three to five days.

Repulsive though these creatures are, most tick bites are harmless.
However, certain species of ticks can transmit serious infectious diseases
to humans. Rocky Mountain spotted fever, Colorado tick fever, and relaps-
ing fever (tick fever) are all spread by ticks.

Scorpion

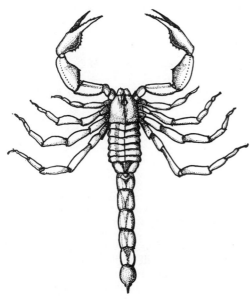

³/₄ to 3 in. long. Yellow to greenish-yellow. Lethal variety found only in Arizona and southern California. Night animal. Hides in shoes, boots, sleeping bags.

Possible Signs & Symptoms
- prickling sensation at time of bite, quickly followed by severe pain
- site becomes extremely sensitive
- restlessness
- severe breathing difficulty
- convulsion
- muscle cramps, nausea, vomiting
- high fever
- headache, dizziness
- abdominal pain
- profuse sweating

FIGURE 8–8
(From *Emergency Medical Procedures for the Backpacker*. Copyright © 1979, Patient Care Publications, Inc., P.O. Box 1245, Darien, Conn. All rights reserved.)

First Aid

Ticks should be removed as quickly as possible without squeezing the tick's body. Ways of removing ticks from the skin include the following:

1. Apply any substance that will smother the tick and cause it to disengage its head, so it can be lifted off with tweezers or a tissue. Heavy oils or greases,

Tick

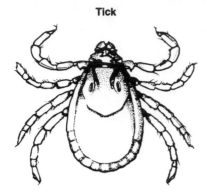

- flat and oval-shaped, with dark head
- grey or brown in color
- 1/8-1/4 inch fully developed

FIGURE 8—9

(From *Emergency Medical Procedures for the Backpacker.* Copyright © 1979, Patient Care Publications, Inc., P.O. Box 1245, Darien, Conn. All rights reserved.)

such as mineral oil or vaseline, will close off the respiratory opening on either side of the tick's body, but it may take as long as half an hour for the tick to back off. If after a half hour the tick has not backed out, gently pull it out with tweezers. Avoid squeezing the body in order to avoid squeezing more toxin into the victim.

2. Put a drop of gasoline or kerosene on the head of the tick at the skin surface. Wait a full 15 to 20 minutes so that the tick will loosen its grip voluntarily. Then, with tweezers, seize the tick gently at the skin surface and pull it off. Avoid squeezing the body, as this may squeeze more toxin into the bloodstream.

3. Apply fingernail polish to cover it completely and leave it on until hardened (two hours or more). Then peel the hardened polish off and the tick will come with it, head and all. This method is criticized because the longer a tick stays embedded, the greater the likelihood for contracting a disease.

4. Place an ice cube directly on the tick. The tick may back out.

CONTROVERSIAL REMOVAL METHODS

1. Apply heat by holding a heated needle or by lighting a match and blowing it out, then immediately touching the glowing end to the tick. The tick may back out or be killed, but the head will remain embedded in the skin thus necessitating the use of tweezers. Also, the human victim may be burned in the process.

2. Pull the tick out with tweezers. Authorities disagree on this technique. Some say there is no medical substantiation of the fact that pulling a tick out will increase the chance of the victim contracting a disease. Nor is there proof that if a piece of the tick's sucker is left in the skin (which rarely happens) the reaction will be any worse than if another foreign body is left in the skin.

   Other authorities say a tick's head can be unscrewed by grasping the body with tweezers and turning it counterclockwise as you pull, but the pressure of the tweezers on the tick's body can inject toxin into the victim. Other experts call this an "old wives' tale." On the other hand, if the tick is dead and embedded, the use of tweezers may be the safest and only way a first aider has of removing it.

After removal. Wash the bite site well with soap and water. Apply alcohol to further disinfect the area. Then apply a cold compress to reduce pain and calamine lotion to alleviate any itching. If unable to remove the tick, seek medical care.

Watch for signs of infection or unexplained symptoms, such as severe headache, fever, or rash, which may develop three to ten days later. If they appear, seek medical care immediately.

Insect Stings

The venom from insect stings kills more people than that of rattlesnakes. The National Safety Council has constructed a useful reference chart on troublesome insects, including spiders, bedbugs, chiggers, ticks, mosquitoes. (See Table 8–5.)

There are four major "offenders" in the insect order *Hymenoptera*: yellow jacket, wasp, hornet, and honeybee (see Figure 8–10).

After a honeybee stings, it is unable to withdraw the barbed stinger from its victim. As the bee tries to remove the stinger, a portion of the abdomen and venom sac remain in the victim; hence the bee dies. The remaining stinger is an indication of a honeybee sting.

Types of reactions. Most stings produce symptoms that may be classified as

A normal reaction to a single sting
A local reaction occurring in proximity to the sting site
A generalized reaction that may culminate in true anaphylaxis
A toxic reaction resulting from multiple stings
A delayed reaction days later.

FIGURE 8–10

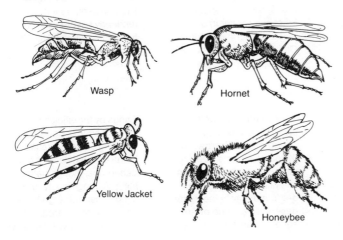

Wasp

Hornet

Yellow Jacket

Honeybee

TABLE 8-5 Facts About Troublesome Insects

DESCRIPTION	HABITAT	PROBLEM
Chigger		
Oval with red velvety covering. Sometimes almost colorless. Larva has six legs. Harmless adult has eight and resembles a small spider. Very tiny—about 1/20-inch long.	Found in low damp places covered with vegetation: shaded woods, high grass or weeds, fruit orchards. Also lawns and golf courses. From Canada to Argentina.	Attaches itself to the skin by inserting mouthparts into a hair follicle. Injects a digestive fluid that causes cells to disintegrate. Then feeds on cell parts. It does not suck blood.
Bedbug		
Flat oval body with short broad head and six legs. Adult is reddish brown. Young are yellowish white. Unpleasant pungent odor. From 1/8- to 1/4-inch in length.	Hides in crevices, mattresses, under loose wallpaper during day. At night travels considerable distance to find victims. Widely distributed throughout the world.	Punctures the skin with piercing organs and sucks blood. Local inflammation and welts result from anti-coagulant enzyme that bug secretes from salivary glands while feeding.
Brown Recluse Spider		
Oval body with eight legs. Light yellow to medium dark brown. Has distinctive mark shaped like a fiddle on its back. Body from 3/8- to 1/2-inch long, 1/4-inch wide, 3/4-inch from toe-to-toe.	Prefers dark places where it's seldom disturbed. Outdoors: old trash piles, debris and rough ground. Indoors: attics, storerooms, closets. Found in Southern and Midwestern United States.	Bites producing an almost painless sting that may not be noticed at first. Shy, it bites only when annoyed or surprised. Left alone, it won't bite. Victim rarely sees the spider.
Black Widow Spider		
Color varies from dark brown to glossy black. Densely covered with short microscopic hairs. Red or yellow hourglass marking on the underside of the female's abdomen. Male does not have this mark and is not poisonous. Overall length with legs extended is 1½ inch. Body is 1/4-inch wide.	Found with eggs and web. Outside: in vacant rodent holes, under stones, logs, in long grass, hollow stumps and brush piles. Inside: in dark corners of barns, garages, piles of stone, wood. Most bites occur in outhouses. Found in Southern Canada, throughout United States, except Alaska.	Bites causing local redness. Two tiny red spots may appear. Pain follows almost immediately. Larger muscles become rigid. Body temperature rises slightly. Profuse perspiration and tendency toward nausea follow. It's usually difficult to breathe or talk. May cause constipation, urine retention.
Scorpion		
Crablike appearance with claw-like pincers. Fleshy post-abdomen or "tail" has five segments, ending in a bulbous sac and stinger. Two poisonous types: solid straw yellow or yellow with irregular black stripes on back. From 2½ to 4 inches.	Spends days under loose stones, bark, boards, floors of outhouses. Burrows in the sand. Roams freely at night. Crawls under doors into homes. Lethal types are found only in the warm desert-like climate of Arizona and adjacent areas.	Stings by thrusting its tail forward over its head. Swelling or discoloration of the area indicates a non-dangerous, though painful, sting. A dangerously toxic sting doesn't change the appearance of the area, which does become hypersensitive.

SEVERITY	TREATMENT	PROTECTION

Itching from secreted enzymes results several hours after contact. Small red welts appear. Secondary infection often follows. Degree of irritation varies with individuals.

Lather with soap and rinse several times to remove chiggers. If welts have formed, dab antiseptic on area. Severe lesions may require antihistamine ointment.

Apply proper repellent to clothing, particularly near uncovered areas such as wrists and ankles. Apply to skin. Spray or dust infested areas (lawns, plants) with suitable chemicals.

Affects people differently. Some have marked swelling and considerable irritation while others aren't bothered. Sometimes transmits serious diseases.

Apply antiseptic to prevent possible infection. Bug usually bites sleeping victim, gorges itself completely in 3 to 5 minutes and departs. It's rarely necessary to remove one.

Spray beds, mattresses, bed springs and baseboards with insecticide. Bugs live in large groups. They migrate to new homes on water pipes and clothing.

In two to eight hours pain may be noticed followed by blisters, swelling, hemorrage or ulceration. Some people experience rash, nausea, jaundice, chills, fever, cramps or joint pain.

Summon doctor. Bite may require hospitalization for a few days. Full healing may take from 6 to 8 weeks. Weak adults and children have been known to die.

Use caution when cleaning secluded areas in the home or using machinery usually left idle. Check firewood, inside shoes, packed clothing and bedrolls—frequent hideaways.

Venom is more dangerous than a rattlesnake's but is given in much smaller amounts. About 5 percent of bite cases result in death. Death is from asphyxiation due to respiratory paralysis. More dangerous for children, to adults its worst feature is pain. Convulsions result in some cases.

Use an antiseptic such as alcohol or hydrogen peroxide on the bitten area to prevent secondary infection. Keep victim quiet and call a doctor. Do not treat as you would a snakebite since this will only increase the pain and chance of infection; bleeding will not remove the venom.

Wear gloves when working in areas where there might be spiders. Destroy any egg sacs you find. Spray insecticide in any area where spiders are usually found, especially under privy seats. Check them out regularly. General cleanliness, paint and light discourage spiders.

Excessive salivation and facial contortions may follow. Temperature rises to over 104°. Tongue becomes sluggish. Convulsions, in waves of increasing intensity, may lead to death from nervous exhaustion. First three hours most critical.

Apply constriction. Keep victim quiet and call a doctor immediately. Do not cut the skin or give pain killers. They increase the killing power of the venom. Antitoxin, readily available to doctors, has proved to be very effective.

Apply a petroleum distillate to any dwelling places that cannot be destroyed. Cats are considered effective predators, as are ducks and chickens, though the latter are more likely to be stung and killed. Don't go barefoot at night.

TABLE 8–5 (Continued)

DESCRIPTION	HABITAT	PROBLEM
Bee		
Winged body with yellow and black stripes. Covered with branched or feathery hairs. Makes a buzzing sound. Different species vary from ½ to 1 inch in length.	Lives in aerial or underground nests or hives. Widely distributed throughout the world wherever there are flowering plants—from the polar regions to the equator.	Stings with tail when annoyed. Burning and itching with localized swelling occur. Usually leaves venom sac in victim. It takes between 2 and 3 minutes to inject all the venom.
Mosquito		
Small dark fragile body with transparent wings and elongated mouthparts. From 1/8- to 1/4-inch long.	Found in temperate climates throughout the world where the water necessary for breeding is available.	Bites and sucks blood. Itching and localized swelling result. Bite may turn red. Only the female is equipped to bite.
Tarantula		
Large dark "spider" with a furry covering. From 6 to 7 inches in toe-to-toe diameter.	Found in Southwestern United States and the tropical varieties are poisonous.	Bites produce pin-prick sensation with negligible effect. It will not bite unless teased.
Tick		
Oval with small head; the body is not divided into definite segments. Grey or brown. Measures from 1/4-inch to 3/4-inch when mature.	Found in all United States areas and in parts of Southern Canada, on low shrubs, grass and trees. Carried around by both wild and domestic animals.	Attaches itself to the skin and sucks blood. After removal there is danger of infection, especially if the mouthparts are left in the wound.

Source: National Safety Council, *Family Safety*, Spring 1980, pp. 20–21.

Local reactions. Itching and pain followed by some redness and swelling at the sting site are the immediate local symptoms of a normal reaction to a single sting. The sting site is gradually surrounded by a whitish zone and a reddish flare, whereupon a wheal forms, which subsides after a few hours.

If the sting occurs around the eyes, nose, or throat, the local reaction may cause more than the common amount of distress. Stings about the eyes are especially dangerous because they can injure the eye.

Anaphylaxis. When generalized reactions occur after an encounter with an insect, medical help must be sought swiftly. These reactions may first be indicated by a dry, hacking cough, a sense of constriction in the throat or chest, swelling and itching about the eyes, massive hives, sneezing and wheezing, a rapid pulse, blush of the skin, and a sense of uneasiness.

SEVERITY	TREATMENT	PROTECTION
If a person is allergic, more serious reactions occur—nausea, shock, unconsciousness. Swelling may occur in another part of the body. Death may result.	Gently scrape (don't pluck) the stinger so venom sac won't be squeezed. Wash with soap and antiseptic. If swelling occurs, contact doctor. Keep victim warm while resting.	Have exterminator destroy nests and hives. Avoid wearing sweet fragrances and bright clothing. Keep food covered. Move slowly or stand still in the vicinity of bees.
Sometimes transmits yellow fever, malaria, encephalitis and other diseases. Scratching can cause secondary infections.	Don't scratch. Lather with soap and rinse to avoid infection. Apply antiseptic to relieve itching.	Destroy available breeding water to check multiplication. Place nets on windows and beds. Use proper repellent.
Usually no more dangerous than a pin prick. Has only local effects.	Wash and apply antiseptic to prevent the possibility of secondary infection.	Harmless to man, the tarantula is beneficial since it destroys harmful insects.
Sometimes carries and spreads Rocky Mountain spotted fever, tularemia Colorado tick fever. In a few rare cases, causes paralysis until removed.	Apply heavy oil over tick. Gently remove with tweezers so none of the mouthparts are left in skin. Wash with soap and water; apply antiseptic.	Cover exposed parts of body when in tick-infested areas. Use proper repellent. Remove ticks attached to clothes, body. Check neck and hair. Bathe.

> While there are accounts of individuals who have survived some 2,000 bee stings, generally 500 or more will bring about death. If a person is severely allergic, a single bee sting can kill.

Toxic reactions.   Toxic reactions result from innumerable insect stings to a single victim, as when a colony of bees or wasps is disturbed. Even when no sensitivity exists, the amount of venom injected from multiple stings may lead to death. The main symptoms are gastrointestinal (including diarrhea and vomiting), as well as faintness and unconsciousness. These are accompanied by edema without hives, headache, fever, drowsiness, involuntary muscle spasms, and sometimes convulsions.

Delayed reactions. Some victims experience delayed reactions to stings. In this case, symptoms of fever, headache, and hives occur as late as 10 to 14 days after the actual sting. If such a victim is stung again, the response may be immediate and anaphylactic. This delay is due to the fact that antibodies have to be formed with the first sting; therefore, they are in production. Thus, a single sting may produce both an immediate and a delayed reaction.

First Aid

The sting site should be carefully examined to determine whether a stinger is still embedded in the skin. If it is embedded, it should be removed to prevent further injection of toxin into the skin. If the stinger is left in the skin (only honeybees leave a stinger), it will continue to inject venom through spasmodic muscle contractions for two or three minutes unless removed immediately. It should be scraped off with the fingernail or a knife. Removal with the fingers or tweezers will exert pressure on the venom sack, and the victim will get the full amount of venom.

After an examination of the sting site and removal of the stinger, an ice or cold pack should be placed over the sting site to slow absorption of the toxin into the bloodstream. An ice pack will also relieve some of the pain associated with the sting. Wash the site with soap and water to cleanse the area of bacteria.

An ammonia (full-strength household ammonia) solution or a sodium bicarbonate paste will usually aid in controlling the pain. Relief can be obtained from rubbing a paste of meat tenderizer applied to the site for 20 to 30 minutes. The tenderizer contains papain, an enzyme that can break down insect venoms. An antihistamine may prevent some local symptoms if administered early, and an analgesic may be needed for pain relief. The victim should be observed for at least 30 minutes for signs of an allergic reaction.

The only effective treatment for insect sting anaphylaxis is the injection of epinephrine. The use of emergency insect sting kits by nonmedical personnel is of concern to many medical experts. Having emergency insect sting kits available for over-the-counter purchase is not accepted because some may use the epinephrine in order to get a "high." Furthermore, epinephrine should not be used to treat a sting unless anaphylaxis ensues, and on many occasions untrained persons might use the drug inappropriately. Finally, epinephrine has a limited shelf life (shelf life expires after three years or when it has turned brown), and over-the-counter kits would become outdated and ineffective. Therefore, such kits are available only through a prescription from a medical doctor.

These emergency insect sting kits contain a preloaded syringe of aqueous epinephrine and an oral antihistamine. Antihistamines are of little value in treating the immediate and life-threatening reaction. The epinephrine (0.3 ml.) is given subcutaneously. Since epinephrine is short-acting, the victim must be watched closely for signs of returning shock, and small doses of epinephrine should be injected as often as every 15 minutes as needed. Many kits also contain a constriction band and a Medic-Alert tag that identifies the potential victim as "allergic to insects."

Victims having past moderate to severe reactions with insect stings should also be told to go to the nearest medical facility after a sting.

MARINE ANIMAL INJURIES

Various injuries may result from many different kinds of marine animals. Refer to Table 8-6 for a listing of injuries and suggested emergency care.

TABLE 8–6 Guide to Diagnosis and Emergency Treatment of Marine Animal Injuries

TYPE OF INJURY	MARINE ANIMAL INVOLVED	EMERGENCY TREATMENT	POSSIBLE COMPLICATIONS
Trauma (bites and lacerations)	Major wounds by: Shark Barracuda Alligator gar	Control bleeding Prevent shock Give basic life support Splint the injury Secure prompt medical care	Shock Infections
	Minor wounds by: Moray eel Turtle Corals	Cleanse wound Splint the injury	
Sting (by tentacles)	Jellyfish Portuguese man-of-war Anemones Corals Hydras	Inactivate the area with alcohol and sprinkle with meat tenderizer, coalesce powder and scrape the area[1]	Allergic reactions Respiratory arrest
Puncture (by spines)	Urchins Cone shells Stingrays Spiny fish (catfish, toad, or oyster fish)	Inactivate with hot water[2]	Allergic reactions Collapse Infections Tetanus Granuloma formation
Poisonous bite (by fangs)	Sea snake Octopus[3]	Give basic life support	Paralysis Myoglobinuria Respiratory arrest

TABLE 8–6   (Continued)

TYPE OF INJURY	MARINE ANIMAL INVOLVED	EMERGENCY TREATMENT	POSSIBLE COMPLICATIONS
Poisoning (by ingestion)[4]	Puffer fish Scromboids (tuna species) Ciguatera (large colored fish) Paralytic shell fish	Give basic life support; prevent self-injury from convulsions	Allergic reactions Asthmatic reactions Paresthesia, numbness Temperature reversal phenomena Respiratory arrest and circulatory collapse
Miscellaneous: Shocks Skin rashes	Electric fish Marine parasites	No treatment required injuries usually self-limiting	Electric fish or electric eel may precipitate a panic reaction

Source: American Academy of Orthopaedic Surgeons, *Emergency Care and Transportation of the Sick and Injured* (Menasha, Wis.: George Banta, 1981), p. 332.

[1]The intense burning pain resulting from the sting of the jellyfish is produced by nematocysts (stinging cells) on the tenacles. Even when the sea creature is washed up on shore, the stinging cells remain potent for several days. In treating the sting, 95-percent alcohol "fixes" the nematocysts on the skin and prevents further stinging, and the meat tenderizer neutralizes the protein toxin of the nematocyst. Powder dries the area and causes the stings to stick together so they can be more readily removed by scraping.

[2]A toxin is introduced with some of the puncture wounds from this group. In any case, the wounds are excruciatingly painful. It appears that the foreign material or poison introduced into the wound is heat-sensitive. Dramatic treatment results occur when soaking in quite hot water for thirty to sixty minutes. Be careful, however, not to scald the patient with water that is too hot, as the pain of the wound will mask his normal reaction to heat.

[3]Only one species of octopus, the blue ringed octopus of Australia, is known to have inflicted fatal bites to persons.

[4]Should ingestion of a poisonous fish be suspected, reference to Halstead's *Poisonous and Venomous Marine Animals of the World* or seeking immediate assistance from poison control centers is suggested.

Chapter 9

Burn Injuries

About two million burn injuries each year require medical attention or restriction of activity. The 90,000 patients admitted to hospitals annually with burns require an average of 12 days of hospital care. About one in every 20 burns that are treated is serious enough to result in hospitalization.

Burns can be very severe, painful injuries that require many months of costly care. They are a leading cause of accidental death in the United States. These injuries are caused by heat, electricity, chemicals, and radiation.

Burns caused by excessive heat are called thermal burns. Injuries from moist heat result from contact with such things as steam and hot liquids. Injuries from dry heat result from contact with such things as lighted cigarettes, open fires, hot metal, and explosions. Faulty wiring often is the cause of electrical burns. The improper use of chemicals such as lye, strong cleaning products, and acids also may result in burns. Radiation burns result from x-rays, radioactive substances, or ultraviolet rays.

Burn injuries often generate extraordinary anxiety, not only in the relatives of the victims but also in the first aider. Inexperience may explain some of the first aider's apprehension, but the urgency which such injuries seem to require may be intimidating even for the most experienced.

Human flesh begins to burn at 113°F (45°C). Three seconds in 146°F (63°C) water, or one second of exposure at 160°F (71°C), or water at 133°F (56°C) for about 30 seconds can result in third-degree burn injury. At 180°F (82°C) third-degree burns result. Third-degree burns can happen after five minutes in 120°F water.

Even after direct contact with a heat source has ceased, human flesh will continue to simmer and burn for minutes afterwards.

The first thing for a first aider to do when confronted with a burned victim is to assess the severity of the burn. It should be stressed, however, that breathing and severe bleeding should be checked and taken care of first.

CLASSIFICATION

Burns may be classified by depth, which may vary in severity in different areas of the body. Depth is spoken of in *degrees* (see Table 9–1).

Even in the most experienced hands, the exact diagnosis of the depth of burn is difficult. Diagnosis of the depth of injury is at times extremely difficult because the skin varies in thickness, depending upon its location on the body and the victim's age, and because burns are frequently of mixed depths. It is particularly difficult to determine the depth of the burn very early after injury. The greater the depth, the greater the fluid loss and, therefore, the more critical the burn.

First-Degree Burns

Normal skin is made up of two main layers: the epidermis and the dermis. The epidermis is the outermost layer of skin. The dermis is a deep inner layer that has nerves, blood vessels, sweat glands and hair follicles, which are important in the regrowth of skin in first-degree and second-degree burns.

First-degree burns affect only the outer epidermal area and are characterized by redness, mild swelling, increased warmth, tenderness, and pain (see Figure 9–1). These burns often are the result of sunburn, scalding by hot water or steam, and sudden flash burns. Although quite painful at first, first-degree burns usually heal without scarring within a week.

TABLE 9-1 Categories of Burn Depth

DEGREE	CAUSE	SURFACE APPEARANCE	COLOR	PAIN LEVEL	HISTOLOGIC DEPTH	HEALING TIME
First: All are considered minor unless victim is under 18 months, over 65, or with severe loss of fluids	Flash, flame, ultraviolet (sunburn)	Dry, no blisters, edema	Red	Painful	Epidermal layers only	2 to 5 days with peeling, no scarring, may have discoloration
Second (partial thickness): Minor—less than 15% in adults, less than 10% in children. Moderate—15 to 30% in adults, or less than 15% with involvement of face, hands, feet, or perineum; minor chemical or electrical; in children, 10 to 30% Severe—more than 30%	Contact with hot liquids or solids, flash flame to clothing, direct flame, chemical	Moist blebs, blisters	Mottled white to pink, cherry red	Very painful	Epidermis, papillary, and reticular layers of dermis; may include fat domes of subcutaneous layer	Superficial—5 to 21 days with no grafting; deep with no infection—21 to 35 days; if infected, converts to full thickness
Third (full thickness): Minor—less than 2% Moderate—1 to 10% any involvement of face, hands, feet, or perineum Severe—more than 10% and major chemical or electrical	Contact with hot liquids or solids, flame, chemical, electricity	Dry with leathery eschar until debridement, charred blood vessels visible under eschar	Mixed white (waxy-pearly), dark (khaki-mahogany), charred	Little or no pain, hair pulls out easily	Down to and includes subcutaneous tissue; may include fascia, muscle, and bone	Large areas require grafting that may take many months; small areas may heal from edges after weeks

Source: *American Journal of Nursing*, November, 1977.

Second-Degree Burns

Second-degree burns involve the entire layer of the epidermis and extend into the under layer of skin (dermis). (See Figure 9–1.) Superficial second-degree burns are characterized by deep reddening, blister formation, considerable swelling, and weeping of fluid (it will be wet-looking). Deep second-degree burns may not be distinguishable from third-degree burns immediately after the injury. There is severe pain because of the irritated and overly sensitive nerve endings: any breeze, pressure, or disturbance to the area will cause increased pain. These burns often are the result of a very deep sunburn, contact with scaling liquid, and flash burns from such things as gasoline and kerosene. If the burns do not become infected, they should heal with little scarring in about three weeks. If infection does occur, the burn may transform into a third-degree type injury.

FIGURE 9–1   Classification of burns according to skin depth damaged.

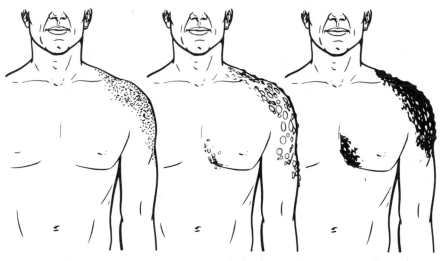

FIRST DEGREE PARTIAL THICKNESS	SECOND DEGREE PARTIAL THICKNESS	THIRD DEGREE FULL THICKNESS

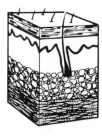  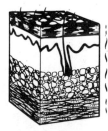

EPIDERMIS

DERMIS

FAT

MUSCLE

SKIN REDDENED   BLISTERS   CHARRING

One of the best ways to differentiate between second- and third-degree areas is by pulling on a hair. If the hair slips out easily and painlessly, it is a third-degree burn.

Third-Degree Burns

Third-degree burns involve the epidermis, dermis, and may extend to the underlying fat, muscle, and bone. (See Figure 9-1.) They are usually characterized by charring of the skin, which may be black or dark brown, hard, cherry-red and dry, milk-white, thick, and leathery. Soot may make a burn appear to be third-degree. Coagulated blood vessels frequently may be identified. Pain may be absent because of the destruction of the nerve endings. These burns may be the result of hot liquids, ignited clothing, explosions, electricity, and gasoline or oil fires. This type of burn will not heal properly by itself, except at the margins of the wound. Early skin grafting must be done to prevent contractures, which may occur as scar tissue covers the damaged area.

In 1832, Dupuytren, the French surgeon, classified burns as to degrees, such as first degree, second degree, third degree.

You can consider as *very rough* rules the following:

Scald burns on nude skin tend to be superficial because the heat dissipates rather quickly; however, in the very young and very old, scalds may well be full-thickness injuries.

Flame burns tend to be at least deep partial-thickness injuries, and often are full thickness.

Grease burns may be full thickness because grease cools slowly and is difficult to remove.

Electrical and chemical burns can be deep, even when at first they appear to be minor. Hospitalization is recommended for almost all electrical and chemical burn victims, if only for observation, because such burns frequently become progressively more serious.

Third-degree burns are usually surrounded by first- and/or second-degree burns.

EXTENT OF THE BURN

The extent of the burn is expressed as a percentage of the total body surface. The amount of burned skin surface in an *adult* can be estimated by using the *rule of nines*. (See Figure 9-2.) The head and neck represent 9

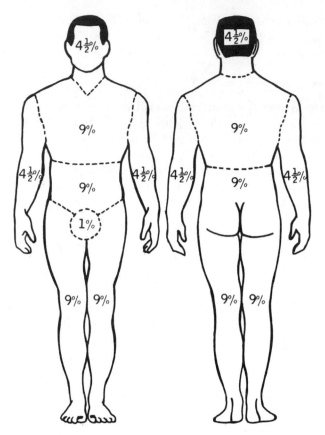

FIGURE 9–2   The rule of nines.

percent of the body surface, as do each arm, the chest, the upper back, the abdomen, the buttocks and lower back, the front of each leg, and the back of each leg. The genitalia represent 1 percent. The knowledge that the victim's hand is about 1 percent of the total body surface is very useful in estimating the size of small or oddly shaped burns. In *children*, the head is larger in relationship to the body and should be counted as 18 percent, and the legs are smaller (14 percent); otherwise, the basic rule may be used.

In the severely burned victim, estimating the percentage of the *unburned* area can sometimes be more accurate than estimating burned areas. It is better to overestimate the extent of a burn than to underestimate.

Generally, an adult with second-degree burns of 15 percent or more of the body surface and a child with second-degree burns of 10 percent or more of the body surface may require hospitalization. Critical burns require immediate examination and hospitalization because of their life-threatening nature. Burn severity is usually considered either minor, moderate, or critical. Refer to Table 9–2 for a definition of these categories.

TABLE 9–2 Burn Severity

Critical Burns

All burns that are complicated by injuries to the respiratory tract, soft tissues and bone structures.
Third-degree burns that involve the critical areas of the body: hands, face, perineum.
Third-degree burns that involve more than 10% of the body surface.
Second-degree burns that involve more than 30% of the body surface.

Moderate Burns

Third-degree burns that involve less than 10% of the body surface, excluding hands, face and feet.
Second-degree burns that involve 15% to 30% of the body surface.
First-degree burns that involve 50% to 75% of the body surface.

Minor Burns

Third-degree burns that involve less than 2% of the body surface, excluding the hands, face and feet.
Second-degree burns that involve less than 15% of the body surface.
First-degree burns that involve less than 20% of the body surface.

Source: Grant and Murray, *Emergency Care* (Bowie, Md.: Robert J. Brady Co.).

Other Factors That Affect the Severity of Burn Injury

The severity of the burn is affected by several other factors, such as the age of the victim, the location of the burn on the body, and associated diseases or injuries. Children under the age of five and adults over the age of 60 tolerate burns poorly. Mortality rates escalate with increasing age; by age 60, a burn that covers more than 20 percent of the total body surface is often fatal.

Burns that involve the respiratory tract are considered critical because breathing may become obstructed as the swelling increases. Respiratory burns can be suspected if the victim has obvious burn injury to the face and neck. This may be identified by singed eyebrows, eyelashes, or hair. More insidious is the respiratory burn suffered by the victim caught in a closed room who inhales super-heated gases and carbonaceous particles. This type of respiratory burn may be identified by hoarseness, increased respiratory rate, and carbonaceous particles in victim's sputum (see page 216). Other critical burns include third-degree burns of 10 percent and second-degree burns of 30 percent or more of the body surface; burns of the face, hands, feet, and perineum; and burns associated with soft tissue injuries and fractures.

The prognosis is poor for victims with third-degree burns that cover 50 percent or more of the body surface. However, the rate of recovery has increased for victims treated in modern burn centers where newer methods of treatment are used. Although a young adult may recover, the very young and the elderly may not recover from burns of the same extent and degree. Victims under four and those over forty should be considered in more danger when burned.

Examine the eyes promptly. Suspect eye damage in victims:

with facial burns

who were involved in flash fires confined to a small, closed room where heat might have caused indirect damage to the conjunctiva, cornea, or sclera

with electrical burns where the current may have traveled to the eye, which is rich in vascular and neural structures.

Prompt eye examination is crucial with facial burns because the eyelids become markedly swollen and close very quickly.

First Aid

First-Degree Burns

First-degree burns that involve only a small area usually require little treatment. To relieve the pain, cold water applications can be applied, or the burned area can be submerged in cold water. Do not use salt or ice water. Continue cold water applications until pain subsides. Unclean areas should be cleansed with soap and water and left open to air or, if desired, covered with a clean dry dressing. If sunburned areas are clean, they should not be washed. Infection seldom occurs unless there is also an abrasion or contact dermatitis, such as poison ivy.

ALOE VERA PLANT FOR BURNS

Extracts of the *Aloe vera* plant are widely believed by the public to be useful in the treatment of sunburn and some types of superficial burns. This is supported by a long history of use in Mexico. *Aloe vera* (70 percent gel) has an aspirinlike compound that may produce analgesia. It has also been shown to have antibacterial properties against many organisms. To be useful, *Aloe vera* has to be used properly. The inner part of the spike, a clear jelly, is to be used. The gel should not be applied before the heat in the burn is out (use cold water treatment first), or the gel will hold the heat in. *Aloe vera* should not be used with caustic or acid burns.

Further evidence is needed to verify conclusively the usefulness of *Aloe vera* for burns.

Avoid topical burn sprays. They generally are ineffective and may cause allergic reactions.

If there is pain, an analgesic such as aspirin is usually sufficient to

TABLE 9–3   First Aid for Burns

BURN	DO	DON'T
First Degree (redness, mild swelling, and pain)	Apply cold water and/or dry sterile dressing.	Apply butter, oleomargarine, etc.
Second Degree (deeper; blisters develop)	Immerse in cold water, blot dry with sterile cloth for protection. Treat for shock. Obtain medical attention if severe.	Break blisters. Remove shreds of tissue. Use antiseptic preparation, ointment spray, or home remedy on severe burn.
Third Degree (deeper destruction, skin layers destroyed)	Cover with sterile cloth to protect. Treat for shock. Watch for breathing difficulty. Obtain medical attention quickly.	Remove charred clothing that is stuck to burn. Apply ice. Use home medication.
Chemical Burn	Remove by flushing with large quantities of water for at least 5 minutes. Remove surrounding clothing. Obtain medical attention.	

Source: U.S. Coast Guard.

relieve it. For mild (first-degree burn) sunburn, calamine lotion may provide relief, but Caladryl, which contains Benadryl, an antihistamine, may cause an allergic reaction when applied on the skin.

Second-Degree (Small) Burns

To relieve pain and reduce blister formation, cold water applications should be used or the burned area of the skin should be immersed immediately in cold water (not salt or ice water) until the pain subsides. Immediate cooling in the treatment of most first- and second-degree burns can mean the difference between extensive deep burns and more limited superficial injuries.

When the skin is burned, the deeper parts of the skin can be further damaged for two to three minutes after the heat contact. During this period of time, coagulation and depth of deeper parts of the skin may occur from the retained heat. This is especially true if clothing has been involved. On the other hand, if the burned skin is immersed in cold water within 30 seconds of being burned, skin temperatures drop to normal within three seconds.

The best cold water temperature is 86°F (30°C). Water from the typical household cold water faucet is between 70° to 77°F (22° to 25°C). Don't waste time attempting to get ice to add to the cold tap water. Healing of burns is most rapid when the burned area is cooled promptly, but even up to 45 minutes after the burn, cooling speeds up the healing process. Little is known about the length of time for cooling. One standard is 20 to 30 minutes; other experts say continue to cool until the pain does not recur when cold is removed from a burned area for a five-minute period. Remember, excessive cooling may be damaging to skin tissues. Don't apply ice directly to the burn, and never soak a burn in ice water. Salt lowers the temperature of ice water and *never* should be added as it may cause further injury. Following the cold treatment, the area should be cleansed with soap and water and blotted dry with either sterile gauze or a clean towel.

> Do *not* put burn ointment, butter, or vaseline on burns. Some first aiders think they must put something—almost anything—on burns. Putting butter or vaseline on burns seals in the heat and the resulting injury may be worse than it would have been without the butter or vaseline. Such substances may contaminate the injury, which could result in an infection. Sometimes, a physician may have to remove the burn ointment in order to treat the burn; therefore, ointment is a waste of time and the removal can be painful. Moreover, ointments don't offer any real pain relief.

No over-the-counter burn ointment is presently acceptable in first aid practice.

> Do *not* break the blisters. The treatment of blisters continues to be a controversial topic among burn-therapy specialists. Blisters provide a protective covering to prevent surface bacteria from penetrating the wound; therefore blisters should be left intact, especially on the soles of the feet and palms of the hands. Wound healing is better under intact blisters—the blister fluid apparently has a healing effect.
>
> Do *not* try to remove pieces of body tissue that adhere to the wound.
>
> Remove all clothing and jewelry from the burn area. Later removal could be difficult and painful if edema (swelling) develops. Exercise great care because tissue may be stuck to clothing.

The dressing may be changed more frequently if it develops an odor or becomes soaked with exudate. When the dressing needs to be replaced, it should *never* be pulled from adhering surfaces; the area should be soaked with large amounts of water to free the material from the wound. Before a new dressing is applied, the burned area should be washed gently with soap and water.

Third-Degree and Extensive Second-Degree Burns

Establish an airway.   The victim should be checked immediately for breathing, and an open airway should be established. Artificial respiration or cardiopulmonary resuscitation should be performed as required (see page 47).

Respiratory problems always should be anticipated if there are burns around the face, head, and neck or if during a fire the victim was caught in an enclosed area.

The tongue of an unconscious victim may drop back into the throat and block the air passage. Usually resuscitation can be accomplished with proper positioning of the head and neck.

Treat for shock.   Although there may be no immediate signs of shock, it should be anticipated and treated. Loss of plasma from severely burned areas lowers the victim's blood volume and causes shock.

If the victim is conscious, does not have a heart problem or high blood pressure, is not vomiting, and if medical care may be delayed for several hours, a weak solution of baking soda (½ level teaspoonful) and salt (one level teaspoonful) to a quart of water may be given every 15 minutes—½ glass for adults; ¼ glass for a child; ⅛ glass for infants. Discontinue if vomiting occurs.

Treat the burned area.   The first aider's hands should be clean. All debris and dirt *around* the burned areas should be removed to avoid additional contamination of the area. When treating the injury, remember:

1. *No attempt should be made to open blisters or to remove pieces of tissue from the burned surface.* The blisters are not harmful; they protect the underlying tissues against the entry of bacteria.
2. *No attempt should be made to apply cold water to extensively burned surfaces.* This may increase the victim's shock reaction or induce hypothermia.

Multiple layers of sterile dressings should be added to absorb the large amount of fluid that is produced. Roller bandages can be used to hold the dressings in place. If adhesive tape is used to fasten the bandage, it should *not* come into contact with the skin. If the burns are extensive and sterile dressings are scarce, a freshly laundered or ironed sheet can be used.

Dressings should be left in place for 24 hours unless they become soaked with drainage. If this should occur before medical attention can be obtained, the dressings should be replaced under as sterile conditions as possible. If there is evidence of infection, the treatment should be the same as for an infected wound (see page 104). Fever following serious burns is common and does not necessarily indicate infection.

Elevate the injured part, where this is possible. Edema (swelling) makes the wound susceptible to infection. Caution the victim to be alert to indications that the dressing is becoming tight. A tight dressing may hinder circulation and affect healing, or it may be an early signal of infection.

Burned hands require a special type of dressing. They should be dressed in the position of function (hand in a cupped position) with pads separating the fingers. It is a good idea to leave the tips of the fingers or toes out of the dressing so that you can observe the circulation in them.

When treating burn injuries, *always* remember to examine the victim for other injuries. If there are fractures and lacerations, they should be treated the same as when burns are not present.

RESPIRATORY BURNS

Respiratory burns (see page 211) are caused by the inhalation of hot gases and air, particles, and smoke. They should be anticipated when burned areas are found around the mouth, nose, face, hair, and neck. However, sufficient heat from a flash fire may cause swelling of the larynx with little evidence of other burns.

The victim with a mild injury to the respiratory passages may have only a cough, hoarseness, or a sore throat. Complete obstruction of the respiratory passage may occur as a result of a severe injury. Also, partial collapse of a lung may occur. The victim first may exhibit cyanosis (blue color of the skin), dyspnea (shortness of breath), coughing, wheezing, and hoarseness.

First Aid

An airway must be maintained. Medical advice should be obtained. Plans should be made to transport the victim to the nearest medical facility.

ELECTRICAL BURNS

The severity of electrical burns is often difficult to determine because the deeper layers of the skin, muscles, and internal organs may be involved. Also, the burns may be followed by a paralysis of the respiratory center and an irregularity in the beat of the heart. Unconsciousness or instant death may occur.

First Aid

The victim must be removed from the source of the electrical current as quickly as possible, without endangering the rescuer. Electrical lines may be removed with a dry wooden pole, chair, or other nonmetal object. Cardiopulmonary resuscitation (see page 57) may be required because the shock may affect the victim's heart and lungs. The treatment of the burn is the same as for any thermal burn of the same extent and depth. This includes relief of pain, prevention and treatment of shock, care of the wound, and control of infection. Be aware that two burn wounds may be present—an entry wound and an exit wound.

CHEMICAL BURNS

Chemical burns occur when acids, alkalis, and other corrosive chemicals come in contact with the skin and mucous membranes.

First Aid

The chemical should be washed away immediately with large amounts of water, using a hose or shower if available. If water is not available, any nonirritating liquid should be used (milk or soda pop). Water is best, however. The washing should be continued for a minimum of 15 minutes. Plunging the injured part into a bucket of water merely dilutes and diffuses the chemical. All of the victim's clothing that has become contaminated with the chemical should be removed. *This washing technique must be modified for dry lime burns.* Before washing, the lime should be brushed away gently. Water mixed with the lime reacts chemically to produce heat, which may further burn the skin.

Do not attempt to neutralize a chemical, because the neutralization process produces heat, which can cause further damage. Additional treatment would be the same as for any thermal burn of the same extent and depth.

MULTIPLE BURN CASES

Give Priority to the Victim Who Can Benefit Most

In disasters and accidents involving a number of burn injuries, you may be responsible for deciding which victims should receive priority in reaching the hospital. To assure maximum salvage of lives, follow these general guidelines:

Send those with facial and extensive chest burns in whom airway obstruction is a high probability before sending those with extremity burns of equal extent.

Send those with 60 to 80 percent burns in preference to those with burns of more than 80 percent. Burns greater than 80 percent are usually fatal, and victims who suffer them should be considered fatalities even though still alive.

When victims' burns are equal in extent, send a victim who does not complain before a victim who complains vigorously. It takes energy to complain, and a third-degree burn is painless; second-degree burns hurt.

RADIATION BURNS

Radiation burns may be nuclear or solar. Because solar burns are basically sunburns, they should be treated like any other first- or second-degree burn. The concern in this section is nuclear burns.

Ionizing radiation (alpha, beta, and gamma rays) affects the body cells.

Alpha and beta particles are dangerous only if swallowed or inhaled—they damage internal organs.

Gamma rays are very penetrating and dangerous.

The amount of radiation damage depends upon:

1. Type of radiation delivered
2. Duration of exposure
3. Area of body affected
4. Distance between person and source
5. Strength of source
6. Shielding between person and source.

First Aid

If a hazardous radiation level exists, the victim should be removed from the area as quickly as possible even if some of the rules of initial emergency care are violated. If there is reason to suspect that there are radioactive materials on the victim's or rescuer's clothes, they should be removed at the edge of the exposed area and disposed of in labeled metal containers with tight lids. Both rescuer and victim should shower and be transported to a medical facility for decontamination.

AFTER-THE-EMERGENCY CARE

Minor burns can be treated at home. Severe burn care should follow a physician's directions. However, many of these cases may be cared for afterward at home.

1. Wash your hands thoroughly with soap and water.
2. Spread ointment (usually silver sulfadiazine) on the bandage.
3. Wash and remove the dressings:

    Remove the old dressings by cutting off the outer layer and then rolling off the rest. Do not pull off the dressing if it is sticking to the wound; soak it off in a basin or tub.

    Soak the burn for 10 to 15 minutes in a mild detergent solution. Gently wash over the burned area with a soft washcloth to remove any old blood, cream, loose skin, or dry, yellow matter.

    Rinse the wound with clear water. Pat the area dry with a freshly laundered soft towel.

    Cover the wound with one layer of dressing treated with ointment (silver sulfadiazine), and wrap snugly with six to seven layers of dry bandage.
4. Physician appointments should be kept regardless of how well the victim may feel.
5. If there is any sign of infection—fever (102°F or higher), yellow pus, a foul smell, increase in pain, and redness or red streaking—consult a physician.
6. As the burn heals, the skin and joints nearby can become stiff. To loosen them up, you should exercise the joints and muscles around the burn as soon as healing begins.

Chapter 10

Cold-
and Heat-Related
Injuries

FROSTBITE

To most people, frostbite (freezing of tissue) may seem like a remote risk.
Yet as more and more people venture outdoors in winter—skiing, hiking,
hunting, snowmobiling—it has become an increasing health hazard.

As the body tries to conserve heat for vital internal organs in bitter
cold, it reduces the flow of warming blood to the extremities. Eventually, if
the temperature in the tissue drops low enough, tiny ice crystals begin to
form in the watery spaces between the cells. Expanding outward in all
directions, the ice ruptures cell membranes and kills the tissue, which turns
white, stiff, and insensitive to touch. Furthermore, the reduced blood flow
due to sludging and clotting of blood inside small blood vessels raises the
possibility of gangrene occurring.

The extent of the injury depends upon such factors as temperature,
duration of exposure, wind velocity, humidity, lack of protective clothing,
or the presence of wet clothing. Also, the harmful effects of exposure to
cold are intensified by fatigue, individual susceptibility, existing injuries,
emotional stress, smoking, and drinking alcoholic beverages. Table 10-1
may be used to estimate wind velocity, and Table 10-2 may be used to
determine the wind-chill factor.

TABLE 10–1 Estimating Wind Velocity From Simple Observations

IF YOU SEE . . .	THE WIND IS PROBABLY BLOWING
Flags or pennants hanging limp from their staffs; smoke rising vertically from chimneys and open fires	0–1 mph
Flags and pennants barely moving; leaves moving slightly on trees; smoke drifting lazily with the wind	0–3 mph
Flags and pennants moving slightly out from their staffs; leaves rustling in trees; if you feel wind on your face	4–7 mph
Flags and pennants standing out from their staffs at an angle of 30° to 40°; or leaves and twigs in constant motion	8–12 mph
Small branches moving in trees; dust and paper being blown about	13–18 mph
Flags and pennants flying at 90° angle; small trees swaying	19–24 mph
Flags and pennants standing straight out from their staffs and fluttering vigorously; large tree branches in motion; or if you hear whistling in power lines	25–31 mph
Flags and pennants whipping about wildly on the staffs; whole trees in motion; loose objects being picked up and blown about; or if you find it somewhat difficult to walk when facing the wind	32–38 mph
Twigs being broken from trees; drivers having a problem in controlling their vehicles; or if you hear power lines whining loudly	39–46 mph
Trees bending sharply; structural damage occurring in buildings; the progress of vehicles and pedestrians alike being seriously impeded	47–54 mph
Trees being uprooted; considerable structural damage occurring	55–63 mph
Buildings suffering severe damage	63–72 mph
Widespread destruction; or if walking is virtually impossible	more than 72 mph

Source: Grant and Murray, *Emergency Care* (Bowie, Md.: Robert J. Brady Co., 1978).

Types of Frostbite

The extent of injury is not usually known when first seen. At one time, some effort was made to describe frostbite injury in terms of degrees, as presently done with burns (first-, second-, third-degree). Frostbite injuries are now classified as either superficial or deep. Even these designations are somewhat limited because it is difficult initially to tell the extent of injury. Classifying may not matter, however, because the treatment for both types is basically the same.

Superficial. Fingers, cheeks, ears, and nose are the most commonly affected body parts. If the exposure is prolonged, the freezing may extend up the arms and legs. Ice crystals in the skin and other tissues cause the area to appear a white or greyish-yellow color. Pain may occur early and

TABLE 10–2 Wind-Chill Factor

ESTIMATED WIND SPEED (IN MPH)	ACTUAL THERMOMETER READING (°F.)											
	50	40	30	20	10	0	−10	−20	−30	−40	−50	−60
	Equivalent Temperature (°F.)											
calm	50	40	30	20	10	0	−10	−20	−30	−40	−50	−60
5	40	37	27	16	6	−5	−15	−26	−36	−47	−57	−68
10	40	28	16	4	−9	−24	−33	−46	−58	−70	−83	−95
15	36	22	9	−5	−18	−32	−45	−58	−72	−85	−99	−112
20	32	18	4	−10	−25	−39	−53	−67	−82	−96	−110	−124
25	30	16	0	−15	−29	−44	−59	−74	−88	−104	−118	−133
30	25	13	−2	−18	−33	−48	−63	−79	−94	−109	−125	−140
35	27	11	−4	−20	−35	−51	−67	−82	−98	−113	−129	−145
40	26	10	−6	−21	−37	−53	−69	−85	−100	−116	−132	−148
(Wind speeds greater than 40 mph have little additional effect.)	Little danger (for properly clothed person.) Maximum danger of false sense of security.			Increasing danger (Flesh may freeze within 1 minute.)			Great danger (Flesh may freeze within 30 seconds.)					

Source: Grant and Murray, *Emergency Care* (Bowie, Md.: Robert J. Brady Co., 1978).

subside. Often the part will feel only very cold and numb, or there may be a tingling, stinging, or aching sensation. The victim may not be aware of frostbite until someone mentions it. When the damage is superficial, the surface will feel hard and underlying tissue soft when depressed gently and firmly. After thawing, the part becomes flushed and sometimes deep purple in color. It later sheds by flaking.

Deep. In a deep, unthawed frostbite, the area (mainly the hands and feet) will feel hard, solid, and cannot be depressed. It will be cold, pale, and numb, and blisters will appear on the surface and in the underlying tissues in 12 to 36 hours. After thawing, it may be blue, purple, or black in color. The area will become swollen when it thaws, and later gangrene may occur and there will be a loss (sloughing) of tissue (necrosis). Time alone will reveal what kind of frostbite has occurred.

First Aid

As late as the 1950s, some doctors and first aid manuals were recommending massage of a frostbitten limb with snow or ice, a treatment that traces back to Baron Larrey, Napoleon's chief surgeon on the Grand Army's disastrous retreat from Moscow during the bitter winter of 1812 to 1813.

All frostbite injuries follow the same sequence in care: initial care, rapid rewarming, and postcare. Also assess the victim for hypothermia, for which priority treatment should be given because of its life-threatening effects.

Initial Care

The principles of emergency care for frostbite injury are relatively few. The two most important aspects are getting the victim to a place of permanent treatment as soon as possible, and then rewarming. If the victim is out in the field—but not too far away from a medical facility—and the part is still frozen, take the victim in as is with no attempt to thaw the injured part. Be sure that the part is kept frozen. If partial thawing and refreezing occurs, ice crystals formed the second time are larger, and therefore, tissue damage is more severe. If in a remote area and the feet are frostbitten, it is important to note that a victim can walk on frostbitten feet if the feet have not started to thaw. Otherwise, do not allow the victim to walk. Once rewarming has started, warming must be maintained. Never thaw frostbite if there is a likelihood of refreezing. Victims with frostbite to the lower extremities are litter cases. Refreezing or walking on a partially thawed part can be very harmful. During transportation and initial treatment, the use of alcoholic beverages should not be permitted because they dilate capillaries and cause a loss of body heat. Do not let the victim smoke because smoking constricts capillaries and thus produces poor circulation.

Do not rub the affected part to restore circulation, and especially do not rub it with snow. Rubbing or massage will increase the injury to frozen tissue; rubbing it with snow just intensifies the damage.

Rapid Rewarming

There are two techniques of *rapid rewarming*: wet and dry.

1. *Wet, rapid rewarming*, which is preferred (because it preserves the greatest amount of tissue), is accomplished by completely immersing the local part in an adequate amount of water at a temperature between 102°F and 106°F (39°C and 42°C). Different authorities have suggested temperatures as low as 90°F to as high as 108°F. The water bath should be tested frequently with a thermometer. If one is not available, some of the water should be poured over the inner portion of the rescuer's wrist or arm to make sure the water is not too hot. Warming should be discontinued when the part becomes flushed, usually within 30 minutes with the wet method. Further rapid wet rewarming is not necessary. For injuries involving the face or ears, warm moist cloths (frequently changed to maintain heat) can be applied.

   The thawing process is quick but usually quite painful. As thawing proceeds, a pink flushing will progress down the extremity; continue thawing until the tip of the thawed part flushes, is warm to the touch, and remains flushed when removed from the warm bath.

TEMPERATURE CONVERSION

Many people have difficulty relating Celsius temperatures to Farenheit temperatures. Here are the formulas to use in converting one to the other:
To convert Celsius into Fahrenheit, multiply Celsius temperature by 9, divide by 5, and add 32:

$$F = \frac{C \times 9}{5} + 32$$

To convert Fahrenheit into Celsius, subtract 32 from Fahrenheit temperature, multiply by 5, and divide by 9:

$$C = \frac{F - 32 \times 5}{9}$$

---

2. *The dry, rapid rewarming technique* takes three to four times as long as the wet technique and is best accomplished by the use of natural body warmth, as exemplified by putting the victim's hands in another person's axilla (armpits) or sharing warm clothing. Also, the victim can be exposed to warm room air.

Do not allow the victim to walk or to massage a body part. Do not use water hotter than 108°F (may cause massive tissue destruction) or recool with ice or snow, and do not expose the extremity near an open flame or fire.

Postcare

After the rewarming of frostbite of a lower extremity, the victim is treated as a litter case. All constricting clothing items should be removed, total body warmth should be maintained, and sleep should be encouraged. Protect the injured part(s) from direct contact with clothing, bedding, and so on.

After rewarming, take care to leave any blisters intact. Dry, sterile gauze should be placed between toes and fingers to keep them separated. Elevate the affected part(s) and protect them from being rubbed or bumped. Seek medical attention for the victim.

HYPOTHERMIA

Hypothermia (low body core temperature) occurs when the body loses more heat than it produces. It can be fatal. Subfreezing temperatures are not needed for hypothermia to develop. Remember that if body temperature falls to 80°F (26.7°C), most people die.

Recognition

Hypothermia gives little warning. Two of the body's initial reactions to cold are goose pimples and shivering. If the heat produced by shivering does not keep up with heat being lost, the body's temperature will fall. The metabolic rate slows, resulting in mental and physical changes. Victims drop out of conversation and appear discouraged or depressed. They will become uncoordinated, with slow, labored movements. Simple tasks such as fastening a zipper are difficult. Judgment will fail completely. Hallucinations may occur.

Accurate recognition of hypothermia requires a thermometer that can reach a low temperature. A low-reading rectal thermometer (not the standard rectal thermometer) of sufficient length for obtaining a true core temperature is not usually available; therefore, a rough estimation of the victim's temperature can be made by using Table 10–3. Use caution when relying on shivering as the key symptom.

There are three types of exposure that cause people to become susceptible to hypothermia:

1. Acute or rapid-onset exposure
2. Subacute exposure
3. Chronic or long-onset hypothermia.

There are two recorded cases of victims surviving body temperatures as low as 60.8°F. Dorothy Mae Stevens (1929–74) was found in an alley in Chicago on February 1, 1951, and Vickie Mary Davis of Milwaukee, Wisconsin, at age 2 years 1 month was admitted to an Iowa hospital, in 1956, each with a temperature of 60.8°F. The little girl had been found unconscious on the floor of an unheated house and the air temperature had dropped to −24°F. Her temperature returned to normal after 12 hours and may have been as low as 59°F when she was first found.

Guinness Book of World Records

Rapid-onset or acute hypothermia most often results with cold water (below 70°F) immersion. Acute exposure is defined as six hours or less in duration. Subacute exposure is defined as longer than six hours but less than 24 hours and involves a land-based experience or immersion in water warmer than 70°F (21°C). Long-onset or chronic hypothermia happens

TABLE 10–3 Levels of Hypothermia

CLASSIFI-CATION	CORE TEMPERATURE	FINDINGS
	98.6° F (37° C)	Normal
Mild	95°–98° F (35°–37° C)	Vigorous shivering. Conscious and alert. Mild hyperventilation. Poor muscular coordination.
Moderate	90°–95° F (32°–35° C)	Uncontrollable shivering to decreased shivering as temperature drops. Level of consciousness declines to confused state. Mild hyperventilation which slows as temperature drops.
Severe	86°–90° F (28°–32° C)	Shivering stops and is replaced by muscle rigidity. Stupor progressing to coma. Respiratory rate slows to below normal. Pupils become dilated.
	82°–86° F (28°–30° C)	Coma. Respirations slow to ½ normal rate and below. Pupils are dilated and do not respond to light. Pulse either becomes slowed to less than ½ normal rate or becomes faster and irregular in rhythm. Cardiac arrest may occur.
	82° F and below (28° C and below)	Barely detectable respiration and pulse. Irregular pulse. Terminal ventricular fibrillation.

Reprinted with permission of *Journal of Emergency Nursing* (January, 1980), and Betty Alexy.

after exposure to cold weather for more than 24 hours on land in a victim who has inadequately prepared for the cold weather. This is how elderly people die in unheated homes or apartments.

First Aid

Victims suffering from hypothermia should *not* be transported in a sitting-up position—the head should be lower than the feet. Apparently the deficiency of oxygen to the brain that has been established by cold exposure is further aggravated by a vertical body position that makes it more difficult, because of gravity, to get blood to the brain. Move the victim to shelter and warmth as rapidly as possible. Gently remove all wet clothing. Apply heat to the central core of the body (head, neck, sides, and groin).

Any of the following warming methods are recommended:

Immerse the conscious victim in a tub of warm water (about 105°F). Keep the arms, legs, and head out of the water, because rewarming shock can occur as the body's circulatory system warms and dilates before the heart.

Apply warm, moist towels (or other clothes) around the victim's head, neck, sides, and groin. As the packs cool, rewarm them by adding warm water (about 105°F). Check the temperature with the elbow—it should be warm but not burn. Hot water bottles and heated blankets can also be used.

An effective method for remote situations is for one or two of the rescuers to remove their own clothing and use their bodies to warm the victim's unclothed body. Modesty should be maintained in both the rescuers and victim. A sleeping bag or blankets should be used to conserve the body heat.

CHANCES OF RECOVERY FROM HYPOTHERMIA:

91°F—Chances of normal recovery good
80–90°F—Victim will recover but there will be some sort of lasting damage
Less than 80°F—Most will not survive

Controversy over starting CPR exists. Refrain from CPR when the pulse (take one full minute to monitor) cannot be felt, *except* in acute hypothermia drownings. In these cases, the heart has not yet become cold and CPR should be given. Whereas, chest compressions can cause a heart to fibrillate in subacute and chronic hypothermia. If CPR has been started, it may have to be continued throughout a long rescue.

Dr. Cameron Bangs suggests the following don'ts and do's regarding first aid:

DON'TS IN HYPOTHERMIA FIRST AID

Do not put an unconscious victim in a bathtub.

Do not give the unconscious victim anything to drink.

Do not give the victim alcohol.

Do not rub frozen body areas, especially with snow.

Do not wrap a hypothermic in a blanket without a source of heat unless it is to protect the victim against further heat loss before treatment. Wrapping hypothermia victims in blankets without a heat source is ineffective because they are not generating sufficient heat to rewarm themselves, and the blanket insulates them from the warm environment.

Do not allow victim to move about, walk, or struggle.

Do not stop resuscitative attempts until the victim has been rewarmed and, preferably, evaluated at a medical facility.

DO'S IN HYPOTHERMIA FIRST AID

Handle the victim gently.

Remove wet clothing immediately.

Protect the victim from the wind.

Rewarm the victim by applying external heat slowly.

Always have the hypothermic victim evaluated at a medical facility as soon as possible.

If there are no heart sounds, no palpable pulse, no visible breathing, and the victim's body is cold, stiff, cyanotic, and pale, the person may be mistaken for dead. The fact that full recovery has been reported after complete cardiac arrest leads to the axiom that "no one is dead until he or she is warm and dead."

HEAT EXHAUSTION

Exhaustion or collapse in the heat is caused by excessive loss of water and salt from the body. It occurs commonly among persons working in hot indoor environments or from exposure to hot, humid heat while outdoors. Most vulnerable are alcoholics, young children, the obese, the elderly, and users of certain drugs. The circulation to such vital organs as the heart and brain is disturbed by the pooling of blood in the capillaries of the skin in order to cool the body. The capillaries constrict to compensate for this deficient blood supply, so the victim's skin appears pale and clammy. (See Figure 10–1.)

Weakness, dizziness, nausea, dim or blurred vision, and mild muscular cramps may signal the attack. There is profuse sweating. The guide to differentiate between heat exhaustion and heatstroke is skin temperature and moisture. The pulse will be fast and weak, the pupils dilated, and the respirations rapid and shallow.

Heat exhaustion needs care, but it is not usually life-threatening.

First Aid

Get the victim to a cool place. Also, remove all nonessential clothing and cool by bathing the victim with cloths soaked in cool water.

To improve the blood supply to the brain when fainting has occurred or seems likely to occur, the victim should be placed in a reclining position (elevate legs 8 to 12 inches) with all tight clothing loosened. Sips of cool water containing one level teaspoonful of table salt per quart should be given orally; approximately one half glassful should be given every 15 minutes for an hour. If the victim vomits, fluids by mouth should be stopped. Victims with heart problems or high blood pressure should receive no salt.

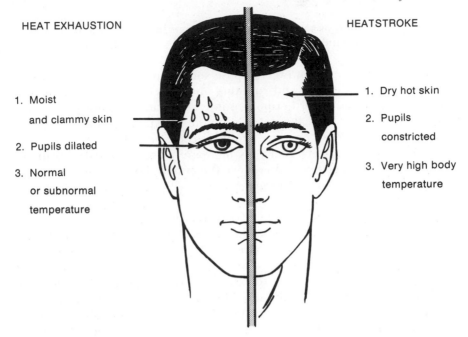

HEAT EXHAUSTION

1. Moist
   and clammy skin

2. Pupils dilated

3. Normal
   or subnormal
   temperature

HEATSTROKE

1. Dry hot skin

2. Pupils
   constricted

3. Very high body
   temperature

FIGURE 10–1 Symptoms of heatstroke and heat exhaustion.

The victim should be instructed to take it very easy for several days, and to avoid exposure to excessively high temperatures during that time.

HEAT CRAMPS

Heat cramps is a condition that affects individuals working in high temperatures. The severe pain and spasms of the abdominal or skeletal muscles occur as a result of profuse sweating and a failure to replace the salt loss. The cramps are usually more severe when the individual has been drinking large amounts of fluids without replacing the salt.

The cramps begin suddenly and occur most frequently in the muscles that bend the arms and legs. The victim may be lying down with the legs drawn up, while crying out from the severe pain. The skin may be pale and wet, and the temperature will be normal or slightly elevated. Usually there is no loss of consciousness. Although an untreated attack may last for hours, the condition is not considered dangerous.

First Aid

Most authorities indicate that salt intake should rapidly reduce the cramping. Sips of salt water in concentrations of one teaspoon of salt per quart of cool or tepid water are recommended. A much saltier concentration of one teaspoon of salt per glass of water at the rate of one half glass of water every 15 minutes up to one hour is suggested by the American Red Cross.

Most researchers, however, oppose such heavy salt solutions because they may promote nausea and vomiting and thus cause additional loss of fluids from the body. Furthermore, some authorities suggest that such a solution will draw cellular fluids and promote cramping. Victims with heart problems or high blood pressure should receive no salt.

Don't use salt tablets; they only increase nausea. Manual pressure to the muscle or massage may help relieve the cramp; however, some experts disagree by claiming that massage may actually aggravate the pain and rarely helps.

Water replenishment alone is probably insufficient, and it appears that some salt must be taken in to maintain the concentration of electrolytes. Heat cramps represent a chemical imbalance. Products such as Gatorade are effective.

Rest should be continued for one or two days depending upon the severity of the attack. The victim should be informed about the cause of the cramps and how to prevent recurrence by including more salt in the diet. This may pose a special problem for those with hypertension, because a common treatment excludes dietary salts.

Sustained body temperatures of much over 109°F are normally incompatible with life, although recoveries after readings of 111°F have been noted. Marathon runners in hot weather attain 105.8°F.

Guinness Book of World Records

HEATSTROKE

Heatstroke is a medical emergency that is associated with a potentially high mortality rate (greater than 50 percent). All untreated victims will die— they may even die when treated. *Heat exhaustion* may be regarded as the end result of overactive heat balance mechanisms that are still functioning. *Heatstroke* results when the body's heat regulatory activities are *not* functional, and the main avenue of heat loss (evaporation of sweat) is blocked. There may be early warning symptoms such as headache, uneasiness, and excessive warmth, or a general picture of heat exhaustion. The onset is usually abrupt, with sudden loss of consciousness, convulsions, or delirium. Sweating is absent in the typical case, and inquiry frequently reveals that this was noted by the victim prior to onset of the other symptoms. To differentiate between heatstroke and heat exhaustion, skin temperature and moisture should be noted.

On physical examination, the skin is hot, red, and dry. (See Figure 10-1.) In severe cases, tiny rounded hemorrhage spots (petechiae) may appear. Deep body temperature is high, frequently in excess of 106°F (41°C). The best indication of heat stroke is body temperature. A rectal temperature above 108°F (42.2°C) is not uncommon and indicates a poor outlook (prognosis) for the victim's future. The pulse will be rapid and strong and may go up to a count of 160 or more. Respiration may be rapid and deep. The pupils of the eyes will first contract, then dilate. Muscular twitching, cramps, convulsions, and vomiting may occur and may be followed by circulatory collapse and deep shock.

Types of Heatstroke

There are two basic types of heatstroke:

1. *Exertional heatstroke* can affect a healthy individual when the person works or plays with intensity. The skin of these victims may feel moist and cool rather than hot and dry. Nevertheless, the body temperature will be elevated to about 105°F or higher. High school athletes and military recruits are stricken most frequently.

2. *Classic heatstroke* is more apt to involve fluid and salt loss; it need not be associated with exertion at all. During periods of hot and humid weather, the disorder commonly affects the aged, the debilitated, the chronically ill, the obese, alcoholics, diabetics, and people with circulatory problems. Medications and drugs can increase the likelihood of heatstroke.

The highest dry-air temperature endured by naked men in U.S. Air Force experiments in 1960 was 400°F and for heavily clothed men 500°F. (Steaks require only 325°F for cooking.) Temperatures of 284°F have been found quite bearable in sauna baths.

Guinness Book of World Records

A temperature of 116°F was recorded for Willie Jones, age 51, of Atlanta, Georgia, on July 10, 1980 during a record-breaking heat wave. The 116°F was recorded after he had been immersed for 25 minutes in cold water. The attending physician said that his body temperature may have exceeded 120°F when first arriving at the hospital.

UPI release

Because of the extreme seriousness of heatstroke, everyone should be taught the importance of recognizing cessation of sweating so that corrective measures can begin at an early, reversible stage.

First Aid

Immediate treatment for heatstroke must be given to reduce the body temperature, or brain damage and death may occur. Critical body temperature is

over 104°F in an adult
over 105°F in a child.

The victim should be undressed and placed in a tub of cold water, covered with continuous cold packs such as wet blankets, or sponged with cold water until the temperature drops. The temperature should be taken every ten minutes and should not be allowed to fall below 101°F (38.3°C) in order to prevent convulsions. The skin should be massaged during this procedure to prevent constriction of the blood vessels, to stimulate return of the cooled blood to the overheated brain and other areas, and to speed up the heat loss. If the body temperature starts to rise, it will be necessary to begin the cooling procedure again.

The idea that prior victims of heatstroke become highly susceptible to later episodes is not medically substantiated. Certain cooling measures that may be considered for reducing body temperature such as aspirin, acetaminophen, and ice water enemas are not effective and should not be used.

Table 10-4 presents a summary of heat emergencies.

TABLE 10-4 Heat Exposure Emergencies

INDICATORS	HEAT CRAMPS (LEAST SERIOUS)	HEAT EXHAUSTION (SERIOUS)	HEAT STROKE (MOST SERIOUS)
Cause	Salt and water loss	Salt and water loss	Failure of heat-regulating mechanisms
Cramping	Present	May be present	Absent
Skin	Cool, moist	Cool, pale, moist	Hot, flushed, dry
Temperature	Normal	Normal or low	Very high
Pulse	Rapid	Rapid, weak	Rapid, bounding
First aid	Salt water solution, if tolerated by the victim	Cooling	Rapid cooling
		Reclining position, elevate legs	Semireclining position
		Salt water solution if conscious	Obtain medical care

Table 10-5 shows the apparent temperature (how hot the weather feels) at various combinations of temperature and humidity. When the apparent temperature rises above 130°F, heatstroke may be imminent. Between 105° and 130°F, heat cramps or heat exhaustion are possible. So is heatstroke, with prolonged exposure and physical activity. Between 90° and 105°F, heat cramps and heat exhaustion are possible with lengthy exposure and activity. Heat stress varies with age, health, and body characteristics.

TABLE 10-5　Apparent Temperature

RELATIVE HUMIDITY	AIR TEMPERATURE										
	70	75	80	85	90	95	100	105	110	115	120
	APPARENT TEMPERATURE*										
0%	64	69	73	78	83	87	91	95	99	103	107
10%	65	70	75	80	85	90	95	100	105	111	116
20%	66	72	77	82	87	93	99	105	112	120	130
30%	67	73	78	84	90	96	104	113	123	135	148
40%	68	74	79	86	93	101	110	123	137	151	
50%	69	75	81	88	96	107	120	135	150		
60%	70	76	82	90	100	114	132	149			
70%	70	77	85	93	106	124	144				
80%	71	78	86	97	113	136					
90%	71	79	88	102	122						
100%	72	80	91	108							

*Degrees Fahrenheit.
Source: National Weather Service.

Chapter 11

Bone, Joint, and Muscle Injuries

The skeleton forms the supporting framework of the human body (Figure 11-1). Injuries to the skeleton and other related parts (joints, tendons, ligaments, and muscles) are often seen by first aiders.

SPRAINS

A *sprain* is an injury to a joint in which the ligaments and other tissues are damaged by violent stretching or twisting. The ankle and knee joints are the ones most often sprained. Sharp pain and marked swelling are characteristic of this type of injury. Attempts to move or use the joint increase the pain. With severe sprains, the victim may be unable to use the injured hand or walk on the injured leg. The skin about the joint may be discolored because of bleeding from torn tissues (see Table 11-1).

It often is difficult to distinguish between a severe sprain and a fracture. The injury should be treated as a fracture until the advice of a physician can be obtained. It may be necessary to obtain an x-ray before the extent of the injury can be determined.

A severe lateral ankle sprain, if not correctly diagnosed and properly treated, will probably cause a chronically unstable ankle.

234

MEDICAL NAMES

COMMON NAMES

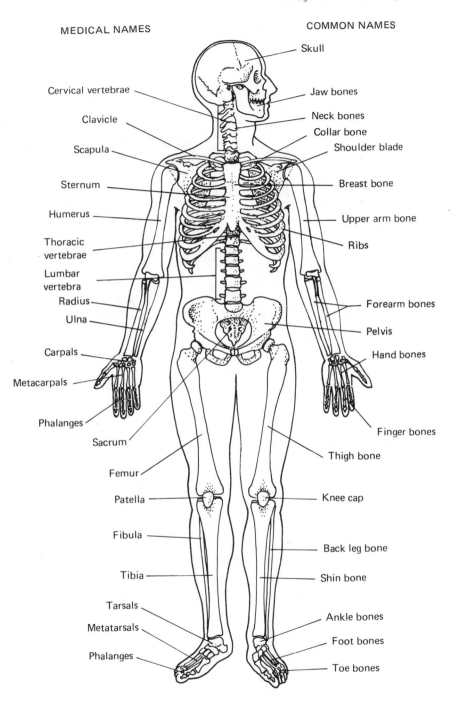

Cervical vertebrae

Clavicle

Scapula

Sternum

Humerus

Thoracic vertebrae

Lumbar vertebra

Radius

Ulna

Carpals

Metacarpals

Phalanges

Sacrum

Femur

Patella

Fibula

Tibia

Tarsals

Metatarsals

Phalanges

Skull

Jaw bones

Neck bones

Collar bone

Shoulder blade

Breast bone

Upper arm bone

Ribs

Forearm bones

Pelvis

Hand bones

Finger bones

Thigh bone

Knee cap

Back leg bone

Shin bone

Ankle bones

Foot bones

Toe bones

FIGURE 11–1   The skeletal system.

TABLE 11–1   Sprains, Strains, Dislocations

TYPE	POSSIBLE CAUSES	SIGNS & SYMPTOMS	EMERGENCY CARE
Sprain (stretching or tearing of ligaments about joint)	Sudden twisting of joint	Tenderness Black and blue Rapid swelling Loss of function Pain upon joint movement	Apply ice, compression, elevation for 24 hours Support injured part Limit exercise Apply heat in 48 hours only after no further swelling Contrast baths (hot/cold)
Strain (overstretching of muscles or tendons)	Heavy unexpected force, exertion of muscle beyond its limits	Stiffness Pain, acute and tearing Spasms	Rest muscle Apply cold first, heat in 24 hours or for back Exercise as tolerated Apply cold immediately after exercise, then heat
Dislocation (complete separation of bones of joint)	Twisting of bone near joint which pulls bone out of its socket	Loss of function Rigidity Deformity Pain about joint Swelling	Immobilize as for fracture Seek medical help

Source: *Emergency: The Journal of Emergency Services*, August, 1979, p. 59, and Alan Rabe. Reprinted with permission.

Classification of Sprains

Sprains may be classified as mild, moderate, or severe, as follows: mild—a stretching injury to a ligament without a tear; moderate—an incomplete tear; severe—complete tear of one or more ligaments.

Each degree of injury requires a specific treatment. However, the diagnosis cannot be made on the basis of appearance or amount of pain. A mild sprain often is considerably more painful than a severe one. A severe sprain frequently has very little swelling.

Initial care consists of elevation, applying cold compresses or ice packs to the injury site, and supporting with an elastic bandage. Remember the mnemonic ICE is a guide to sprains: Ice, Compression, Elevation. Refer to page 239 for details.

Swelling is like glue and can lock up a joint within a matter of hours. It is vitally important to prevent swelling by using cold promptly; it is even more important to make the swelling recede as quickly as possible with a compression bandage (elastic bandage).

Ligaments are bands of tissue that connect bone to bone or bone to cartilage, and serve to support and strengthen joints.
Tendons are cords that attach a muscle to bone.
Cartilage is tissue found in joints, at the developing ends of bones, and in specific areas such as the nose and ear.

It is better to break an ankle than to sprain it. Easier to diagnose and predictable in healing, the fracture is more easily dealt with.

Sir Reginald Watson-Jones

MUSCLE INJURIES

Muscle injuries are hard to explain to most first aiders because little solid information is available and there are misconceptions and disagreement on proper emergency care. For example, coaches and athletes frequently avoid medical attention and resort to "running it out" for almost any type of muscle injury.

Though muscle injuries pose no real emergency, first aiders and other emergency personnel have ample opportunities to care for them.

Muscle Strains

Another term often used for muscle strain is muscle pull. Skeletal muscles can both stretch and contract. However, if the muscle is stretched while attempting to contract, or it is stretched beyond its normal range of motion, a tear of the muscle fibers may occur.

Muscle strains are of various degrees of severity, depending on the degree of the actual muscle tear. One classification scheme uses four types of muscle strains. A *grade one* muscle tear is a tear of a few muscle fibers, with the fascia (protective covering of the individual muscle fibers) remaining basically intact. There is little loss of function, but some pain may be present.

A *grade two* muscle tear occurs when a moderate number of muscle fibers are involved in the tear, and most of the fascia remains intact. There will be some localized hematoma (inflammation and rupture of blood vessels), leading to swelling and discoloration in the area. There is a loss of function and more pain with a grade two strain.

A *grade three* is a muscle tear of many of the muscle fibers and also a partial tearing of the fascia. Diffuse bleeding often accompanies the grade three tear. A grade three muscle strain exhibits much more discoloration and indicates greater internal damage. Pain is often very severe and there is a significant loss of muscle function.

A *grade four* muscle tear is a complete tearing of the muscle and the fascia. There is much discoloration and pain with this type of injury. Muscle strength and range of motion may be totally lost at the particular joint involved. Though physicians may recommend surgical reattachment of the muscle, most physicians give little support to surgical repair of the completely torn muscle. A complete tear of a normal muscle is unusual, and few physicians have ever encountered one.

Signs of a muscle strain include the following:

1. The victim may have heard a snap when the tissue was torn.
2. A sharp pain may have been felt immediately after the injury.
3. There was a spasmodic muscle contraction of the affected part.
4. Extreme point tenderness occurs upon palpation.
5. Disfigurement may be seen either in the form of an indentation or cavity where tissues have separated or a bump indicating contracted tissue.
6. There is a severe weakness and loss of function of the injured part.

Muscle Contusions

Another category of muscle injury is the blow to the muscle or contusion. This injury is also known as a *charley horse*.

The term *charley horse* was derived from baseball players who experienced blows to muscles in the early twentieth century. At that time, the outfield grass of some of the major league ballparks was mowed by horses pulling lawn mowers. At Ebbit's Field in New York, the horse that did this chore was known as "Charley." Charley had a continual limp. When a baseball player was hit in the leg with a ball or received a blow to the leg muscle sliding into the base, which subsequently caused him to limp, it was said that the baseball player was limping like Charley the horse. Consequently, the muscle blow and contusion which caused an athlete's pain and limping was referred to as a charley horse injury. This term is still quite popular in America today.

Muscle Soreness

There are several theories about what actually happens when a muscle is sore. Probably the best known is that the muscle has a buildup of lactic acid. Lactic acid is a waste product of metabolism and is removed by the venous flow from the muscle. Another theory says that continued hard use of a particular muscle causes minute tears and irritation to some muscle fibers.

Much of the muscle soreness a person experiences may be the result of exposing the muscles to too much work for too long. It has been shown that gentle stretching exercises seem to relieve muscle soreness.

Muscle Cramps

Another category of muscle injuries is the muscle cramp, in which the muscle goes into uncontrolled spasm or contraction, resulting in severe pain and a restriction or loss of movement. Muscle cramps can occur in any skeletal muscle that is overworked.

When the cramp occurs in a leg or hand muscle, the victim may attempt to relieve it by gradually stretching or massaging the muscle. Because a muscle cramp is really an uncontrolled spasm or contraction of the muscle, a gradual lengthening or kneading of the muscle may help to lengthen those muscle fibers and relieve the cramp. Other experts have implicated diet or lack of fluids as possible reasons for muscle cramps.

First Aid for Muscle Strains and Contusions

Muscle injuries must receive prompt care to avoid delay in recovery. This is especially true of muscle strains. It is well known that a severely injured muscle does not regenerate itself. Healing is by scar formation. In fact, no muscle tear can heal completely in less than 25 days even though there may be no pain.

Even though the ice, compression, and elevation (ICE) protocol is used universally for immediate care of acute muscle strains and contusions, many first aiders and even emergency room personnel continue to treat fresh muscle injuries with heat packs.

Ice. The first initial in the acronym ICE stands for ice. Ice should be applied to the injured area for 20 to 30 minutes out of each hour for the first day if possible. This procedure may be used into the second day of injury. Frostbite will not occur if cold is applied for the suggested time periods.

Cold does not accelerate the healing process, but it does reduce the metabolic rate of the damaged tissue and thus limits the damage somewhat. Cold also constricts the blood vessels to and in the injured area, which helps reduce the swelling and at the same time dulls the pain and relieves muscle spasms.

Cold should be applied as soon as possible after the injury because healing time is often directly related to the amount of swelling that occurs. However, care must be taken to avoid tissue damage from the cold itself (frostbite).

There are several different ways to use cold on an injury:

1. Ice bags. Put crushed ice (or cubes) into a plastic bag or hot water bottle, wrap with a towel, and place over the injury. Apply a new bag for 20 to 30 minutes each hour for the first 24 hours. Hold the bag in place with an elastic wrap to help provide some compression as well as cold.
2. Refreezable ice packs. Use as described above. Never place directly on skin.
3. Cold packs. Chemical cold packs are convenient and can be used as described above, but quickly lose their cooling power and can be used only once. They may be impractical because of expense and the danger of breakage.
4. Immersion. Place injured part in cold tap water or ice slush for about 10 minutes. Vary the temperature for the person's comfort. Repeat throughout the day.
5. Ice massages. Freeze water in a styrofoam cup and peel the cup away to expose ice. Rub ice directly on and around the injured site for 3 to 10 minutes. Repeat throughout the day.
6. Frozen vegetable bag. As a last resort, use a frozen bag of vegetables (for example, peas) as described above. It quickly loses its cooling power and can be used only once.

A common error is the early use of heat. Heat will result in swelling and pain if applied too early. A minimum of 24 hours and preferably up to 48 or even 72 hours should pass before any heat is applied.

Compression.   The second initial, *C*, stands for compression. In an attempt to limit internal bleeding, a compression bandage is applied to the injured area. Often the compression bandage is applied directly to the site, ice is placed over the first layer of elastic bandage wrap, and more compression elastic wrap is put over the ice. The ice, together with the compression, helps limit internal bleeding, which is associated with all acute muscle injuries. Compression of the injured area may also aid in squeezing some fluid and debris out of the injury site. The victim should wear the elastic wrap continuously for 18 to 24 hours.

Elastic bandages may be applied too tightly and thus inhibit circulation. Leave fingers and toes exposed to allow observation of possible color change. Pain, pale skin, numbness, and tingling are all signs of a too-tight bandage.

Elevation.   The *E* stands for elevation. Elevating the injured area limits circulation to that area and, hence, further limits internal bleeding. It is simple to prop up an injured leg or upper extremity to limit bleeding. The aim is to get the injured part above the level of the heart, if possible. This should aid venous return to the heart.

DISLOCATIONS

A *dislocation* occurs with severe wrenching or twisting of a joint. The ligaments holding the bones in position are stretched and sometimes torn, and the bone ends are forced into an abnormal relationship. A dislocation is generally caused by a blow or a fall, or by strenuous lifting, pulling, or twisting in which a sudden, violent strain is placed on a joint.

Severe pain, rapid swelling, discoloration, and loss of ability to use the joint are characteristic symptoms of this injury (Table 11–1). The joint has a deformed appearance (a sprain does not) and is generally stiff and immobile. Although a fracture and dislocation can occur at the same time, fractures usually occur between joints. The joints most frequently dislocated are the shoulders and the fingers. The ankle joint often is dislocated and fractured at the same time.

Cold compresses may help to relieve the pain and to keep the swelling down. Treatment for specific dislocations will be discussed later.

FRACTURES

A fracture means a break in a bone. Fractures are classified as closed or open (see Figure 11–2).

A *closed (simple) fracture* is an injury in which the bone has been broken

FIGURE 11–2 Closed fracture (left) and open fracture (right).

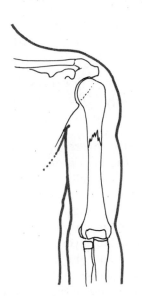

but does not break the skin. Surrounding tissues and blood vessels may suffer damage. Closed fractures that do not produce obvious deformities may be very difficult to detect and may not be discovered without an x-ray. Fractures should always be suspected following a severe injury. The type of accident that is most likely to cause a fracture is a sudden twist, sharp blow, fall, or crushing injury. A fracture may occur even though the injury seems relatively slight. For example, a fracture of the anklebone often is confused with a sprained ankle.

An open (compound) fracture is an injury in which the bone is broken and there is a wound through the soft tissues and skin. The skin is pierced by the bone end or by the external source that caused the fracture, such as a gunshot wound or penetrating materials. Careless handling of a victim may cause a closed fracture to become an open fracture by forcing the jagged ends of bone through intact overlying skin. An open fracture should be considered to be present when an open wound is located at or near the site of a fracture.

Extensive bleeding can accompany a major fracture, especially those of the pelvis and femur. This blood loss may be slow, so vital signs must be checked frequently to recognize the early appearance of shock. The following list demonstrates the amount of blood that can be lost within six hours after a fracture:

1. Pelvis—   1000–2000 cc (2.11–4.22 pints)
2. Femur—   500–1000 cc (1.05–2.11 pints)
3. Tibia-Fibula—   250–600 cc (0.52–1.26 pints)
4. Radius-Ulna—   250–500 cc (0.52–1.05 pints
5. Humerus—   150–350 cc (0.31–0.73 pints)
6. Ribs—   125 cc per rib (0.26 pints)

There are several types of closed and open fractures. Fractures are classified according to the appearance of the broken bone (Figure 11-3). Obviously, the first aider will not be able to identify the type of fracture a victim may have—in fact, such classification requires an x-ray.

Fractures, whether closed or open, usually cause severe pain. Although pain is generally present at the fracture site, the area around the injury may be tender to the touch. The best way for a first aider to determine a fracture is by palpation. Swelling almost always occurs immediately (although even a serious fracture may have little or no swelling when first seen) and discoloration of the skin may follow. It may be difficult or impossible for the victim to move the part beyond the injury. However, the fact that the part can be moved does not rule out the possibility of a fracture. The victim may be reluctant to move the part because of the severe tenderness and throbbing pain. Even if the bone is cracked, the part may be moved without difficulty. When the part is moved, the victim may feel a

TYPE OF FRACTURE		DEFINITION
1. Transverse		1. Usually produced by angulating force; once the fragments are aligned and immobilized, stability is assured
2. Oblique		2. Fragments tend to slip by one another unless traction is maintained
3. Spiral		3. Produced by twisting or rotary force; reduction difficult to maintain
4. Greenstick		4. Caused by compression force in long axis of the bone; often seen in children under age of ten
5. Compression		5. Usually produced by severe violence applied to cancellous bone, such as the spine
6. Comminuted		6. Always more than two fragments
7. Impacted		7. Produced by severe violence, driving bone fragments firmly together
8. Avulsion		8. Produced by forcible contraction of a muscle which pulls off a fragment of bone
9. Fracture dislocation		9. In addition to fracture there is a dislocation of the joint

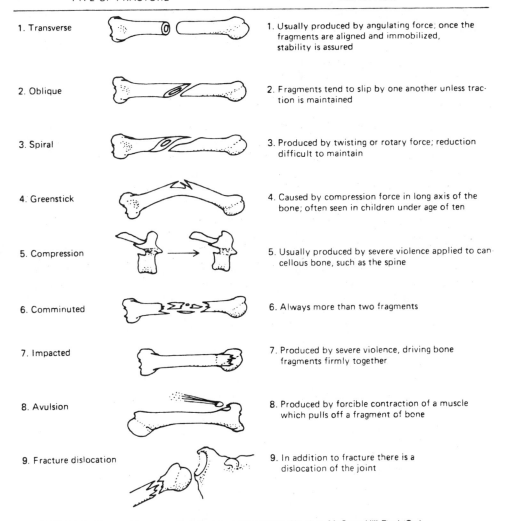

FIGURE 11–3 Types of fractures. (Adapted from *Emergency Nursing*, McGraw-Hill Book Co.)

grating sensation (crepitus) as the ends of the bones rub together. Unnecessary movements should be avoided because the grating may increase the damage to the bone ends, blood vessels, nerves, and soft tissue. The injured part may be deformed or may be in an unnatural position. One limb may be shorter than the other if the broken ends of the bone overlap. Open fractures may be accompanied by serious bleeding and shock is likely to develop, especially if a large bone is involved.

If a long bone in the arm or leg has been severely fractured, it should be straightened carefully before splinting. Traction should be applied on the hand or the foot, and the limb moved back into position. (See Figure 11–4). This tension should be maintained until the splint is in place. If any firm resistance occurs, terminate immediately and splint in the position in which it was originally found. During the straightening process, pain may be experienced—this is usually temporary and should be relieved once the splint is in place. Fractures of joints, such as the elbow, knee, shoulder, or wrist, should not be manipulated because of possible damage to nerve and blood vessels. They should be gently splinted as they are found; if straight, splint them straight, if angulated, splint them in the position found. Inflatable splints (see Figure 11–5) may be used for some fractures. However, many orthopedic surgeons do not like air splints because of first aider misuse. To provide adequate stability, the splint should be long enough to extend beyond the joints at the end of the fractured bone. Splinting will be covered in more detail later.

Uncorrected misalignment at fracture and dislocation sites can cause continued compression of the nerves. Damage to the blood vessels rarely occurs during the fracture manipulation associated with splinting and transport. For this reason, limbs and fractures and/or dislocations are best treated by restoring them to normal anatomic alignment and splinting them adequately.

Experienced orthopedic surgeons have never seen a case of blood vessel damage resulting from straightening a limb prior to splinting, and they advise first aiders to realign and splint extremity injuries in the correct anatomic position.

To treat extremity fractures and/or dislocations with associated vascular injury, first realign the limb to the normal anatomic position (do not use force) and then splint securely. This maximizes protection for both injured

FIGURE 11–4 Straightening a fractured limb.

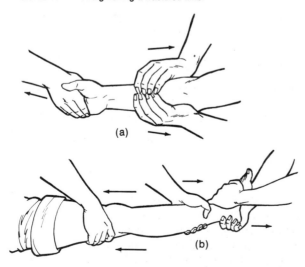

(a)

(b)

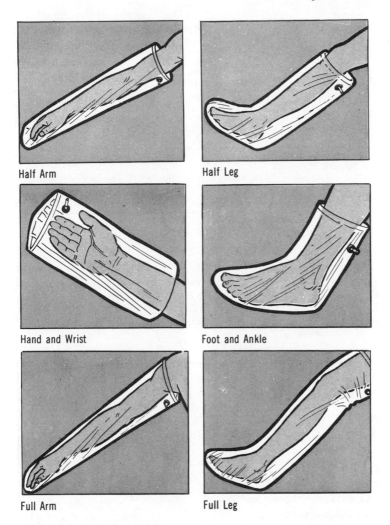

Half Arm

Half Leg

Hand and Wrist

Foot and Ankle

Full Arm

Full Leg

FIGURE 11–5 Inflatable air splints.

vessels and limbs during transport. The adage "Splint them where they lie" can be interpreted: Before transporting an accident victim, carefully return injured limbs to anatomic alignment by traction, and splint them adequately.

Angulations can be straightened by grasping the limb above and below the fracture site and gently pulling with the hand placed below the site. Do *not* attempt to straighten angulations involving the shoulders or wrists. Make one gentle attempt to straighten angulations of the elbow or knee only if there is no pulse below it. Do not attempt to straighten an ankle angulation if there is a pedal pulse.

When a bone is broken, a splint should:

1. Reduce the possibility that a closed fracture will be converted to an open one
2. Minimize the damage to nerves, muscles, and blood vessels that might otherwise be caused by the broken bone ends
3. Prevent the bone ends from moving around in the lacerated tissues and causing more bleeding
4. Lessen the pain that is generally associated with the unrestricted movement of broken bone ends.

Splint them where they lie.

Old first aid axiom

General splinting rules are as follows:

1. Straighten any severely angulated fractures of the long bones that can be straightened safely. The exceptions are those fractures involving joints (elbow, shoulder, wrist or knee). Fractures of the joints should be splinted where they lie. Never attempt to straighten fractures involving the spine.

AIR SPLINTS

Pros:
Comfortable
Easy to use

Cons:
Expensive
Easily punctured
Overinflation can hinder circulation
Circulation is hard to monitor
Skin sweats inside splint and if victim is outside in the cold, frostbite may occur
When brought from outside cold to warm room, the air tends to expand, making the splint tighter
If stored in cold surroundings, moisture may bind splint's walls together unless stored in a partly inflated condition

---

2. Do not attempt to reduce the fracture or push back any bone ends.
3. Immobilize the extremity before moving the victim and leave in place until medical care is begun.

4. Apply slight traction during splinting.
5. Splint firmly but not so tightly that circulation is impaired.
6. Pad splints to prevent excessive pressure and discomfort. Padding also helps hold the splint firmly in place.
7. When in doubt, splint.
8. Immobilize the joints above and below the fracture site as well as the injury itself.
9. Periodically check for tightness—pulse (radial for arm fractures and pedal for leg fractures), cyanotic color, skin temperature.
10. Listen to the victim's complaints about numbness or tingling.
11. Treat the more important injuries first—breathing, bleeding, shock. Fractures and dislocations of the extremities occasionally cause serious complications; they are rarely a threat to life.

Skull Fractures

A fracture of the skull may be caused by a fall, direct blow, crushing injury, or a penetrating injury such as a bullet wound. The victim may be conscious, unconscious, or dizzy, and may have a headache or nausea.

Skull fractures are usually determined by x-rays. They correspond to the classification of other bone fractures—either open or closed.

Specific types are

1. *Linear*—A linear fracture is a thin line crack in the skull.
2. *Comminuted*—In a comminuted fracture, cracks radiate from the center of impact similar to the pattern seen in a cracked egg.
3. *Depressed*—A depressed fracture has bone fragments pushed inward against the brain.
4. *Basal*—A basal (at the bottom or lower edge) skull fracture is difficult to detect even with x-ray. The loss of cerebrospinal fluid through the ears and nose is one of the best signs of a basal skull fracture.

When a head injury occurs—but an obvious wound is not present—these signs may indicate a skull fracture:

Pain, tenderness and swelling at the injury site.
Deformity of the skull.
Bleeding from ears, nose, or both.
Loss of cerebrospinal fluid (CSF) from ears, nose, or both, or a scalp wound, if present. Blood and cerebrospinal fluid will separate on a gauze pad in the "halo test," where CSF diffuses out away from a central spot of blood.
Discoloration of the soft tissues under the eyes.
Unequal pupils—an important sign of brain damage.
Bruise over the mastoid region (behind the ear)—called "Battle's sign."

Serious brain injury is more common when there is no skull fracture.

First Aid

The victim with a head injury should receive immediate attention to prevent additional damage to the brain. The victim should be kept lying down. If the face is flushed, the head and shoulders should be elevated slightly. If the face is pale, the head should be kept level with the body or slightly lower. Bleeding can be controlled by pressure bandages or from the edges of the wound. The victim should be moved carefully with the head supported on each side. Do not attempt to control the flow of CSF, as this may cause intracranial pressure to rise. Refer to page 127 for more information on skull injuries.

Upper Jaw

In all injuries of the face, an adequate airway must be considered first.

First Aid

If there are wounds, bleeding should be controlled. Dental consultation should be obtained after the victim has been transported to a medical facility. Preserve any knocked-out teeth because they sometimes can be reinserted (see page 137 for details).

Lower Jaw

A dislocation or fracture of the lower jaw may occur as a result of a direct blow or fall. The pain from the injury is likely to become severe when an effort is made to open or close the jaw. A fracture may cause a deformity of the jaw, missing or uneven teeth, bleeding from the gums, swelling, and difficulty in swallowing. Dental consultation should be obtained after the victim has been transported to a medical facility. Dislocation of the lower jaw may be associated with a fracture of the lower jaw and other facial injuries. A lower jaw dislocation may occur simply from opening the mouth too wide while yawning or eating. In the most common type of acute dislocation, the lower jaw is locked open, making eating and talking almost impossible. Medical advice should be obtained on the proper course of action.

First Aid

The injured jaw may interfere with breathing. If this occurs, the jaw and tongue should be pulled forward and maintained in that position. If unconscious, the victim should be placed on the side or on the stomach, with the face tilted to one side to avoid aspiration of blood, mucus, and vomitus.

Application of cold compresses may reduce the swelling and pain. The victim's jaw must be immobilized by closing the person's mouth as much as possible (depending on the degree of deformity) and applying a bandage [See Figure 11-6 for method (a) or method (b)]. If the victim is unconscious or bleeding from the mouth, or if there is danger of vomiting, an attendant must be present at all times to loosen the bandage in case of vomiting.

Nose

A fracture of the nose usually is caused by a direct blow. Generally, there will be pain, swelling, bleeding, and a deformity that is easy to detect.

First Aid

The victim should be positioned so the head is tilted slightly forward. If the bleeding does not stop in a few minutes, cold compresses or an ice bag should be applied to the injury (see page 133 on nosebleed). A permanent deformity of the nose may occur as a result of the fracture, so medical attention should be obtained.

FIGURE 11-6 Bandages for a fracture of the jaw.

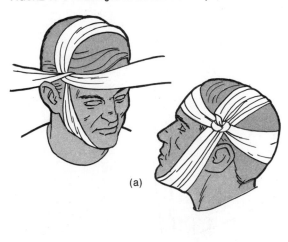

(a)

(b)

Clavicle

Fractures of the clavicle (collarbone) are common and are usually the result of falling with the hand outstretched. The force from the fall is transmitted to the shoulder. Usually the fracture is easy to detect because the clavicle lies immediately under the skin and a deformity can be seen easily. Also, the fracture can be detected by feeling the bone with the fingers and noting a tender or swollen area. There is pain and tenderness, and a grating sensation can be felt. The shoulder on the injured side may droop downward and forward.

First Aid

The fracture should be treated by supporting the arm in a simple sling on the injured side. The sling will remove weight from the clavicle, which helps to support the arm. The arm and sling should be secured to the body with a wide cravat bandage (swath). (See Figure 11-7.) Check

FIGURE 11–7   Applying a sling and cravat bandage.

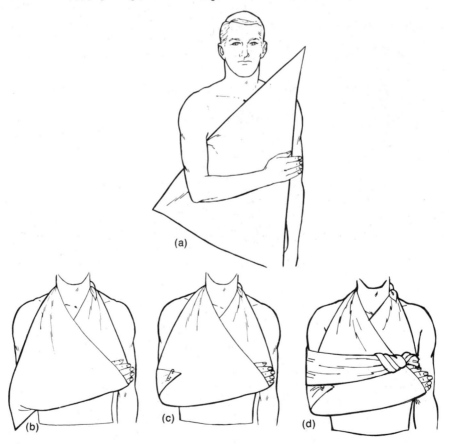

(a)

(b)   (c)   (d)

circulation at the radial pulse and neurological status by sensation in the fingers.

Some first aid books recommend a figure-of-eight bandage. This bandage may cause damage if the shoulder is dislocated rather than the clavicle broken.

Scapula

Fractures of the scapula (shoulder blade) are generally due to direct trauma and are not common. Usually they are simple fractures with little displacement. There is pain and swelling, usually coupled with inability to swing the arm. The victim should be examined further; associated injuries from the blow may be present.

First Aid

A sling should be applied to the arm on the injured side, and the sling and arm secured to the body by a wide cravat bandage (swath). (See Figure 11-7.)

Dislocation of Shoulder

An injury to the shoulder that results in complete loss of function is more apt to be a dislocation than a fracture. There is a sagging of the shoulder, with the elbow held away from the body at an awkward angle. Extreme pain is present in the shoulder region. The head of the humerus often may be felt in an abnormal position. A history of previous dislocations may be described by the victim.

First Aid

No attempt should be made to reduce the dislocation. The arm should be placed in a sling (see Figure 11-7) or splinted in the position found. Place a small pillow, folded towels, or some type of pad under the person's armpit. Secure sling and arm to the body by a wide cravat bandage (swath). Check circulation at the radial pulse and neurological status by sensation in the fingers.

Humerus (and Elbow)

Complications may occur in fractures of the humerus (upper arm and elbow) because of the closeness of the nerves and blood vessels to the bone. There is pain and tenderness at the fracture site and an obvious deformity may be present. Victims may be unable to lift the arm or bend the elbow.

First Aid

If there is no resistance, flex the arm to 90 degrees at the elbow and place in a sling, with the sling and arm secured to the body by a wide cravat bandage (swath). (See Figure 11-7.) One or two short padded splints, applied from elbow to armpit inside the arm and from elbow to the shoulder from the outside, may be used in addition to the previous procedure. (See Figure 11-8.) Do not extend the splint too far into the armpit. The elbow should not be bent if it does not bend easily. If there is any possibility that the elbow is involved in the fracture, the joint should be immobilized as found with a splint. This is because of potential damage to nerves and arteries caused by bone ends. (See Figure 11-9.) If straight, splint straight; if bent, splint bent.

Check the radial pulse and color and temperature in the fingers for signs of circulatory impairment. If the radial pulse has disappeared, carefully straighten or bend the elbow a *little* in an attempt to restore the pulse.

Radius and Ulna (Forearm)

There are two large bones (radius and ulna) in the forearm, and either one or both bones may be broken. When only one bone is broken, the other acts as a splint and there may be little or no deformity. However, a marked deformity may be present in a fracture near the wrist. When both bones are broken, the arm usually appears deformed. In any fracture of the forearm, pain, tenderness, swelling, and inability to use the forearm may be present.

First Aid

The fracture should be straightened carefully by applying gentle traction on the hand. (See Figure 11-4.)

Two well-padded splints should be applied to the forearm—one on the top and one on the bottom. (See Figure 11-10.) The splints should be long enough to extend from beyond the elbow to the middle of the fingers. The hand should be raised about four inches higher than the elbow, and

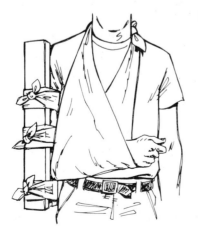

FIGURE 11-8 Splinting a fractured humerus.

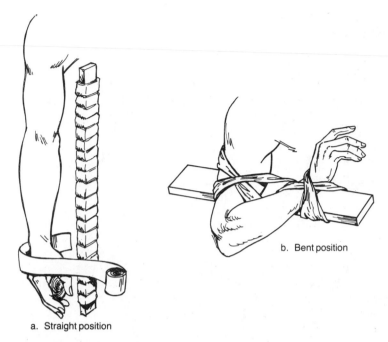

b. Bent position

a. Straight position

FIGURE 11-9 Dislocated or fractured elbow.

the arm should be supported in a sling. (See Figure 11-10.) An improvised splint (for example, folded pillow, newspapers, and so forth) can be applied if other splints are not available. Check for circulation at the radial (wrist) pulse.

Wrist

The wrist usually is broken by falling with the hand outstretched. Often a lumplike deformity occurs at the back of the wrist, along with pain, tenderness, and swelling.

First Aid

A fracture of the wrist should *not* be manipulated or straightened. In general, the fracture should be managed like a fracture of the forearm.

Hand

Crushed hand. The hand may be fractured by a direct blow or may receive a crushing injury. There may be pain, swelling, loss of motion, open wounds, and broken bones.

When there are open wounds, refer to Wounds and Bleeding (page 85). The hand should be placed on a padded splint that extends from the

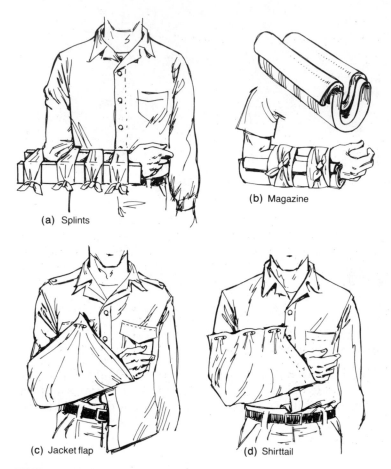

(a) Splints

(b) Magazine

(c) Jacket flap

(d) Shirttail

FIGURE 11-10 Splinting a fractured forearm.

middle to the lower arm to beyond the tips of the fingers. A firm ball of gauze should be placed under the fingers to hold the hand in a cupped position (position of function). Roller gauze, elastic bandage, or cravats may be used to secure the hand to the splint. (See Figure 11-11.) The arm and hand should be supported in a sling. (See Figure 11-7.) Often, further treatment is urgent, regardless of the severity of the injury, to preserve as much of the function of the hand as possible.

Finger fracture. Each of the four fingers has three bones, and the thumb has two bones. The fracturing of a finger is rather common. When it occurs, it is evident because there is pain, deformity, swelling, and inability to use the part. The finger or thumb may be fractured by a direct blow, a crushing injury, a blow to the end of the finger, or when forced into sudden flexion or hyperextension. Finger fractures are common in physical activities, especially football, basketball, and baseball.

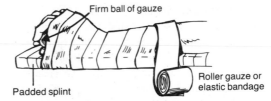

FIGURE 11-11
Splint for crushed or fractured hand. Padded splint

Firm ball of gauze

Roller gauze or
elastic bandage

If the finger is injured, it could be a sprain, a dislocation, or a fracture. Only an x-ray can tell for certain the nature of the injury. In all three situations, the finger should be immobilized. The finger can be immobilized with a splint in the position the finger is found. If the finger is straight, a padded tongue blade can be placed under the finger and secured in place with a roller gauze bandage or adhesive tape (see Figure 11-12).

Most injured fingers will be found in the position of function (cupped). Place a ball of gauze or pad of cloth under the victim's fingers to hold them in a cupped position (Figure 11-11). Roller gauze, elastic bandage, or several cravat bandages may be used to secure the hand and fingers to the splint.

Taping the injured finger to an adjacent finger is another alternative procedure recommended by some authorities. After splinting, the arm should always be placed in a sling with the hand slightly elevated above the height of the elbow.

Unattended broken fingers and injured joints may leave permanently crippled fingers.

To aid in identifying a fractured finger, some experts suggest that in a suspected finger fracture the victim should be asked to place the hand palm down on a table with fingers extended. Exert light pressure over the victim's fingers and tap each fingertip with your finger in the direction of the finger's long axis. If no sharp pain results in the area under suspicion, there is probably no fracture. Nevertheless, the finger should be x-rayed and a physician should make the diagnosis.

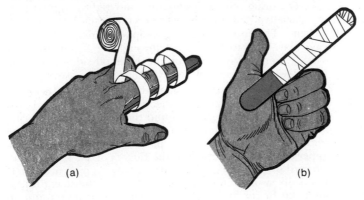

(a)

(b)

FIGURE 11-12 Dislocated or fractured finger.

Dislocated finger.   The fingers are injured easily, and even a minor injury may cause a dislocation. The injury is recognized readily by the abnormal position of the two adjoining bones (looks like a lump at the joint). There will be pain, swelling, and shortening of the finger, and the victim may be unable to bend the finger in the injured area.

Unskilled efforts to correct a finger dislocation can easily damage blood vessels and nerves or even produce fractures. In most situations, any attempt to correct the deformity should be avoided. However, correction is justified in certain circumstances or in relatively remote areas.

Most finger dislocations occur at the second joint and may be easily corrected immediately after the dislocation by pulling on the injured finger.

Thumb dislocations are usually accompanied by a fracture of the bone at the base of the thumb.

The injured finger should be immobilized with a splint using a procedure described earlier for a fractured finger. The victim should be examined by a physician as soon as possible.

Ring-strangulated finger.   Most rings stuck on fingers are removed with a combination of lubrication and gentle tugging. Sometimes a finger is too swollen for the ring to be removed in the usual manner. A ring cutter makes removal simple. But if the ring is valuable or you don't have a ring cutter, the following techniques might be tried:

1. Slide the ring off after lubricating the finger with grease, oil, butter, petroleum jelly, or some other slippery substance.
2. Immerse the finger in ice water for several minutes in an effort to reduce the swelling. Move the ring to a point on the finger where it is loose. Gently massage the finger from tip to hand; this may move the fluid from the swollen area. After a few minutes of massaging, lubricate the finger again and try to slip the ring off.
3. Start about three-quarters of an inch from the ring edge and smoothly wind string around the finger going toward the ring with one strand touching the next (Figure 11–13). Continue winding smoothly and tightly right up to the edge of the ring. The advantage of this method is that it tends to push the swelling toward the hand. The end of the string is slipped under and through the ring. The string may have to be pushed through by a matchstick or toothpick. The string is then slowly unwound on the hand side of the ring while the ring is gently twisted off the finger over the spiraled string.
4. Slide three or four inches of thin string under the ring toward the hand (Figure 11–13). The string may need to be pushed through with a matchstick or toothpick. Then wrap the string tightly around the finger below the ring for about three-quarters of an inch. Each wrap should be right next to the one before. While holding the wrapping snugly in place with the fingers of one hand, grasp the upper end of the string with the fingers of the other hand. Pull the string downward over the ring. This starts an unwrapping process. If the finger is not too badly swollen, the ring may slide over the string that is still wrapped around the finger and continue to move as you continue to

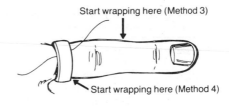

Start wrapping here (Method 3)

Start wrapping here (Method 4)

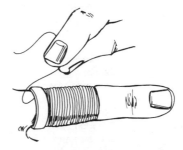

FIGURE 11–13 Removing a ring.

unwrap. It may be necessary to repeat the procedure several times to get the ring completely off the finger.

5. Carefully cut the thinnest portion of the ring with a ring cutter, ring saw, jeweler's saw, or a fine hacksaw blade. If anything other than a ring saw is used, take care to protect exposed portions of the finger.

It should be remembered that gangrene may result within four or five hours.

Spine

The treatment of a fractured spine should minimize shock and prevent further injury to the spinal cord. If a victim complains of acute pain in the back or neck following an injury, it is advisable to treat the injury as a fracture, even if no other symptoms appear.

Cervical (neck). The victim usually will complain of severe pain at the site of the fracture, with tingling or numbness. If the spinal cord has been damaged, there may be paralysis down from the site of the fracture (see Table 11–2). Usually there is severe shock, which may not be observed for a period of time.

A cervical spine injury must be suspected in all accident cases. Each year about 10,000 to 15,000 new spinal cord injuries occur. There is 50:50 ratio between quadriplegia (all four extremities paralyzed) and paraplegia (lower extremity paralysis).

TABLE 11-2   Signs and Symptoms of Spinal Cord Injury: Summary of Observations and Conclusions

EXTREMITY	OBSERVATION	CONCLUSION
Legs	Can feel touch Can wiggle toes Can raise legs	Probably no injury to spinal cord
Arms	Can feel touch Can wiggle fingers Can raise arms	
Legs	Cannot feel touch Cannot wiggle toes Cannot raise legs	Probable injury to cord somewhere below neck
Arms	Can feel touch Can wiggle fingers Can raise arms	
Legs	Cannot feel touch Cannot wiggle toes Cannot raise legs	Probable injury to cord in area of neck
Arms	Cannot feel touch Cannot wiggle fingers Cannot raise arms	

Source: Grant and Murray, *Emergency Care* (Bowie, Md.: Robert J. Brady Co., 1978).

Any forceful blow to the head or neck must be expected to result in spinal injury. Falls from more than 20 feet and motor vehicle accidents are the leading causes of such damage. Assessment of conscious victims poses few problems. However, assessment of unconscious victims does present difficulties.

Unconscious victims with cervical spine injuries often exhibit one or more of the following signs:

Abdominal breathing. Although abdominal breathing is a normal finding in the healthy, sleeping person, exaggerated movement of the abdominal area for the purpose of respiration warns of cervical trauma.

Penile erection. Rarely looked for, erection of the penis in the unconscious victim strongly suggests spinal injury.

Hand-up posture. Victims lying either supine or prone, with arms and hands raised over their heads, often have spinal damage.

Trapezius pinch. If pinching the victim's trapezius muscle (side of the neck) does not cause the same side pupil to dilate, spinal or head injury should be suspected.

First Aid

To treat a fractured neck, one person should hold the victim's head straight and apply gentle traction while another person applies a cervical collar (see Figure 11-14). Using several people, the victim should be rolled onto the side while the neck is supported; a long spine board is placed alongside (see Figure 11-15). The victim should be rolled onto the board in a supine (face-up) position and strapped securely to it. An unconscious person with suspected cervical spinal injury should be immobilized and transported on the side or in prone position (see page 40).

If a spine board is not available, any long board may be used. This board should be long enough and wide enough to contain completely the victim's head and body. If a cervical collar is not available, the victim's head should be held straight and gentle traction applied during turning and positioning on the spine board. Traction should be maintained until the head is immobilized completely. Clothing, about the thickness of a rolled bath towel, should be placed under the neck to support it. A sandbag or similar material should be placed on each side of the head, and the head should be secured to the board with cravat bandages.

For cervical fractures, a short spine board also can be used, depending on the position and location of the victim. It should be placed behind the victim, and all straps secured. (See Figure 11-16.) Then the victim should be placed on a long spine board and transferred. Moving a victim with spinal injuries is dangerous. We are not talking about a victim's discomfort but about the difference between the person walking again or being a quadriplegic. In most cases the first aider should *not* move the spinal injured victim unless the victim's life is endangered. Waiting for the

FIGURE 11-14 Cervical collar.

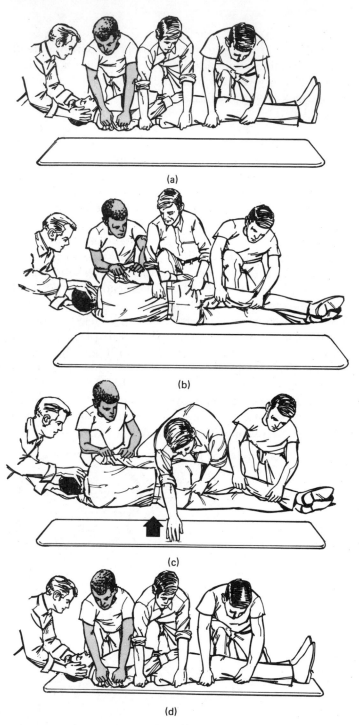

(a)

(b)

(c)

(d)

FIGURE 11–15   Application of a full backboard.

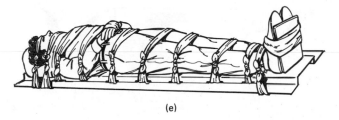

(e)

FIGURE 11-15 *(cont.)*

paramedics or emergency medical technicians is well worth it because of their training and equipment.

Thoracic and lumbar (back). The symptoms of a fractured back are similar to the symptoms of a fractured neck. If the spinal cord is damaged, paralysis may occur below the site of the injury (Table 11-2). Pain may be severe, or there may be a little discomfort with only a tender area around the spine. As with all spinal fractures, the danger lies in the possibility of damage to the spinal cord. *Correct handling of the victim is crucial.* The slightest displacement of a fractured vertebra may damage the spinal cord, producing paralysis below the point of injury.

Contrary to popular opinion, a person can be paralyzed for life even though the spinal cord has not been completely cut in two.

First Aid

Refer to Cervical (Neck) First Aid, page 259, for rolling and positioning of the victim on a long spine board. *The victim's body must not be twisted or bent when moving, or further damage may occur to the spinal cord.* It is best to splint the back in the original position of deformity. The proper position must be maintained, and the victim should be cautioned against undue movement. First aiders should normally wait for paramedics or other rescue squads to transport the victim because of their training and equipment. If the victim needs transporting before paramedics or other rescue squads arrive, and if there is time, practice first on an uninjured person.

Rib

A fractured rib is a common chest injury and is usually caused by a direct blow or crushing injury. There will be pain at the fracture site, with little displacement or deformity. There may be severe pain when breathing, bending, or coughing. The victim may press the hands against the chest to prevent painful movement. If the lung has been punctured, bright

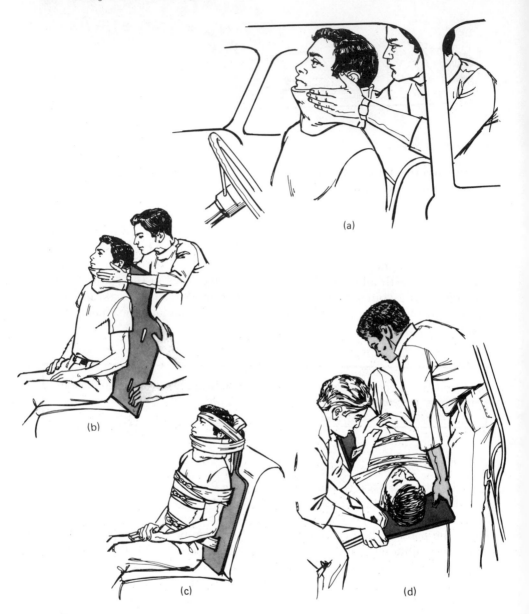

FIGURE 11–16   Application of a half backboard.

red, frothy blood may be coughed up. Asking the victim to place a finger at the injured site can often help determine the injury location.

First Aid

If the victim is fairly comfortable, it will not be necessary to apply anything to the chest. If there is severe pain, the ribs can be immobilized somewhat by placing the arm of the injured side across the chest as shown in Figure 11–17. Apply overlapping cravats around the body. Tighten the cravats as the victim exhales. Place in a sling for elbow support. Refer to page 117 for treatment of a punctured lung.

Hip

Dislocation of hip.   A hip may be dislocated by a fall, a blow to the thigh, or direct force to the foot or knee. There will be severe pain and loss of motion, and a marked deformity may be present. The most common deformity has the victim's leg rotated inward with the knee bent. The foot may hang loose, and the victim is unable to flex the foot or lift the toes.

First Aid

No attempt should be made to reduce a dislocation of the hip. The injury is serious and should be treated only by a physician. The victim should be transported on a long spine board. (See Figure 11–15.) A blanket, pillow, or other suitable padding should be used to support the legs in the position of the deformity.

Fracture of hip.   A fractured hip is usually caused by a fall. There is severe pain in the groin area, and the victim may not be able to lift the injured leg. The leg may appear shortened and be rotated, causing the toes to point abnormally outward. Shock generally will accompany this type of fracture.

FIGURE 11–17   Care for rib fractures.

Place arm of injured
side across chest

Bind arm to chest with
wide cravat

Repeat with two additional
cravats, overlapping
bandages slightly

Tie fourth cravat along
angle of arm for support

First Aid

A fracture of the hip can be splinted with a half-ring traction splint—a Thomas or Hare Traction Splint. (See Figure 11–18 and page 267 under Femur First Aid.) If one is not available, a well-padded board splint should be placed from the armpit to beyond the foot. Another well-padded splint should be placed on the inner side of the leg from the groin to beyond the foot. The splints should be secured in place with an adequate number of ties, and both legs tied together to provide additional support. (See Figure 11–19.) Still another method is to place pillows or folded blankets between

FIGURE 11–18   A traction splint is the best emergency treatment for a femur fracture. The proper application requires two trained rescuers with previous practice. The sequence of steps in applying a traction splint is given here.

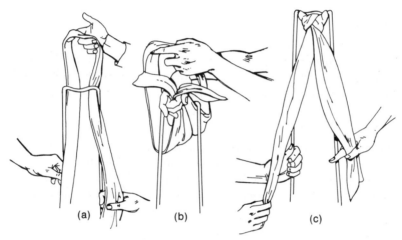

(a)   (b)   (c)

Step 1. Prepare the splint

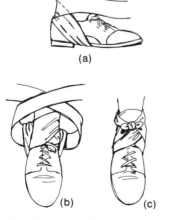

Step 2. Apply sprained ankle bandage   Step 3. Apply traction

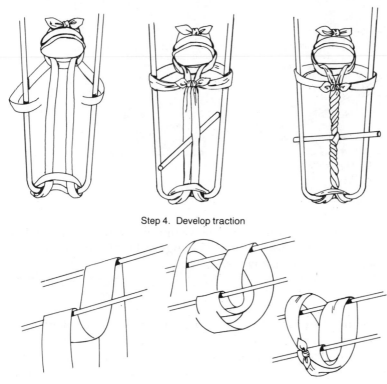

Step 4. Develop traction

Step 5. Form cradle hitches

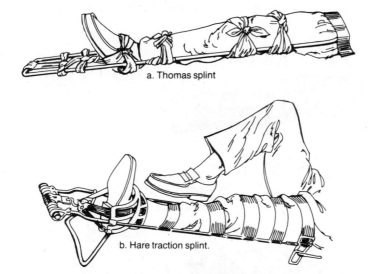

a. Thomas splint

b. Hare traction splint.

Step 6. Secure support hitches

FIGURE 11–18 *(cont.)*

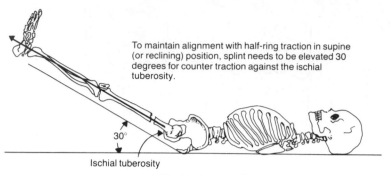

To maintain alignment with half-ring traction in supine (or reclining) position, splint needs to be elevated 30 degrees for counter traction against the ischial tuberosity.

30°

Ischial tuberosity

Step 7. Elevate splint

FIGURE 11–18   *(cont.)*

the legs and then tie the legs together. The victim should be transported on a long spine board to a medical facility. (See Figure 11–15.) If a backboard is not available, a stretcher may be used.

Pelvis

Pelvic fractures are usually caused by falls, crushing accidents, and sharp blows. Severe pain, shock, internal bleeding, and the loss of ability to use the lower extremities may be present. The bladder may be injured or ruptured, as well as other organs that are protected by the pelvis. Victims will have massive internal bleeding.

Compressing the sides of the pelvis at the iliac crests (hip pointers) with your hands should produce pain in the fractured pelvis and help confirm the diagnosis. (See page 34.)

FIGURE 11–19   Femur fixation splint.

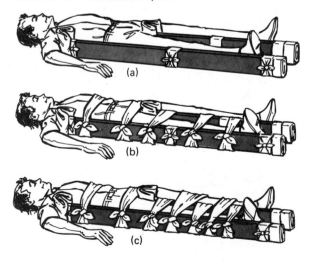

(a)

(b)

(c)

First Aid

The victim with a fractured pelvis should be treated for shock but not placed in a shock position. A long spine board or rigid stretcher will provide the necessary support during transportation. If possible, three to four people should be used to lift the victim onto the spine board. (See Figure 11-15.) Rolling the victim may cause additional internal damage. A pad should be placed between the victim's thighs, and the knees and ankles should be bandaged together. The victim may be placed on the spine board with the knees straight or bent, whichever position is more comfortable. If the knees are flexed, padding should be placed under them for support. The victim should be secured firmly to the spine board both above and below the pelvis. (See Figure 11-20.)

If medical care by a physician is to be delayed, the victim with a pelvic fracture is best treated by placing the person on a bed that has a firm mattress or a board under the mattress.

Femur

A fracture of the femur (thigh) is usually caused by a fall or direct blow. There is severe pain, a shortening of the leg, deformity, and a grating sensation. The limb has a wobbly motion, and below the fracture there is a complete loss of control. Severe damage to the nerves and blood vessels may occur. Victims may lose nearly a quart of blood, so treatment for shock should be given.

First Aid

The injured leg should be straightened carefully by applying gentle traction on the leg. (See Figure 11-18, Step 3.) If a long period of time will elapse before medical attention is available, the fracture should be splinted with a half-ring traction splint—a Thomas or Hare Traction Splint—which uses the ischial tuberosity as the point for countertraction. To be effective, the victim must either sit up or elevate the leg in a 30-degree position (Figure 11-18, Step 7). The traction of the limb will reduce pain and tissue damage during transportation because it counteracts the spasm and pull of

FIGURE 11-20 Pelvis fixation splint.

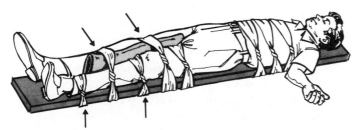

the large, powerful thigh muscles. Traction will align the bone and minimize nerve, blood vessel, muscle, and bone damage. Padding between the upper thigh strap and the leg are essential in allowing proper circulation. A traction splint is difficult to apply, and specific training is needed by a first aider. If a traction splint is not available, the fracture may be splinted with long, well-padded board splints (Figure 11-21). For the procedure, see fracture of the hip, page 264.

There are two rules to remember when using a mechanical traction splint: First, once traction is applied, it should not be released; second, apply only enough traction to immobilize and realign the bone ends.

Knee

A fracture of the knee generally occurs as a result of a fall or a direct blow. Besides the usual signs of a fracture, a groove in the kneecap may be felt. There will be an inability to kick the leg forward, and the leg will drag if an attempt is made to walk.

First Aid

The leg should be immobilized in the position found to prevent further damage to nerves and blood vessels. If the leg is straight, a padded board splint can be used under the leg to keep it straight, or two board splints (one on the inside and the other on the outside) can be placed on the leg. If bent, the knee should be immobilized in the bent position. When splints are not available, a pillow or a blanket may be used to immobilize the knee. Check the pedal pulse for signs of circulatory impairment. If there is no pulse, try moving the leg to a straight anatomical position. Do not force the leg. Stop if there is any resistance. Make only one attempt to straighten.

The broken bone, once set together, is stronger than ever.

John Lyly (1554–1606)

Tibia and Fibula (Lower Leg)

Fractures of the tibia and fibula (lower leg) are common and occur as a result of various accidents. There is a marked deformity of the leg when both bones are broken. When only one bone is broken, the other acts as a splint and little deformity may be present. When the tibia (the bone in the front of the leg) is broken, an open fracture is likely to occur. Swelling may be present and the pain usually is severe.

First Aid

The leg should be straightened carefully, to normal position if possible, using slight traction. (See Figure 11-4.) Do not use force. A well-padded splint should be applied to each side of the leg. The splints should extend from the middle of the thigh to beyond the heel. (See Figure 11-21.)

Check for circulation after immobilization is complete by palpating the pedal pulse (see page 35).

Ankle and Foot

A fracture of the ankle or foot is usually caused by a fall, twist, or a blow. Pain and swelling will be present, along with marked disability.

It is often difficult to differentiate between a fracture and a sprain of the ankle. If you cannot tell, splint the part. Treat any injury to the foot or ankle as a fracture.

For fractures of the ankle and foot, shoes or boots should be removed to allow for a better examination and for checking pulse and temperature. The following is a suggested procedure for taking off boots.*

1. Tell the victim that the boot needs to be removed and explain how you will do it.
2. Obtain consent, if possible, from the victim to cut the boot.
3. Have another person elevate and support the knee and ankle during the boot removal.

*Adapted from the *Journal of Emergency Nursing*, January 1980.

FIGURE 11-21 Splinting fractures of tibia and fibula.

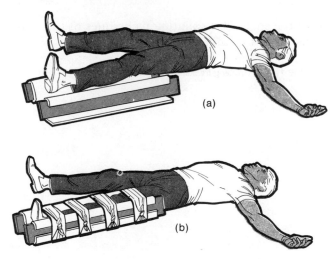

(a)

(b)

4. It is usually best to cut the boot at an inner seam for two reasons: (1) seams can be resewn, thus preserving the boot for future use and (2) boot decoration is usually on the outer side of the boot and thus won't be destroyed.

5. To prevent laceration of the victim's skin, position your hand adjacent to the knife or scissors, depressing the skin while cutting the stitching. Do this slowly. The seam should be cut to the sole of the boot.

6. After the seam is cut to the sole, with another person supporting the ankle and knee and elevating the leg, slip your hand carefully under the heel and slowly remove the boot over the toes.

First Aid

If conventional splints are applied, the ankle should be well-padded with a pillow. If wood splints are used, apply them to each side of the leg, extending from the midcalf to beyond the foot.

Molding a pillow carefully around the foot and ankle, and then securing it with cravat bandages or safety pins, is the recommended splint for ankle and foot fractures. (See Figure 11–22.)

Toe

A fractured toe is usually caused by a crushing injury or by kicking the foot against a hard object. There is pain and swelling, and a deformity may be present.

First Aid

If necessary, the injured toe can be bandaged to the next toe to provide support or splinted with a tongue depressor.

Splinting Summary

For a quick review of the suggested splinting techniques of the most common fracture locations, refer to Table 11–3.

FIGURE 11–22 Splinting fractures of ankle and foot.

TABLE 11–3 Splinting Fractures

SITE	SUGGESTED IMMOBILIZATION
Clavicle	Sling and swath
Humerus	One or two short board splints with wrist sling and swath
Elbow	Splint it as found—*Straight:* One board splint on inside of arm—*Bent:* One or two board splints to create triangle with elbow being apex; wrist sling
Radius/ulna	Two board splints/newspaper and sling and swath
Hand	Splint in position of function, sling
Finger	Tongue depressor splint, splint in position of function, or tape injured finger to adjacent finger, sling
Ribs	Place arm of injured side across chest; bind arm to chest with three wide swathes, and sling elbow for support
Pelvis	Tie legs together and use long spine board or rigid stretcher
Hip	Same as for femur (see following), and use long spine board or rigid stretcher
Femur	Traction splint or one long board splint from ankle to armpit and another board splint from groin to ankle; or, for short distance, tie injured leg to uninjured leg
Knee	Splint it as found—*Straight:* One board splint from buttocks to ankle—*Bent:* One or two board splints to create triangle with knee being apex
Tibia/fibula	Two board splints—one on inside and other on outside of leg
Ankle/foot	Pillow splint
Toe	Tape injured toe to adjacent toe or tongue depressor splint

Chapter 12

Sudden Illness

HEART ATTACK (Acute Myocardial Infarction)

A history of hypertension, angina pectoris, or a previous heart attack will help confirm the diagnosis of a heart attack. Chest pain centered behind the breastbone is the most significant sign and is not intermittent or pulsating. Generally it is described as a pressure or squeezing sensation. The pain builds in intensity over the first minutes and lasts from a half hour to several hours. Pain may travel to the left shoulder or left arm, the lower jaw, or upper abdomen. Less often, it radiates to the right shoulder or right arm. Sweating, nausea, and a feeling of impending death are often associated features. The pain is not relieved by changes in body position or affected appreciably by breathing. A victim who goes into shock or acute heart failure may not survive. (See Figure 12-1.)

About one million people in the United States experience acute myocardial infarction each year. More than 650,000 of these result in death, and 350,000 of these deaths occur outside the hospital, usually within two hours after onset of symptoms. Sudden death from heart attack is the most important medical emergency today.

American Heart Association

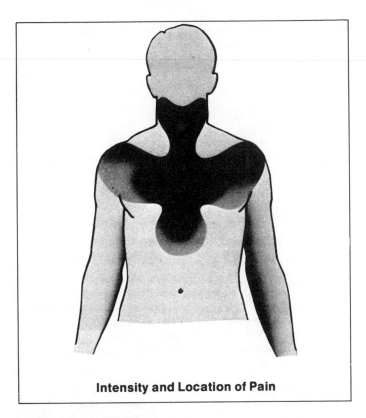

Intensity and Location of Pain

KNOW THE SIGNALS

The Signals of Heart Attack

- ■ Uncomfortable pressure, fullness, squeezing or pain in center of chest lasting 2 minutes or more.

- ■ Pain may spread to shoulders, neck or arms.

- ■ Severe pain, dizziness, fainting, sweating, nausea or shortness of breath may also occur.

FIGURE 12–1 Heart attack. (Reproduced with permission, © *Heart Facts 1985*, American Heart Association)

PREDICTOR OF HEART DISEASE

Several studies have found a statistical link between the incidence of heart disease and the creases on the ear lobe. Paramedics responding to heart attacks have also noticed a preponderance of victims having ear lobe creases. The person may be more likely to have gummed-up coronary arteries, which increase the risk of a heart attack.

Some victims with heart attacks do *not* have chest pain. They may have fainting, shortness of breath, or palpitations. Because belching and vomiting are common with heart attacks, one should not be misled and attribute the chest pain to indigestion.

First Aid

The conscious victim suspected of having a heart attack should be placed in a half-sitting position. Heart attack victims should not be allowed to move themselves. Comfort and reassure the victim, and loosen clothing

Medical attention always should be obtained. Evacuation should be arranged as soon as possible. Monitoring respiration and circulation is essential if the victim is unconscious because mouth-to-mouth or cardiopulmonary resuscitation (CPR) may be needed.

---

*HOW TO HELP A POSSIBLE HEART ATTACK VICTIM.**

You can best help—possibly save a life—if you know in advance: (1) The nearest hospital equipped to handle heart attack emergencies. (2) How to do Cardiopulmonary Resuscitation (CPR). (3) How quickly to call a doctor, the hospital and/or an ambulance. (4) The fastest route to the hospital. Knowing these things, you should:

1. Help victim to least painful position—usually sitting with legs up and bent at knees. Loosen clothing around neck and midriff. Be calm, reassuring.
2. Quickly call ambulance to get victim to hospital via local rescue squad, police, fire or other available service. Once the ambulance is on the way, notify family physician, if you have one.
3. If ambulance is coming, comfort victim while waiting. Otherwise, help victim to car, trying to keep victim's exertion to minimum. If possible, take another CPR-trained person with you. Victim should sit up.
4. Drive cautiously to hospital. Watch victim closely (or have other passenger do so). If he or she loses consciousness, check for breathing, and feel for neck pulse under side angle of lower jaw to check for circulation. If no pulse, start CPR. Continue CPR until trained help arrives to take over.
5. If victim retains consciousness to hospital, make sure he or she is carried, not walked, to emergency room.

*Courtesy of the Metropolitan Life Insurance Company.

ANGINA PECTORIS

Angina pectoris occurs when the blood flow to the heart is temporarily inadequate to meet its oxygen needs. The major importance of angina pectoris is that it indicates a person is prone to a heart attack.

The pain of angina pectoris resembles that of a heart attack. Usually it is a squeezing, steady pain, centered behind the breastbone. Pain may radiate to the same body areas as in a heart attack. However, the pain is different in that it is brought on by physical exertion, exposure to cold, emotional stress, or by the ingestion of food. It seldom lasts longer than ten minutes and almost always responds to nitroglycerin. A heart attack is as likely to occur at rest as during activity. This pain lasts much longer than ten minutes and does not respond to nitroglycerin. Table 12–1 describes the differences between angina and heart attack.

First Aid

Nitroglycerin dissolved under the tongue is the most commonly used medication for angina pectoris. Nitroglycerin tablets should not be swallowed because the acid juices of the stomach destroy the therapeutic effect.

Victims suffering their first attack of angina pectoris should be treated the same as victims of a heart attack. The same treatment should be given to victims with a long history of angina pectoris whose attacks are more frequent or more easily triggered. Frequent easily provoked attacks often precede a heart attack. Medical advice should always be obtained. The pain is usually relieved by rest and lasts three to eight minutes and rarely longer than ten minutes.

STROKE

A stroke occurs when the blood supply to some part of the brain is interrupted. This generally is caused, as shown in Figure 12–2, by:

TABLE 12–1   Chest Pain—Differences Between Angina and Heart Attack

CHARACTERISTIC	ANGINA	HEART ATTACK
Intensity	Mild to moderate pressure; tightness; "squeezing," "viselike"	Severe pressure; "crushing," "stabbing," "viselike"
Duration	Usually less than 15 minutes and not more than 30 minutes. Average is 3 minutes	Last ½ to 2 hours
Precipitating factors	Exercise, stress, cold weather	May occur at rest or with exercise or stress
Relieving factors	Rest	Not relieved by rest
Effect of nitroglycerin	Often relieves	No effect
Associated symptoms	May be none	Often shortness of breath, nausea, vomiting, sweating, dizziness, feeling of impending death

Adapted from Nancy Caroline, *Emergency Care in the Streets*, 2nd ed. Copyright © 1983, Little, Brown and Company, p. 248.

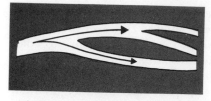

Hemorrhage

The wall of an artery of the brain may break, permitting blood to escape and thus damage the surrounding brain tissue.

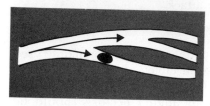

Thrombosis (clot formation)

A clot of blood may form in an artery of the brain and may stop the flow of blood to the part of the brain supplied by the clot plugged artery.

Embolism (blocking of a vessel by a clot floating in the blood stream)

A clot from a diseased heart or, less commonly, from elsewhere in the body may be pumped to the brain and stop up one of the brain's arteries.

FIGURE 12–2 Mechanism of a cerebral vascular accident.

A blood clot forming in the blood vessel (cerebral thrombosis)

A rupture of the blood vessel wall (cerebral hemorrhage)

Obstruction of a cerebral blood vessel by a clot or other material from another part of the vascular system that flows to the brain (cerebral embolism)

Pressure on a blood vessel, as by a tumor

Tightening of a blood vessel.

A stroke usually occurs suddenly, without warning signs. In more severe cases, there is a rapidly developing loss of consciousness and a flabby, relaxed paralysis of the affected side of the body. Headache, nausea, vomiting, and convulsions may be present. The face usually is flushed but may become pale or ashen. The pupils of the eyes are often unequal in size. The pulse is usually full and rapid, and breathing is labored and irregular. The mouth may be drawn to one side, and often there is difficulty in speaking and swallowing. (See Figure 12–3.)

The specific symptoms will vary with the site of the lesion and the extent of brain damage. Mild cases may experience no loss of consciousness, and paralysis may be limited to weakness on one side of the body.

The outcome of a stroke will depend upon the extent of brain compression or damage. When stroke is fatal, death usually occurs in two to 14 days and seldom at the time of the attack. Most victims with first or second

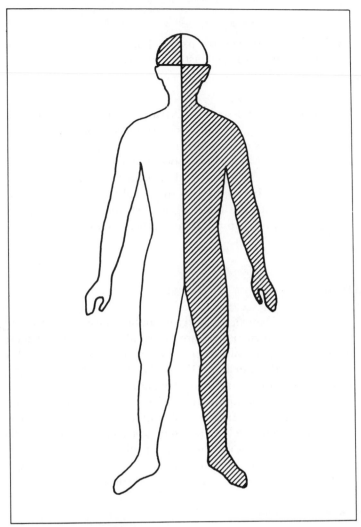

KNOW THE SIGNALS

The Warning Signals of Stroke

- ■ Sudden, temporary weakness or numbness of the face, arm and leg on one side of the body.

- ■ Temporary loss of speech, or trouble in speaking or understanding speech.

- ■ Temporary dimness or loss of vision, particularly in one eye.

- ■ Unexplained dizziness, unsteadiness or sudden falls.

FIGURE 12–3   Stroke. (Reproduced with permission, © *Heart Facts 1985*, American Heart Association)

attacks recover, but recurrent attacks are likely. The extent of permanent paralysis will not be determined for at least six months.

First Aid

Good care is essential after a stroke. Extra care should be taken to prevent the victim from choking on saliva or vomitus. The unconscious victim should be placed on one side face down so fluids can flow out of the mouth. Keep the airway open. Mucus and food debris should be removed from the mouth with a piece of cloth wrapped around a finger. If there is a fever, cold compresses should be applied to the forehead. The conscious victim should be laid down with the head slightly elevated—don't elevate the legs. Do not give any liquids. Immediate medical advice must be obtained.

DIABETES MELLITUS

In diabetes mellitus (sugar diabetes), the body is unable to use or to store all of the sugar derived from the carbohydrates normally eaten. The excess sugar remains in the blood and spills over into the urine, carrying water with it. This loss of sugar and water from the body causes increased appetite and thirst, frequent urination, and loss of weight.

Diabetics do not produce enough insulin, which is a hormone secreted into the blood by the pancreas. The function of insulin is to take sugar from the blood and carry it into the body cells to be used. The excess sugar remains in the blood, and the body cells must rely on fat for fuel. For a diagrammatic explanation, refer to Figure 12-4. Adjustments in the metabolism of sugar have to be made by changing the diet and/or the amount of insulin.

Insulin Shock (Hypoglycemia)

Insulin shock will occur if too much insulin is given, too little food eaten, a meal delayed too long, or an unusual amount of exercise or work is done (Figure 12-5). Prior to becoming unconscious, the victim may have emotional changes, a headache, numbness and tingling, poor coordination, a staggering gait, and slurred speech. Also, convulsions may occur. When the blood sugar falls below the normal level, the victim may appear pale, break out in a cold sweat, and have a rapid heartbeat (see Table 12-2).

First Aid

When an insulin reaction occurs or when there is doubt as to the cause of unusual behavior or unconsciousness, the conscious victim should be given sugar or sugar-containing substances or beverages. Many diabetics

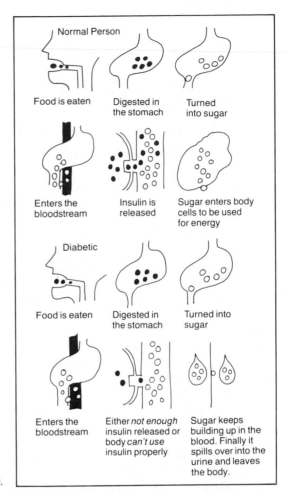

Normal Person

Food is eaten   Digested in   Turned
                the stomach   into sugar

Enters the   Insulin is   Sugar enters body
bloodstream   released   cells to be used
                                for energy

Diabetic

Food is eaten   Digested in   Turned into
                the stomach   sugar

Enters the   Either *not enough*   Sugar keeps
bloodstream   insulin released or   building up in the
                 body *can't use*   blood. Finally it
                 insulin properly   spills over into the
                                        urine and leaves
                                        the body.

FIGURE 12–4
Insulin and the utilization of food.

carry candy for such an occasion. An appropriate dose is four heaping teaspoons of sugar in some water. Diet soft drinks are ineffective.

For an unconscious victim, give nothing by mouth because the victim cannot swallow without the risk of mouth contents entering the airway. However, a cube of sugar or loose sugar may be placed under the tongue of an unconscious person because some sugar is absorbed through the lining of the mouth. Observe the victim closely until the sugar is dissolved because it could become displaced from under the tongue and lodge in the victim's trachea. Anyone with a disoriented state of consciousness should be suspected of being in insulin shock. If untreated, brain damage or death can occur rapidly.

Emergency treatment *must be administered first*, and immediate transportation to a medical facility is required.

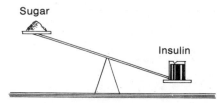

FIGURE 12–5
An excess of insulin is the cause of insulin shock.

Diabetic Coma (Hyperglycemia or Ketoacidosis)

Overindulgence in food that contains or produces sugar, too little insulin, injury, or decreased activity can lead to increased blood sugar (hyperglycemia) and an increased loss of sugar and water in the urine (Figure 12-6). With insufficient insulin, the body is not able to convert all of this sugar into energy. Then fat normally stored in the body is broken down for energy, and poisonous acidlike substances accumulate.

Some of these substances excreted in the urine as acetone or ketones can be detected with commercial products. Some of these acid products are exhaled from the lungs and give the breath a peculiar sweetish odor. These substances also cause dryness of the mouth and rapid, deep respirations (air hunger). The victim may be thirsty, the skin dry, and the eyeballs soft and sunken due to the loss of fluid. Abdominal pain, slight fever, nausea, and vomiting may occur. Many of these signs also suggest alcoholic intoxication. The treatment for diabetic coma occasionally has been delayed, with either irreversible damage or fatal results, because the breath odor was thought to be that of alcohol.

First Aid

If not treated, diabetic acidosis may cause unconsciousness (diabetic coma) and eventually death. *The most important step in treatment is to give fluids if the victim is conscious and to transport the victim to a medical facility.*

If the rescuer cannot distinguish between diabetic coma and insulin shock, and sugar is available, have the victim take it. It cannot appreciably hurt the victim in diabetic coma, and it may save the life of a victim or avoid brain damage in insulin shock.

EPILEPSY (And Other Convulsive Seizures)

Epilepsy is a chronic nervous disorder characterized by muscular convulsions with partial or complete loss of consciousness. Epilepsy may vary from mild to severe. In the mild form (petit mal), there is momentary loss of consciousness or confusion and slight muscular twitching without falling.

TABLE 12–2   Diagnostic Signs in Diabetic Emergencies

	DIABETIC COMA	INSULIN SHOCK
History:		
Food	Excessive	Insufficient
Insulin	Insufficient	Excessive
Onset	Gradual—days	Sudden—minutes
Appearance of patient	Extremely ill	Very weak
Skin	Red and dry	Pale and moist
Infection	May be present	Absent
Gastrointestinal system:		
Mouth	Dry	Drooling
Thirst	Intense	Absent
Hunger	Absent	Intense
Vomiting	Common	Uncommon
Abdominal pain	Frequent	Absent
Respiratory system:		
Breathing	Exaggerated air hunger	Normal or shallow
Odor of breath	Acetone odor usual (sweet, fruity)	Acetone odor may be present
Cardiovascular system:		
Blood pressure	Low	Normal
Pulse	Rapid	Normal, may be rapid
Vision	Dim	Diplopia (double vision)
Nervous system:		
Headache	Present	Absent
Mental state	Restlessness merging into unconsciousness	Apathy, irritability merging into unconsciousness
Tremors	Absent	Present
Convulsions	None	In late stages
Urine:		
Sugar	Present	Absent
Acetone	Present	May be present
Improvement	Gradual, within 6 to 12 hours following administration of insulin	Immediate improvement following oral administration of carbohydrates (glucose, candy, orange juice, gingle ale, sugar)

Source: American Academy of Orthopaedic Surgeons, *Emergency Care and Transportation of the Sick and Injured* (Menasha, Wis.: George Banta, 1981).

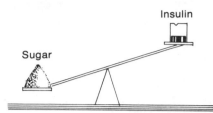

FIGURE 12-6
Insufficient insulin is the cause of diabetic coma.

In the severe form (grand mal), the victim suddenly falls as if struck by an overwhelming blow. Grand mal seizure is characterized by convulsions due to a sudden abnormal stimulation of brain cells (see Table 12-3). An epileptic may have a seizure any time and frequently may have some forewarning of the attack.

First Aid*

Although petit mal is a common type of epilepsy, it does not generally require emergency treatment. On the other hand, both grand mal and psychomotor seizures may generate fear and anxiety in persons who are unaware of their cause.

Grand Mal

An individual suffering a grand mal seizure normally should not require special assistance. Most seizures last only a few minutes. In many cases, the convulsions may have ended by the time competent help is available. Victims who are conscious should be allowed to rest and then be encouraged to go about their regular activities. If the victim is unconscious, neckties, tight clothing, and belts should be loosened. The face should be turned gently to the side to allow drainage of saliva and mucus from the mouth. A responsible person should stand by until the victim has fully recovered consciousness. No special efforts should be made to arouse or restrain the victim. Awakening should be voluntary. If the victim is still convulsing when help comes, he or she should, again, not be restrained or held in any way. Victims should be allowed to remain in the same place for the duration of the seizure, unless this is a precarious location, such as a busy street. If necessary, the person may be moved to prevent injury from hard or sharp objects. If possible, however, these hazards should be moved and not the victim.

In certain cases, it may be necessary to apply a minimum restraint to the person, generally because of a potentially dangerous environment. In these circumstances, the victim may be turned on the side and held by a firm grip on the shoulder until the convulsions have ended.

*Reprinted with permission from "Recognition and First Aid for Those with Epilepsy," by the Epilepsy Foundation of America.

TABLE 12–3 Epilepsy

INDICATORS	PETIT MAL	GRAND MAL	PSYCHOMOTOR
		TYPES	
Convulsions	NO	YES	Probably NOT
Appearance	Staring, day-dreaming	Unconscious, convulsions	Inappropriate or purposeless behavior
Loss of body control	Minor convulsive movements of eyes or extremities	Convulsions—loses control of faculties —may defecate, vomit or urinate.	
Duration of attack	Less than one minute	2 to 5 minutes	2 to 5 minutes
Conscious of surroundings	YES	Probably	NO
Premonition prior to attack	NO	YES	
Emergency care	Lay victim down with coat under head Do *NOT* restrain victim (allow seizure to run its course) Do *NOT* force object between victim's teeth Protect victim from injury Maintain airway (use mouth to nose if necessary) Protect from on-lookers and peers Provide rest after seizures.		

Prepared by Alan N. Rabe. Reprinted with permission.

It is physically impossible for the victim to swallow the tongue during a seizure. However, the victim may bite the tongue or cheek as the teeth become tightly clenched. Never force anything between them. By this time the tongue has or has not already been bitten and there is no point in forcing the mouth open. Attempts to do so often cause damage to the teeth and/or gums. Further damage may result if fragments of broken teeth are taken into the lungs during a deep breath before the victim becomes fully conscious.

A special type of grand mal epilepsy is known as *status epilepticus*. In this type, the victim goes from one grand mal seizure into another without regaining consciousness. This condition may last for several hours and is a definite medical emergency. The victim should be placed in a hospital or under the immediate attention of a physician.

Psychomotor

The major problem in the handling of psychomotor cases is the recognition of the symptoms. The unusual behavior of the psychomotor victim is often mistaken for that of a drunk. A cardinal rule in the handling of any epileptic seizure is that the victim should not be restrained in any way unless it is essential for the person's personal safety. This is particularly true in the case of psychomotor epilepsy. Here the victim may react violently to the restraint although unaware of his or her actions.

The observable effects of an average psychomotor seizure last about 15 to 20 minutes. During the seizure the victim is in a confused mental state but is usually amenable to suggestions and comments made in a pleasant and friendly manner. It is possible to control the actions of the person in this way for the duration of the seizure unless it is a very long one. If any question still remains, the victim should be examined by a physician, preferably a neurologist.

First Aid for Grand Mal Seizure

1. *Keep calm* when a major seizure occurs. You cannot stop a seizure once it has started. Do not restrain or try to revive the person.
2. *Clear the area* of hard, sharp, or hot objects that could cause the victim injury.
3. *Do not force anything between the teeth.* If the victim's mouth is open, you may place an airway between the side teeth. (*Author's note:* Most first aiders neither know how to use an airway nor will they have one.)
4. *Turn the victim on the side*, and make sure breathing is not obstructed. Loosen necktie and tight clothing but do not interfere with the person's movements.
5. *Do not be concerned* if the victim seems to stop breathing *temporarily. Do be concerned* if the victim seems to pass from one seizure to another without gaining consciousness. This is rare, but it is a true emergency that requires a doctor's immediate attention.
6. Carefully observe the victim's actions during the seizure for a full medical report later. When the seizure is over, let the victim rest if he or she wishes.

Almost no one with known seizures who is not having great difficulty with seizures needs to go to the emergency room. The person should go to an emergency room if seizures are uncontrolled, if there is breathing difficulty, or if the person has never had a seizure before.

Other Conditions That May Cause Convulsions

Convulsive seizures do not occur only with grand mal epilepsy. They may indicate an unsuspected illness or poisoning by any of a variety of chemical agents. In the case of children, particularly those under the age of ten, convulsions may develop as a consequence of high temperatures associated with many diseases. These feverish convulsions do not always indicate epilepsy, although they do indicate a predisposition to the disorder. Infections of the brain, for example, meningitis or encephalitis, may result in fever and convulsions. Hence, adequate medical attention is required to rule out presence of any of these major diseases.

Many common household chemicals, as well as most insecticides, fungicides, germicides, and rodenticides, are highly toxic. They give rise to a variety of symptoms, often including convulsions, depending on their composition and ultimate concentration in the body. Ingestion may occur through swallowing, inhalation of dust or fumes, or absorption through the skin. Early symptoms include nausea, vomiting, weakness, pallor, respiratory difficulty, and headache, depending on the particular poison. These in turn may be followed by convulsions and prostration or coma.

The appearance of unusual symptoms prior to the onset of convulsions is a possible indication of some type of acute poisoning. A grand mal seizure invariably occurs without warning to others, apart from a sharp cry some individuals may utter at the onset of the seizure. Therefore, any history or complaints of physical discomfort by the victim before going into convulsions should be considered as possibly indicative of poisoning. The first aid rendered would then be based on the presence of a toxic agent in the body rather than the relatively simple procedures required for grand mal epilepsy.

Summary

Persons experiencing an epileptic seizure can easily be mistaken for drunks or drug addicts. They should be searched immediately for emergency medical information (necklace, bracelet, or wallet card) and checked for alcoholic breath.

Epileptic seizures cannot be stopped, and the victim should not be restrained in any way. If the victim is unconscious, clear away hard, hot, or sharp objects that could cause injury, and loosen tight clothing, necktie and belt. Gently turn the person on the side to permit saliva to escape. Do not force anything between the teeth. Protect the head if it is against a hard surface. Let the seizure run its course and permit the victim to rest afterward.

Medical assistance is generally not necessary except in rare cases of status epilepticus, in which the victim goes from one grand mal seizure into another. This may last for hours and is a definite medical emergency requiring a doctor or hospitalization.

Not all seizures indicate epilepsy. Toxic agents and high temperatures may also result in convulsions. In rare instances, convulsions may be associated with a major heart problem.

BLEEDING (Respiratory and Digestive Tracts)

It is sometimes difficult to differentiate between bleeding from the respiratory tract and bleeding from the digestive tract. Blood from the nose, throat, or lungs may be swallowed; thereafter it will have the same appearance in the stool as blood from the digestive tract. To find the source of blood discharged from either the mouth or rectum, the factors that follow must be considered.

The blood may be bright red, leaving no doubt that it is blood; or it may not look like ordinary blood. If vomited and partly digested, the blood will appear dark and granular like coffee grounds. The vomitus mixed with partly digested food and other stomach contents makes for further confusion. Also, blood may give a stool a black appearance like tar.

There may be much or only a little bleeding. Sputum may be only blood-streaked, as in some mouth diseases. A teaspoonful or more of bright blood may be coughed up or vomited if the trouble is farther down the throat, in the lungs or in the stomach. A pint or more of partly digested material like coffee grounds may be vomited. Or there may be smaller or larger amounts of bright red blood usually from a local disease of the anus or rectum, such as piles or a tumor. Digested blood in tarry stools usually occurs in large amounts.

Bleeding from the digestive or respiratory tract usually does not produce pain or other obvious signs or symptoms, except those associated with considerable loss of blood, such as faintness, weakness, dizziness, pale moist skin, and rapid thready pulse.

Tables 12–4 and 12–5 list some of the usual characteristics of respiratory and digestive tract bleeding.

The cause of the bleeding will determine treatment. In all cases of bleeding from the lungs or the gastrointestinal tract, the victim should see a doctor. Unless the bleeding stops promptly, immediate evacuation may be necessary.

TABLE 12–4   Blood in Stools

COLOR AND APPEARANCE	AMOUNT AND METHOD	MOST LIKELY SOURCE	CAUSE	REMARKS ON TREATMENT
Bright red	Streaked feces	Lower end of digestive tract: hemorrhoids, anal fissure	Constipation (hard fecal matter that injures mucous membrane), local injuries, fissures, piles, cancer	If present with every stool and not reduced by cathartics which soften stools, see doctor.
Bright red	Teaspoonful or more	Lower end of digestive tract	Ulcer or tumor of rectum, ulcerative colitis, dysentery, typhoid	See doctor.
Tarry	Abundant	Upper part of digestive tract	Stomach or duodenal ulcer; gastritis; liver; kidney or heart disease; typhoid; dysentery; tumor; cancer	Symptomatic treatment. See doctor.

Source: U.S. Public Health Service, *The Ship's Medicine Chest and Medical Aid at Sea*, U.S. Department of Health, Education, and Welfare.

TABLE 12-5 Bleeding From the Mouth

COLOR AND APPEARANCE	AMOUNT AND METHOD	MOST LIKELY SOURCE	CAUSE	REMARKS ON TREATMENT
Bright red	Blood-streaked sputum	Local: From mouth tissues, gums, throat, back of nose	Pyorrhea, cold in head, laryngitis, pharyngitis	Mouthwash or other symptomatic treatment. See dentist.
Bright red	Coughed up (teaspoonful or more)*	Lungs	Tuberculosis of lung, cancer	Symptomatic treatment (see below). See doctor.
Bright red	In sputum or phlegm: Coughed up, frothy, bubbly, pink or red	Lungs	Heart disease	Symptomatic treatment (see Heart Disease). See doctor.
Brown (like prune juice)	In phlegm: Coughed up (½ to 1 teaspoonful)	Lungs	Pneumonia	See doctor.
Bright red	Vomited (cupful or more)	Stomach	Hemorrhage from ulcer, cancer, ruptured vessel. Probably very recent or still continuing	Symptomatic. Use icebag.
Dark brown (like coffee-grounds)	Vomited (usually considerable in amount; one pint or more)	Stomach (old blood, mixed with partly digested food)	Stomach or duodenal disease, or blood swallowed after extraction of tooth. Bleeding probably occurred 2 or 3 hours previously, and has stopped or lessened in amount	Ulcer, cancer.

Source: U.S. Public Health Service, *The Ship's Medicine Chest and Medical Aid at Sea*, U.S. Department of Health, Education, and Welfare.

*Coughed-up blood may result from a paroxysm of coughing or it may come from the back of the throat without any great amount of coughing, until the blood actually is in the mouth.

ASTHMA

There are about 10 million asthmatics in the United States, over half of them children. Ninety-five percent of all chronic respiratory disease in children is asthma, and 5 to 10 percent of the population are believed to be affected at some time in their lives. Because it is a chronic disease, asthma accounts for many absences from school and work. Asthma kills 4,000 to 5,000 of its victims each year.

There is nothing new about asthma. The Egyptians knew about it as early as 5000 B.C. The early Greeks named it *asthma*, meaning "panting" or "breathing hard." In 460 B.C. Hippocrates discovered that cold and dampness can cause asthma. Fifth-century Romans prescribed breathing exercises, long walks, and fresh air to relieve the condition. By the mid-seventeenth century, doctors had learned that dust, pollen, and certain foods could trigger an attack.

The treatment of asthma was dictated by superstitions. Past "cures" included eating raw cat meat, eating only boiled carrots for two weeks, and collecting spider webs, which were rolled into a ball in the palms of the hands and then swallowed.

Even today asthma is surrounded by myths. The U.S. Public Health Service cites examples of current folk remedies: rubbing tomato paste on the chest, carrying around a small dog, stroking a Chihuahua toward the head of the victim, eating a diet of chicken livers, tilting the head back and balancing a penny on the forehead, hanging certain aromatic wood from the ceiling or above the door, standing on one's head, and boiling herbs so that the odor permeates the room.

Types of Asthma

Asthma can be divided into two major types: *extrinsic* (allergic) and *intrinsic* (nonallergic). Extrinsic asthma is common in children and is often an allergy to pollen and dust, among other things. Intrinsic asthma is more common in adults and is largely due to such factors as lung infections. Some asthmatics may have a combination of both types.

All asthmatics, regardless of their disease classification, have hyperirritable airways, thus making the bronchial tree sensitive and overreactive to substances and conditions that do not normally affect other people adversely.

Although extrinsic and intrinsic asthma are precipitated by various "triggers," the result is the same—an airway obstruction due to

Bronchospasm
Swelling of mucous membranes in the bronchial walls
Plugging of bronchi by thick, mucus secretions.

See Table 12–6 for a comparison of these two categories of asthma. The distinction between the two groups is arbitrary and somewhat over-simplified, but it is a useful classification.

Status asthmaticus is a severe, prolonged asthmatic attack that even a physician using epinephrine cannot control. It is a true emergency. The chest is greatly distended and the victim has great difficulty in moving air. There may be inaudible breath sounds and wheezes because of the little air movement. The victim is usually exhausted and dehydrated.

Signs

Asthma is characterized by a sudden narrowing of the smaller air passageways in the lungs. The victim becomes acutely short of breath, and a wheezing will be heard during exhalation.

Wheezing is the most obvious sign of this condition. It is a whistling, high-pitched sound produced by air being forced through a constricted airway. Wheezing is usually quite audible, but wheezes may be absent if the attack is very severe and there is very little movement of air. Not all wheez-

TABLE 12–6 Extrinsic and Intrinsic Asthma Compared

	EXTRINSIC	INTRINSIC
Age at onset	In childhood or adolescence	After 35 years of age
Personal or family history of allergy	Positive	Negative
Periodicity of attacks	Often seasonal, associated with environmental changes; symptoms sometimes disappear entirely after childhood	Is unpredictable, often chronic and severe
Precipitation of attacks ("triggers")	By pollens, animal danders, feathers, mold, dusts, and some foods	By inhaled fumes (e.g., cigarette smoke, chemicals), cold air, dust, respiratory infection (usually viral), aspirin (in certain cases), emotional stress, exercise)

ing is related to asthma. Other causes of wheezing include heart failure, smoke inhalation, and chronic bronchitis.

Other important signs leading to suspicion of asthma include:

Victim has a known history of severe allergies or a family history of allergies.

Victim has had previous attacks of acute dyspnea (shortness of breath).

Victim may have had a recent respiratory infection.

Victim has prescription medications in the form of pills and/or inhaler.

Victim has an unproductive cough.

Victim has a rapid respiration rate.

Victim's chest appears hyperinflated. During an acute attack, the person has relatively more obstruction during exhalation than during inhalation. The result is a trapping of air in the lungs, with consequent hyperinflation of the chest.

First Aid

The first aider may be called upon to assist a person who is suffering from an acute asthmatic attack. In most cases there is little the first responder can do other than to recognize the nature of the ailment and, if needed, obtain medical assistance. One should consider the following when providing emergency care:

Adequate fluid intake is important. Doubling the intake of liquids will benefit the victim. Water, given orally if possible, is warranted.

Often steam or vaporized inhalations are beneficial.

Inhalation of nebulized medication should not be done more than every one or two hours, and should rarely be used for more than one day. Many asthmatics carry a nebulizer or inhaler or at least know which one is effective.

Help the victim to choose a comfortable breathing position. Don't make the victim assume a position that *you* think will be comfortable. The best position is usually sitting straight up. Asthmatics probably won't let you position them in any other way. They know better than you what position enables them to breathe most comfortably.

Place the victim in a room that is as free as possible of common allergens (dust, feathers, animals). It should also be free of odors (tobacco smoke, paint, and so forth).

Panic is often present in the acute asthmatic attack. A calm and caring attitude and a comforting voice can prevent panic from escalating.

Keep all questioning of the victim as brief as possible. The victim may be struggling merely to breathe. Attempt to find out when the onset of the attack began and if previous attacks have occurred.

Observe skin and nailbed color for cyanosis, and note wheezing patterns.

Home therapy may not be sufficient if the asthma attack has been present for several hours or if there have been recurrent attacks within a few days. Therefore, medical advice should be obtained.

First aiders will have neither access to nor the background for administering humidified oxygen. Epinephrine is usually the first drug used in the treatment of an acute asthmatic attack. Both require medical administration either by paramedics and/or at a hospital emergency department.

Unconscious victims may need to be resuscitated. Provide prompt, gentle transportation to the hospital emergency department.

FOOD ALLERGY EMERGENCIES

Allergy to food can occasionally produce a life-threatening situation. There are accounts in medical literature of fatal reactions to foods. For example, a young boy severely allergic to peanuts died when he ate chocolate ice cream that contained peanut butter as a filler and smoother—an ingredient no one would have suspected.

Three situations in which food allergy may require immediate emergency treatment are:

Angioedema (giant hives) of the larynx
Anaphylactic shock
Status asthmaticus (continuous asthma attacks).

Angioedema of the larynx is dangerous because it can obstruct the airways. Sometimes the victim is warned by sudden hoarseness or loss of voice, but there may be no symptom other than a sudden sense of suffocation. The victim may appear to be choking on a foreign object, and this possibility must be considered. Immediate transportation to a medical facility is advised since a tracheostomy or intubation could be necessary.

It is obvious that the food or foods provoking this condition should be avoided once they are identified. The victim must learn to read carefully the labels on all food products.

Anaphylactic shock is another potentially fatal consequence of allergy to food. Symptoms may begin mildly enough with a cough, widespread hives, flushing, sweating, but they can intensify rapidly with abdominal pain, wheezing and breathing difficulties, cyanosis (blueness of skin), and unconsciousness.

As in a severe reaction to insect venom or drugs, epinephrine is the treatment; thus, immediate transportation to the nearest medical facility is essential.

Foods most often associated with anaphylactic shock reactions are peanuts (legumes), nuts, shellfish, and fish.

Some victims who respond to food allergens with severe asthma may develop status asthmaticus. Medical assistance is essential for this condition.

The possibility that a reaction to food is the cause of any of these three emergencies is not great, but it is wise to be prepared to deal with such emergencies by being knowledgeable about them.

ACUTE ABDOMEN

The *acute abdomen* occurs when a severe, nontraumatic condition develops that usually requires surgery. It is important to assess the severity of the victim's complaints and to determine if immediate transport is needed. If the pain does not appear to be serious, the victim can be reassured and transported under less hurried circumstances.

Many diseases in many different organs result in the same signs of pain and tenderness in the abdomen. It is frequently difficult for a skilled physician or surgeon to determine exactly what is causing an acute abdomen. The first responder should be able to recognize the existence of such an abdominal condition but need not know the exact cause.

Acute abdomen conditions may quickly result in death. Such conditions require correction of life-threatening problems and prompt transportation to a hospital, where emergency surgery may be needed.

Causes

It is not useful to distinguish among the dozens of conditions that cause acute abdomen because in general the emergency care will be similar regardless of the cause. However, the first responder should have a general idea about the types of disorders thay may cause abdominal pain and should know which of these may progress to life-threatening situations.

Because it is generally of little practical importance for first responders to distinguish among the many causes, they should be alert to the possibility of an aortic aneurysm. An aneurysm is a sac formed by dilatation of the walls of an artery leaving it vulnerable to rupture. Aortic aneurysms resulting from arteriosclerosis occur most frequently in men in their fifties or sixties and are manifested by mild to moderate midabdominal or lumbar pain. The most characteristic physical finding is a mass in the abdomen, usually in the epigastric area.

An episode of acute abdominal pain is often frightening because it is well known that conditions causing such pain often require immediate surgical treatment. However, the most common disorders producing abdominal pain do not require any specific therapy; many others can be effectively treated without surgery. Medically unattended abdominal emergencies nave a mortality rate approaching 100 percent.

Signs and Symptoms

The general signs and symptoms of an acute abdomen may include either singly or in combination any of the following:

1. Abdominal pain, local or widespread.
2. Abdominal tenderness, local or widespread.
3. Rapid pulse (tachycardia).

4. Rapid and shallow breathing. The victim is not breathing deeply, because a deep breath hurts.
5. Abdomen is tense, often distended.
6. Nausea and vomiting may be present.
7. Fever or chills.
8. Change in bowel habits, (that is, constipation, diarrhea, stool color change, or bloody or black stools).

For women of child-bearing age, an ectopic pregnancy should be considered. Always suspect poisoning if the victim is a child.

It may be possible to distinguish abdominal wall pain from intraabdominal pain by placing the victim in a head-up position. Pain from abdominal organs usually is lessened in an upright position, but abdominal wall pain would be unaltered. Pain from hollow organs (bowel or gallbladder) tends to be intermittent. Pain from solid organs (spleen, liver) tends to be more constant. There are exceptions to these rules, naturally.

When the peritoneum has been inflamed or irritated by leaking blood, feces, urine or gastric juices, this condition is termed *peritonitis*.

The vomiting of blood is called *hematemesis*. Vomiting of bright red blood indicates bleeding in the upper gastrointestinal tract. If the vomit contains dark material that resembles coffee grounds, this suggests that there is bleeding and that the blood has been retained in the stomach long enough to be acted upon by the digestive juices. This condition is classic with the victim who has bleeding from a peptic ulcer. Blood in the gastrointestinal tract that has not been vomited passes through the bowel where further chemical processes act on it, producing feces that are dark and tarlike in consistency. Bright red bleeding from the rectum may occur from trauma but typically occurs from hemorrhoids that have been irritated.

Assessment

First aiders can examine the abdomen by observation and palpation. Palpation of the abdomen is a skill that requires years of practice and experience to perfect. A primary principle is that the first responder must be gentle.

Areas of tenderness must be accurately located. Spasm in the abdominal muscles over tender areas should be identified. Rebound tenderness, which is a sudden sharp pain occurring when the pressure over a tender area is suddenly released, should be sought.

Severe pain that lasts for more than six hours or prevents the victim from sleeping is usually indicative of a condition requiring surgery.

The examination can be done very quickly and will yield much information. Do not prolong this examination; the physician will do it in much more detail at the hospital. Carry out all abdominal palpation very gently. Rough palpation can rupture aneurysms of the aorta or lacerate an enlarged spleen.

For our purposes, the abdomen is divided into four quadrants, with one dissecting line down the midline and the other crossing at the umbilicus. These sections are called the upper left quadrant (ULQ), upper right quadrant (URQ), lower left quadrant (LLQ), and lower right quadrant (LRQ). See Figure 12–7.

The victim will tell you where the pain is. After this, first examine the other three quadrants so that any pain you elicit from the trouble spot doesn't tighten the rest of the abdominal muscles. Except for examining the painful area last, the order in which you examine the quadrants isn't important.

Try to make the victim relax by explaining what you're doing. If possible, have the person urinate before the examination begins. Remove all clothing from the abdomen. Place the victim comfortably on the back, knees bent and arms at the sides. This will keep the abdominal muscles from tensing. Your hands must be warm; keep the victim covered and warm except for the part you are examining.

Everyone has a favorite technique for palpating abdominal organs. The most frequently used techniques are *light palpation* and *deep palpation*. In light palpation, you use your fingertips to depress the abdominal wall a little more than a half inch. Light palpation will reveal skin temperatures, large masses, and tender areas. This type of palpation will elicit any guarding of the abdominal wall when a sensitive area is reached. Most victims will guard (hold the muscles of their abdomen tight) to protect the abdomen from the pressure of the examiner's hand. First aiders should perform only light palpation.

With deep palpation, a paramedic assesses to find organ position and any masses. Deep palpation is done with the fingers of one hand pressed in

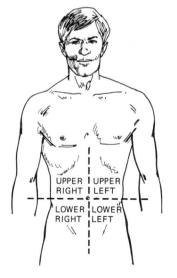

FIGURE 12–7 The four abdominal quandrants.

UPPER RIGHT UPPER LEFT

LOWER RIGHT LOWER LEFT

about 3 inches with the aid of the other hand. Deep palpation is a more advanced technique than light palpation, and unless you know how to perform it, don't attempt it without prior demonstration and practice. Avoid deep palpation over tender areas.

Deep palpation includes rebound tenderness, evoked when you suddenly withdraw your fingertips. This occurs only when the peritoneum is inflamed. Rebound tenderness is often used to test for appendicitis, but this should not be done repeatedly.

Assessment should include attention to the ABCs, a brief medical history, a complete physical review for associated injuries, and a check of vital signs.

Don't evaluate the abdomen extensively. Extensive palpation is of little value. Sophisticated palpation of the abdomen will delay transportation and may cause unnecessary pain, which will be repeated in the hospital emergency department. If an undetected abdominal aneurysm is the cause of the pain and is palpated, it could rupture and the victim might die.

A helpful means of evaluating the victim's level of pain tolerance is that, if the sigmoid colon is not the area of discomfort, mild pressure over this area usually elicits a certain amount of pain. Most victims will say that this makes them uncomfortable. This is a low-grade pain and may be used as a reference for the victim's pain level tolerance during the palpation of the rest of the abdomen.

First Aid

The acute abdomen most often requires surgery, although some acute abdomens may be treated medically. In either case, immediate care by a physician is mandatory for this is a medical emergency.

Emergency care is limited. Most assistance is supportive and includes

Monitoring the ABCs, especially if vomiting has occurred.

Not giving anything to eat or drink. Food or fluid can aggravate many of the symptoms. If emergency surgery is needed, food in the stomach will make the surgery much more dangerous. In some cases, food will not pass out of the stomach and will only incrase distention and vomiting.

Not giving any pain medication. Pain medication will mask the symptoms and delay the diagnosis at the hospital.

Not giving an enema or a laxative for abdominal pain, nausea, or vomiting, because of the risk of rupturing an appendix due to the stimulation of the intestine.

Recognizing the possibility of vomiting and being prepared for it by transporting victims on their side so that any vomitus material can be quickly cleansed from the mouth or can drain out by gravity.

Maintaining the victim in a comfortable position, usually with knees bent.

Not wasting time palpating the abdomen extensively.

Saving any stool, urine, or vomitus so it can be tested in the hospital for the presence of blood.

Transporting the victim as soon as possible.

Not delaying transportation for extensive diagnostic maneuvers.

Not attempting to diagnose the victim's condition. However, do obtain a description of the pain and tenderness and other signs and symptoms so the physician may know what these were when the victim was first seen.

Treating for shock by making the victim as comfortable as possible, conserving body heat with blankets, and transporting the victim gently and quickly to the emergency department.

If stable vital signs are present and there is no guarding and no other associated illness, reassure the victim and advise the person to seek help through his or her own physician or the nearest hospital emergency department.

FEVER

Fever is a body response to infection that is probably more useful than it is harmful. If the person is uncomfortable, fever should be treated with aspirin or similar antifever medicines, lukewarm sponging, and a cool environment. The source of the infection should be evaluated by a physician if the feverish victim looks very sick or if the fever has been above 101°F for more than 24 hours.

COLDS (Upper Respiratory Infections)

Many unnecessary visits to a physician are made because of colds. Since colds and flu are viral illnesses, they cannot be cured by antibiotics or any other drugs. However, several things are helpful in relieving the symptoms.

Most colds have an uncomplicated course of seven to ten days, but they may appear to last longer when they occur in sequence. Any symptom that is persistent and appears to be worsening should be evaluated by a physician.

Aspirin or acetaminophen is useful for the fever and muscular aches of the cold. Drinking a lot of fluids aids in keeping the mucus more liquid, thus preventing complications such as bronchitis and ear infection. Moreover, a fever requires more fluids. Rest is also helpful.

WHAT CHICKEN SOUP CAN REALLY DO

Scientific studies indicate that chicken soup *does* have value.

One example: Expectorant drugs are often used for bronchitis and other respiratory diseases because they stimulate secretions and increase expectoration. At UCLA Medical Center, Dr. Irwin Ziment has shown that chicken soup—if it has pepper, garlic, and maybe some curry powder in it—has the same effect.

Another example: At Mt. Sinai Medical Center, Miami Beach, Dr. Marvin A. Sackner, using special measuring instrumentation, has demonstrated that chicken soup speeds nasal mucus organisms. Other hot beverages also speed the flow, but chicken soup works best.

SORE THROAT

A sore throat can result from a variety of causes: allergy, low humidity, toxic fumes, yelling, an unusual amount of talking or singing, or bacterial or viral infection. To ease discomfort, follow these suggestions:

Use a saltwater gargle—about a half teaspoon of salt to a cup of warm water.
Dissolve throat lozenges, hard candy, or honey slowly in your mouth.
Use aspirin or acetaminophen.
Drink lots of fluids to moisten the throat.
Get as much rest as you possibly can until you feel well.

When To Call the Doctor

If bacterial infection is the cause of a sore throat, a prescribed antibiotic is often needed. And that is especially important if the infection is caused by strep bacteria, which can be determined through a culture of a small amount of mucus taken from the back of the throat. Consult a physician if any of the following signs appear:

Pain is severe enough to affect swallowing.
A fever or a skin rash accompanies the sore throat.
In a child, the sore throat is accompanied by fever, headache, vomiting, stomach pain, or swollen glands.
A mild sore throat lasts for more than 48 hours.
A sore throat develops after exposure to someone with a strep throat.
A sore throat occurs in anyone with a history of rheumatic fever or kidney disease.

EARACHE (Otitis)

Earache is caused by a buildup of fluid and pressure in the middle ear (behind the eardrum). Normally, the middle ear is drained by a short narrow tube (eustachian tube) into the nasal passages. During a cold or allergy, the eustachian tube will become swollen and closed. Fluid begins to accumulate, resulting in pain.

Consult a physician; a prescription antibiotic may need to be prescribed. Aspirin or acetaminophen may be used. Nasal decongestants may also be helpful. Heat can be applied to the ear using a heating pad or warm washcloth. Use a vaporizer or steamy shower to promote drainage in the eustachian tube.

COUGH

A cough is desirable because it is the body's method of ridding foreign substances. Most coughs are caused by colds or postnasal discharge of mucus.

Increased humidity in the air will help; a vaporizer or a steamy shower can increase the humidity. Drinking large quantities of fluids is helpful. Dry, tickling coughs can often be relieved by sucking on hard candy or honey.

Expectorants are usually advised; they liquefy secretions and help get rid of unwanted material. Suppressants should be avoided as long as the cough brings up material or if there is a lot of mucus. Later, if the cough becomes dry and hacking, a suppressant may be useful.

Read labels. Expectorant action is provided by such compounds as glyceryl guaiacolate, potassium iodide, and chloroform. Suppressant action comes from codeine or a codeine relative such as dextromethorphan hydrobromide.

A cough of short, dry quality suggests that there may be an underlying infection; consult a physician. If the person has difficulty breathing and looks ill, a physician should be contacted.

HEADACHE

Headache is a very common complaint. The main causes are tension and muscle spasms in the neck, scalp, and jaw. Aspirin or acetaminophen are quite effective in relieving headache. Massaging the neck muscles may also help. Applying heat to the back of the upper neck or simply resting with eyes closed and head supported may alleviate the headache. Any headache that is persistent or occurs frequently should be discussed with a physician to determine its cause and treatment. Headaches associated with difficulty in using arms or legs or slurring of speech should also be discussed with a physician.

ABDOMINAL PAIN

Abdominal pain can be a sign of something serious. Appendicitis is often suspected. Symptoms of appendicitis include: (1) pain at first around the navel and later in the right lower quarter of the abdomen; (2) nausea or vomiting; (3) fever between 100°F to 102°F.

Avoid solid foods; sips of water or other clear fluids may be taken. A warm bath may help. Do not give laxatives or enemas. (See page 292.)

VOMITING

Viral infections are the most common cause of vomiting. The threat of most vomiting is dehydration. All food intake should be stopped until vomiting has ceased for two to four hours. Ginger ale or 7-Up in small amounts may be given. Then the *BRAT* diet may start. BRAT stands for bananas, rice, applesauce, and toast. The objective of this diet is to provide as much fluid as possible without upsetting the stomach any further. Sipping water or sucking on ice chips may also be done. Avoid milk products. Call a physician if the symptoms persist for more than 72 hours or if signs of dehydration appear.

DIARRHEA

The considerations for diarrhea are very much the same as those for vomiting. The most serious complication, especially in children, is dehydration. Avoid milk and milk products. Neither eat nor drink for two to four hours. Then, give ginger ale or 7-Up until the diarrhea stops. Later, utilize the BRAT diet discussed in the section on vomiting. Watch for dehydration.

CONSTIPATION

Although constipation can be a symptom of disease, it rarely is. Common constipation is correctable, usually without drugs. Try the following:

Add fiber to your diet: vegetables, fruits, whole-grain breads and cereals, and bran (the kind available in health food stores). This is a most important step.
Exercise daily: walk, jog, swim, or do another activity.
Drink plenty of fluids: eight or more glasses daily.
Cut down and eliminate any laxatives that you might be taking.
Use a bulk preparation, such as Metamucil, if a laxative is required.

PAIN DURING URINATION

Pain or burning upon urination is not always caused by infection due to bacteria. It can be due to a viral infection, excessive use of caffeine-containing beverages (coffee, tea, and cola drinks), or bladder spasm. Bladder infection is more common in women than in men.

Drink more fluids, especially fruit juices. This puts more acid into the urine, and it may help. Cranberry juice is the most effective because it contains a natural antibiotic.

Seeing a physician is important. Antibiotics for this ailment have become standard medical practice.

DEHYDRATION

Dehydration is the result of water imbalance in which the output exceeds the intake, thus causing a reduction of body water below normal. Dehydration results when the body loses more fluid than it takes in.

People of any age can become dehydrated, but it develops most quickly and is most dangerous in small children. This is because the kidneys of infants are less able to consume water than those of adults. Elderly persons also are more susceptible to developing water imbalances because the sensitivity of their thirst mechanisms tends to decrease with age, and physical disability may make it difficult to obtain adequate fluids.

Therefore, dehydration can occur as a result of two basic situations: decreased fluid intake or increased fluid output.

Decreased fluid intake: Restriction of fluid intake can occur under many circumstances, such as mental patients who refuse to drink water, those in an unconscious state or coma, those who find themselves in a hazardous situation with no water (lost in the desert or adrift on the ocean), and those paralyzed or physically handicapped who may find water consumption difficult.

Increased fluid output: Abnormal losses of fluids can be caused by increased perspiration from high fever, warm environments, and increased physical activity (especially in warm, humid conditions). Vomiting, diarrhea, and excessive use of laxatives can produce a dehydrated body condition. In cases of vomiting and diarrhea, children, especially young children, are more likely to have significant dehydration. Uncontrolled diarrhea, advanced kidney disease, and overuse of diuretics lead to body fluid loss through excessive urination.

Signs and Symptoms of Dehydration

Military survival manuals describe three levels of dehydration, based on percent loss of body weight. The signs and symptoms resulting from these differing degrees of dehydration are listed in Table 12-7 in their usual order of appearance.

Several indications of dehydration are:

Little or no urine; the urine is dark yellow.
Sunken, tearless eyes.

TABLE 12–7   Signs and Symptoms of Dehydration

1%–5% OF BODY WEIGHT	6%–10% OF BODY WEIGHT	11%–20% OF BODY WEIGHT
Thirst	Dizziness	Delirium
Vague discomfort	Headache	Spasticity
Economy of movement	Dyspnea (labored breathing)	Swollen tongue
Anorexia (no appetite)	Tingling in limbs	Inability to swallow
Flushed skin	Decreased blood volume	Deafness
Impatience	Increased blood concentration	Dim vision
Sleepiness	Absence of salivation	Shriveled skin
Increased pulse rate	Cyanosis (blue skin)	Painful urination
Increased rectal temp.	Indistinct speech	Numbness of the skin
Nausea	Inability to walk	Anuria (decreased or deficient urination)

Dry, sticky saliva.

Sunken "soft spot" of an infant's head.

Loss of elasticity of skin. Pinch a small amount of skin and hold it up for a second, like a little tent of flesh, and then release it. Normally, the skin pops down instantly to its previous position. If a person is dehydrated, the skin will remain raised and will *slowly* return to its previous position.

First Aid for Dehydration

Care of mild dehydration is simple. A dehydrated person should drink large amounts of liquid. A potassium-salt electrolyte solution or brand name drinks like Gatorade or Pripps may be used instead of water because they will restore some of the salts lost with the fluids. If a commercial product is not available, concoct a solution in about 3 ounces (half a glass) of water by putting a teaspoon of sugar and a pinch of salt in it. Give the dehydrated victim sips of this drink every five minutes. A small child may drink up to 1 quart daily, and a large adult may consume up to 3 quarts in a single day.

Medical care should be sought if the eyes appear sunken, if there has been little or no urination for 12 hours, if the skin feels "doughy," and if a temperature of 102°F develops. Although in most instances of dehydration, providing fluid by mouth is satisfactory and adequate, the first aider should not hesitate in acquiring the services of emergency medical personnel who can provide assistance.

Chapter 13

Emergency Childbirth

Occasionally, a person without medical training has to deliver a baby outside a hospital. A baby is normally born without any complications. The first aider should be able to receive the baby, tie and cut the umbilical cord, receive the placenta (afterbirth), and provide proper care for the mother and baby following delivery. The first aider's role is to assist—in no way does the first aider deliver the child. A very important function is to reassure the mother and make her feel that there is someone close at hand upon whom she can rely. This feeling of confidence by the mother will increase in proportion to the calmness and efficiency that the first aider exhibits.

When confronted with a woman in labor, the first aider should be able to evaluate the mother properly and, if delivery is imminent, prepare to assist her in giving birth. If possible, the mother should be transported to a hospital where a well-trained staff is available with the appropriate equipment and supplies.

In order to decide whether or not to transport the mother to the hospital, certain information should be obtained by questioning and examination. Ask the mother:

How many months pregnant is she?
Has she had a baby before?

How long has she been in labor?
How frequent are the contraction pains? How long do they last?
Has the "bag of waters" broken?
Does she feel as though she has to strain to move her bowels?

Then:

Examine the mother for *crowning* (top of the baby's head appears).
Determine if time is available to evacuate her to the nearest hospital.

Because some women do not look as if they are near term, always ask how many months pregnant the woman is.

The average time of labor for the mother of a first child is 10 to 12 hours, but labor is considerably shorter for subsequent babies (5 to 6 hours is not uncommon). However, it should be remembered that no two cases are alike. Thus, if the mother says that she is having her first baby and that she has not been in labor long, there may be time to transport her to a hospital. However, the decision should not be based on this information alone without finishing the evaluation.

The mother's indication that she feels she must strain or move her bowels means that the baby has moved from the uterus into the birth canal, a reliable sign that birth is imminent. This sensation is caused by the baby pressing the wall of the vagina against the rectum. When birth seems imminent, the woman should not be allowed on the toilet. Excessive bearing down by the mother will cause early delivery and may result in the death of the child in the toilet.

The first aider also should examine the vaginal opening for crowning before making a final decision about transporting the mother. "Crowning" is when the head may be seen and is a sign that birth is imminent. This procedure may be embarrassing to the mother, and it is important that the first aider fully explain what is being done and why. Every effort should be made to protect the mother from embarrassment during both the examination and delivery.

In many cases a hasty decision to transport the mother means that the delivery could take place under the worst possible circumstances. Therefore, it is very important to weigh this information before deciding to evacuate the mother.

As the mother's contractions increase in intensity and frequency, she may become restless, moan, and cry out. As labor progresses, the contractions will cause the mother to "bear down," as she would if straining to have a bowel movement. She should be encouraged to relax and rest between contractions.

False contractions or "false labor" may begin as early as three or four weeks before actual delivery. During true labor the interval between contractions gradually diminishes from 10-minute intervals to 2- or 3-minute intervals. The duration of the contractions is usually 45 to 90 seconds.

Precautions include not holding the mother's legs together and not letting the mother go to the bathroom when birth seems imminent. The attendant should look but not touch. Holding the mother's legs together causes undue pressure and may result in the death of or permanent injury to the infant.

To give intelligent assistance to the woman in labor, the first aider should know something about what is happening to the body as labor progresses, as well as the symptoms that will occur.

STAGES OF LABOR

Labor, which is the process of childbirth, consists of contractions of the wall of the uterus (womb). These contractions force the expulsion of the baby into the outside world. (See Figure 13-1.) Labor is divided into three general stages. The *first stage* usually lasts several hours (10 to 12 hours or more for a first baby), from the first contraction to full dilation of the cervix. The small opening at the lower end of the uterus (the cervix) gradually stretches until it is large enough to let the baby pass through. The contractions usually begin as an acutely aching sensation in the small of the back; in a short time, they turn into cramplike pains recurring regularly in the lower abdomen. At first, these contractions are from 10 to 15 minutes apart, are not very severe, and last but a few moments. Gradually, the intervals between contractions grow shorter and they increase in intensity. Delivery is imminent when regular contractions of about two minutes last 45 to 90 seconds. A slight, watery, bloodstained discharge from the vagina may accompany contractions or occur before the labor begins.

At the end of the first stage of labor, the *bag of waters* (amniotic sac), which encases the baby in the uterus, breaks. A pint or more of watery fluid discharges. Sometimes the bag of waters breaks during the first stage of labor. This should not cause the first aider any concern, because it does not usually affect labor. If the bag of waters breaks prematurely and labor does not begin within 12 hours, the danger of infection to mother and baby is potentially greater.

The *second stage* lasts usually about 30 minutes to two hours or more. It begins when the neck of the cervix is fully open, and it ends with the actual birth of the baby.

During the *third stage*, beginning 5 to 20 minutes after the birth of a child and lasting about 15 minutes or more, the afterbirth (placenta) is expelled.

SUPPLIES AND EQUIPMENT

The supplies and equipment that could, with time allowing, be assembled are:

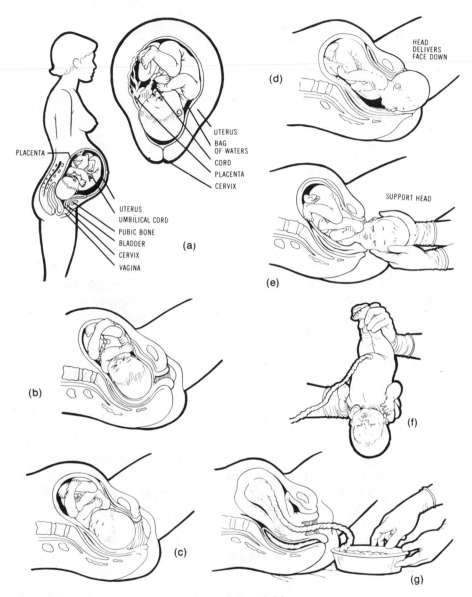

FIGURE 13–1 Anatomy of pregnancy and normal stages in labor.

Freshly laundered towels.

Four pieces of one-inch-wide sterile, gauze bandage, about nine inches long, to be used in tying the baby's cord. Usually only two are used; the other two are extra. New white shoelaces or strips of clean sheeting could also be used if boiled for 30 minutes. Do not use string. The ties may be used even if wet.

Several sterile gauze dressings, four inches square, to wrap around the stump of the cord.

Sterile scissors for cutting the cord. If sterile scissors are not available, scissors can be cleaned with soap and water and boiled for five minutes in a clean container. A new razor blade could also be used.

A soft, warm blanket or towel to wrap around the baby.

A basin with a cover or heavy plastic bag (1 gallon size) to receive the afterbirth.

Rubbing alcohol (isopropyl alcohol, 70 percent or equivalent) for the cord dressing.

A roll of two- or three-inch gauze bandage.

Sanitary pads (uncontaminated) from an unopened package, to catch the vaginal discharge.

Clean sheets and blanket for the mother.

Newspapers to spread on the floor.

A small rubber bulb or ear syringe to remove excess mucus from the baby's mouth.

DELIVERY OF BABY AND PLACENTA

When the labor contractions occur regularly every five minutes, the mother should get into bed. The first aider should lay out the supplies in a convenient place, ready for use. Then the first aider's hands should be scrubbed thoroughly with soap and water.

Because of the danger of introducing infection into the vagina, one never should attempt to clean or disinfect the area between the mother's thighs or around the openings of the vagina, either before or after delivery. Any gross contamination such as feces should be wiped away. However, care must be taken not to introduce any additional bacteria into the vagina. The mother should remain covered with a sheet until just before the baby is born.

It is important to keep calm. it should be remembered that most babies are born without undue difficulty. If there is any marked divergence from the following description of the baby's birth, or for any reason there seems to be cause for alarm, *medical advice should be sought (CB radio, telephone).*

The bag of waters (amniotic sac) will probably break shortly before the child is born; this may go unnoticed, or a pint or more of clear or blood-stained fluid may come from the vagina. If the bag of waters does not break, puncture the sac and push it away from the baby's mouth and nose when the face appears.

The lowest birth weight for a surviving infant of which there is definite evidence is 10 oz. in the case of Marion Chapman, born on June 5, 1938, in England. She was 12¼ inches long. She was fed hourly through a fountain pen filler. Her weight on her 21st birthday was 106 lbs.

Guinness Book of World Records

The mother should lie on her back with her knees bent and spread apart. If she is in an automobile, one foot may be placed on the floorboard. If possible, the bed should be well lighted. Normally, the baby's head comes out first, with the face downward. The first aider should place one hand under the baby's forehead and have the other ready to receive the body. As soon as the head is born, the body and limbs usually follow quickly after another contraction. Do not pull or twist the head.

After the baby is born, a fold of towel should be wrapped around its ankles to prevent slipping. With one hand, the baby should be held up by the heels, taking care that the umbilical cord is slack. To get a good grip, insert one finger between the baby's ankles. *Don't spank the baby.* If breathing does not start spontaneously, snap the forefinger of your hand on the sole of the baby's foot. The baby will be very slippery, and should be held over the bed in case it slips from the first aider's grasp. The first aider's other hand should be placed under the baby's forehead with its head bent back slightly, so that fluid and mucus can run out of its mouth. A small rubber bulb or ear syringe may be used to remove excess mucus from the mouth, if necessary (see Figure 13–2). Remember—always squeeze the bulb before inserting the tip of the syringe into the baby's nose or mouth, and gently release the bulb to remove the mucus. If a bulb syringe is not available, use a finger wrapped in gauze or clean cloth, and gently wipe out the baby's mouth. Do not wipe out ears, eyes, or nose, and do not wipe off the film on the baby's body. When the baby begins to cry, lay it on its side on the bed close enough to itsmother tokeep the cord slack. Note the time of delivery.

Tie a strip of sterile gauze around the cord about three to six inches from the baby's body, and another piece of sterile gauze tied about two to three inches farther along toward the mother. Do not use any material so thin that it will cut through the cord when tightened. Make square knots and *be sure the ties are tight*. Using sterile scissors or new razor blades, cut the cord between the two knots. (See Figure 13–3.)

FIGURE 13–2

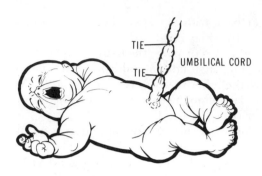

FIGURE 13-3
Tying and cutting the umbilical cord.

A pad of sterile gauze, moistened with rubbing alcohol, should be placed under and over the stump. Shortly after cutting the cord, examine the cut end attached to the baby for signs of continued bleeding. If there is evidence of bleeding from the cord, do not attempt to adjust or tighten the existing knot or clamp. Tie or clamp the cord again a short distance from the original closure. It is very important that the cord be closed off completely. The baby should be wrapped in a warmed blanket and placed on its left side in its bed where an assistant can watch it. The baby should be observed carefully during the first 24 hours.

The Placenta

Continue to observe the mother. Contractions usually stop after the birth of the baby but will begin again to expel the placenta. This usually occurs in 5 to 20 minutes, and is accompanied by a gush of blood. *Do not pull on the cord.* When the placenta is delivered, it should be wrapped in a towel, placed in a plastic bag or basin with a cover, and refrigerated until it is transported with the mother and baby to the hospital. The physician will want to examine the placenta for completeness because any portion of the placenta that was not delivered must be removed. Any tissue remaining in the mother's uterus could lead to infection, continued bleeding, and, in extreme cases, fatal hemorrhaging.

CARE OF MOTHER AFTER DELIVERY

After the placenta has been delivered, the first aider's hand should be placed on the mother's abdomen, just below the naval. The contracted uterus feels like a hard lump about as big as a grapefruit. If a hard lump is not felt, the abdomen should be massaged firmly and gently until one forms under the hand. Gentle massage will stimulate a relaxed uterus, causing it to contract. This should be continued every five minutes for one hour. If the uterus does not contract, there is danger of hemorrhaging. Therefore, the uterus should be felt every 15 minutes for hardness to assure that it is contracted. *If the uterus does not become hard, continue the massage and seek medical advice.*

The heaviest normal newborn child reported in modern times was a boy weighing 24 lbs. 4 oz., born in southern Turkey. A major news agency reported it, but it still should not be considered reliable.

Guinness Book of World Records

When one knows that the uterus has contracted, the mother's thighs and buttocks should be bathed with soap and water and dried. A sanitary pad should be applied. The mother should lie on her back with a pillow beneath her knees and her legs together. She may have a slight chill, so she should be kept warm with blankets.

CARE OF BABY AFTER DELIVERY

The baby should be observed every half hour for the first three hours and then every hour for the next 24 hours. Skin color and breathing rate should be noted.

Resuscitating the Newborn Baby

If the baby is not breathing spontaneously within 30 seconds after delivery (about the time it takes to clear the blood and mucus from its nose and mouth), or if it is born limp and apparently lifeless, resuscitative measures must be initiated without delay. The following procedure should be used.

Again, quickly suction the infant's mouth and nose to assure that there is no blockage due to blood or mucus. Replace the baby on its side, with the head lower than the body. Grasp the baby's feet between the second, third, and fourth fingers of one hand, and snap the forefinger of your other hand sharply against the soles of its feet. This stimulation should cause the infant to gasp and breathe, and perhaps to cry lustily. If not, begin mouth-to-mouth resuscitation (see page 55). Quickly blow four small puffs of air from your cheeks into the baby's mouth and nose, and then check for signs of breathing and a pulse at the brachial artery. If you cannot locate a pulse, start cardiopulmonary resuscitation (see page 60). Remember to use only two fingers on the sternum and to apply very little pressure.

COMPLICATIONS OF PREGNANCY AND DELIVERY

The majority of births are normal and uncomplicated and pose no particular threat to either the mother or baby. There are, however, numerous complications that can occur. Some of these can be alleviated by the first aider, but others require the skill of trained professionals in a hospital with the necessary equipment and supplies.

This book does not provide information on all possible complications of pregnancy and delivery. There are possible complications that would require immediate care by a physician. The following complications are examples of some of the abnormal conditions that might occur. The use of a CB radio or telephone to obtain medical advice provides the best approach in dealing with these problems:

> *Vaginal bleeding at any time* during the last three months of pregnancy usually constitutes an emergency. The mother should be taken to a medical facility as soon as possible for evaluation by a physician. The mother should also consult a physician if vaginal bleeding occurs anytime during the first trimester of pregnancy.
>
> *Excessive bleeding after birth* requires placing a sterile sanitary napkin at the vaginal opening—save blood-soaked pads for a physician to estimate blood loss. Do not hold the mother's legs together or put your hand or anything in the vagina. Preserve for physician inspection any tissue passed and transport immediately to a medical facility.
>
> *Rupture of the bag of waters* without labor and with no labor within 12 hours also is considered an emergency. The danger of infection to mother and baby is potentially greater. *Seek medical advice.*

Breech: The Anglo-Saxon words "brec or breek" designated a garment covering the thighs or buttocks. In about the sixteenth century, the term *breech* came to be applied to the part encased in the garment, and hence "breech" came to designate the "hinder-part" of anything. Thus, in obstetrics we have the "breech presentation," where the buttocks or hinder-part of the baby presents itself first.

The breech presentation is the most common of abnormal deliveries. This is when the buttocks are delivered first rather than the head-first presentation as in normal delivery. In a breech presentation, the same procedures should be followed as in normal delivery. Let the baby deliver with as little interference as possible. If the head does not deliver in three minutes, transport to a medical facility immediately. The baby will need an airway created for it because the umbical cord will be compressed by the head and will receive little or no blood and therefore no oxygen. Some experts recommend the creation of an airway by either placing a finger in the baby's mouth or forming a V with your fingers on either side of the baby's nose, and pushing the vaginal wall away from the baby's face until the head is delivered. (See Figure 13–4.) Do not pull the baby out. If only a foot or arm protrudes, transport to a hospital immediately. (See Figure 13–5.)

A *prolapsed umbilical cord* occurs when the cord comes out of the vagina before the baby is born (see Figure 13–6). Because the cord is already in the birth canal and the uterine contractions are pushing the baby into the canal, the cord will be squeezed between the baby's head and the wall of the vagina and the underlying pelvic structure. Because the baby still is dependent on the blood circulating through the cord for its oxygen supply, the danger of suffocation develops very quickly. Without facilities and a physician to perform an emergency Caesarian section, there is virtually nothing that can be done to save the baby. The delivery should be handled in the usual manner. Put the mother in shock position—legs elevated, keep warm, and have her lay on one side. Do not attempt to push the cord back in. Wrap a sterile towel around the visible portion of the cord with no pressure on the cord. As a very last resort some experts suggest gently pushing the baby up the vagina several inches. Transport immediately to a medical facility.

Multiple birth procedures are the same as for single births.

Abortion (miscarriage) procedures include preventing shock, saving any passed tissue, and immediate transportation of the woman to a medical facility.

FIGURE 13–4 Maintenance of an airway in a breech delivery.

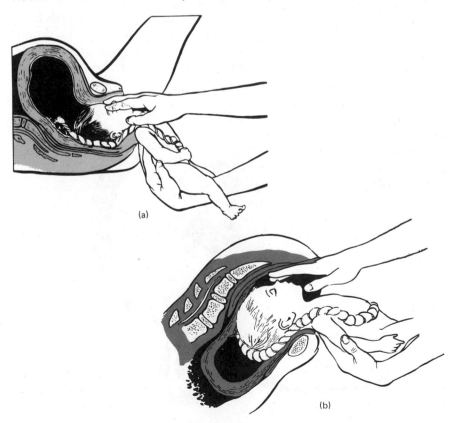

(a)

(b)

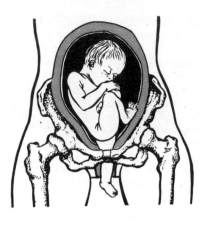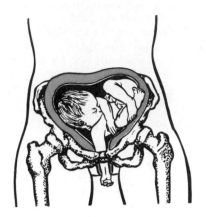

FIGURE 13–5

Immediate Delivery

There are occasions when time will not allow for the gathering and preparing of sterile supplies and equipment.

Have the mother lie down on clean sheets and towels (to absorb fluid expelled during delivery). Wash your hands. Let the baby come out naturally onto a clean towel or sheet; support the baby's head during birth.

If the bag of waters is not broken, carefully break it; keep fluid away from the baby's face so that normal breathing may begin. Wipe out the

FIGURE 13–6   Prolapsed cord delivery.

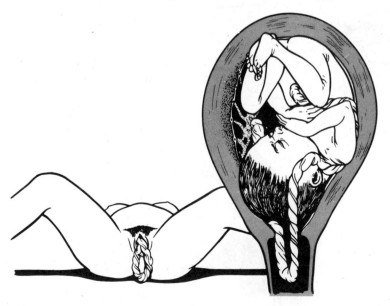

baby's mouth by using a clean towel but being careful not to initiate vomiting.

Do not tie or clamp the cord, and do not cut the cord. Keep the baby at the side of the mother's buttocks but out of the pool of fluid and blood. When the placenta is delivered, wrap it in a towel, leaving it attached to the baby, and place it with the baby, who can now be moved. The placenta should always be slightly above the baby. Keep the baby warm but don't cover its head. Both baby and placenta can now be transported safely.

Chapter 14

Alcohol and Drug Emergencies

ALCOHOL

Ethyl alcohol is the substance that makes fermented and distilled liquors intoxicating. Other commonly used alcohols are methyl, denatured, and isopropyl.

Methyl alcohol, also known as wood alcohol or methanol, is a fuel and has industrial usage as a solvent. Wood alcohol is a poison that *must not be taken internally* because it can cause blindness or death.

Isopropyl alcohol is used as a rubbing alcohol and often as a disinfectant. It is poisonous if taken internally.

Denatured alcohol is ethyl alcohol to which other materials (denaturants) have been added to make it unfit for drinking. *For external use only*, it can be applied to the skin as a disinfectant and cooling agent.

Ethyl alcohol (also known as grain alcohol or ethanol) is given special attention in this chapter because it is the active intoxicant of alcoholic beverages. It is a colorless, flammable liquid that is classed as a food by some authorities because it supplies calories, but it has no nutritive value. It acts as an irritant, antiseptic, drying agent, sedative, anesthetic, and hypnotic agent. It is a pain-reliever that, unlike other analgesics such as aspirin, reduces pain by putting the brain to sleep. Ethyl alcohol is considered a drug because of the profound effects it has on the central nervous system. Like barbiturates and narcotics, it causes addition.

Alcohol in the Body

Unlike other foods that require slow digestion, alcohol is absorbed rather quickly into the bloodstream, directly through the walls of the stomach and the small intestine. The blood carries it to all body tissues, including the brain, where it has an immediate effect. The liver slowly changes the alcohol into carbon dioxide and water. A small amount of it goes out through the lungs, skin, and kidneys. If alcohol is consumed faster than the body can dispose of it, its concentration in the blood increases and it acts as a depressant or anesthetic on the central nervous system.

Initially alcohol seems to produce feelings of stimulation. Alcoholic "numbing" of the judgment center of the brain, which controls our inhibitions and restraints, makes one feel buoyant and exhilarated. Continued drinking on a given occasion increases the percentage of alcohol in the bloodstream. This causes depression of various areas of the brain that affect judgment, emotions, behavior, and physical well-being.

First the man takes a drink, then the drink takes a drink, then the drink takes the man.

Japanese proverb

Sudden death may occur (1) when the individual has ingested so much alcohol that the brain center that controls breathing and heart action is depressed to a fatal level; (2) when some other depressant drugs, used as sleep preparations, are taken along with alcohol; (3) during an accident (one-half of all fatal traffic accidents involve the use of alcohol); or (4) as a result of suicide or murder (many self-inflicted deaths as well as homicides involve the use of alcohol).

Acute intoxication.   Episodes of excessive drinking may be manifested as mild drunkenness or serious drunkenness (stupor or coma).

Mild intoxication.   Mild intoxication is usually self-limiting, and its treatment requires only rest and the cessation of drinking alcoholic beverages. The victim may show poor control of muscles, poor coordination, double vision, flushing of the face, bloodshot eyes, and vomiting. Behavior

TABLE 14–1 Effects of Alcoholic Beverages

AMOUNT OF BEVERAGE	CONCENTRATION OF ALCOHOL ATTAINED IN THE BLOOD	EFFECTS	TIME REQUIRED FOR ALL ALCOHOL TO LEAVE THE BODY
1 highball or 1 cocktail or 3½ oz. of fortified wine or 5½ oz. of ordinary wine or 2 bottles (24 oz.) of beer	0.03%	Slight changes in feeling	2 hrs.
2 highballs or 2 cocktails or 7 oz. of fortified wine or 11 oz. of ordinary wine or 4 bottles of beer	0.06%	Increasing effects with variation among individuals Feeling of warmth—mental relaxation Slight decrease of fine skills—less concern with minor irritations and restraints	4 hrs.
3 highballs or 3 cocktails or 10½ oz. of fortified wine or 16½ oz. of ordinary wine or 6 bottles of beer	0.09%	and in the same individual at different times	Buoyancy—exaggerated emotion and behavior—talkative, noisy or morose	6 hrs.
4 highballs or 4 cocktails or 14 oz. of fortified wine or 22 oz. of ordinary wine or 8 bottles (3 quarts) of beer	0.12%	Impairment of fine coordination—clumsiness Slight to moderate unsteadiness in standing or walking	8 hrs.
5 highballs or 5 cocktails or 17½ oz. of fortified wine or 27½ oz. of ordinary wine or ½ pint of whisky	0.15%	Intoxication—unmistakable abnormality of gross bodily functions and mental faculties	10 hrs.

Reproduced with permission from Leon A. Greenberg, "What the Body Does with Alcohol." *Popular Pamphlets on Alcohol Problems*, No. 4. Rutgers University, Center of Alcohol Studies, New Brunswick, New Jersey, 1955.

varies greatly. It is hard to predict what an intoxicated person will do next. The person may cry bitterly, show unexplained happiness, change moods rapidly, or just pass out. Inappropriate behavior, such as urinating in public and loud or abusive speech, is also common. Occasionally an intoxicated individual exhibits marked excitement and/or combativeness, and restraints may be needed.

It is impossible to walk off an excess of liquor. Alcohol is metabolized by the body at a constant rate regardless of activity. Black coffee, a cold shower, and fruit juice may make a drinker feel better, but the person's reaction time will still be slowed. He or she will be a wide-awake drunk instead of a sleepy one.

First Aid

For hangover symptoms of jitters, thirst, nausea, and severe headache, the victim should be allowed to remain quiet. A single dose of an antacid may help the nausea. One or two cups of salted tomato juice and a glass of fruit juice, sipped slowly, also may help. A pain reliever may be given every four hours by mouth for headache, if it can be retained without vomiting.

Serious intoxication.   If a very large amount of an alcoholic beverage is taken in a short period of time, especially if taken on an empty stomach, serious acute intoxication may develop. Symptoms are drowsiness that might progress rapidly to coma; slow-snoring breathing; blueness of the face, lips, and fingernail beds; involuntary passage of urine or feces; dilated pupils; and rapid weak pulse.

A suspected alcoholic stupor or coma is a medical emergency. The signs or symptoms of drunken stupor are much like those of such conditions as insulin shock or diabetic coma (see page 278 on these two opposite conditions that may cause unconsciousness in diabetics), stroke, poisoning with other drugs, some kinds of food poisoning, and brain injury. A person may have an odor of alcohol on the breath and yet be suffering primarily from a condition unrelated to drinking. The fruity or sweet odor of the breath in *diabetic coma* may be mistaken for alcohol. In diabetic coma, the onset is usually slower than in alcoholism, and rapid, deep breathing is almost always present. This distinction is very important because *diabetic coma requires prompt and aggressive treatment.* The victim's clothing or wallet should be checked for identification cards or tags that might identify medical problems that need special medical attention, such as allergies or diabetes. The individual's friends should be questioned on whether the victim might have taken drugs, been injured, or been overexposed to fumes or poisons. Try to find out specifically what, when, and how much alcohol was taken.

First Aid

The alcoholic stupor victim's airway should be kept clear by placing the person on the side, then on alternate sides frequently to avoid accumulation of secretions. Unconscious victims should not be allowed to sleep on their back, because a deepening of stupor or coma may cause choking on the tongue or vomitus. The condition of the victim should be observed often for vomiting and changes in respiration. Do not leave the person alone. If there is sleepiness or breathing problems, try to keep the person awake.

If the victim is hostile, never attempt to handle the victim by yourself.

DRUG ABUSE

A drug is any substance that produces an effect on the mind or body. Undesirable reactions can occur with the use of any drug. Harmful reactions result when a person accidentally or intentionally misuses any of the following:

1. Prescription drugs
2. Nonprescription drugs (over-the-counter medicine)
3. Illegal drugs ("street" drugs)
4. Household or industrial chemicals.

Most drugs that are knowingly misused are taken for their stimulating, depressing, or hallucinatory effect on the mind (see Table 14–2). Often the physical effects of these drugs are extremely unpleasant and even life-threatening.

Stimulants

Stimulants, also called "uppers," include amphetamines, cocaine, some antiasthmatics, and antihistamines. Characteristic symptoms include excitement, restlessness, irritability, and talkativeness. If the person is unconscious, check for cardiorespiratory failure. Respiratory failure is common among cocaine abusers.

Depressants

Depressants, also called "downers," include narcotics, sleeping pills, tranquilizers, and alcohol. Characteristic symptoms include depression, sleepiness, poor reflexes, and "driftiness." Because all these agents depress respiration, care must be taken to ensure an open airway. Changes in respiration should also be watched: Often respiratory failure is not recognized because it is assumed that the victim just "fell asleep."

Hallucinogens

Hallucinogens are drugs that affect how people mentally see themselves, others, and their surroundings. These drugs (LSD, STP, mescaline) can cause emotional symptoms that range from ecstasy to horror ("bad trip"). Another problem that occurs with using hallucinogens is called "flashback." Flashback can occur *anytime* after the drug has been used. These episodes mimic and may intensify the original drug experience. Persons experiencing hallucinogen drug symptoms often display behavior that is dangerous to themselves and others.

Handling Drug Abuse Victims

As with all emergency victims, priorities of care must be set. Situations involving breathing or heart failure must receive immediate attention. First aid should be administered in the following order:

1. Ensure adequate breathing and heart function (cardiopulmonary resuscitation–CPR).
2. Treat for shock if necessary.
3. If the victim is drowsy, keep victim awake by using cold wet towels, gentle shaking, walking, and conversation.
4. Attempt to make victim vomit if conscious. If victim is semiconscious or unconscious, *no* attempt should be made to cause vomiting. Vomiting should be induced if the overdose was taken within the preceding 30 minutes.
5. Semiconscious or unconscious victims should be positioned on their sides so that materials in the mouth can drain out instead of into the lungs.
6. Victims who have taken drugs that cause severe excitement and/or hallucinations should be handled in such a way as to protect them from self-injury. Use physical restraints only when absolutely necessary.
7. Attempts should be made to calm down excited and/or hallucinating victims by "talking them down" with quiet, reassuring conversation.
8. If the victim is bleeding or appears to have a bone injury, administer the appropriate first aid.
9. Collect all materials (empty bottles, packages, vomitus, and so forth) and information available at the scene to assist medical personnel in identifying the abused drug and treating the victim. Try to find out specifically what, when, and how much drug was taken.
10. Get the victim to medical assistance as soon as possible.
11. Brief medical personnel on all information and materials collected concerning the incident.
12. Leave police functions to police authorities.
13. Do not risk personal injury if at all possible; obtain professional assistance for such dangerous circumstances.

TABLE 14–2　Controlled Substances: Uses & Effects

DRUGS	TRADE OR OTHER NAMES	MEDICAL USES	PHYSICAL DEPEN-DENCE
Narcotics			
Opium	Dover's Powder, Paregoric, Parepectolin	Analgesic, antidiarrheal ⎫	
Morphine	Morphine, Pectoral Syrup	Analgesic, antitussive ⎬ High ⎭	
Codeine	Codeine, Empirin Compound with Codeine, Robitussin A-C	Analgesic, antitussive	Moderate
Heroin	Diacetylmorphine, Horse, Smack	Under investigation	
Hydromorphone	Dilaudid	Analgesic ⎫	
Meperidine (Pethidine)	Demerol, Pethadol	Analgesic ⎬ High	
Methadone	Dolophine, Methadone,	Analgesic, heroin substitute ⎭	
Other Narcotics	LAAM, Leritine, Levo-Dromoran, Percodan, Tussionex, Fentanyl, Darvon*, Talwin*, Lomotil	Analgesic, antidiarrheal, antitussive	High-Low
Depressants			
Chloral Hydrate	Noctec, Somnos	Hypnotic	Moderate
Barbiturates	Amobarbital, Phenobarbital, Butisol, Phenoxbarbital, Secobarbital, Tuinal	Anesthetic, anticonvul-sant, sedative, hypnotic	High-Moderate
Glutethimide	Doriden	⎫	
Methaqualone	Optimil, Parest, Quaalude, Somnafac, Sopor	Sedative, hypnotic ⎬	High
Benzodiazepines	Ativan, Azene, Clonopin, Dalmane, Diazepam, Librium, Serax, Tranxene, Valium, Verstran	Antianxiety, anti-convulsant, seda-tive, hypnotic	Low
Other Depressants	Equanil, Miltown, Noludar Placidyl, Valmid	Antianxiety, seda-tive, hypnotic	Moderate
Stimulants			
Cocaine†	Coke, Flake, Snow	Local anesthetic ⎫	
Amphetamines	Biphetamine, Delcobese, Desoxyn, Dexedrine, Mediatric	Hyperkinesis, nar-colepsy, weight control ⎬	
Phenmetrazine	Preludin	Weight control ⎬	Possible
Methylphenidate	Ritalin		
Other Stimulants	Adipex, Bacarate, Cylert, Didrex, Ionamin, Plegine, Pre-Sate, Sanorex, Tenuate, Tepanil, Voranil	⎭	

TABLE 14–2   (Continued)

PSYCHO-LOGICAL DEPEN-DENCE	TOLER-ANCE	DURA-TION OF EFFECTS (HOURS)	USUAL METHODS OF ADMINIS-TRATION	POSSIBLE EFFECTS	EFFECTS OF OVERDOSE	WITHDRAWAL SYNDROME
High Moderate High High-Low	Yes	3–6 12–24 Variable	Oral, smoked Oral, injected, smoked Oral, injected Injected, sniffed, smoked Oral, injected	Euphoria, drowsiness, respiratory depression, constricted pupils, nausea	Slow and shallow breathing, clammy skin, convulsions, coma, possible death	Watery eyes, runny nose, yawning, loss of appetite, irritability, tremors, panic, chills, and sweating, cramp, nausea
Moderate High-Moderate High Low Moderate	Possible Yes	5–8 1–16 4–8	Oral Oral, injected	Slurred speech, disorientation, drunken behavior without odor of alcohol	Shallow respiration, cold and clammy skin, dilated pupils, weak and rapid pulse, coma, possible death	Anxiety, insomnia, tremors, delirium, convulsions, possible death
   High	Possible Yes	1–2 2–4	Sniffed, injected Oral, injected Oral	Increased alertness, excitation, euphoria, increased pulse rate and blood pressure, insomnia, loss of appetite	Agitation, increase in body temperature, hallucinations, convulsions, possible death	Apathy, long periods of sleep, irritability, depression, disorientation

TABLE 14–2 (Continued)

DRUGS	TRADE OR OTHER NAMES	MEDICAL USES	PHYSICAL DEPEN- DENCE
Hallucinogens			
LSD	Acid Microdot		None
Mescaline and Peyote	Mesc, Buttons, Cactus	None	
Amphetamine Variants	2.5-DMA, PMA, STP, MDA, MMDA, TMA, DOM, DOB		Unknown
Phencyclidine	PCP, Angel Dust, Hog	Veterinary anesthetic	Degree unknown
Phencyclidine Analogs	PCE, PCP, TCP		
Other Hallucinogens	Bufotenine, Ibogaine, DMT, DET, Psilocybin, Psilocyn	None	None
Cannabis			
Marihuana	Pot, Acapulco Gold, Grass, Reefer, Sinsemilla, Thai Sticks	Under investigation	Degree unknown
Tetrahydrocannabinol	THC		
Hashish	Hash	None	
Hashish Oil	Hash Oil		

*Not designated a narcotic under the CSA.
†Designated a narcotic under the CSA.
Source: U.S. Department of Justice.

TABLE 14–2 **(Continued)**

PSYCHO-LOGICAL DEPEN-DENCE	TOLER-ANCE	DURA-TION OF EFFECTS (HOURS)	USUAL METHODS OF ADMINIS-TRATION	POSSIBLE EFFECTS	EFFECTS OF OVERDOSE	WITHDRAWAL SYNDROME
Degree unknown	Yes	8–12	Oral			
		Up to days	Oral, injected	Illusions and hallucinations, poor percep-tion of time and distance	Longer, more intense "trip," episodic psychosis, possible death	Withdrawal syndrome not reported
High			Smoked, oral, injected			
Degree unknown	Possible	Variable	Oral, injected, smoked, sniffed			
Moderate	Yes	2–4	Smoked, oral	Euphoria, re-laxed inhibi-tions, increased appetite, dis-oriented be-havior	Fatigue, para-noia, possible psychosis	Insomnia, hyperactivity, and decreased appetite occa-sionally re-ported

Chapter 15

Emotional Emergencies

Emotional emergencies may be independent problems, or they may arise as the result of an accident, injury, illness, or disaster. As a first aider, always consider the emotional needs of the victim. Be aware also of the emotional problems that sometimes confront the first aider and those working as rescuers in disasters.

RESCUER REACTION

The sight of blood and the cries of the injured can be very upsetting to those attempting to rescue and assist the injured. Grotesque sights such as amputations, being splattered with vomitus, and disagreeable odors from urine and feces can be quite unnerving.

More than one rescuer has regurgitated, felt nauseated and weak, or fainted at an accident scene. Even the toughest of physicians will have difficult moments when exposed to certain situations.

It may be essential that rescuers stay conscious and working at a trauma scene. Rescuers who collapse while aiding the injured are of no value in rendering aid. Moreover, their condition will detract attention from the original victim(s) who is usually more seriously affected. All the knowledge and skills obtained may be rendered useless if the rescuer collapses or has to be removed from the trauma scene because of nausea and weakness.

There are those in the emergency care field who seem to have ice in their veins. They always appear calm and unaffected by even the worst traumatic injury. Such people may be called "calloused" by some, but the proper psychological term is desensitized. A specialty within psychology deals with desensitization and suggests a way to overcome anxieties caused by unpleasant sights and sounds at accident scenes. Desensitization can be viewed as a *deconditioning* or a *counterconditioning* process. The procedure can be effective in eliminating fears and anxieties. The idea is to weaken an undesirable response (nausea, vomiting, fainting) by strengthening an incompatible response. In other words, when responses are incompatible (that is, calm vs. anxiety), the occurrence of either one prevents the occurrence of the other. In desensitizing, the person learns to associate relaxation with situations that elicit anxiety so that eventually the anxiety is no longer experienced.

Thus, people first need to learn how to invoke relaxation and then gradually expose themselves to the anxiety situations (the sight of blood, for example).

Some simple ways of desensitizing (calming) yourself while aiding another include

1. Closing your eyes for a moment and taking several long, deep breaths. Let your mind be blank; just count the breaths. Count one as you breathe in, two as you breathe out, and so on.
2. Changing your thought patterns from the unpleasant to the pleasant by mentally singing a favorite song to yourself (not out loud, for the obvious reason of how you might appear to observers around you).

Once a relaxation response technique is learned, then gradual exposure might start with the viewing of films, 35 mm slides, and/or pictures of traumatic injuries in medical journals. Another step in the process of conditioning oneself against fainting might be to volunteer service to a hospital emergency department where injuries may be seen.

In a number of cases, a fainting rescuer had failed to eat breakfast. Therefore, a strong recommendation is the maintenance of an adequate blood-sugar level through proper eating habits.

Another technique that sometimes works is to remind yourself that "if I don't do it, no one else will." While rendering first aid, remembering to concentrate on the injury and not upon the person is another suggestion. Exercise caution when attempting to be calm by using discretion in your comments and avoid joking, which may be offensive to some of the victims and/or bystanders.

Two conclusions can be drawn: (1) The more exposure to traumatic injuries one has, the less likelihood there will be of fainting or collapsing at an accident scene while attempting to aid the injured; and (2) the next time you are aiding an injured victim where there are unpleasant sights and sounds, try one of the calming and relaxing techniques if you feel you might be adversely affected by what you see and hear.

PSYCHOLOGICAL FIRST AID

Another kind of injury frequently occurs: psychological injury, a form of damage to human beings that requires its own kind of first aid.

Psychological first aid really means nothing more than helping people with emotional injuries, whether those injuries result from physical injury or from excessive or unbearable strain on the victim's emotions.

Psychological first aid often goes hand in hand with physical first aid, because a physical injury and the circumstances surrounding it may actually cause an additional emotional injury. On the other hand, psychological injury may occur even when there is no real danger of physical injury. Emotional injuries are not as apparent as physical injuries, but both can be severe and both require first aid.

Although emotional reactions are temporary, lasting only for minutes, hours, or at the most a few days, they are seriously disabling, often contagious, and may result in danger not only to the emotionally upset person but also to others. For these reasons, it is very important for you to know that first aid can be applied to injuries of the mind as well as to those of the body and that you can understand the basic principles of this psychological first aid.

Typical Reactions

With few exceptions, all people feel fear in the face of an emergency. In such a situation you should not be surprised if you feel shaky, perspire profusely, and become a little nauseated and confused. These reactions are normal and are no cause for concern. Most people are able to collect themselves within a short time. After a while, if you get busy, your heart will stop pounding, your breath will come back, and you will feel less tense.

Some reactions, however, can be easily recognized as abnormal. The following are the most usual types:

Physical Reactions. Sometimes bodily reactions such as rapid breathing, fast pulse, and shakiness go far beyond mere "butterflies." When these physical symptoms become severe, they may result in violent nausea and vomiting and a kind of psychological paralysis that inhibits the effective performance of normal duties.

Depressed Reactions. Most people are dazed, shocked, or numb after an emergency, but this condition promptly clears up. Sometimes, however, a person will not be able to "shake it off." The person acts as if he or she were alone in the world. When the person moves, if at all, bodily movements are slow and aimless. Such people will respond faintly to anyone or anything and will show no emotion at all—only a vacant stare. A person like this is completely helpless and unaware of his or her surroundings.

Overactive Reactions. In emergency situations you can expect "running about" and confusion. Some people, however, seem to run about excessively, creating additional confusion and doing things that are of no value or even harmful. They talk a lot, make silly jokes, or may be demanding, critical, and overly confident. They jump from job to job, brush aside any directions, and make a spectacle of themselves.

Panic Reactions. Perhaps you can understand how overwhelming fear can cause some people to act in abnormal ways. You can remember how you felt or how others have acted when severely frightened. Some people seem to lose all control and do things in a blind, unreasonable way. They may run aimlessly with complete disregard for their safety, weep so severely that they become exhausted and unable to care for themselves even when their lives depend upon it, or recklessly go about doing things that make no sense.

We fear things in proportion to our ignorance of them.

Livy

You do not need much training to recognize severe abnormal reactions. Some victims, however, will have reactions that are less severe and more difficult to detect. To determine whether or not a person needs help, find out if the person is doing something that makes sense and is able to perform duties and take care of him or herself. Furthermore, you should stop from time to time and carefully assess your own emotional condition. You may need to either slow down or get yourself going.

First Aid

Table 15-1 lists the typical kinds of emergency reactions and summarizes the most important aspects of administering psychological first aid. For the most part, these psychological first aid measures are simple and easy to understand. However, improvisation is in order, just as it is in splinting a fracture. Whether or not you use good judgment depends largely upon your ability to observe the casualty and truly understand the needs that have to be met.

Whatever the situation, you will have your own emotional reactions (consciously or unconsciously) toward the victim. These reactions are very important—they can either enhance or hinder your ability to help the person. Especially when you are tired or worried, you may very easily become impatient with the person or persons who seem to be "dragging their heels" or "making mountains out of molehills." You may even feel resentful toward them for being such a nuisance.

TABLE 15-1   Psychological First Aid for Emergency Reactions

REACTION	SYMPTOMS	DO	DON'T
Normal	Trembling Muscular tension Perspiration Nausea Mild diarrhea Urinary frequency Pounding heart Rapid breathing Anxiety	Give reassurance Provide group identifica- tion Motivate Talk with victim Observe to see that individ- ual is gaining composure, not losing it	Don't show resent- ment Don't overdo sym- pathy
Individual Panic (flight reaction)	Unreasoning at- tempt to flee Loss of judgment Uncontrolled weep- ing Wild running about	Try kindly firmness at first Give something warm to eat or drink Get help to isolate if necessary Be emphathetic Encourage victim to talk Be aware of your own limi- tations	Don't use brutal restraint Don't strike Don't douse with water Don't give sedatives
Depression (underactive reactions)	Stands or sits with- out moving or talking Vacant expression Lack of emotional display	Get contact gently Secure rapport Get victim to tell you what happened Be empathetic Recognize feelings of re- sentment in victim and yourself Find simple, routine job Give warm food, drink	Don't tell victim to "snap out of it" Don't overdo pity Don't give sedatives Don't act resentful
Overactive	Argumentative Talks rapidly Jokes inappropri- ately Makes endless sug- gestions Jumps from one ac- tivity to another	Let victim talk about it Find victim jobs which re- quire physical effort Give warm food, drink Supervision necessary Be aware of own feelings	Don't suggest that victim is acting abnormally Don't give sedatives Don't argue with victim
Physical (conversion reaction)	Severe nausea and vomiting Can't use some part of the body	Show interest in victim Find small job for victim to make him forget Make comfortable Get medical help if possible Be aware of own feelings	Don't tell victim that there's nothing wrong with him Don't blame Don't ridicule Don't ignore disa- bility openly

Source: Modified from M 51–400–603–1, Dept. of Non-resident Instruction, Medical Field Service School, Brooke Army Medical Center, Fort Sam Houston, Texas.

On the other hand, do not be overly sympathetic. Excessive sympathy for an incapacitated person can be as harmful as negative feelings. The person needs strong help but does not need to be overwhelmed with pity.

Above all, you must guard against becoming impatient, intolerant, resentful, or overly solicitous. Remember that such emotion will rarely help the victim and can never increase your ability to make clear decisions. Victims who can see in you calmness, confidence, and competence will be reassured and feel greater security in the world around them.

HOSTILE VICTIMS

The angry, hostile victim is not difficult to recognize: Such a person is ready to fight with anyone and may be shouting threats and verbally abusing others. If alcohol and/or drugs are known to be involved, be especially careful because extreme and bizarre behavior can result. Observe the following precautions:

1. If possible, transport the person to a medical facility immediately. Also, if possible, have someone that is known to the person (family member, friend, neighbor) remain nearby.
2. Never approach a violent person by yourself. It is best to wait for help and better still to wait for the police.
3. Avoid getting hurt. Vacate the premises; call for help.
4. If the person is armed, call the police. Stay away from the person entirely.

SUICIDE

Suicide, the ninth leading cause of death in the United States, is increasing, and the reported ratio of eight attempts to one completed suicide is believed to be an underestimate. Moreover, many other people contemplate the act but never carry it out.

Information about suicides can be useful in identifying those people who are at risk of attempting suicide. However, remember that the information that follows is about groups of people and doesn't always predict individual risk.

Based upon studies of suicide, elderly white men who are socially isolated or who live alone are at greatest risk of attempting suicide. These men will most often use an active form (for example, firearm, explosive), whereas women most often use a passive form (for example, overdose of medication). This helps explain why men complete more suicides than women do: Rescue and resuscitation are more successful with the passive forms. People with alcohol problems, those experiencing hallucinations (for example, voices directing the person), and those suffering from depression are at greater risk of committing suicide. Persons with a physical or emotional health problem are thus more likely to take their own lives. Also, people who have experienced a recent loss or disappointment are often more suicidal. Finally, those who have attempted suicide in the past are more likely to try it again.

Guidelines for managing suicidal victims include the following:

1. Do not leave the person alone. Staying and listening to the person's pain may help the individual through a suicidal crisis. Remain calm and kind, and don't become excited. Never argue.
2. Locate and discard pill bottles or other implements of self-destruction (for example, poison, knives).
3. Communicate with the person such things as:
    What conflicts and concerns the person has
    Why suicide is the answer to the person's problems
    What alternatives there are.
4. Always get professional help. If the person resists assistance, it may be necessary to involve the police. Transportation to a hospital is always necessary even though the person says everything is all right.
5. If the person has already attempted suicide, render first aid to the injury.

CHILD ABUSE

What is child abuse and neglect? According to Public Law 93–247, the Child Abuse Prevention and Treatment Act, ". . . child abuse and neglect" means the "physical or mental injury, sexual abuse, negligent treatment, or maltreatment of a child under the age of 18 by a person who is responsible for the child's welfare."

Extent of Child Abuse and Neglect

Because child abuse and neglect usually occur in the privacy of the home, no one knows exactly how many children are affected. Estimates of the total number of abused and neglected children in the United States per year vary widely, ranging from 500,000 to 4.5 million, but these figures are unproven. The National Center on Child Abuse and Neglect estimates that approximately one million children are maltreated by their parents each year. Of these children, as many as 100,000 to 200,000 are physically abused, 60,000 to 100,000 are sexually abused, and the remainder are neglected. And each year, more than 2,000 children die in circumstances suggestive of abuse or neglect.

A recent study found that boys are abused about as often as girls, that women were responsible for the maltreatment in 60 percent of the cases, and that although child abuse and neglect is known to exist in all racial and ethnic groups and at every level of society, lower income families, which are more visible to reporting agencies, are overrepresented in the reports. Another finding was that, although child abuse and neglect affects children of all ages, fully half of the reported cases concern children under the age of six. This is especially significant because the physical consequences of abuse and neglect are more crucial in younger children; nearly 60 percent of fatalities reported in the study were of children under the age of two.

Effects of Child Abuse and Neglect

Child abuse and neglect can result in permanent damage to the child's physical, emotional, and mental development. The physical effects of child abuse and neglect may include damage to the brain, vital organs, eyes, ears, arms or legs. These injuries may in turn result in mental retardation, blindness, deafness, or loss of a limb. Abuse or neglect may cause arrested emotional development. At its most serious, of course, abuse or neglect can result in the death of a child.

Child abuse and neglect can be as damaging emotionally as they are physically. Impaired self-concept, ego competency, and thought processes; higher levels of aggression; low impulse control; and self-destructiveness are all characteristics of abused and neglected children.

Recognizing Child Abuse and Neglect

Child abuse and neglect is usually divided into four major types: physical abuse, neglect, sexual abuse, and emotional maltreatment. Each has recognizable characteristics, and all may be encountered by the first aider.

Physical and behavioral indicators are set forth in Table 15–2. The list is not intended to be exhaustive; many more indicators exist than can be included. In addition, the presence of a single indicator does not necessarily prove that child abuse or neglect has occurred. However, the repeated occurrence of an indicator, the presence of several indicators in combination, or the appearance of serious injury or suspicious death should alert the first aider to the possibility of child abuse or neglect.

Reporting Child Abuse and Neglect

Every state has child abuse and neglect-reporting statutes.

Who reports? Most states mandate reporting of suspected child abuse and neglect by professionals who work with or are in contact with children.

To emphasize the mandatory or required reporting of suspected child abuse and neglect, many states provide penalties for those who fail to perform their required duties under the law. Penalties can be severe: fines of up to $1,000 and prison sentences of up to one year in some states. For

TABLE 15-2 Physical and Behavioral Indicators of Child Abuse and Neglect

TYPE OF CHILD ABUSE/NEGLECT	PHYSICAL INDICATORS	BEHAVIORAL INDICATORS
PHYSICAL ABUSE	Unexplained Bruises and Welts: on face, lips, mouth on torso, back, buttocks, thighs in various stages of healing clustered, forming regular patterns reflecting shape of article used to inflict (electric cord, belt buckle) on several different surface areas regularly appear after absence, weekend, or vacation especially about the trunk & buttocks be particularly suspicious if there are old bruises in addition to fresh ones Unexplained Burns: cigar, cigarette burns, especially on soles, palms, back or buttocks immersion burns (sock-like, glove-like doughnut shaped on buttocks or genitalia) patterned like electric burner, iron, etc. rope burns on arms, legs, neck or torso Unexplained Fractures: (particularly if multiple) to skull, nose, facial structure in various stages of healing multiple or spiral fractures Unexplained Lacerations or Abrasions: to mouth, lips, gums, eyes to external genitalia	Wary of adult contacts Apprehensive when other children cry Behavioral extremes: aggressiveness, or withdrawal Frightened of parents Afraid to go home Reports injury by parents The child who is apathetic and *does not cry* despite his injuries The child who has been seen by emergency personnel recently for related complaints The child whose injury occurred several days before you were called
PHYSICAL NEGLECT	Consistent hunger, poor hygiene, inappropriate dress Consistent lack of supervision, especially in dangerous activities or for long periods Unattended physical problems or medical needs Abandonment	Begging, stealing food Extended stays at school (early arrival and late departure) Constant fatigue, listlessness, or falling asleep in class Alcohol or drug abuse Delinquency (e.g., thefts) States there is no caretaker

TABLE 15-2   (Continued)

TYPE OF CHILD ABUSE/NEGLECT	PHYSICAL INDICATORS	BEHAVIORAL INDICATORS
SEXUAL ABUSE	Difficulty in walking or sitting Torn, stained, or bloody underclothing Pain or itching in genital area Bruises or bleeding in external genitalia, vaginal, or anal areas Venereal disease, especially in pre-teens Pregnancy	Unwilling to change for gym or participate in Physical Education class Withdrawal, fantasy, or infantile behavior Bizarre, sophisticated, or unusual sexual behavior or knowledge Poor peer relationships Delinquent or runaway Reports sexual assault by caretaker
EMOTIONAL MALTREATMENT	Speech disorders Lags in physical development Failure-to-thrive	Habit disorders (sucking, biting, rocking, etc.) Conduct disorders (antisocial, destructive, etc.) Neurotic traits (sleep disorders, inhibition of play) Psychoneurotic reactions (hysteria, obsession, compulsion, phobias, hypochondria) Behavior extremes: complaint, passive aggressive, demanding Overly adaptive behavior: inappropriately adult inappropriately infant Developmental lags (mental, emotional) Attempted suicide

Source: National Center on Child Abuse and Neglect.

those who do report cases of child abuse or neglect, however, the law provides protection. If done in good faith, people who report suspected child abuse and neglect are immune from civil liability and criminal penalty. The person reporting cannot be successfully sued for notifying proper authorities of possible instances of child abuse and neglect. However, in many states persons who are required to report and refuse to do so can be successfully sued.

What to report?   It is necessary to consult state statutes to be certain just what is considered child abuse and neglect in a particular jurisdiction.

Most states require the reporting of *suspected* child abuse and neglect; no state requires the reporter to have absolute proof of child abuse and neglect before reporting. *Waiting for proof may involve grave risk to the child.*

Where to report?   Each state specifies one or more agencies as recipients of reports of suspected child abuse and neglect. In 30 states a law-enforcement agency is specified as one of the receiving agencies, with the local social services department usually cited as the other. In some states the district attorney's office or juvenile or district court is the designated agency.

How to report?   State statutes vary with regard to the form and content of reports required. Individual statutes specify the information that must be submitted in a report. Usually this includes:

> Child's name, age, and address
> Child's present location
> Parents' names and addresses
> Nature and extent of injury or condition observed
> Reporter's name and location.

In some states, additional information is required. Some states and local jurisdictions have developed forms to facilitate the making of written reports of suspected abuse and neglect. To facilitate the making of an oral report of suspected abuse and neglect, some states maintain a toll-free, 24-hour telephone line just for receipt of reports of suspected maltreatment. Anyone may use this "hotline" to report an incident of suspected child abuse and neglect anywhere in the state.

First Aid

Emergency care for an abused child's injuries is similar to the care for accidental injuries. Recognizing physical and behavioral indicators (see Table 15-2) of child abuse and neglect is an important aspect in the care of abused children. Once abuse is suspected—based on the history and primary survey—the victim should be examined from head to toe for injuries. The victim examination should be conducted in a matter-of-fact fashion; keep all suspicions to yourself. Provide appropriate emergency care for all injuries before moving the victim, and do *not* delay transporting the victim to a medical facility.

Hospitalization may protect the child from additional injuries. If the parents are confronted with the accusation of child abuse and neglect, they may refuse care and transportation of the child. Moreover, it is not your responsibility to confront the parents with your own suspicion of child abuse.

Immediate medical attention is necessary when any of the following conditions are present:

> Any type of fracture
> Head injuries
> Serious infections

Serious burns
Severe bruising
Sexual abuse
Failure to thrive (failure to grow vigorously)
Unattended medical problems; for example, high fever or difficulty in breathing.

Other than the physical and behavioral indicators identified in Table 15-2, other factors indicating possible child abuse and neglect include (1) a repeated history of trauma; (2) discrepancy between the history and the injury; (3) a third party being blamed for injuries (especially siblings); and (4) blame of the child for the injury.

Do not expect to obtain correct information from the child, who may have been taught not to tell the truth, be afraid of parental retaliation, or fear getting the parents in trouble. Therefore, do not ask the child more than once about the cause of the injuries.

Parents or guardians of abused children are often fearful of using emergency services. They fear that this action may expose themselves or their spouse.

When you arrive at the medical facility, privately convey your suspicions and findings to the physician. It will be of particular value to the doctor to learn what you have observed in the home because this information is otherwise unavailable to the physician.

RAPE

Perhaps one of the most difficult emergency situations that the first aider may have to deal with is sexual assault. Rape is the fastest growing violent crime in the United States. Authorities suspect that only a small proportion of actual rape cases are reported.

In most cases, the victim of rape is a woman. It should be noted, however, that men, both heterosexual and homosexual, may also be raped.

There are many definitions of rape, but in general rape involves attempted or actual sexual intercourse that is carried out forcibly, against the will of the victim. Related physical injury is common, but more damaging is the psychological trauma. It is essential that the first aider be calm and sympathetic when dealing with sexually assulted victims.

A first aider's job is to care for the victim—not to collect evidence or even to notify law-enforcement officials. Confine questions to important assessment of the injuries; not a detailed description of the events. Ask general, open-ended questions such as: "Does anything hurt?" "Where?" "How are you doing?"

Determine those injuries that require immediate care. If disrobing of a female victim is necessary, it should be conducted with another woman present. Better still, a female first aider should do the examining. Do not expose the genitalia unless there is injury there that requires immediate care (for example, profuse bleeding). Examining female genitalia, except in some cases of emergency childbirth, has serious legal implications and therefore should usually not be done.

Try if possible to preserve evidence. However, leave the investigation to the police. The victim should be encouraged not to change her clothes, wash, urinate, defecate, douche. Explain to the victim in a sympathetic way the reasons why it would be best not to "clean up." Keep in mind that a rape victim, like any other victim, has the right to refuse first aid and transport to a medical facility.

If the victim refuses aid, be sure that she or he is not simply left alone. Emotional support is vital. Most large communities have rape crisis centers, and furnishing this number (found in the telephone directory) is recommended.

Try to have a friend or relative of the victim stay with the person. *Do not* abandon rape victims at the scene. Do protect the privacy of the victim.

DYING VICTIM

A dying person presents a difficult situation. Suggestions for assisting such a victim include:

1. Avoiding negative statements about the victim's condition. Even a semiconscious person can hear what is being said.
2. Assuring the victim that you will locate and inform the family of what has happened. Attempt to have family members present because they can provide great comfort to the victim and will want to talk to the person before he or she dies.
3. Allowing some hope. Don't tell the victim that he or she is dying. Instead, say something like, "I don't know for sure. I won't give up on you, and don't give up on yourself. Keep trying."
4. Not volunteering information about the victim or others who may also be injured. However, if the victim asks a question about a family member, you must tell the truth. Provide simple, honest, clear information if it is requested, and repeat it as often as necessary.

Survivors of the Dead

1. Leave the confirmation of death to a physician.
2. Allow survivors to grieve in whatever way seems right to them (anger, rage, crying).
3. Provide simple, honest, clear information as it is requested, and repeat it as often as necessary. However, the survivors should be told everything at once.
4. Offer as much support as possible, both by presence and by words. Do not leave an individual survivor alone, but do respect that person's rights to privacy.

DISASTER VICTIMS

Emotional health needs have recently been recognized as a major problem confronting disaster victims. Mistaken ideas about the problems during the aftermath of a disaster still persist despite exhaustive study. For example, it has been determined that panic does not generally follow a major catastrophe; people rarely disintegrate and become incapable of coping; mental illness does not suddenly appear on the scene in full-blown states; and people do not become shells of their former selves—incapable, ineffective, self-centered, and thoughtless.

When a person is experiencing an emotional crisis, it is usually apparent even to the casual observer. In a disaster it might be expected that the direct and indirect effects of the catastrophe might produce severe emotional crises for some people. Precipitating causes could be the death of or separation from loved ones, sudden loss of possessions, loss of contact with friends and familiar routines and settings, or simply the physical force of the disaster itself. The last-mentioned situation can in some cases trigger overwhelming feelings of inadequacy in victims who are suddenly confronted with their own feelings of helplessness and mortality.

The following principles should make the job of the first aider easier.

Understand that people are the products of an enormous variety of factors. We are all different and we don't all react the same way to the same situation. You may be impressed with how well you made it through a disaster in comparison with someone else, but there is no guarantee that the situation will not be reversed next time. Victims do not want to be upset and worried any more than you would; they would "snap out of it" if they could. Your job, therefore, is to help people in this tough situation, not to be their critic—you would appreciate the same kind of consideration if you were in the other person's place.

Realize that emotional injuries are just as real as physical injuries. Such expressions as, "It's all in your head," "Snap out of it," "Buck up," and "Get a hold of yourself," are often used by people who believe they are being helpful. Actually, these goading terms are often expressions of hostility because they show a lack of understanding. They only emphasize weakness and inadequacy and are of no use in psychological first aid.

Realize that every physically injured person has some emotional reaction to the fact that he or she is injured. A slight injury such as a cut finger gives most people a start. But damage to a highly valued part of the body, such as the eyes, is likely to be severely upsetting. Injured people feel less secure, more anxious, and more afraid, not only because of what has happened to them but also because they imagine more dire things may still happen as a result of their injuries. This fear and insecurity may cause people to be irritable, stubborn, or unreasonable; they may seem uncooperative, unnecessarily difficult, or even emotionally irrational. As you help victims, always keep in mind that such behavior has little or nothing to do with you personally. Victims need your patience, reassurance, encouragement, and support. Even though they seem disagreeable and ungrateful at first, get across the idea you want to help them.

Realize that there is more strength in most disturbed people than appears at first glance.   No injured or sick person puts his or her best foot forward. The strong points of the personality are likely to be hidden beneath fear, anguish, and pain. It is easy to see only the victim's failures, even though the person may have worked efficiently alongside of you only a short time ago. With your aid, that person's "real self" will soon resurface.

Keeping these principles in mind, consider the following first aid measures as you seek the right combination of tactics to bring about the victim's recovery.

Getting through to the victim.   Persistent efforts to make the victim realize that you want to understand will be reassuring. Familiar things such as the use of the person's name or the sight of familiar people and activities, will add to the victim's ability to overcome fear and other emotional problems. By your words, attitude, and behavior, let the person know your willingness and ability to understand his or her feelings. Show patience and a real desire to help. No victim will respond if you are excited, angry, or abrupt.

Venting emotions.   In the terror of injury or catastrophe, many casualties give up. By being calm, patient, and willing to listen to a victim, you can get across the idea that you believe in that person, that you respect him or her as a human being, and that you think the person is worthwhile. Then perhaps the person will begin to talk. There is no better medicine for fear and feelings of isolation than a chance to talk with a friendly person. Encourage talk and be a good listener. People will frequently solve their own problems when they are encouraged to put them into their own words and to examine how they really feel about them.

Activity.   After you help victims get over their initial fears, regain some self-confidence, and realize that their job is to continue to function as best they can, you should then help them find something to do. Get them to help load trucks, clean up debris, or assist others. Avoid having people just sit around. Your instructions to others should be clear and simple. They should be repeated, and they should be reasonable and obviously possible. A person who has panicked is likely to argue. Respect their feelings, but point out more immediate, obtainable, and demanding needs. Do not argue. If you cannot get someone interested in doing something profitable, it may be necessary to enlist aid in controlling the individual's overactivity before it spreads to the group and results in more panic.

Rest.   There are times when physical exhaustion is a principal cause of emotional reactions. For the weary disaster victim, adequate rest, warm food, and a change of clothing with an opportunity to bathe may provide spectacular results.

Benefits of the group spirit.   You have probably noticed that a person works better, faces danger better, and handles serious problems better in a group. Each individual in a group supports the others and seems to be strengthened in turn by the group. This group spirit is so powerful that it is one of the most effective tools you have in psychological first aid. Make sure that victims do not become isolated from others and thus reinforce their emotional problems.

Finally, once you have helped victims to regain their confidence and to feel more secure, assure them that you expect them to recover fully, that there is much they can do, and that there is a pressing need for their help. Just as with the physically injured casualty, medical personnel will take over the care of the psychological casualty as soon as possible. The first aid that victims have received from you will be of great value to their complete recovery.

DISASTER RESCUERS

Disaster workers expose themselves to unprecedented personal demands in their desire to help meet the needs of disaster victims. For many the disaster takes precedence over all other responsibilities and activities, and the workers devote all their time to the disaster-created tasks. As some order returns, many of the workers, especially volunteers, return to their regular jobs, at the same time attempting to continue with their disaster work. The result of this overwork is *burnout*, a state of exhaustion, irritability, and fatigue that creeps up unrecognized and undetected upon the individual and markedly decreases the person's effectiveness and capability.

The best way to forestall burnout is to expect it, be alert to its early signs, and act in relieving the stress that burnout triggers. Being relieved from duties for a short period of time is helpful. In some cases a supervisor must order the rescuer to take time off.

Chapter 16

Rescuing, Lifting, and Moving Victims

In general, victims should not be moved until they are ready for transportation to a medical facility. All necessary first aid should be provided first.

Victims should be moved only if there is an immediate danger to them or others if they are not moved. Immediate moving should occur when:

> There is a fire or danger of fire
>
> Explosives or other hazardous materials are involved
>
> It is impossible to protect the accident scene (traffic hazards)
>
> It is impossible to gain access to other victims who need lifesaving care
>
> A cardiac-arrest victim must be moved to the ground or floor in order to have a firm surface for giving cardiopulmonary resuscitation (CPR)
>
> There is danger of asphyxia due to lack of oxygen or due to gas
>
> There is exposure to cold, intense heat, or other severe weather conditions
>
> There is an electrical injury or potential injury
>
> There is danger from possible collapsing walls or building.

When faced with the problem of rescuing a threatened person, do not take any action until you have had time to determine the extent of the danger and your ability to cope with it. In a large number of accidents, the rescuer rushes in and becomes the second victim. Do not take unnecessary chances. Do not attempt any rescue that needlessly endangers a life.

Heroism that is unsupported by ability—natural or acquired—often
ends disastrously.

RESCUES

If there is a fire or any of the other situations just cited, the victim should be
pulled away from the area as quickly as possible.

The major danger in moving a victim quickly is the possibility of spine
injury. In an emergency, every effort should be made to pull the victim in
the direction of the long axis of the body to provide as much protection to
the spine as possible. It is impossible to remove a victim quickly and, at the
same time, provide protection for the victim's spine.

A victim who is on the floor or ground can be dragged away from the
scene by tugging on the clothing in the neck and shoulder area. It may be
easier to pull the victim onto a blanket and then drag the blanket away from
the scene. Such moves are emergency moves only. They do not really
protect the spine from further injury.

Rescue from Fire

If you must go to the aid of a person whose clothing is on fire, try to
smother the flames by wrapping the person in a coat, blanket, or rug. Leave
the victim's head uncovered. First beat out the flames around the head and
shoulders, and then work downward toward the feet. If you have no
material with which to smother the fire, roll the victim over and beat out
the flames with your hands. If the victim tries to run, catch the person and
throw him or her down. Remember that the victim must lie down while you
are trying to extinguish the fire. Running will cause the clothing to burn
more rapidly. Sitting or standing may cause the victim to be killed instantly
by inhaling flames or hot air.

Inhaling flame or hot air can kill. Don't get your face directly over the
flames. Turn your face away from the flame when inhaling.

If your own clothing catches fire, roll yourself up in a blanket, coat, or
rug. Keep your head uncovered. If material to smother the fire is not
available, lie down, roll over slowly, and beat at the flames with your hands.

While trying to escape from an upper floor of a burning building, be
very cautious about opening doors into hallways or stairways. When a
building is on fire, hot air often collects in halls and stairwells. Always feel a
door before opening it: If it feels hot, don't open it if there is any other
possible way out. Remember also that opening doors or windows will create
a draft and make the fire worse; don't open any door or window until you
are actually ready to get out.

If faced with the problem of removing an injured person from an upper story of a burning building, improvise a lifeline by tying sheets, blankets, curtains, or other materials together (use square knots). Secure one end around some heavy object inside the building, and fasten the other end around the victim under the arms. Lower the victim to safety, and then let yourself down the line. Do not jump from an upper floor of a burning building. If forced to remain in a room, stay near a slightly opened window.

It is often said that the "best" air in a burning room or compartment is near the floor, but this is true only to a limited extent. There is less smoke and flame down low near the floor, and the air may be cooler, but carbon monoxide and other deadly gases are just as likely to be present near the floor as near the ceiling. Cover your mouth and nose with a wet cloth to reduce the danger of inhaling smoke, flame, or hot air. Remember, however, that a wet cloth gives you no protection against poisonous gases or lack of oxygen.

Rescue from Electrical Contact

Rescuing a person who has received an electric shock is likely to be difficult and dangerous. Extreme caution must be used, or you may be electrocuted.

You must not touch the victim, the wire, or any other object that may be conducting electricity. Look for the switch first of all and, if you find it, turn off the current immediately. Don't waste too much time hunting for the switch, however; every second is important. If the switch cannot be found, try to remove the wire from the casualty with a dry broom handle, branch, pole, oar, board, or similar nonconducting object (Figure 16–1). It may be possible to use dry rope or dry clothing to pull the wire from under the victim. When trying to break an electrical contact, always stand on some nonconducting material such as a dry board, dry newspapers, or dry clothing.

Rescue from the Water

A drowning victim must be rescued as quickly as possible. Most incidents occur within reach of a bystander; thus, even a nonswimmer can be of assistance. The adage of "reach, throw, row, then go" should be followed. The life of the rescuer should not be endangered while attempting to rescue a drowning person. Too many cases of double and triple drownings have happened when the above recommendation was not followed. Never attempt to swim to the rescue of a drowning person unless you have been trained in lifesaving methods—and then only if there is no better way of reaching the person. A drowning person may, because of panic, fight so violently that you will be unable either to rescue the person or to save yourself. Even if you are not a trained lifesaver, however, help a drowning

FIGURE 16-1

person by holding out a pole, oar, branch, or stick for the person to catch hold of; by throwing a lifeline; or by throwing some buoyant object with which the person can be supported in the water.

EMERGENCY MOVES

In an emergency, you may have to hoist, carry, or drag an injured person away from a position of danger. In some instances you will be able to do this by using the fireman's carry, the tied-hands crawl, the blanket drag, the pack-strap carry, the chair carry, or some type of arm carry. Sometimes it is necessary to move the victim with all possible speed, without regard to the severity of the person's injuries. Remember, however, that when moving an injured person you are taking a calculated risk of further injuring or even killing the person. Justification in taking such a risk occurs only when it is evident that the victim will die if not moved.

Fireman's Carry

One of the easiest ways to carry an unconscious person is by means of the fireman's carry. Figure 16-2 shows the procedure:

1. Turn the victim face down, as shown in Figure 16-2a. Kneel on one knee at the victim's head, facing the person. Pass your hands under the armpits; then slide your hands down the victim's sides and clasp them across the back.
2. Raise the victim to the knees, as shown in Figure 16-2b. Take a better hold across the victim's back.

FIGURE 16–2 Fireman's carry.

3. Raise the victim to a standing position and place your right leg between the legs, as shown in Figure 16-2c. Grasp the right wrist in your left hand and swing the arm around the back of your neck and down your left shoulder.

4. Stoop quickly and pull the victim across your shoulders and, at the same time, put your right arm between the victim's legs, as shown in Figure 16-2d.

5. Grasp the victim's right wrist with your right hand and straighten up, as shown in Figure 16-2e.

   The procedure for lowering the victim to the deck is shown in Figure 16-2f and g.

Fireman's Drag

The fireman's drag, shown in Figure 16-3, may be used to drag an unconscious person for a short distance: it is particularly useful when you must crawl underneath a low structure.

To carry someone by this method, turn the person so that he or she is lying flat on the back. Cross the wrists and tie them together. Kneel astride the victim and lift the victim's arms over your head so that the wrists are at the back of your neck. When you crawl forward, raise your shoulders high enough so that the victim's head will not bump against the floor or ground.

Blanket Drag

The blanket drag, shown in Figure 16-4, can be used to move a person who is so seriously injured that he or she should not be lifted or carried by one person alone. Place the victim face up on a blanket and pull the blanket along the floor. Always pull the victim's head first, with the victim's head and shoulders slightly raised, so that the head will not bump against the ground.

Pack-Strap Carry

With the pack-strap carry, shown in Figure 16-5, it is possible to carry a heavy person for some distance. Use the following procedure:

1. Place the victim lying down, face up.
2. Lie down on your side along the victim's uninjured or less-injured side. Your shoulder should be next to the victim's armpit.
3. Pull the victim's far leg over your own, holding it there if necessary.
4. Grasp the victim's far arm at the wrist and bring it over your upper shoulder as you roll and pull the victim onto your back.
5. Rise up on your knees, using your free arm for balance and support. Hold both the victim's wrists close against your chest with your other hand.
6. Lean forward as you rise to your feet and keep both of your shoulders under the victim's armpits.

FIGURE 16-3 Fireman's drag.

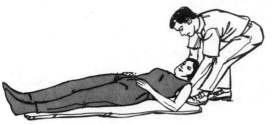

FIGURE 16–4

One-rescuer emergency transfer.

Do not attempt to carry a seriously injured person by means of the pack-strap carry, especially if the victim's arms, spine, neck, or ribs are fractured.

Chair Carry

The chair carry can often be used to move a sick or injured person away from a position of danger. The victim is seated on a chair, as shown in Figure 16–6, and the chair is carried by two rescuers. This is a particularly good method to use when you must carry a person up or down stairs or through narrow, winding passageways. It must *never* be used to move a person who has an injured neck, back, or pelvis.

Arm Carries

Several kinds of arm carries can be used in emergency situations to move an injured person to safety. Figure 16–7 shows how one person can carry the casualty alone. However, you should never try to carry a seriously injured person in this way. Unless the victim is considerably smaller than you are, you will not be able to carry the victim very far by this method.

FIGURE 16–5 Pack-strap carry.

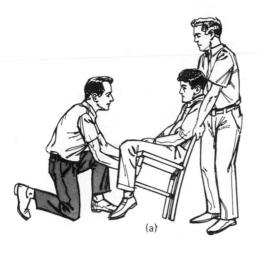
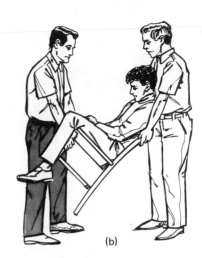

FIGURE 16–6 Chair carry.

Extremity Lift

The two-rescuer extremity carry, shown in Figure 16-8, can be used in some cases to move an injured person. However, it should not be used to carry a person who has serious wounds or broken bones.

This technique requires two rescuers to lift a victim with no fractures or whose fractures have been splinted.

1. One rescuer kneels at the head of the victim and one at the side by the victim's knees.

FIGURE 16–7 One-rescuer arm carry.

FIGURE 16–8 Two-rescuer carry by arms and legs.

2. The head rescuer places one hand under each of the victim's shoulders while the foot rescuer grasps the victim's wrists.

3. The foot rescuer pulls the victim to a sitting position; the head rescuer assists by pushing the victim's shoulders up and supporting the victim's back and head with his body.

4. The head rescuer slips his or her hands under the victim's arms and grasps the victim's wrists.

5. The foot rescuer slips his or her hands under the victim's knees.

6. Both rescuers crouch on both feet.

7. They stand simultaneously and move with the victim to a stretcher.

Another two-rescuer carry that can be used in emergencies is shown in Figure 16-9. Two rescuers kneel beside the victim at about the level of the victim's hips and carefully raise the victim to a sitting position. Each rescuer puts one arm under the victim's thighs; hands are clasped and arms braced as shown in Figure 16-9. This carry must not be used to move seriously injured persons.

TRANSPORTATION OF THE INJURED

Thus far in this chapter we have dealt with emergency methods used to get an injured person out of danger and into a position where the person can receive first aid. As we have seen, these emergency rescue procedures often involve substantial risk to the victim and should be used only when clearly necessary.

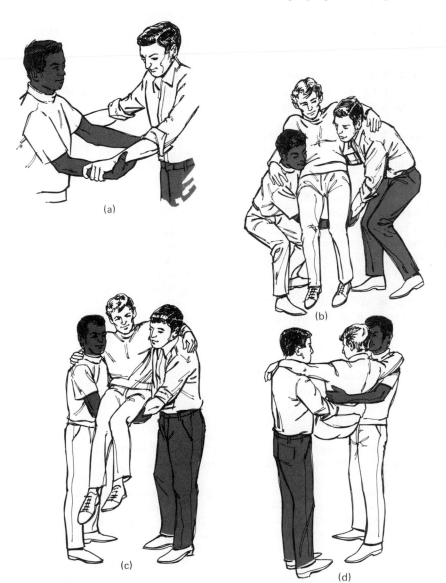

(a)

(b)

(c)

(d)

FIGURE 16–9 Two-rescuer carry.

Once you have rescued the victim from immediate danger, slow down! From this point on, handle and transport victims with every regard for the injuries that they have sustained. In the excitement and confusion that almost always accompany an accident, you are likely to feel rushed, as though you must do everything rapidly. To a certain extent, this is a reasonable feeling to have: Speed is essential in treating many injuries and in getting the victim to medical help. However, it is not reasonable to let yourself feel so hurried that you handle victims roughly or carelessly, or transport them in a way that will aggravate their injuries.

All injured parts should be immobilized as much as possible prior to moving and should be protected as much as possible during moving.

In order to protect themselves, the first aiders should use the following principles in all nonemergency moves:

> Keep in mind physical capabilities and limitations, and do not try to handle too heavy a load. When in doubt, seek help.
>
> Do not attempt to lower a victim if you feel you could not lift the person.
>
> Keep yourself balanced when carrying out all tasks.
>
> Maintain a firm footing.
>
> Maintain a constant and firm grip.
>
> Lift and lower by bending the legs and not the back—keep the back as straight as possible at all times; bend knees and lift with one foot ahead of the other.
>
> When holding or transporting, keep the back straight and rely on shoulder and leg muscles; tighten muscles of the abdomen and buttocks.
>
> When performing a task that requires pulling, keep the back straight and pull using the arms and shoulders.
>
> Carry out all tasks slowly, smoothly, and in unison with any helpers.
>
> Move body gradually; avoid twisting and jerking when conducting the various victim-handling tasks.
>
> When handling a victim, try to keep the arms close to the body in order to maintain balance.
>
> Do not keep muscles contracted for a long period of time.

General Precautions

The basic precautions that must be observed in transporting an injured person may be summarized as follows:

1. Give necessary first aid before attempting to transport the victim. Be sure that all injuries have been located. Treat serious breathing problems, bleeding, and shock, in that order. Immobilize all fractures, sprains, and dislocations. Do whatever you can to reduce the victim's pain and to make the person as comfortable as possible under the circumstances.
2. Use a regular stretcher, if one is available; if using an improvised stretcher, be sure that it is strong enough. Be sure, also, that there are enough rescuers to carry the stretcher, so that you will not run any risk of dropping the victim.
3. Whenever possible, bring the stretcher to the victim instead of the other way around.
4. Fastening the victim to the stretcher so that the victim cannot slip, slide, or fall off may be necessary for long distances or in rugged terrain.
5. Use blankets, clothing, or other material to pad the stretcher and to protect the victim from exposure.
6. As a general rule, injured people should be lying face up while being moved. However, in some instances the type of location of the injury will necessitate

the use of another position. A person who is having difficulty in breathing because of a chest wound may be more comfortable if the head and shoulders are slightly raised. A person who has a broken bone should be moved very carefully, so that the injury will not be made worse. Victims who have received a severe injury to the head should be kept lying on the side to prevent them from choking on saliva. blood, or vomitus while being transported. Heart attack victims should be semireclining. Unconscious victims should be on their side with their head down. Persons with suspected spine injuries should be maintained in the position found. Legs should be elevated to prevent shock. In all cases, it is important to place victims in the position that will best protect them from further injury.

7. The stretcher should be carried in such a way that the victim will be moved feet first, so that the rear stretcher bearer can continually watch the victim for signs of breathing difficulty. See Figure 16–10.

8. If using a motor vehicle to transport a seriously injured person, the best means is an ambulance; if no ambulance is available, however, a truck or station wagon makes a fairly good substitute. If it is necessary to use a passenger car to transport a seriously injured person, wait until you have figured out how to place the victim without undue bending, twisting, or turning before placing the victim in the car.

9. Do not turn the victim over to anyone without giving a complete account of the situation. Be sure that the person taking over knows what caused the injury and what first aid treatment has been given. If a tourniquet has been applied, make sure that this is known to the person who is taking charge of the victim.

Army Litter

The Army litter, shown in Figure 16–11, is a collapsible stretcher made of canvas and supported by wooden or aluminum poles. It is very useful for transporting victims. However, it is sometimes difficult to fasten the victim onto the Army litter. Open the Army litter with a foot if wearing shoes or, if not, with the palm of the hand.

FIGURE 16–10 Stretcher carry.

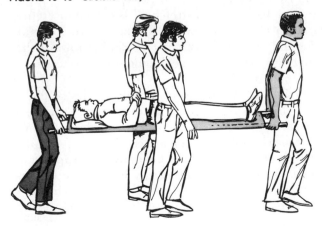

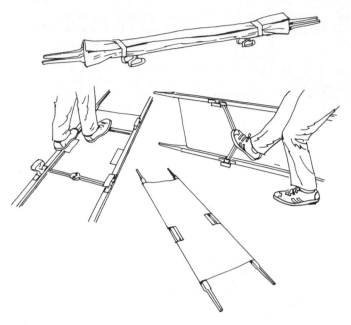

FIGURE 16–11   Army litter.

Improvised Stretchers

A stretcher or the Army litter should be used, if possible, whenever it is necessary to transport a seriously injured person. If these are not available, it may be necessary for you to improvise some way of carrying the seriously injured.

Shutters, doors, boards, and even ladders may be used as stretchers. All stretchers of this kind must be very well padded, and great care must be taken to see that the victim is fastened securely in place.

Sometimes a blanket may be used as a stretcher, as shown in Figure 16–12. The victim is placed in the middle of the blanket. Three or four people kneel on each side and roll the edges of the blanket toward the victim. When the rolled edges are tight and large enough to grasp securely, the victim should be lifted and carried.

Stretchers may also be improvised by using two long poles (about 7 feet long) and any strong cloth, such as a rug, a blanket, a sheet, a mattress cover, two or three gunny sacks or two coats. Figure 16–13 shows an improvised stretcher made from two poles and a blanket.

Caution: Many improvised stretchers do not give sufficient support to be used in cases where there are fractures (especially in the case of suspected spinal injury) or extensive wounds of the body. They should be used only when the victim is able to stand some sagging, bending, or twisting without serious consequences.

FIGURE 16–12 Blanket lift.

Two- or Three-Rescuer Lift

This technique may be used to transfer a victim from the ground or floor onto a stretcher. No spine injury should be present and two or three rescuers may be used. (See Figure 16–14.)

1. Rescuers line up on one side of the victim.
2. Rescuers drop one knee to the ground (the same knee for each rescuer—preferably onto the knee closer to the victim's feet).
3. The victim's arms are placed over the chest if possible.
4. The head rescuer places one arm under the victim's head.
5. The head rescuer places his or her other arm under the victim's lower back.
6. A second rescuer places one arm under the victim's knees and one arm above the buttocks. *Note:* If there is a third rescuer, this person places both arms in the waist area, and the other two rescuers slide their arms up to the midback or down to the buttocks as appropriate.
7. On signal, rescuers lift the victim to their knees and roll the victim in toward their chests (rescuers' backs are now straight and they are supporting the victim by their arms and chests).

FIGURE 16–13
Stretcher made from poles and a blanket.

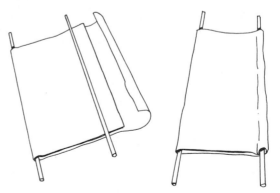

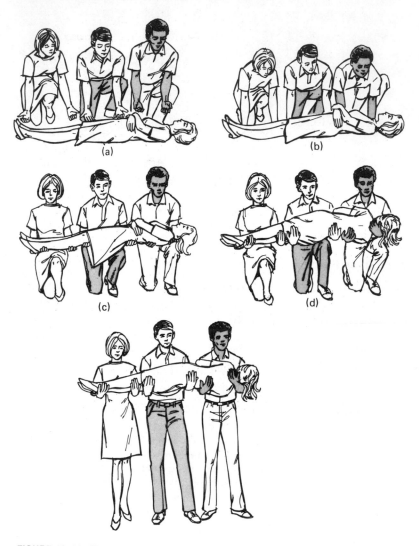

FIGURE 16–14 Three-rescuer lift and carry.

8. On signal, the rescuers stand and move the victim to a stretcher.
9. To replace the victim on the ground or on a low cot, the procedure would be reversed.

Moving Victim with Spine Injury

To move a victim suspected of having a spine injury, a long backboard or scoop stretcher is preferred. Such devices are available on most ambulances and rescue squad vehicles. If at all possible, the victim with a spine injury should not be moved until proper equipment (a long backboard) is available. Those providing the long backboard will usually have the training to lift and move the victim. Such moving should be left to those trained in the use of a long backboard. See page 257 for details on transporting a victim with spinal cord injury.

IN CONCLUSION

If you have systematically read and studied this book, you can save a life and assist people with a wide variety of injuries and sudden illnesses.

The term *first aid* should not conjure up visions of young Boy Scouts bandaging imaginary wounds in yard after yard of gauze and tape. Today's first aid course still includes bandaging and splinting skills, but the emphasis is on using good observation skills and practicing sound judgment.

In fact, any intelligent person can learn to perform a quick, systematic, head-to-toe examination of an injured victim in order to identify the simplest and most direct assistance required. The trick is to develop a plan of action before emergencies arise so that fast action can occur when the unexpected need is at hand. In a real emergency there is too much excitement and too little time to read more than a few lines of a first aid book. But the first step in preparing for trouble should be the reading of a good first aid book.

A good first aid book can be used as a reference during actual first aid situations. Memory is not always dependable and should not be relied on when other sources of information are available and there is time for a quick review.

Another use of a good first aid book is as a reference for periodically reviewing first aid procedures. An individual's competence in first aid can decrease over time. Review becomes more crucial as new information and methods become available, thus rendering previously learned first aid techniques obsolete.

Index